Debating the Issues in Colonial Newspapers

Primary Documents on Events of the Period

DAVID A. COPELAND

Greenwood Press
Westport, Connecticut • London

Library of Congress Cataloging-in-Publication Data

Copeland, David A., 1951–
   Debating the issues in colonial newspapers : primary documents on events of the period
/ David A. Copeland.
      p. cm.
   Includes bibliographical references and index.
   ISBN 0–313–30982–5 (alk. paper)
      1. United States—History—Colonial period, ca. 1600–1775—Sources. 2. United
States—Politics and government—To 1775—Sources. 3. United States—Politics and
government—To 1775—Public opinion. 4. Public opinion—United States—History—17th
century—Sources. 5. Public opinion—United States—History—18th century—
Sources. 6. American newspapers—Abstracts. I. Title.
   E187.C78 2000
   973.2—dc21   99–089070

British Library Cataloguing in Publication Data is available.

Library of Congress Catalog Card Number: 99–089070
ISBN: 0–313–30982–5

First published in 2000

Greenwood Press, 88 Post Road West, Westport, CT 06881
An imprint of Greenwood Publishing Group, Inc.
www.greenwood.com

Printed in the United States of America

The paper used in this book complies with the
Permanent Paper Standard issued by the National
Information Standards Organization (Z39.48–1984).

10 9 8 7 6 5 4 3

Contents

Introduction: Newspapers in Colonial America

In 1690 Boston printer Benjamin Harris decided it was time to publish a newspaper. He believed Massachusetts needed one so that people could have a better understanding of public affairs, business, and, in fact, all the occurrences that take place and affect everyone. He called his paper, quite appropriately, *Publick Occurrences Both Forreign and Domestick*. Even though the Massachusetts Bay government did not like the idea of Harris publishing *all* the information that he received and shut down the newspaper after one issue, the love of Americans for news of all sorts could not be denied or controlled through censorship. Sixty years later, another printer, James Parker of New York, wrote that the taste Americans had for news could not be understood by foreigners, and then added, news was something that Americans "can't be without."[1]

For more than 250 years, newspapers served as the principal source of news for Americans, and despite the introduction of numerous other media in the last 100 years, newspapers still offer the most in-depth analysis of events of all media. But what were newspapers like in their infancy in America? Were they like today's newspapers, or were they different? Today's reader would find many things about America's newspapers before the Revolution to be familiar. The same reader would also sometimes find it difficult to understand the language, arrangement, and content of the early newspapers. Still, the newspapers of colonial America established all of the newspaper practices in use today with the exception of color printing and photographs, techniques not yet invented.

Even though the printing press arrived in America in 1636 and Harris printed *Publick Occurrences* in 1690, the first continually published paper in America did not appear until 1704, when the *Boston News-Letter* was begun, and it had no competition until 1719. Newspaper production in America then began to grow and prosper. By 1736 printers had begun weekly newspapers in seven of the American colonies with multiple newspapers in Massachusetts, New York, and Pennsylvania. A dozen newspapers existed in America at that time, a number that remained constant for the next twenty years.

In the mid-1750s, American newspapers experienced a growth spurt fueled by the French and Indian War, which lasted from 1754 to 1763. The desire for all the information available about the war that threatened the very existence of the British American colonies led directly to more newspapers throughout America. Newspaper starts from 1754 to 1760 increased by about 73 percent, from eleven to nineteen. The population increased only about 36 percent, from slightly more than 1.17 million inhabitants to slightly more than 1.59 million. By 1763 there were twenty-three papers in America.[2] The number of newspapers grew again with the Stamp Act crisis of 1765. By 1775 and the beginning of the American Revolution, forty newspapers provided Americans with news, and every colony except Vermont had at least one newspaper by that time.

With the increase in newspapers came an increase in circulation, as well. Newspapers in 1750, for example, had an average circulation of about 600 copies per week. By the Stamp Act crisis, these figures topped 1,500 in some towns and grew to more than 3,500 in some cases before the Revolution. It must be remembered that no colonial town had more than 15,000 inhabitants by 1750, and only three could boast populations between 20,000 and 30,000 by 1775. Also, most large colonial towns—Boston, New York, and Philadelphia, for example—had four or five newspapers; obviously, newspaper readership was sizable. Most literate people had access to newspapers, and newspapers, which were sold by subscription, were read aloud in taverns, making their information available to all within hearing.

American newspapers before the Revolution were weeklies, but several printers attempted multiweek publications. For printers, producing papers more than once a week proved difficult because of the limited amount of news, paper, and advertising revenue available to them. Still, nearly every printer in America would issue supplements between regular publication dates when important news was received.

Newspaper production essentially followed the same printing process that Johannes Gutenberg used in 1455 when he invented the printing press. Printers and their apprentices used lead type. Each letter of type was handset by sliding it into a "stick," a piece of metal designed to hold letters. Once a line of type was completed, it was placed in an iron frame, which was approximately the size of the newspaper page. When the frame

The Print Shop. Printers worked in various-sized shops, ranging from one to three printing presses, in colonial America. Apprentices, journeyman printers, and master printers all worked to produce publications as depicted in this portrayal of the Franklin print shop. Because printers often sold other items in addition to newspapers and pamphlets, the print shop was often a busy place with customers inquiring on items offered for sale by the printer.

was filled, the sticks were locked into place and the frame placed on the press. Using a dauber made of animal skin, an apprentice inked the letters. The printer then transferred the impression of the letters in the frame to the piece of paper. After one side of the paper was printed, it had to be hung up to dry. Once dry, the other side could be printed. Most printers required the workers in their shops to produce up to 250 impressions per hour. Generally, if the shop could not meet its quota, no one was paid.

Colonial newspapers were usually two to four pages in length. Four-page papers were made by taking a piece of paper and folding it so that pages one and four were on one side of the sheet and pages two and three on the other. Even though most papers were of this length, printers sometimes ran papers six to ten pages in length weekly. In order to print a paper of this length, a printer usually needed more than one press. Only the most successful of printers, such as Benjamin Franklin, had multiple-press shops.

Printers' resources were often in short supply. Printers imported lead type from England. Ink could be made in the colonies, but the process was not easy. It involved boiling linseed oil and mixing it with lampblack, the soot produced from burning oil or tar. Paper was not always easy to obtain, either, and its size varied because paper was made of cloth, not wood. *Publick Occurrences* was printed on pages 7.5 inches by 11.5 inches, but later papers approached the size of today's supermarket tabloids. Printers often asked readers to donate old rags to be turned into newsprint. *Virginia Gazette* printer William Parks made this request cleverly in a poem:

> Nice Delia's Smock, which, neat and whole,
> No man durst finger for his Soul;
> Turn'd to Gazette, now all the Town,
> May take it up, or smooth it down.
> Whilst Delia may with it dispense,
> And no Affront to Innocence.[3]

Even though lead type wore out and ink and paper were sometimes in short supply, printers before the Revolution produced their newspapers on a regular basis. Printers rarely missed a week or changed the day of publication, even if it happened to fall on Christmas.

Printers—and society in general—did not have a standard grammar or dictionary. Spelling and punctuation in newspapers therefore varied. Nearly all nouns were capitalized in newspapers through the first half of the eighteenth century. Run-on sentences were common, and commas were dashed about in stories much as one uses salt or pepper to season food. Words could appear in stories spelled in a variety of ways. While these grammatical errors might be a distraction to readers of later eras, they do not appear to have distracted readers in the eighteenth century. In this work, the original capitalization, spelling, and punctuation are preserved. Some of the newspaper selections, then, will seem archaic in construction while others will appear quite modern.

A year's subscription to the first colonial newspapers cost about 11 percent of the average person's yearly salary, about $1.54 out of an income of $14.30 in today's money.[4] Carriers—usually one of the printer's apprentices—delivered the papers to subscribers in town, and postal riders carried them to neighboring communities. The high cost of newspapers may help to explain why circulation was not large during the newspapers' beginning years in America. Printers in the eighteenth century—as well as publishers today—depended on advertising as the newspaper's chief source of revenue. Colonial advertisements looked more like today's classified advertisements. Advertising usually appeared on the last page of the paper, but printers such as Benjamin Franklin wisely began to insert advertisements throughout the paper, even on the front page, which meant readers were more likely to see them because they were not separated from the news. As part of the advertisements, printers used woodcuts to provide readers with visuals. The woodcut could be a carving of a ship, book, person, or anything else in a small block of wood. The block was placed into the frame with the lettering, and its highlights were inked, which produced a picture to draw the attention of readers to the advertisement. Most newspaper advertisements dealt with commodities. The most prominent advertisements centered on the slave trade and runaway slaves. These advertisements listed the slave and her or his attributes. The runaway ads often listed the reward for return of the slave.

The news in papers before the Revolution depended on a number of sources. In some ways, the information-gathering process differed greatly from today's practices. In other ways, eighteenth-century papers paved the way for later publications. Newspapers depended on letters, people arriving in town by land or sea, other newspapers, official government announcements, and correspondents for news. The correspondent, a person who lived somewhere in or near a town, wrote to the printer telling him about local occurrences. The idea of a reporter who went out and gathered the news did not exist in America until the French and Indian War, and even then, references to the "weekly news writer" were rare.

As important events in the colonies took place, the sharing of news from paper to paper became even more important. Printers in Boston, for example, counted on Southern newspapers for information on the Cherokee War of 1759 to 1761, which was fought in the South but had repercussions for Native American relations in other regions. Southern printers, in turn, expected the same from New England printers in the 1770s, during the British blockade and occupation of Boston. Patriot printers started the "Journal of Occurrences," a distribution service for news that chronicled the city's occupation. What was being created by printers was a news distribution service much like today's Associated Press.

To be sure the information they printed was accurate, printers sought out verification for their important stories. Two Boston printers, William and John Fleet, for example, assumed accuracy in a story from Jamaica because it had originally appeared in the island's newspapers. The brothers also would not report that France had surrendered Canada in the French and Indian War until the story could be verified from another source. Through the "colonial wire service" and verification of important facts, the newspapers of the colonial period established important precedents for the media that followed.

Even though printers developed methods of newsgathering and verification that are still in use, news moved slowly. In an age when news is dispersed in a matter of minutes, it is hard to understand how news of events that sometimes happened six months earlier could be of value. News of an occurrence that is new to you and affects your life is of value, however, no matter when it is received. This fact was especially true in colonial America. News from Europe often took six months to reach

America, and the fastest news could move from one end of the colonies to the other was about three weeks. The speed of sharing news would not increase until the invention of the telegraph in the nineteenth century.

Much of the news contained in colonial newspapers centered upon political topics. Just as today, what happened in the world and in government affected colonial Americans. Newspapers did not limit the scope of their content and discussion to politics, however. America's first newspapers discussed every imaginable topic, and many printers placed the slogan "the freshest Advices Foreign and Domestic" below the paper's name. Philadelphia printer William Goddard summed up the content of newspapers in 1767 by placing the following in the nameplate of his *Pennsylvania Chronicle*: "Containing the freshest Advices, both Foreign and Domestic; with a Variety of other Matter; useful, instructive and entertaining."

The news of the eighteenth century was often more graphic than today's news. Descriptions of rapes, murders, executions, and other events were often printed with intricate detail. To read this news, however, one had to search through newspapers. Newspapers rarely contained headlines as we think of them today. Instead, news changed from paragraph to paragraph, which meant one had to read the entire newspaper to discover all the news; one could not selectively jump from one story to another based on interest generated by headlines. Furthermore, the latest news was rarely found on the front page; it usually appeared on the inside of the paper, often the last part to be printed.

The front page of colonial newspapers was usually reserved for letters, essays, and news that could be set well before press day. Following the practice of English printers, the front page generally featured material on issues that could be discussed or debated by readers, such as opinion pieces or editorials, although the word "editorial" was never used during the colonial era.

The front page was not the only place that opinions appeared in newspapers nor was the shaping of public opinion necessarily the central purpose of printers during the colonial period. Printers initially regarded their products as journals of occurrences or as a record of events. In two of America's earliest papers, *Publick Occurrences* and the *Boston Gazette*, the printers announced their chief purpose was to present the latest news to help people understand public affairs or trade.

Competition for readers ended the notion that newspapers were solely journals of record. With multiple papers in towns, printers needed to find an edge to increase circulation and income. Dealing in controversy was one answer. Again following the British example, printers from 1720 on increasingly added opinion essays to their newspapers. The subject matter of opinion pieces varied, but before the middle of the eighteenth century, most opinion pieces dealt with education, medicine, religion, and gender issues including marriage.

As America grew more populous and economically independent, political issues became the central focus of opinion in newspapers. But politics also played a role in many of the issues surrounding education, medicine, and religion. When the citizens of Boston began arguing about the validity of inoculating against smallpox in 1721, for example, an underlying issue dealt with political and religious control of the colony. Congregationalists such as Cotton Mather supported inoculation, while Anglicans such as Dr. William Douglass opposed it. While the two sides argued about inoculation, they also were positioning themselves for political power in Massachusetts.[5] Even though political debate became the central focus of opinion articles in newspapers in the twenty-five years before the Revolution, writers of opinion still used the press in attempts to sway readers on almost all imaginable subjects. When women began to petition courts for divorces in the 1770s, both sexes wrote to papers in an attempt to sway public opinion. One female writer closed her argument with a long poem that said abuse of wives by husbands should always be grounds to end a marriage. "Tho' husbands are tyrants, their wives will be free," she declared.[6]

Even though printers may have held opinions on the myriad of subjects discussed in their papers, the authors of the opinions usually were not the printers. As Boston printer Thomas Fleet said in 1733 in the *Weekly Rehearsal*, "The Publisher declares himself of no Party, and Invites all Gentlemen of Leisure and Capacity, inclined to either side, to write anything of a political Nature, that tends to enlighten and serve the Public."[7] Printers, especially in the first half of the eighteenth century, may have proposed an open and impartial press for a number of reasons. First, they may have considered themselves as purely artisans or tradesmen who produced a product for public consumption.[8]

Second, printers may have opened their presses to the citizens for financial reasons. A newspaper with from 300 to 500 weekly subscriptions probably could not support a printer if its news alienated half of those readers. Printers, therefore, would welcome opinions from all sides of an issue to use their newspapers as forums for the community and to stimulate circulation and profits. Similarly, printers might reject opinion articles if they felt the message was too highly charged or morally or ethically offensive to most readers.

Even though printers sometimes refused to publish controversial letters and essays, writings were usually inserted regardless of topic. That may have been because printers often charged a fee for printing essays and letters in newspapers. The acceptance of money to publish an opinion piece does not lessen its persuasive power; it merely supports the concept that printers kept their presses open to all for financial reasons.

When South Carolina printer Lewis Timothy began printing a series of essays in 1735 written by a group of Charleston citizens known as the "Meddler's Club" that intruded upon the affairs of the town's citizens, he no doubt received compensation. Later, his son Peter noted that an anonymous political essayist had failed to pay "the Price notified for publishing the same."[9]

The content of newspapers was not always open to all sides. Boston citizens opposing the use of inoculation to fight smallpox in Boston in 1721 hired James Franklin to publish a newspaper opposing the practice. Franklin's *New-England Courant* never proposed itself to be an unbiased publication, only that it would not directly attack the clergy or the government, two promises the paper's writers broke in less than two years. Similarly, some New York politicians initiated the *New-York Weekly Journal* purely as a means to attack the government of Governor William Cosby, which culminated in the arrest of the paper's printer, John Peter Zenger.

If printers did not write the opinion pieces in newspapers, who did? The answer to this question is hard to determine because most letters and essays during the colonial era were either unsigned or attributed to a writer who chose to close them with a pseudonym that often described the author's intentions. Often, the pseudonym was a Latin or Greek term or phrase such as "Philo-Patria," or lover of country. Despite the use of pseudonyms, the identity of anonymous writers was sometimes known to readers, which was the case with a series of letters titled "Letters from a Pennsylvania Farmer" that sought to unify colonial opposition to the British. Americans knew the writer was John Dickinson. At other times, authors of letters and essays remained a mystery. In 1756 a series of essays appeared first in the *Virginia Gazette*, soon to be reprinted in nearly every town in America. The essays by the "Virginia Centinel" sought to increase solidarity among colonials to defeat the French and Indians during the French and Indian War. While the author of the essay series may have been known by the *Gazette*'s printer, all that was revealed about the writer was that he was a minister, speculated by some to be James Maury. Maury never admitted to writing the series, however.[10] Most of the letters or essays that appeared in the papers, then, were written by influential and educated members of a community. Dickinson was not a farmer but a lawyer and politician, and the "Virginia Centinel" was probably a minister who occupied a place of importance in Virginia society. Anonymity, no doubt, allowed writers to speak more freely in an age when criticizing the government was considered a crime even if the offenders were not always prosecuted.

Even though printers in general did not write opinion articles in the first half of the eighteenth century, they increasingly did so in the twenty-five years before the Revolution. The most well-known of America's early printers, Benjamin Franklin, however, was one printer who honed his opinion-writing skills at an early age, contrary to the habit of printers not to write lengthy opinion essays. Serving as an apprentice in Boston, the teenaged Franklin used the name "Silence Dogood" to write a series of opinion essays on Massachusetts politics and life in his brother's *New-England Courant* in 1723. He did the same as "The Busy-Body" in Philadelphia in the *American Weekly Mercury* in 1729.

As America's situation changed, so, too, did Franklin's opinion writing. In the May 9, 1754, *Pennsylvania Gazette*, Franklin used his persuasive skills to warn Americans that their way of life was in danger of being destroyed if they did not unite "for our common Defence and Security" and "under one Direction, with one Council, and one Purse." Even though Franklin's "JOIN, or DIE" essay or editorial was unsigned, all who read the *Gazette* knew the paper's owner was the author. Other printers quickly copied the woodcut of a disjointed snake—America's first editorial cartoon—and Franklin's essay.

The French and Indian War seemed to bring out the editorial skills of printers. New York printer Hugh Gaine, for example, echoed Franklin's sentiments when he added the following editorial note to a piece titled "*The* PRESENT STATE *of this Continent*":

I hope, and pray the Almighty, That the British Colonies on this continent, may cease impolitically and ungenerously to consider themselves as distinct States . . . that they unite like Brother Protestants, and Brother Subjects . . . and secure to themselves and their Posterity, to the Ends of Time, the inestimable Blessings of Civil and Religious Liberty, and the Possession and Settlement of a great Country, rich in all the Fountains of human Liberty.[11]

The same kinds of insertions aimed at changing public opinion were made by printers from the Stamp Act crisis of 1765, when printers and other Americans protested British taxes on paper, through the beginning of the Revolution and beyond. During the Revolutionary period, three Boston printers—Benjamin Edes, John Gill, and Isaiah Thomas—consistently wrote invectives for their papers. Edes and Gill railed against the British after the Boston Massacre, where an American mob confronted British soldiers in 1770 and five citizens were killed, and Thomas put the Battle of Lexington into the American perspective when he wrote in the *Massachusetts Spy* on May 3, 1775, "AMERICANS! Forever bear in mind the BATTLE OF LEXINGTON!—where British troops, unmolested and unprovoked, wantonly and in a most inhuman manner, fired upon and killed a number of our countrymen, then robbed, ransacked, and burnt their houses!"

All of these printers—Franklin, Gaine, Edes, Gill, and Thomas, as well as others—were making intentional personal efforts to sway public opinion with their newspapers. From the inception of newspapers in America, printers had been expressing personal opinion with statements appended to stories or through their choices of news to print. But they often encountered opposition. *Publick Occurrences*, for example, was published only once in part because its printer, Benjamin Harris, inserted hearsay into a news article about shipping and military problems with France. The Massachusetts council reckoned that hearsay was libelous and ordered Harris never to print in Boston again. Harris' assertion that the French king Louis XIV "used to lie with the Sons Wife,"[12] although not an opinion article, was no doubt an effort to further colonial dislike and distrust of France and was intentionally placed in the paper by Harris for that purpose. Boston printer Thomas Fleet did the same in 1740 when he inserted the following sentence after a story about the itinerant minister George Whitefield's departure from Boston: "the town is in a hopeful Way of being restor'd to its former State of Order, Peace and Industry."[13] Printers also made editorial comment about events by inserting scripture, poetry, and parody before and after news items.

Whether written by printers or others, the essays and letters in colonial newspapers helped shape the opinions of Americans. The news selected by printers to appear in their newspapers also helped mold thoughts in eighteenth-century America.

This book presents debates on issues of importance in colonial America as they were discussed in newspapers. Each chapter focuses upon a specific event or issue during the colonial period, from the introduction of newspapers in 1690 through the signing of the Declaration of Independence in 1776. It presents writings on both sides of an issue as printers and other colonists used newspapers to sway public opinion. Material is drawn from many of America's newspapers during this period, but newspapers located in the larger towns of the colonies—Boston, New York, Philadelphia, and Charleston—often are central to issues of the times, especially if the event or issue centered in that city or its colony.

The selection of events and issues for such a book is subjective to a certain extent but also limited by newspaper content. The work is organized chronologically by issue or event. Some broader issues, such as the role of women in society, are also included. The newspaper articles selected reflect a variety of stances on events and issues. Thirty-one issues of concern in the colonial era are featured in this work. Each issue concludes with questions for discussion.

NOTES

1. *New-York Gazette Revived in the Weekly Post-Boy*, 22 January 1750, 1.

2. David A. Copeland, "JOIN, or DIE: America's Newspapers in the French and Indian War," *Journalism History* 24 (1998): 118.

3. *Virginia Gazette* (Williamsburg), 26 July 1744.

4. Monetary figures based on conversions found in John J. McCusker and Russell R. Menard, *The Economy of British America 1607–1789* (Chapel Hill: University of North Carolina Press, 1985), 57, 61.

5. See Wm. David Sloan, "The *New-England Courant*: Voice of Anglicanism," *American Journalism* 8 (1991): 108–41.

6. *New-York Journal*, 25 October 1770, 4. For the arguments put forth by both sides, see David A. Copeland, "Virtuous and Vicious: The Dual Portrayal of Women in Colonial Newspapers," *American Periodicals* 5 (1995): 72–76.

7. *Weekly Rehearsal* (Boston), 2 April 1733.

8. See Stephen Botein, " 'Meer Mechanics' and an Open Press: The Business and Political Strategies of Colonial American Printers," in *Perspectives in American History*, vol. 9, ed. Donald Fleming and Bernard Bailyn (Cambridge: Harvard University Press, 1975), 127–225.

9. Quoted in Hennig Cohen, *The South Carolina Gazette* (Columbia: University of South Carolina Press, 1953), 10.

10. See J. A. Leo Lemay, *A Calendar of American Poetry* (Worcester, Mass.: American Antiquarian Society, 1972), 183–84.

11. *New-York Mercury*, 23 September 1754, 2 (emphasis included).

12. *Publick Occurrences Both Forreign and Domestick* (Boston), 25 September 1690, 3.

13. *Boston Evening-Post*, 29 September 1740, 2.

CHAPTER 1

Censorship, Printing Control, and Freedom of the Press, 1690

When an American hears the terms freedom of the press and freedom of speech, his or her thoughts turn immediately to the First Amendment, which reads, "Congress shall make no laws . . . abridging the freedom of speech, or of the press." Not all people, however, interpret of the First Amendment in the same way. Some people believe that because the amendment states "no laws," no constraints should be placed on media or the speech of anyone. Most people believe that the media's rights guaranteed by the First Amendment should be balanced with other rights enjoyed by Americans.

The concept of what media may print or broadcast is constantly undergoing revision. The ultimate decision of what receives protection under the First Amendment comes from rulings made by the U.S. Supreme Court. Any notion that we might have of what freedom of the press means for media today would have been unacceptable to almost all Americans living in the colonial period. Americans operated under British law, under which many kinds of speech were illegal, especially criticism of government. Most American colonists believed in freedom of speech and the press. Many of the settlers who colonized what would become the United States came here to escape religious persecution, and they talked and wrote of free speech in relation to their rights to publish religious material that supported their understanding of the Bible.

Dissension from the religious rules set up in America by groups such as the Puritans occurred in the colonies just as it did in England. Because of this criticism, England established laws that required printers to have all that they printed approved by government officials. Known as licensing, all colonial governors received directions in 1686 "that no person keep any printing-press for printing, nor that any book, pamphlet, or other matter whatsoever be printed without your especiall leave and license first obtained."[1]

In 1690 printer Benjamin Harris violated that law. Harris, who came to America the same year that the licensing law went into effect, believed that Boston needed a newspaper so that its citizens could be kept apprised of all events that affected them. On September 25, 1690, he published *Publick Occurrences Both Forreign and Domestick*. The three-page newspaper contained no attacks on the licensing law or complaints about the government; it simply related to its readers what was going on—a smallpox outbreak, a murder, a good harvest among the "Christianized" Indians, the execution of Native American prisoners of war, and a report that the king of France, Louis XIV, might be sleeping with his son's wife. Massachusetts officials would probably never have approved the printing of the last two items, and therein lay the problem for Harris. His publication and its contents were never approved by the governor. On September 29, the governor ordered that Harris never publish *Publick Occurrences* again. America's first newspaper printed but one issue before it died at the censor's hand.

Newspaper success in the early eighteenth century was tied directly to governmental approval of content, but the idea that a newspaper needed the endorsement of a political body did not last long. Printers of Boston's *New-England Courant* and Philadelphia's *American Weekly Mercury* both experienced run-ins with the authorities in the early 1720s when the printers published material critical of some aspect of leadership in their colony.

By 1735 America's colonies had grown large enough to foster political dissension. No longer was press control proposed for religious reasons. The trial of John Peter Zenger (Chapter 5) revolved around who would control New York politics. Zenger's paper, the *New-York Weekly Journal*, attacked the government of Governor William Cosby and defended its right to do so as freedom of the press. Another New York printer, James Parker, defied the colony's government and published objectionable material in 1747. In 1756 Parker called into question the results of an election. He defended his right to do so as freedom of the press. Slowly, Americans were developing the concept of freedom of the press as a means of checking government actions, stirring agitation for causes, and fighting laws some believed to be tyrannical. When England attempted to impose a tax on paper in 1765, the colonists, regarding the tax as an attack on American freedoms, erupted in protest.

By the 1770s, newspapers were regarded as a principal instrument in the fight for freedom from England, but not all printers thought independence was proper. Tory printers, who felt America should remain part of Britain, found their presses destroyed and their likenesses hanged in effigy by angry Patriots who supported America's separation from Great Britain. Even though the majority of Americans demanded a free press to criticize government, minority opposition was often suppressed. Freedom of the press—even though it had left behind religious restraints—was still meant principally for those in control. The *Massachusetts Spy* proclaimed in 1772, "However lordly fools would be!! FOREVER shall the PRESS be FREE!!"[2] But the author of the lines no doubt never intended that the "fools" be given press access to espouse opposing viewpoints, even though many printers in the 1770s claimed they believed in the concept of an open and unbiased press by declaring in their nameplates that their papers were "Open to all Parties, but Influenced by None," as did printer John Pinkney's *Virginia Gazette*.

Even if printers consciously limited the information presented in their newspapers to one side of an issue, publishing articles that called for limiting free speech were rare. This chapter includes one newspaper essay from the 1730s that explains why limiting the press was necessary. It also contains two pieces from the 1770s that call for limiting press freedom, one an essay in the pro-British newspaper the *Censor*, the other a letter from a person signing himself "Tory." Both attack the freedom of the press as it was used by American Patriots to attack British officials when these same Patriots used whatever means possible to silence Tory or Loyalist publications.

The chapter begins with a selection of pieces advocating limitations on freedom of the press. The first two are statements by seventeenth-century policymakers, Virginia Governor William Berkeley in 1671 and the Massachusetts Bay governing council in 1690. The section ends with a statement by jurist Francis Hopkinson on the dangers of criticizing government, which includes self-interest, partisanship, and sedition.

A selection of pieces defending freedom of the press begins with an essay that appeared over a four-week period in the *Pennsylvania Gazette* in 1737. The author of the essay was probably James Alexander, the person behind the printed attacks on New York Governor William Cosby in 1733 and 1734. Alexander wrote in response to essays from Barbados criticizing the trial of John Peter Zenger. This piece is followed by a series of essays on freedom of speech and of the press printed by Benjamin Edes and John Gill after they assumed control of the *Boston Gazette* in April 1755. The series included "An Apology for the LIBERTY of the PRESS" and was probably printed by the Patriot-minded printers to establish the agenda of the paper under their tenure. The series is followed by a 1767 *Boston Gazette* essay that may well have been a collaboration with the printers' good friend Samuel Adams. Adams, Edes, and Gill were outspoken opponents of British intervention in the colonies. While the three advocated free speech and a free press, their opponents claimed "they would confine it wholly to themselves."[3] The chapter closes with a *New-Hampshire Gazette* statement on the value of a free press to society shortly before the signing of the Declaration of Independence.

IN FAVOR OF CENSORSHIP AND PRESS LIMITATIONS

WILLIAM BERKELEY: "ENQUIRIES TO THE GOVERNOR OF VIRGINIA"

British law required colonial governors to issue reports on the state of their colonies and to reply to any questions that might arise concerning the colonies. In 1671 the Lords Commissioners of Foreign Plantations sent Virginia Governor William Berkeley a questionnaire on the state of religion in his province. In his reply, the governor lamented the fact that religious life in Virginia could be better, and he added the statement below on the state of the press there. Berkeley's statement accurately describes the perception of most colonial governments on the potential dangers of a press not controlled by government licensing, especially in matters of religion and politics.

"Enquiries to the Governor of Virginia," 1671

I thank God, there are no free schools nor printing; and I hope we shall not have these hundred years; for learning has brought disobedience, and heresy, and sects into the world, and printing has divulged them, and libels against the government. God keep us from both!
William Berkeley

THE GOVERNOR'S COUNCIL OF MASSACHUSETTS: "THE SUPPRESSION OF *PUBLICK OCCURRENCES*"

The political situation in Boston during 1690 was chaotic. Taxpayers had revolted against the colony's policies, the French and their Indian allies were at war with the British, and many of the farms and plantations throughout the colony lay in ruin. In order to separate rumor from fact, Benjamin Harris began a newspaper, Publick Occurrences. *Four days after its publication, the governing council ordered the newspaper suppressed and Harris never again to print a newspaper in Massachusetts. The decree stated that any future printing must be licensed by the colony's government. As a result, the newspapers printed in Bos-*

ton that followed Publick Occurrences *carried "Printed by Authority" in their nameplates.*

By the Governour & Council

WHEREAS some have lately presumed to Print and Disperse a Pamphlet Entitled, Publick Occurrences, both Forreign and Domestick: Boston, Thursday, Septemb. 25th. 1690. *Without the least Privity or Countenance of Authority.*

The Governour and Council having had the perusal of the said Pamphlet, and finding that therein is contained Reflections of a very high nature: As also sundry doubtful and uncertain Reports, do hereby manifest and declare their high Resentment and Disallowance of said Pamphlet, and Order that the same be Suppressed and called in; strickly forbidding any person or persons for the future to Set forth any thing in Print without License first obtained from those that are or shall be appointed by the Government to grant the same.

By Order of the Governour & Council.

Isaac Addington, Secr.

Published in Boston, September 29th. 1690.

AN ANONYMOUS NEW YORKER: "THE DANGERS OF PAPERS AND PAMPHLETS"

In January 1734, the assault on New York Governor William Cosby by writers in the New-York Weekly Journal *was at full force. The attack on Cosby was part of a political power play in the colony, and citizens lined up on both sides of the argument. In this selection, an anonymous writer requests that printer William Bradford run an essay that the writer claims comes from the pen of Joseph Addison, the British satirist and printer of a much-emulated London newspaper, the* Spectator. *Addison's words were most often used to support the concept of freedom of the press, but here, a selection has been gleaned that points out the dangers of allowing printers to publish newspapers and pamphlets without any governmental control.*

New-York Gazette, 28 January 1733 (1734)

THERE is nothing so scandalous to a Government, and detestable in the Eyes of all good Men, as defamatory Papers and Pamphlets; but at the same Time there is nothing so difficult to tame, as a Satyrical Author. An angry Writer, who cannot appear in Print, naturally vents his Spleen in Libels and Lampoons. . . .

IT has been proposed, *to oblige every Person that writes a Book, or a Paper, to swear himself the Author of it, and enter down in this a publick Register his Name and Place of abode.*

THIS, indeed, would have effectually suppressed all printed Scandal, which generally appears under borrowed Names, or under none at all. But it is to be feared, that such an Expedient would not only destroy Scandal, but Learning. It would operate promiscuously, and root up the Corn and Tares together. Not to mention some of the most celebrated Works of Piety, which have preceeded from Anonymous Authors, who have made it their Merit to convey to us so great a Charity in secret: There are few Works of Genius that come out at first with the Author's Name. The Writer generally makes a Tryal of them in the World before he owns them; and, I believe, very few, who are capable of Writing, would let Pen to Paper, if they knew, before hand, that they must not publish their Productions but on such Conditions. For my own part, I must declare the Papers I present . . . shall last no longer than while the Author is concealed. . . .

I have never yet heard of a Ministry, who have inflicted an exemplary Punishment on an Author that has supported their Cause with Falshood and Scandal, and treated in a most cruel manner, the Names of those who have been looked upon as their Rivals and Antagonists. Would a Government set an everlasting Mark of their Displeasure upon one of those infamous Writers, who makes his Court to them by tearing to Pieces the Reputation of a Competitor, we should quickly see an End put to this Rate of Vermin, that are a Scandal to Government, and a Reproach to Human Nature. . . .

I cannot but look upon the finest Strokes of Satyr which are armed at *particular Persons*, and which are supported even with the Appearance of Truth, to be the Marks of an evil Mind, and highly Criminal in themselves. Infamy, like other punishments, is under the Direction and Distribution of the *Magistrate*, and not of any private *Person*. Accordingly we learn from a Fragment of Cicero, that tho' there were very few Capital Punishments in the Twelve Tables, a Libel or Lampoon which took away the *good Name* of another, was to be punished by Death.

BUT this is far from being our Case. Our Satyr is nothing but *Ribaldry*, and *Bilingsgate*. Scurrilty passes for Wit; and he who can call Names in the greatest Variety of Phrase, is looked upon to have the shrewdest Pen. By this Means the Honour of Families is ruined, the *highest Posts* and greatest Titles are render'd cheap and vile in the Sight of the People; the noblest Virtues, and most exalted Parts, exposed to the Contempt of the Vicious and Ignorant. Should a Foreigner, who knows nothing of our private Factions, or one who is to act his part in the World, when our present *Heats and Animosities are forgot*, should, I say, such an one form to himself a Notion of the greatest Men of all Sides in the *British* Nation, who are now suffering from the Characters which are given them in some or most of those abominable Writings which are daily published among us, what a Nation of Monsters must we appear!

AS this cruel Practice tends to the utter Subversion of all Truth and Humanity among us, it deserves the utmost Detestation and Discouragement of all who have either the Love of their Country, or the Honour of their Religion, at Heart. I would therefore earnestly recommend it to the Consideration of those who deal in these pernicious Arts of Writing. . . . Every honest Man sets as high a Value upon a *good Name*, as upon Life it self; and I cannot but think that those who privily assault the one, would destroy the other, might they do it with the same *Secrecy and Impunity*.

AN ANONYMOUS BOSTONIAN: "CONDEMNATION OF THE PARTY PRESS"

Following the Boston Massacre in 1770, divisions along political lines in Boston became obvious in the press. The sole purpose of one newspaper, the Censor, *was to support the policies of the British administration of the colony. As a result, the newspaper's writers, who wrote in anonymity, attacked the partisan nature of the writings that appeared in some Boston newspapers, particularly the* Boston Gazette. *The essay suggests that the rise of partisanship is synonymous with lies and threats to legitimate government. As a result, freedom of the press must be controlled. It is worth noting that although this essay was unsigned, its author may well have been Massachusetts Lieutenant Governor Peter Oliver or Dr. Benjamin Church. Church, who was appointed surgeon general of America at the start of the Revolution, was later confined because of correspondence with the British army that occupied Boston.*

The Censor (Boston), 7 March 1772

THE advantages resulting from the art of Printing are acknowledged to be as important and interesting to mankind, as from any mechanical invention, as no method is so well fitted to preserve the production of the learned, and to extend useful knowledge to every order of the species with such surprizing facility and exactness; an art unknown to the ancients. . . . So long as the Press is directed to the valuable purposes of extending literature, promoting arts, improving the morals and correcting the vices of mankind, so long it hath a just claim to the patronage of every friend to science and liberty: But if, by the ascendency and influence of a *party*, it becomes a vehicle in the hands of the licentious to calumniate the amiable and virtuous, and by insidious arts to create fears, jealousies, and distractions, to the great interruption of publick peace and happiness; such prostitution of the Press I am persuaded every judicious man must condemn; and wish that measures might be taken to prevent. I am constrained to say, that no country hath so wantonly abused the freedom of the Press as this; on this account it is notorious.

FRANCIS HOPKINSON: "WHEN GOVERNMENT CAN SUPPRESS THE PRESS"

Philadelphia lawyer Francis Hopkinson signed the Declaration of Independence and was a member of the Constitutional Convention, but in 1776 he used "Tory" as a pen name to write a letter supporting press suppression. Hopkinson believed, as did many Patriots, that freedom of the press was needed in America, but he also believed that there were limits on what could be said. In this letter, he defines those limits to any threat that might undermine the foundations of government.

Pennsylvania Evening Post (Philadelphia), 16 November 1776

The liberty of the press hath been justly held up as an important privilege of the people. . . . But when this privilege is manifestly abused, and the press becomes an engine for sowing the most dangerous dissensions, for spreading false alarms, and undermining the very foundations of government, ought be not that government, upon the plain principles of self-preservation, to silence by its own authority, such a daring violator of its peace, and tear from its bosom the serpent that would sting it to death. *A Tory*

DEFENDING FREEDOM OF THE PRESS

ANDREW HAMILTON: "A *PRINCIPAL PILLAR* OF A FREE GOVERNMENT"

Andrew Hamilton defended John Peter Zenger in his famous libel trial in 1735 (see Chapter 5 for a full description of the trial), but other than Zenger's own printings, nothing about the trial appeared in American newspapers until years later. That does not mean that printers did not discuss the free press ramifications of the trial. In this extended essay, which appeared over four weeks in the Pennsylvania Gazette, *an unsigned essay describes the value of freedom of press and speech for the success of government by placing the concepts into a historical concept. In it, the author emphasizes the concept of truth in printing, the mainstay in the Zenger defense. Even though printer Benjamin Franklin did not attribute the essay to Hamilton, who in addition to being a lawyer was an elected Philadelphia official, the* Barbados Gazette *named Hamilton its author when it reprinted the essay in January 1738.*

Pennsylvania Gazette (Philadelphia), 17 November 1737–8 December 1737

To the Author of the Pennsylvania Gazette
SIR,

THE FREEDOM OF SPEECH is a *principal Pillar* in a free Government: when this support is taken away the Constitution is dissolved, and Tyranny is erected on its Ruins. Republics and limited Monarchies derive their Strength and Vigor from a *popular Examination* into the Actions of the Magistrates. This Privilege in all Ages has been and always will be abused. The best Princes could not escape the Censure and Envy of the Times they lived in. But the Evil is not so great as it may appear at first Sight. A Magistrate who sincerely aims at the *Good* of the Society will always have the Inclinations of a great Majority on his side; and impartial Posterity will not fail to render him Justice.

These Abuses of the Freedom of Speech are the Excrescences of Liberty. They ought to be suppressed; but to whom dare we commit the Care of doing it? An evil Magistrate entrusted with the POWER to *punish Words* is armed with a WEAPON the most *destructive* and *terrible*. Under pretense of pruning off the exuberant Branches, he frequently destroys the Tree. . . .

Augustus Caesar under the specious Pretext of preserving the Characters of the Romans from Defamation introduced the Law whereby Libeling was involved in the Penalties of *Treason* against the State. . . .

Henry VII, a Prince mighty in Politics, procured that ACT to be passed whereby the Jurisdiction of the Star Chamber was confirmed and extended. . . . The Subjects were terrified from uttering their Griefs while they saw the Thunder of the Star Chamber pointed at their Heads. This Caution, however, could not prevent several dangerous Tumults and Insurrections. For when the Tongues of the People are restrained, they commonly discharge their Resentments by a more *dangerous Organ*, and break out into open Acts of Violence.

During the Reign of Henry VIII . . . every light Expression which happened to displease him was construed by his supple Judges into a Libel, sometimes extended to high Treason. . . .

IN the two former Papers the Writer endeavored to prove by historical Facts the fatal Dangers that necessarily attend a Restraint on Freedom of Speech and the Liberty of the Press: Upon which the following Reflection naturally occurs, viz., THAT WHOEVER ATTEMPTS TO SUPPRESS EITHER OF THOSE, OUR NATURAL RIGHTS, OUGHT TO BE REGARDED AS AN ENEMY TO LIBERTY AND THE CONSTITUTION. *An Inconveniency is always to be suffered when it cannot be removed without introducing a Worse.* . . .

To infuse the Minds of the People an ill Opinion of a just Administration is a Crime that deserves no Mercy: But to expose the evil Designs or weak Management of a Magistrate is the Duty of every Member of Society. . . . No Law could be better framed to prevent People from publishing their Thoughts on the Administration than that which makes no distinction whether a Libel be true or false. . . .

The Punishment for writing Truth is Pillory, loss of Ears, branding the

Face with hot Irons, Fine and Imprisonment at the Discretion of the Court. Nay, the Punishment is to be heightened in proportion to the Truth of the Facts contained in the Libel. . . .

Upon the Whole. To suppress Enquiries into the Administration is good Policy in an arbitrary Government: But a free Constitution and freedom of Speech have such a reciprocal Dependence on each other that they cannot subsist without consisting together.

W. K.: "OF FREEDOM OF SPEECH"

When Benjamin Edes and John Gill bought the Boston Gazette *in 1755, the pair opened publication with a series of letters and essays on the significance of the freedom of speech and the press. The letter written by the unnamed W. K. was probably taken from an English newspaper, or it may have been produced by the printers. Either way, its appearance was to let readers know the stance of the paper's new owners. In this letter, freedom of press and speech are equated with the preservation of liberty.*

Boston Gazette, or Country Journal, 21 April 1755

Of Freedom of SPEECH.

WITHOUT Freedom of Thought, there can be no such Thing as Wisdom, and no such Thing as publick Liberty, without Freedom of Speech: Which is the Right of every Man, as far as by it he does not hurt and controul the Right of another; and this is the only Check which it ought to suffer, the only Bounds which it ought to know.

This sacred Privilege is so essential to free Government, that the Security of Property: and the Freedom of Speech, always go together; and in those wretched Countries where a Man cannot call his Tongue his own. Whoever would overthrow the Liberty of the Nation, must begin by subduing the Freedom of Speech; a Thing terrible to publick Traytors. . . .

Freedom of Speech, therefore, being of such infinite Importance to the Preservation of Liberty, every one who loves Liberty ought to encourage Freedom of Speech.

AN ANONYMOUS LONDON WRITER: "AN APOLOGY FOR THE LIBERTY OF THE PRESS"

Boston printers Edes and Gill continued their series supporting free speech and press freedom through their first nine issues in 1755. In this essay, taken from a London newspaper, the concept that all Englishmen are born with these rights is declared.

Boston Gazette, or Country Journal, 26 May 1755

An Apology *for the* LIBERTY *of the* PRESS

THE Freedom of the Press, by which I mean the *Freedom which every Subject has to communicate his Sentiments to the Publick, in that Manner, which may make them most universally known*, is a Freedom which does not proceed from any Peculiarity in the Frame of the *English* Constitution, but is essential to and coeval with all free Governments, into which it is not adopted, but born.

. . . the people of *England* without *the Liberty of the Press* to inform them of the fitness and unfitness of measures, approv'd or condem'd by those whom they have trusted, and whom they may trust again, would be in as blind a state of subjection, as if they lived under the most arbitrary and inquisitorial government; nay their condition would be aggravated by the melancholly consideration, that they lent their own helping hands both to forge and rivet their chains.

FREEBORN AMERICAN: "THE NATURE OF POLITICAL LIBERTY"

In 1767 Americans were abuzz with talk of a new set of taxes about to be imposed upon them. Named collectively for Charles Townshend, Chancellor of the Exchequer (treasury), the new duties taxed tea, paint, lead, paper, and glass. The Boston Gazette *served as the principal voice of protest against British taxes in New England. Here, the anonymous writer asserts that freedom of speech is essential to the preservation of liberty.*

Boston Gazette, and Country Journal, 9 March 1767

Man, in a state of nature, has undoubtedly a right to speak and act without controul. In a state of civil society, that right is limited by the law— Political liberty consists in a freedom of speech and action, so far as the laws of a community will permit, and no farther: all beyond is criminal, and tends to the destruction of Liberty itself.—That society whose laws least restrain the words and actions of its members, is most free.—There is no nation on the earth, where freedom of speech is more extensive than among the English: This is what keeps the constitution in health and vigour, and is in a great measure the cause of our preservation as a free people: For should it ever be dangerous to exercise this privilege, it is easy to see, without the spirit of prophecy, slavery and bondage would soon be the portion of Britons.

Freeborn American

ROBERT FOWLE: "A SACRED RIGHT"

Late in 1775, printer Robert Fowle established a newspaper in Exeter to serve as a voice for Tories in New Hampshire. Like many other printers

with British leanings during the Revolutionary period, Fowle found it
necessary to print statements on freedom of the press as a way to justify
the rights of all printers and citizens—despite their political positions—
to publish newspapers or have letters and essays printed. In this state-
ment, Fowle sees free speech as a sacred right. Without it, he believes,
all freedoms and privileges that Americans love will be lost.

New-Hampshire Gazette (Exeter), 25 May 1776

The liberty of the Press has ever been held as one of the most sacred rights of a free people, and when we are abridged of that invaluable priviledge, farewell to Peace, Liberty, and safety, farewell to Learning Knowledge and Truth, farewell all that is dear to us; we must ever after grope in darkness, thick darkness, that may even be felt: may Heaven forbid such deprivation, and long continue to us this invaluable blessing.

QUESTIONS

1. The First Amendment of the Constitution says, "Congress shall make no laws . . . abridging the freedom of speech, or of the press." In what ways did Americans through 1776 believe government could control speech and the press?
2. What was licensing, and why do you think governments felt they needed to license the press?
3. How did Americans view the relationship between government and the press?
4. What relationship did Americans see between freedom of the press and a free society?
5. Why do you think political leaders in the seventeenth and early eighteenth centuries feared printing?
6. Do you think that free speech and freedom of the press were meant for all people in colonial America? Who do you think the essay writers would have protected, and who might have been omitted from protection?
7. How do our concepts of free speech and press today differ from those of colonial Americans? Explain.
8. Should speech and press freedoms be limited? How would colonial Americans argue the issue?

NOTES

1. "Commissions to Massachusetts Governors," quoted in *Massachusetts Historical Society Proceedings* (June 1893): 273.
2. *Massachusetts Spy* (Boston), 27 February 1772.
3. Quoted in Leonard W. Levy, *Freedom of the Press from Zenger to Jefferson: Early American Libertarian Theories* (Indianapolis: Bobbs-Merrill Company, 1966), 95.

The Inoculation Controversy, 1721

Settlers in America faced many hardships in the seventeenth and eighteenth centuries, but the greatest threat to them did not come from Native Americans, harsh weather, or dangerous ocean voyages. Americans' greatest enemy was disease, especially smallpox. From the beginning of colonization in Jamestown in 1607 to 1625, for example, more than 80 percent of the settlers died from disease. Smallpox and other European illnesses also killed more than 90 percent of all Native Americans who came in contact with European settlers.[1]

In the eighteenth century, people did not understand that diseases such as smallpox were viruses. Medical science attributed diseases to the body's "humours" or its fluids, such as blood and urine. To treat someone for an ailment, a doctor sometimes bled the patient to drain the "bad" blood from the ailing person. This practice often left the sick much weaker than they were before and actually hindered recovery or even hastened death.

Smallpox was a new disease in America, but it was not a new disease to the European settlers who unknowingly brought it with them. Having had experience with the disease did not make it any less feared. Contracting smallpox frightened not only the person who contracted the disease but also everyone in the region because half the people who contracted the disease died from it. Smallpox begins with symptoms similar to influenza, but, within a week, a rash appears on the face, hands, and feet and soon turns into pus-filled blisters that often burst. The open wounds leave the patient vulnerable to other infections. Smallpox can lead directly to blindness, pneumonia, and brain and kidney damage.

In 1721 Boston faced its seventh major smallpox outbreak in less than a century. There had been dozens of lesser outbreaks. People fled the Massachusetts town on the Charles River. Those who stayed could be assured that someone in their family would contract the disease. In fact, 6,000 of Boston's approximately 10,500 residents contracted smallpox during the next eighteen months, and 899 of them died from the disease.[2]

The 1721 outbreak of smallpox in Boston was unlike any previous epidemic, however, because the city's leading Puritan minister, Cotton Mather, advocated a radical procedure. He suggested that people *not* afflicted with the disease be given it through inoculation. The concept of inoculation—or the giving of a weakened form of a disease to a well person so that the body can build resistance to the illness—was not accepted by most European physicians and had never been practiced in America. Mather had learned about inoculation through his readings and from his African slave.[3] Inoculating people as a preventative had been practiced in the Middle and Far East for a number of years, and Mather, who lived through a case of smallpox in 1702 and had studied medicine before entering the ministry, believed inoculation could stop the suffering and death caused by the disease.

Mather began to crusade for inoculation by contacting Zabdiel Boylston, a Boston doctor, who agreed to inoculate individuals. In the early eighteenth century, few of the physicians in America were educated in medicine. They were mostly well-read individuals, or they dabbled in folk remedies and improvised with potions and drug mixtures and experienced some success. Mather's plan for inoculation was immediately opposed by Dr. William Douglass, Boston's only university-trained physician. He called inoculation "a Wicked and Criminal Practice" and the uneducated Boylston a "quack."[4] The controversy concerning inoculation captured center stage in Boston's press in August 1721 with the introduction of the *New-England Courant*, Boston's third newspaper, which was printed by James Franklin with the assistance of his apprentice brother, Benjamin. One of the principal reasons for the establishment of the *Courant* was to fight inoculation.

The Franklins served primarily as the paper's printers; its financial backers included John Checkley, who was a staunch supporter of the Church of England. Checkley's disdain of inoculation no doubt was fueled by his dislike for Puritans and Mather. He and Douglass wrote most of the anti-inoculation articles that appeared in the *Courant*. Before founding the *Courant*, they used the *Boston News-Letter*, the town's oldest newspaper, as their mouthpiece. The pro-inoculation forces used the *Boston Gazette* to present their ideas to the citizens of Boston. Mather and Boylston's minister, Benjamin Colman, wrote letters supporting inoculation. As was the case throughout the colonial era, the writers often used pseudonyms rather than their own names or left their letters un-

signed. In this controversy, Mather, Colman, and several other Puritan ministers sometimes signed letters using their own names, a rarity. Douglass often used the pseudonym "W. Philanthropos," which means "lover of mankind."

The inoculation controversy of 1721 produced some of the most heated newspaper debate in colonial America. Even though medicine eventually proved Mather and Boylston to be correct in the use of inoculation as the way to stop smallpox, inoculation was controversial in the eighteenth century because it was not understood. Those inoculated did sometimes die, but the death rate among those inoculated was significantly lower than that of those who were infected through the normal spread of the disease. As a *Maryland Gazette* writer pointed out during a smallpox outbreak in that colony, "of the 3434 Persons Inoculated in the Inoculating Hospital, only Ten have died; whereas of the Number of 6000 and odd having the Small Pox in the natural Way, dying the same Hospital, upon the lowest Computation is Twenty-Five in an Hundred."[5] Even though inoculation reduced the odds of dying from smallpox, the inoculation controversy continued. In 1760 in Charleston, South Carolina, for example, the *South-Carolina Gazette* ran stories explaining how to inoculate against smallpox at home. At the same time, the paper printed petitions that asked that the practice be outlawed in the province because it threatened to spread the disease.[6]

The Boston newspaper battle concerning inoculation lasted for months. The anti-inoculation writers often belittled their counterparts in print but rarely used complete names. The pro-inoculation forces generally avoided name-calling but did refute attacks on Boylston. The first two anti-inoculation letters included in this chapter were written by Douglass. He used his pseudonym on the first; the second appeared unsigned. The first letter is a response to the initial inoculations performed in Boston by Boylston. The second anti-inoculation letter was a response to a letter that appeared in the *Boston Gazette* and was signed by Mather and five other ministers. The third anti-inoculation letter writer used the pseudonym "Absinthium," which literally means wormword, a bitter liquor that could make the drinker quite ill. "Absinthium" was probably George Steward, another Boston doctor who helped finance the founding of the *Courant*.

The first pro-inoculation entry was written by Mather and signed by his father, Increase Mather, and four other Boston clergymen, including Colman. It is a defense of Boylston and his decision to inoculate against smallpox. The *Boston Gazette* letter begins, "To the Author of the Boston News-Letter," in reference to the Douglass' *News-Letter* attack on Boylston. The second pro-inoculation letter is an account of the success of smallpox inoculation. The third pro-inoculation entry, taken from the *Pennsylvania Gazette* and a later smallpox outbreak, explains how to perform an inoculation and why inoculation generally produces a less harsh form of the disease.

ANTI-INOCULATION

WILLIAM DOUGLASS: "THE HISTORY OF INOCULATION"

Dr. William Douglass was Boston's only university-trained physician in 1721. University training, however, did not necessarily mean that Douglass knew more about curing diseases than nonacademically trained doctors. The best knowledge of the age said diseases were caused by the "humors," bodily fluids such as blood, bile, urine, and spittle. Cures included bleeding and blistering. The first drained "bad blood" from the body; the second raised blisters with red-hot tools in certain spots on the body such as behind the ears. Douglass' history of inoculation attempted to portray the practice of inoculation as originating among the uneducated and the heathen, old Greek women, and Muslims. He also pointed out that the wisest doctors and religious divines in England viewed inoculation as contrary to God's providence.

Boston News-Letter, 24 July 1721

To the Author of the Boston NEWS-LETTER.
Sir,
   The *Inoculation* ingrafting or Transplantation *of the Small Pox* having lately so much amused this Country, it may be agreeable to some of your readers to know the History of this affair from its Origine; how it came to be divulged here, The Success of the first Essay to put it in Practice, with the Character of the Operator; some loose hints from the accounts our Turkey Royal Society Communicators give of it, tending to discourage this Wicked and Criminal Practice, concluding with a disswasive from the same.
   Its Origine was in *Thessaly in Greece*, from thence spreading to Constantinople, began to be practised there by *Old Greek Women* on Turks and others above 50 Years ago. By private Letter commerce and information of Travellers, this Method has been among the Learned Universally known in England above 20 Years, but being deemed *Wicked* and *Fellonious*, was never practised there. . . .
   A Gentleman of *Boston* . . . who upon the first Appearance of the Small Pox here, of a Pious & Charitable design of doing good, applyed to the Practioners of the Place, to put this far fetched and not well vouched Method into Practice, they all in Prudence and Conscience declined . . .

(excepting a certain *Cutter for the Stone*, who this without any serious thought undertakes.)

B——*n*'s first Practice was on his own Child and two Negro's, *the Child narrowly escaped* with his Life, had the Fever so violent that our Operator was obliged to have recourse to a confused course of Methods and Medicines, viz Blistering, Suppedanea (Kidneys to the Feet) Vomits, Saffron, Cordials &c. One of the Slaves also suffered much, he doubts the others receiving the Infection. . . .

His *rashness* appears in every Circumstance, First *His mischievous propogating* the Infection in the most Publick Trading Place of the Town, then entirely free from the same; next, his excusing his first bad Success from *his Negligence*, in not preparing the Bodies of his Subjects. Our Levant Gentlemen tells us, it is to be done only in the Winter and spring Season; he does it in the *stifling heat of Summer*; and in his second Essay on the bodies of robust Men in the full Vigour of their Age, to whom in this Season the *least Fever* may be of bad Consequence. *Inconsiderably* he does not separate his Subjects from all Communication with Infection in the common way; which last if it should take (tho' only by Inspired Particles from his morbisick Magazine) and kill the Patient during the Days of Inoculation, he will be deem'd to Die of the Inoculation, and our *Operator* be Indicted for *Felony*, which would prove an additional Misery. . . .

Pylarnius says, that for many Years it was practised only amongst the *Meaner* sort of people, till the end of Winter 1701, the Small Pox being then Malignant and Mortal; a Greek Nobleman desired his Opinion of Inoculation, he *faintly*, and with *Hesitation* assented; accordingly it was practised by an *Old* Greek *Woman* on his Four Children whereof the eldest eighteen Years of Age, *narrowly escaped after fourteen Days illness, having a continual Malignant Fever, with a Train of difficult Symptons*. Wine and Flesh are forbid for 40 Days. *A small error in the Regimen has produced new Pustles and many hazardous Symptoms.* Sometimes it does not catch by incision; and these Inoculated have afterwards had it the common way of Infection. Sometimes Inoculation *occasions troublesome Ulcers* in the glandulous parts of the Body, like PLAGUE SORES.

The Determination of this as a *Case of Conscience*, I refer to Divines, how the trusting more the extra groundless *Machinations of Men* than to our Preserver in the ordinary course of Nature, may be consistent with the Devotion and Subjection we owe to the *all-wise Providence* of GOD Almighty. . . . So far as I can understand (to speak in a *Medical sense*) this extraneous Substance without any previous Concoction, received immediately into the mass of Blood produces only an eruptive Fever (Petcehial, Pustular; or like Chicken or Swine Pox) or putrid Fever, but nothing analogous to the Small Pox; and therefore these Sufferers *may*

notwithstanding receive the Small Pox in the ordinary way, that it has in fact sometimes happened so, some confidently affirm.
I am Your's, &c.
W. Philanthropos.

WILLIAM DOUGLASS: "THIS IS A DESPERATE REMEDY"

Despite Douglass' warnings, many people in Boston believed Cotton Mather and requested inoculation by Zabdiel Boylston. In this unsigned letter, Douglass tried to diminish the seriousness of the current smallpox epidemic in Boston. In fact, about 60 percent of Boston's residents contracted the disease during the 1721 outbreak. In this letter, Douglass warned readers that mishandled inoculations would be worse than contracting smallpox naturally.

New-England Courant (Boston), 21 August 1721

To the Author of the New England Courant.
Sir,
Finding the Infatuation of ingrafting the Small Pox *not altogether stifled*, we present the Town with some Animadversions on a *late Advertisement*, published by the four inoculated Men; and a further *Dissuasive* from that rash, sometimes hazardous, and always dubious Practice. . . .

They begin by insinuating, that the Town may think this a *desperate Remedy*; the Small Pox being a *very desperate Disease*, required no less. *The Small Pox in Boston* (they say) *is a terrible Distemper, whereby many were severely and dreadfully handled, and whereof so many died, as gave an awful Prospect*. This would better suit the *Plague* at *Marseilles*, and is more than sufficient to occasion that worst of Symptoms in the small Pox, *Fear & Dejection of Spirits*: And as a *false Rumour* may tend to obstruct the Towns being supplied with Provisions from the Country, and interrupt all Trade, Commerce and Communication with our Neighbouring Colonys; we reckon it our Duty to expose this as *imprudent*, and *notoriously false*. We find that from the Arrival of the Small Pox here about the middle of *April* last, to the Date of this Advertisement, the *Burials* in Town have not *exceeded* those . . . of other Years, for the same space of time. Few Epidemick or Popular *Fevers* of any sort, have been *more favourable*. . . .

How boldly do they tell the greatest Part of the Town, that tho' many asserted Inoculation to be a Case of Conscience, &c. few if any really believed it: This in plain English (pardon the Indecency of the Expression) is *calling the Town Lyar*. . . .

By Affidavit and Declarations lately published, we find that the Inconveniencys of *Diseases* proceeding from Inoculation, are . . . high Fevers, and other dangerous Symptoms *immediately attending the Inoculation*.

M. Delbonde deposeth that some have died in that State. The Town knows the violence of *B——n*'s Son's Inoculation-Fever, the narrow Escape of old Mr. *W—b*, the heigth [*sic*] of *C—*'s Fever, the great Degree of Despair in Mr. *H——r* while ill; these being four in ten of the Inoculated, and three of the four Advertisers.

ABSINTHIUM: "WHY YOU SHOULD NOT INOCULATE"

Absinthium was an elixir that often made its drinker sick, so its use as a pseudonym fit the situation, according to the anti-inoculation forces. The writer of this letter was probably George Steward, one of Boston's nonuniversity-trained physicians who opposed inoculation. In this letter, the writer outlined all the reasons not to inoculate people.

New-England Courant (Boston), 18 December 1721

To *the Author of the* New-England Courant.
Sir,
Since in your last *Courant* you was pleased to say, *That both Anti-Inoculatiors and Inoculators should be welcome to speak their Minds in your Paper*, I send the following Reasons against inoculating the Small Pox, which I hope in pursuance of your Promise, you will insert in your next if you have Room.

The First Reason then is, That this Operation being perform'd upon none but such as are in perfect Health, and who, for any thing the Doctor or Patients know, may be such who may never have that Distemper in their Lives, or if they have, not to that Degree as to make it mortal to them: and then it must be needless to the last Degree, for any Man to have himself made sick in order to prevent that which for any thing he knows, he is no Danger of.

But in the Second Place, much more so, when the Persons that are for that Operation, cannot answer this Small Question to the Satisfaction of any rational Creature, viz. *Whether this Operation is Infallible, so that hitherto there is not any Body has perished, that has had the Small Pox produced by it.* I say, this is a Point the World will find them for ever tender upon: And altho' they would fain insinuate that it is infallible, yet they will never give you a direct Answer, but will put you off with this, *That there is nothing infallible in Physick; for that they have known Persons dye by a Vomit, and other by Bleeding*, &c. But allowing what they say to be true, for once; these Gentlemen never distinquish betwixt making a *well Man sick*, and endeavouring to make a *sick Man well*; for certainly there is not any thing will defend any Man's bringing a Sickness on himself, unless he is sure that he cannot die of that Illness he does so bring upon him; for we are obliged to preserve the Health we have; as much as we are obliged to preserve our Lives: Whereas on the other

Hand, in giving of *Vomits*, &c. it is never done by wise Physicians, but to Persons who have *usually lost their Healths*, and of Course it is allowable to run a little Risque to recover that Health which it has pleased God to take from him. . . . I have seen Physick practised by some of the ablest Physicians that ever the World saw, and have been practising of it my self this twenty Years past. But I must say, I never saw any Man die by *Bleeding* or *Blistering*, or by *Vomiting* or *Purging*, provided they were given in proper Doses. But if ignorant People, who neither understand Physick not the Doses of Medicines, will be doing what they should not do, no Wonder if we see Instances of these innocent Things proving Mortal. . . .

And the third Reason is, that if they should say, *Inoculating the Small Pox is an infallible way to preserve Life*. I say, if they should say so, yet it is false in Fact; For Dr. *Emanuel Timonius* in his Letter to the Royal Society, owns, that he saw Two die that were inoculated; but at the same Time would fain insinuate, that they died of some other Distemper, which is the very Error his Disciples on this side the Great *Atlantick* fall into. . . .

My fourth Reason is, that althou' we see sundry Persons have the Small Pox favourably that are inoculated, and so escape; yet we see, (and these Gentlemen own it themselves) that they are capable of infecting their Neighbours to as great a Degree as those that are smitten the Common Way . . . I say, how lawful or commendable it may be for any person so to act, must be left to those Gentlemen, who have wrote in Favour of Inoculation, who are certainly *excellent Commentators* on the Sixth Commandment.

And now, Sir, if this may find a Place in your Paper, I will take leave to subscribe my self,
Your well Wisher,
ABSINTHIUM.

PRO-INOCULATION

COTTON MATHER: "IN DEFENSE OF DR. ZABDIEL BOYLSTON"

One way the anti-inoculation forces in Boston fought the practice of inoculation was to belittle Dr. Boylston and others who supported the practice. In this letter, written by Cotton Mather and signed by other ministers of the city, Boylston's medical abilities are defended along with the practice of inoculation.

Boston Gazette, 31 July 1721

To the Author of the Boston News-Letter.
SIR,

It was a grief to us the *Subscribers* among Others of your Friends in the *Town*, to see Dr. *Boylston* treated so unhandsomely in the *Letter* directed to you last Week, and published in your Paper. He is a Son of the *Town* whom Heaven (we all know) has adorn'd with some very peculiar *Gifts* for the Service of his Country, and hath finally own'd in the Successes which he has had.

If Dr. *Boylston* was too suddenly giving into a new practice and (as many apprehend) dangerous Experiment, being too confident of the Innocence and Safety of the Method, and of the Benefit which the Publick might reap thereby; Altho' in that Case we are highly obliged to any Learned and justicious Person who kindly informs us of the hazard and warns against the practice, yet what need is there of injurous Reflections, and any mean detracting from the known worth of the *Doctor?*

Especially how unworthy and unjust, (not to say worse) is it to attempt to turn *that* to his reproach, which has been and is a singular honour to him, and felicity to his Country? We mean those words in the Letter,—*a certain Cutter for the Stone*—Yes, Thanks be to GOD we have such a One among us, and that so many poor *Miserables* have already found the benefit of his gentle and dextrous Hand. . . .

The Town knows and so does the Country how *long* and with what *Success* Dr. *Boylston* has practis'd both in *Physick* and *Surgery*; and tho' he has not had the honour and advantage of an *Academic* Education, and consequently not the *Letters* of some *Physicians* in the Town, yet he ought by no means to be call'd *Illiterate, ignorant* &c. Would the Town hear that Dr. *Cutler* or Dr. *Davis* should be so treated? no more can it endure to see *Boylston* thus spit at.

Nor has it been without considerable *Study*, expence in *travel*, a good *Genius*, diligent Application, and much Observation, that he has attain'd unto that knowledge and successful practice, which he has to give thanks to GOD for; and wherein we pray GOD that he may improve and grow with all humility. . . .

As to the *Case of Conscience* referr'd to the *Divines*, we shall only say——What *Heathens* must they be, to whom *this* can be a question. . . .

Who know not the profanity and impiety of trusting in *Men* or *Means* more than in GOD? be it the best learn'd Men, or the most proper Means? But we will suppose what in fact is true among us at this Day, that Men of Piety . . . accept it with all thankfulness and joy as the gracious Discovery of a *Kind Providence* to Mankind for that end:——And then we ask, Cannot they give into the method or practice without having their *devotion and subjection to the Allwise Providence of GOD Almighty* call'd into question? . . .

In a word, Do we not in the use of all means depend on GOD's *blessing?* Which are all consistent with a *humble Trust in our Great Preservers, and a due Subjection to His All wise Providence.*

Boston, July 27, 1721

Increase Mather, Cotton Mather, Benjamin Colman[,] Thomas Prince[,] John Webb[,] William Cooper.

AN ANONYMOUS BOSTONIAN: "AN ACCOUNT OF THE SUCCESSES OF SMALLPOX INOCULATION"

Dr. William Douglass, in a letter in the anti-inoculation section, belittled the origin and practice of inoculation. An anonymous supporter of the practice provided his own history of inoculation in Boston during the recent smallpox epidemic. In it, the writer explains the diversity of those receiving inoculation and its rate of success, and he rebukes misconceptions that have been spread concerning inoculation.

Boston Gazette, 30 October 1721

A Faithful account of what had occur'd under the late Experiments of the *Small-Pox* managed and governed in the way of *Inoculation*. Published, partly to put a stop unto that unaccountable way of Lying, which fills the Town & Country on this occasion, and partly for the Information & Satisfaction of our Friends in other places.

I. The Operation within these four Months past has been undergone by more than Threescore Persons. Among which there have been *Old & Young; Strong* and *Weak*; *Male* and *Female*; *White & Black*, many serious and vertuous people; some the Children of Eminent Persons among us.

II. Concerning five or six of these . . . they *first* received the Infection of the *Small Pox* in the *Common Way*; and these (as none would imagine otherwise,) underwent the Distemper in the *Common way*: However, there is cause to think, that the Discharge at their *Incisions* was of use unto them. Only One Gentlewoman so Circumstanced died. . . .

III. Of all the Number that have passed under the Operation, there has *Not so much as One miscarried*. It has done well in *all*; and even beyond Expectation in the most of them.

IV. Some few, have had a considerable Number of *Pustules*, beyond what is reported as usual in the *Levant*. . . . But these have undergone so little Sickness, that they declare, *They would much rather come under the Operation many time over*, than suffer the *Small-Pox* as they see it suffered in the *Common way*. . . .

VI. The Stories, about the peculiar *Stench* attending these Persons, are malicious Invention; There is *not a Syllable of Truth* in them.

VII. The Patients return to their *perfect Health immediately*; and suppose themselves rather better than they were before the Operation.

VIII. The Formidable Stories we have had about their *Sores*, are Egregious Fictions and Falsehoods. . . .

X. Some under Terrors of Death have wish'd that they might have leave to save their Lives, by coming under the *Inoculation*. Their obstinate Friends have unreasonably hindered them; and, *They are dead!*

XI. In *Africa*, the manner is, That in a Village, where the *Small Pox* has already seized upon six or seven Families, and it is like to spread; presently all the rest of the Town at once, fetch the *Inoculations* from them. The Families first Infected, generally dye; But the *Inoculated Live....* But it is hoped, that besides the *Precious Lives* of so many pious and worthy People, which have been saved here, what has been done *here* may prove an Introduction to the saving of some hundreds of thousands of Lives, in other Places, where the *Arts of Self-Destruction* will not hinder it....

Had this offered Mercy of a Gracious GOD been timely and thankfully received by the Town of Boston, it appears to many wise and good Men among us that some hundred of Lives might have been saved: GOD grant that other Towns, if indangered, may take warning by us, and come timely into this Means of Preservation from noisomeness, corruption, distress and death; with devout and humble dependance on GOD for His Blessing: And to His Blessed Name be all the Glory.

But let us beseech those that have call'd this Method—*the Work of the devil*, or a *going to the devil*, no more to allow the cursed thought, or utter the horrid word, lest they be found *Blasphemous* of a most merciful and wonderful Work of GOD.

CHAMBERS'S DICTIONARY: "AN ACCOUNT OF INOCULATION"

Every region of colonial America suffered smallpox outbreaks, and in 1730, Benjamin Franklin provided readers of the Pennsylvania Gazette *with a description of what inoculation was and how one might perform it without a doctor. Newspapers throughout the colonial era continued to provide similar instruction for readers.*

Pennsylvania Gazette (Philadelphia), 28 May 1730

The Small-Pox *spreading very much in a neighbouring Colony, and it being not unlikely to reach us,'tis thought the following Account of* INOCULATION *in that Distemper, taken from Chambers's Dictionary, will not be unacceptable to the curious Reader.*

In a Physical Sense, *Inoculation* is used for the Transplanting of Distempers from one Subject to another, particularly for the Ingraftment of the *Small-Pox*, which is a new Practice among us, but of ancient Original in the Eastern Countries. The best Method of performing the Operation is as follows: After the Body is rightly disposed and prepared, by proper Diet and Evacuations, Two small Incisions are made, one in the muscular Part of the Arm, about the Place where an Issue is usually cut, and the other in the Leg of the opposite Side: Then being provided of a small

Quantity, as a Drop of less of well-concocted *variolous Matter*, chose from the distinct or best Sort of Pustules, before the Turn of the Distemper, and imbibed by two small dissils of Lint; these are immediately put into the Incisions, whilst the *Matter* remains warm, and are kept on by a proper Bandage. In a Day or two the Bandages are opened, the Lint thrown away, and only Colewort Leaf applied over the Incisions. This dressing is continued daily. The Incisions usually grow sore, inflame and inlarge of themselves, and discharge Matter more plentifully as the Distemper rises. The Eruption generally appears within eight or ten Days after the Operation, during which Time the Patient is not confined, or obliged to observe a very strict Regimen. The Practice seems to be useful, because most proper Age, the most favourable Season of the Year, the most regular Method of Preparation, and all possible Precaution may here be used, according to the Wishes of the Patient, his Parents, and Physician Advantages impossible to be had when the Distemper is caught in the natural Way. It has also been constantly observed . . . that the Patient is equally secured from this Distemper for the future, as he would be by having gone thro' it in the natural Way.

QUESTIONS

1. Part of the anti-inoculation argument is based in fear of what the unaccepted practice of inoculation might to do those receiving it. How successful is the use of fear as a persuader, and was its use valid in this controversy? Why?

2. In the second letter, Douglass intimates that smallpox hysteria will harm Boston's economy; and, therefore, news of the outbreak should not be broadcast by the inoculators. Is it ever legitimate to hide certain information in order to ensure one's own security even if doing so endangers others?

3. How does prejudice against certain ethnic groups affect the anti-inoculation argument?

4. The anti-inoculation forces often based their arguments against inoculation on fallacies. A fallacy may be defined as a mistake in reasoning. What are the fallacies in the anti-inoculation argument? Even though incorrect logically, can fallacies be persuasive? How?

5. On what logic did the pro-inoculation forces base the practice as a means to prevent smallpox?

6. Is fallacy of reasoning involved in the pro-inoculation argument? Is it persuasive?

7. Religion was a vital part of life in colonial America. How was religion used by the anti- and pro-inoculation forces?

8. According to these newspaper articles and letters, what was the understanding of the purpose of inoculation in colonial America?

9. Considering what you can tell of the medical knowledge of the day, was Douglass correct to question inoculation? Why?

NOTES

1. James H. Cassedy, *Medicine in America: A Short History* (Baltimore: Johns Hopkins University Press, 1991), 4–5.

2. John Duffy, *Epidemics in Colonial America* (Baton Rouge: Louisiana State University Press, 1953), 51.

3. Wm. David Sloan and Julie Hedgepeth Williams, *The Early American Press, 1690–1783* (Westport, Conn.: Greenwood Press, 1994), 25.

4. *Boston News-Letter*, 24 July 1721, 3.

5. *Maryland Gazette* (Annapolis), 14 March 1765, 1.

6. See, for example, *South-Carolina Gazette* (Charleston), 23 February 1760, 26 April 1760, and 31 May 1760.

CHAPTER 3

Impartiality, Objectivity, and the Press, 1729

For most of its more than three hundred years of existence, the press in America has claimed to be an objective and impartial observer and reporter of the events that affect and shape the lives of people and country. Benjamin Harris made such a promise in 1690 when he published *Publick Occurrences* (see Chapter 1). When he produced his first and only issue on September 25, he said he would report important events of the times to the people of Massachusetts Bay. Harris promised to *"take what pains . . . to obtain a* Faithful Relation *of all such things."*

Benjamin Franklin did the same when he declared that his *Pennsylvania Gazette* would publish opinions and let truth rise from the varying beliefs.[1] Similarly, William Bradford told *New-York Gazette* readers, "That it was by strong Importunity they were induced to give the fore-going Letter a Place herein. And since we have done it, we could not avoid incerting this which follows."[2] By the end of the era, printers were inserting statements of impartiality into their nameplates that promised the space in the paper and its news were "Open to ALL PARTIES, but influenced by NONE."[3]

Even as the press has changed into media with instantaneous broadcasts from all over the globe, the same promises have been made. "Our reporters do not cover stories from *their* point of view. They are presenting it from *nobody's* point of view," the president of CBS News has said. CNN, likewise, promises, "We give *both* sides."[4]

Objectivity and impartiality to current reporters and media outlets usually means allowing the media access to both sides in a dispute. In such a situation, the media allow the facts, not the opinions of the media outlet, to do the explaining. But objectivity and impartiality may well have meant something different in the colonial era than they do today. According to NBC News anchor Tom Brokaw, "Journalism is a reflection of the passions of the day."[5] Producing an outlet for news in the eighteenth century was a new and developing concept, and it reflected current issues just as media do today.

When newspapers began in America, they were sometimes considered to be minor commercial ventures with outdated information. The freshest news was obtained not from them, but by word of mouth or through letters written by influential people in one region to similar people in another. The controlling of knowledge was the key to power. Knowledge continues to remain a source of power, but printers in the eighteenth century improved the method of sharing it so that it was available to most Americans. In 1750, printer James Parker published these words in his newspaper, "This Taste . . . for News, is a very odd one; yet it must be fed; and tho' it seems to be a Jest to Foreigners, yet it is an Amusement we can't be without."[6]

This chapter looks at how printers and others viewed the objectivity and impartiality of the press. Understanding how printers and the rest of society perceived newspaper bias is vital to this book because each of its chapters looks at how public prints were used to influence people. The fact that some people in Boston felt they needed to start a newspaper in 1721 to oppose smallpox inoculation and that a group of New Yorkers financed the *New-York Weekly Journal* to attack the government of Governor William Cosby in 1733 supports the idea that impartiality was not the motivating force in the dissemination of news in the eighteenth century.

Still, the fact that newspapers began in Boston and New York in opposition to a radical medical procedure and a government whose supporters already had access to the press through existing outlets is part of the development and maturation of objectivity and impartiality. If a town had two newspapers and each printed opposing information on the issues, people could read both and weigh for themselves the validity of both arguments, which is exactly what Franklin proposed when he suggested letting all opinions be heard with truth rising from errors, even though he proposed airing the opposing views in a single newspaper.

The idea that a town's newspaper might align itself with one side of an issue while the town's other paper might support a differing viewpoint and both still claim impartiality may have more ties to modern media than is imagined. In an age where most Americans have access to dozens of media outlets, ranging from local to national newspapers, news magazines, radio stations, and television stations to a host of cable television news sources and innumerable Internet news sites, people can consult multiple sources to gather opinions on the issues that affect them. The fewer the media outlets available to people, however, the more important it is for the source to be impartial and objective. Boston, at times during the colonial era, had five newspapers. The printer of each no doubt claimed impartiality, but citizens surely recognized that the writers and correspondents of most of those papers had an agenda that might differ from that of writers in other papers. The readers considered these biases as they weighed the arguments. Sometimes, especially in towns with single newspapers, the conflicting sides of an issue used the same newspaper to wage their polemical battles, just as Bradford felt he was obligated to do in 1739. The newspapers became conduits for ideas; they merely flowed through different papers. Printers rarely considered this a bias. They simply did it, as *Boston Evening-Post* printer Thomas Fleet once said of the objectionable material he published, because "I had a prospect of getting a Penny by it."[7]

The selections in this chapter begin with claims made that printers and their correspondents were biased and not objective in their presentation of the news. They include statements made by printers that support the notion that they would not print carte blanche just any piece of information presented to them by just anyone. Readers should note that many of the selections that insinuate that the press was biased also contain statements made by printers declaring that their presses are open to all parties and all sides in a conflict.

The section on a partial and biased press begins with writings from Boston during the inoculation controversy (see Chapter 2). The first announces that the *New-England Courant* will be suppressed for printing opinions that oppose the standing order of Massachusetts Bay. The next entry, a letter probably written by Mather Byles, nephew of Congregational minister and author Cotton Mather, attacks the *Courant* as scandalous and horrid. Byle's uncle was the principal proponent of smallpox inoculation—the opposition to which was the *Courant*'s initial purpose. The next entry is the official notice of the *Courant*'s suppression.

The next group of readings on a biased press begins with William Bradford's statement that he must publish a response to an earlier letter attacking George Whitefield (see Chapter 8). After publishing part of a series of letters written by Jonathan Arnold and William Smith, Bradford states he will no longer allow his paper to be used to print information on this controversy, even for money. A similar Boston statement is also included. The next selection is an essay by a New York lawyer and printer, William Livingston, on the liberty of the press and published by James Parker. It is, in part, an attack on another printer, Hugh Gaine, for refusing to print information sent to him. The essay is full of references to a free and independent press, but, as seen here, press freedom for Livingston, and no doubt Parker, meant certain limitations to an open and uncontrolled press. Compare this to Livingston's statement in the *Independent Reflector* in the impartial press readings.

The final statement in this section is a statement by Williamsburg printer Clementina Rind, accused in an entry in the next section of readings of running a closed and biased newspaper. Her response is an interesting step in the process of creating an open press in America. Rind declares she will publish the piece when the author identifies himself. She will not, however, open her press to a potential libel for anonymous writings.

The writings advocating an impartial and objective press begin with essays written by Benjamin Franklin. The first was penned under an early Philadelphia pseudonym, Busy-Body. The second is Franklin's "Apology for Printers." The third is a later statement on truth, which advocates opening the press to all because the truth will always rise from error, a concept given the title the "marketplace of ideas" in the early twentieth century.

The next two selections come from politically charged publications from the middle of the century. The first was printed by Gamaliel Rogers and Zechariah Fowle and the second by James Parker for William Livingston. Both promise their new publications will be open to all. Interestingly, neither of the two publications did so. Both were published for about one year before folding. These writings are followed by an essay by New Hampshire printer Daniel Fowle, who explains the values and significance of a free, open, and impartial press to society. The next entry is Purdie and Dixon's *Virginia Gazette* attack on printer Clementina Rind, whose response is in the first section of chapter readings.

The chapter closes with two printers' statements from the Revolutionary period. The first comes from Loyalist printer James Rivington; the second, from printers John and Thomas Fleet, Jr. The brothers truly attempted to maintain an impartial press in Boston. They closed down their business shortly after this piece was written rather than continue to print during the Revolution, something that would have forced the brothers to take sides.

IN FAVOR OF A PARTIAL AND BIASED PRESS

THO. PENSHALLOW: "PROHIBITION OF THE *COURANT*"

In 1721 smallpox raged through Boston. The doctors of the city, as well as its citizens, took sides on whether inoculation was a legitimate way to stop the spread of the deadly disease. The New-England Courant *sprang into existence at this time to fight inoculation. This letter, written using the pseudonym Tho. Penshallow, was written by a Mr. Gardner, according to the notes Benjamin Franklin added to his copy of the* Cour-ant*. The letter discusses how the paper may be censored for the ideas its writers have discussed during the controversy. Although the paper's printer, James Franklin, was not arrested during this controversy, he was arrested in June 1722 for criticizing Massachusetts' handling of pi-rates.*

New-England Courant (Boston), 18 December 1721

It is whispered, that we are to have a Law prohibiting the Reading your Courants, *under severe Penalties; but for what Reason is not yet known; tho' some conjecture it is because your Paper sometimes sets forth the Right and Liberties of Mankind; Doctrines which are not calcu-lated to our Meridian: And possibly, our People by reading them, may too boldly perswade themselves, that they are* Englishmen, *and under Priviledges.* Tho. Penshallow

AN ANONYMOUS BOSTONIAN: "THE MOST AUDACIOUS AND BRAZEN-FAC'D LIARS IN THE WORLD"

As smallpox continued to claim lives in Boston, writings in the town's newspapers grew more hostile with each side attacking not only the other's position on inoculation but also the character of the leaders of each side. This letter calls for the suppression of the Courant *because of its assassination of the character of those who supported inoculation.*

Boston Gazette, 15 January 1721 (1722)

Mr. Musgrave,

WHEN I read the Crimes laid to your Charge in the Scandalous *Courant* last Monday I was in some danger of entertaining an hard Character of you; but when I read a little further, the danger was over. . . . Every one said, That if these Words were indeed there, the Publishers of this Im-pious and Abominable Courant, must be the most Audacious and Brazen-fac'd Liars in the World; not a Word is to be believed that shall be uttered by Fellows of such matchless and uncommon Impudence. . . .

Every one sees that the main intention of this Vile Courant, is to Vilify and Abuse the best Men we have, and especially the Principal Ministers of Religion in the Country. . . .

If such an horrid Paper, called, The *New England Courant*, should be seen in other Countries, what would they think of *New-England*! . . . But there is a Number of us, who resolve, that if this wickedness be not stop'd, We will pluck up our Courage, and see what we can do in our way to stop it.

ASSEMBLY OF MASSACHUSETTS: "THE SUPPRESSION OF JAMES FRANKLIN"

In June 1722, James Franklin was arrested for criticizing the handling of pirates by Massachusetts officials. In January 1723, he further irritated the colony's leaders by attacking what the printer saw as hypocritical religious practices by some of the colony's clerics and public officials. Franklin's observations evoked the ire of the Assembly of Massachusetts, which locked Franklin up again and forbade him to publish the Courant *for a year. Franklin did not stop printing his paper, however. Instead, he placed the name of his apprentice brother, Benjamin, in the masthead and continued printing.*

New-England Courant (Boston), 21 January 1723

The Committee appointed to consider of the Paper called, The New-England Courant, *published Monday the fourteenth Currant,* are humbly of Opinion *that the Tendency of the said Paper is to mock Religion, and bring it into Contempt, that the Reverend and faithful Ministers of the Gospel are injuriously Reflected on, His Majesty's Government affronted, and the Peace and good Order of his Majesty's Subjects of this Province disturbed, by the said courant; And for prevention of the like Offence for the Future, the Committee* humbly propose, *That* James Franklin *the Printer and Publisher thereof, be strictly forbidden by this Court to Print or Publish the* New-England Courant, *or any Pamphlet or Paper of the like Nature, except it be first supervised by the Secretary of this Province; And the Justices of his Majesty's Sessions of the Peace for the County of Suffolk, at their next Adjournment, be directed to take Sufficient Bonds of the said* Franklin *for Twelve Months Time.*

WILLIAM BRADFORD: "NO MORE CONTROVERSIAL ARTICLES"

In 1739 and 1740, Americans became enamored with the itinerant preacher George Whitefield, but his preaching also created riffs among many. In New York, Jonathan Arnold and William Smith had differing opinions on Whitefield and used the New-York Gazette *as their battleground. After allowing Arnold to respond to Smith, printer William Bradford added this note that declared he would no longer allow his paper to used for the controversy. Bradford announced he would suppress any more letters or essays on the subject of Whitefield.*

New-York Gazette, 22 January 1739 (1740)

[The Publishers of this Gazette, hereby inform their Readers, That it was by strong Importunity they were induced to give the fore-going Letter a Place herein. And since we have done it, we could not avoid incerting this which follows, without displeasing several of our constant Readers, whom we have refused, for several Weeks past, to Print it in our Paper. But upon their hearing, that we had agreed to Print Mr. Arnolds Letter, we could not (upon their reiterated Requests) refuse. And we hereby give Notice, that for the future we do not think to incert any *more* of these Controversies, not being proper for this Paper.

THOMAS FLEET: "THE TRUTH WILL BE PUBLISHED"

Printers often were paid for inserting letters or essays into newspapers. In 1740 many people wanted to voice their opinions on George White-field. Boston printer Thomas Fleet, an Anglican, disliked Whitefield, but he refused to print everything he received, even if the writer paid for the space. Fleet, in his remarks below, effectively stated that people were allowed to have opinions on all sorts of subjects, but he was not obli-gated to give them a voice in his Evening-Post *unless the remarks could be proved true. Freedom of the press, in effect, was left to the discretion of the printer.*

Boston Evening-Post, 13 October 1740

Boston: The Publisher of this Paper hereby acknowledges the Receipt of a Paper of Queries sign'd A.B. with the Money; and although he is entirely of the ingenious Author's Opinion, as to the Reasonableness of them, yet he is obliged to inform him, that he does not think it safe for him to print them at present, having sufficient Proof, that the TRUTH is not to be spoke at all Times. The Money shall be return'd by any Person that tells the Sum, without Question.

WILLIAM LIVINGSTON, WITH WILLIAM SMITH JR., AND JOHN MORIN SCOTT: "OF THE USE, ABUSE, AND LIBERTY OF THE PRESS"

In 1753 controversy in New York swirled around the opening of a public college in the colony that would be controlled by a religious denomina-tion (see Chapter 13). William Livingston, a prominent lawyer and pol-itician, and his friends opposed Anglican ties to the college and said so first in the Independent Reflector *and later in the* New-York Mercury *"Watch-Tower" series. In 1753, however, printer Hugh Gaine refused to give Livingston space in the* Mercury *for his opinions. Livingston, therefore, attacked Gaine with this essay printed in the* Reflector, *but at the same time he admitted there were legitimate constraints upon free-dom of the press.*

Independent Reflector (New York), 30 August 1753

WHETHER the Art of PRINTING has been of greater Service or Detriment to the World, has frequently been made the Subject of fruitless Controversy. The best Things have been perverted to serve the vilest Purposes, their being therefore subject to Abuse, is an illogical Argument against their Utility. . . . The most inferior Genius, however impoverished, can spread his Thoughts thro' a Kingdom. The Public has the Advantage of the Sentiments of all its Individuals. Thro' the Press, Writers of every Character and Genius, may promulge their Opinions; and all conspire to rear and support the Republic of Letters. . . .

The wide Influence of the Press is so dangerous to arbitrary Governments, that in some of them it is shut up, and in others greatly restrained. . . .

No Nation in *Europe*, is more jealous of the *Liberty of the Press* than the *English*, nor is there a People, among whom it is so grossly abused. . . . The *Liberty of the Press*, like Civil Liberty, is talked of by many, and understood by few; the latter is taken by Multitudes, for an irrefrainable Licence of acting at Pleasure; an equal Unrestraint in Writing, is often argued from the former, but both are false and equally dangerous to our Constitution. Civil Liberty is built upon a Surrender of so much of our natural Liberty, as is necessary for the good Ends of Government; and the Liberty of the Press, is always to be restricted from becoming a Prejudice to the public Weal. . . .

The Press is for ever in the Mouths of Printers, and one would imagine, that as they live by its Liberty, they would understand its true Limits, and endeavour to preserve its rightful Extent. But the Truth is, there is scarce one in Twenty of them; that knows the one or aims at the other.

A PRINTER ought not to publish every Thing that is offered him; but what is conducive of general Utility, he should not refuse, be the Author a Christian, Jew, Turk or Infidel. Such Refusal is an immediate Abridgement of the Freedom of the Press. When on the other Hand, he prostitutes his Art by the Publication of any Thing injurious to his Country, it is criminal,—It is high Treason against the State. The usual Alarm rung in such Cases, the common Cry of an Attack upon the LIBERTY OF THE PRESS, is groundless and trifling. The Press neither has, nor can have such a Liberty, and whenever it is assumed, the Printer should be punished. . . . I could name a Printer, so attached to his private Interest, that for the sake of advancing it, set up a Press, deserted his Religion, made himself the Tool of a Party he despised, privately contemned and vilified his own Correspondents, published the most infamous Falsehoods against others, slandered half the People of his Country, promised afterwards to desist, broke that Promise, continued the Publication of his Lies, Forgeries and Misrepresentations; and to compleat his Malignity, obstinately refused to print the Answers or Vindications of the Persons he had abused; and yet even this Wretch, had the Impudence to talk of the *Liberty of the Press*. God forbid! that every Printer should deserve so infamous a Character. . . .

CLEMENTINA RIND: "I WILL NOT PUBLISH ANONYMOUS PIECES"

Clementina Rind assumed the printing duties of her husband William's Virginia Gazette *in August 1773 following his death. Tea taxes and religious liberty and toleration were the principal subjects of discussion in Virginia's newspapers. In the December 23 issue of Purdie and Dixon's* Gazette, *a writer accused Rind of violating the freedom of the press by refusing to print a letter. Rind, no doubt remembering that her husband had been charged with libel in 1766, refused to publish the unsigned letter. With her note below, Rind introduced a new concept for opinion in newspapers: Writers must take responsibility for their words by signing their letters, not with a pseudonym, but with their true names. Rind declared that until that occurred the press would truly not be open to all.*

Virginia Gazette (Williamsburg, Rind), 30 December 1773

I shall ever feel a very sensible concern at being obliged to enter into altercations of any nature whatever; but the severe reprimand I received in Messieurs Purdie & Dixon's *last paper, from* AN ATTENTIVE OBSERVER, *makes it absolutely necessary to say something in my own vindication. The motto of this paper has hitherto been, and ever shall be strictly attended to: but, as the* OBSERVER *very justly remarks, "that the press should not be made a vehicle for the conveyance of slander," so neither can it be justifiable to publish indiscriminately, every piece that may be offered . . . besides, as I am in some measure, amenable to the public for what appears in my Gazette, I cannot think myself authorized to publish an anonymous piece. . . . When the author gives up his name, it shall, however repugnant to my inclination, have a place in this paper. . . . I am not conscious of having deviated from that spirit of freedom which I shall always think it my duty to maintain.*

CLEMENTINA RIND.

IN FAVOR OF AN IMPARTIAL AND OBJECTIVE PRESS

BENJAMIN FRANKLIN: "THE BUSY-BODY, NO. 8"

In his long career, Benjamin Franklin assumed many pen names as a means of presenting his opinions to the public. By 1729 Franklin wanted

*a newspaper of his own but did not yet have the means to begin one.
Instead, he initiated an attack on the printer of the* Pennsylvania Gazette, *Samuel Keimer, with a series published in the* American Weekly
Mercury *called "The Busy-Body." Franklin quickly turned the series into
a sounding board for the issues of the day. Number 8 discusses frugality
as a means of acquiring wealth, but buried within Franklin's observations are his opinions on the impartiality and objectivity that are necessary for the press to have in order to serve the public.*

American Weekly Mercury, 27 March 1729

Every Man will own, That an Author, as such, ought to be try'd by the
Merit of his Productions only; but Pride, Party, and Prejudice at this Time
run so very high, that Experience shews we form our Notions of a Piece
by the Character of the Author. Nay there are some very humble Politicians in and about this City, who will ask on which Side the Writer is,
before they presume to give their Opinion of the Thing wrote. This un-
generous Way of Proceeding I was well aware of before I publish'd my
first Speculation; and therefore concealed my Name. And I appeal to the
more generous Part of the World, if I have since I appear'd in the Character of the *Busy-Body* given an Instance of my siding with any Party more
than another, in the unhappy Divisions of my Country; and I have above
all, this Satisfaction in my Self, That neither Affection, Aversion or Interest, have byass'd me to use any Partiality towards any Man, or Sett of
Men. . . . I am forsooth, bound to please in my Speculations, not that I
suppose my Impartiality will ever be called in Question upon that Account.

BENJAMIN FRANKLIN: "APOLOGY FOR PRINTERS"

*After being chided for publishing an advertisement that criticized the
Anglican clergy of Philadelphia, Franklin published the "Apology for
Printers." In it, he outlined what he saw as the essence of impartiality
and objectivity in printing.*

Pennsylvania Gazette (Philadelphia), 10 June 1731

Being frequently censur'd and condemn'd by different Persons for
printing Things which they say ought not to be printed, I have sometimes
thought it might be necessary to make a standing Apology for my self,
and publish it once a Year, to be read upon all Occasions of that Nature.
Much Business has hitherto hindered the execution of this Design; but
having very lately given extraordinary Offence by printing an Advertisement with a certain *N. B.* at the End of it, I find an Apology more particularly requisite at this Juncture, tho' it happens when I have not yet
Leisure to write such a thing in the proper Form, and can only in a loose

manner throw Considerations together which should have been the Substance of it.

I request all who are angry with me on the Account of printing things they don't like, calmly to consider these following Particulars

1. That the Opinions of Men are almost as various as their Faces; and Observation general enough to become a common Proverb, *So many Men so many Minds*.

2. That the Business of Printing has chiefly to do with Mens Opinions; most things that are printed tending to promote some, or oppose others.

3. That hence arises the peculiar Unhappiness of that Business, which other Callings are no way liable to; they who follow Printing being scarce able to do any thing in their way of getting a Living, which shall not probably give Offence to some, and perhaps to many. . . .

4. That it is unreasonable in any one Man or Set of Men to expect to be pleas'd with every thing that is printed, as to thing that nobody ought to be pleas'd but themselves.

5. Printers are educated in the Belief, that when Men differ in Opinion, both Sides ought equally to have the Advantage of being heard by the Publick; and that when Truth and Error have fair Play, the former is always an overmatch for the latter: Hence they chearfully serve all contending Writers that pay them well, without regarding on which side they are of the Question in Dispute.

6. Being thus continually employ'd in serving all Parties, Printers naturally acquire a vast Unconcernedness as to the right or wrong Opinions contain'd in what they print. . . .

7. That it is unreasonable to imagine Printers approve of every thing they print, and to censure them on any particular thing accordingly; since in the way of their Business they print such great variety of things opposite and contradictory. It is likewise as unreasonable what some assert, *That Printers ought not to print any Thing but what they approve*; since if all of that Business should make such a Resolution, and abide by it, and End would thereby be put to Free Writing, and the World would afterwards have nothing to read but what happen'd to be the Opinions of Writers.

8. That if all Printers were determin'd not to print any thing till they were sure it would offend no body, there would be very little printed. . . .

10. That notwithstanding what might be urg'd in behalf of a Man's being allow'd to do in the Way of his Business . . . yet Printers do continually discourage the Printing of great Numbers of bad things, and stifle them in the Birth. I my self have constantly refused to print any thing that might countenance Vice, or promote Immorality; tho' by complying in such Cases with the corrupt Taste of the Majority, I might have got much Money. . . .

I consider the Variety of Humours among Men, and despair of pleasing every Body; yet I shall not therefore leave off Printing. I shall continue my Business. I shall not burn my Press and melt my Letters.

BENJAMIN FRANKLIN: "TRUTH WILL PREVAIL OVER FALSEHOOD"

Every so often, Franklin printed an editorial statement concerning his policies as a printer. In his 1740 statement, Franklin discussed the nature of truth in what was published. His contention was that the very nature of printing sometimes means that falsehoods are printed by unknowing printers. That, according to Franklin's statement here, was all right because in the course of presenting information on issues, truth would always prevail over falsehood.

Pennsylvania Gazette (Philadelphia), 24 July 1740

It is a Principle among Printers, that when Truth has fair Play, it will always prevail over Falshood; therefore, though they have undoubted Property in their own Press, yet they willingly allow, that any one is entitled to the Use of it, who thinks it necessary to offer his Sentiments on disputable Point to the Publick, and will be at the Expence of it. If what is publish'd be good, Mankind has the Benefit of it: If it be bad . . . the more 'tis made publick, the more its Weakness is expos'd, and the greater Disgrace falls upon the Author, whoever he be; who is at the same Time depriv'd of an Advantage he would otherwise without fail make use of, *viz.* Of Complaining, *that Truth is suppress'd, and that he could say MIGHTY MATTERS, had he but the Opportunity of being heard.*

The Printers of this City have been unjustly reflected on, as if they were under some undue Influence, and guilty of great Partiality in favour of the Preaching lately admir'd among us, so as to refuse Printing any Think in Opposition to it, how just or necessary soever. A Reflection entirely false and groundless, and without the least Colour of Fact. . . .

[T]he greatest and best of Men may have *some* Errors, and have been often found averse to *some* Truths, it was justly esteem'd a National Grievance, that the People should have Nothing to read by the Opinions, or what was agreeable to the Opinions of *ONE MAN*. But should every petty Printers . . . presume to erect himself into an Officer of this kind, and arbitrarily decide what ought and what ought not to be published, much more justly might the World complain.

GAMALIEL ROGERS AND DANIEL FOWLE: "PROSPECTUS OF THE *INDEPENDENT ADVERTISER*"

When printers started newspapers, they usually published a prospectus just before the first issue or with the initial newspaper. Gamaliel Rogers and Daniel Fowle were no different. They printed the prospectus below in their first Boston newspaper as a way to let people know that the Advertiser *would be a paper that would discuss the issues of the day. The printers promised a free paper, open to all to improve the situation of those in Boston and New England.*

Independent Advertiser (Boston), 4 January 1748

As our present political state affords Matter for a variety of Thoughts, of peculiar Importance to the good People of *New-England*, we purpose to insert every thing of that Nature that may be pertinently and decently wrote. For ourselves, we declare we are of no Party, neither shall we promote the narrow and private Designs of any such. We are ourselves free, and our Paper shall be free—free as the Constitution we enjoy— free to Truth, good Manners, and good Sense, and at the same time free from all licentious Reflections, Insolence and Abuse. Whatsoever may be adapted to State and Defend the Rights and Liberties of Mankind, to advance useful Knowledge and the Cause of Virtue, to improve the Trade, the Manufactures, and Husbandry of the Country, whatever may tend to inspire this People with a just and proper Sense of their own Condition, to point out to them their true Interests, and rouse them to pursue it, as also any Piece of Wit and Humor, shall at Times find (free of Charge,) a most welcome reception. And although we do not altogether depend upon the casual Benevolence of the Publick to supply this Paper, yet we will thankfully receive every Thing from every quarter conducing to the Good of the Publick and our general Design.

WILLIAM LIVINGSTON: "THE DESIGN OF THE *INDEPENDENT REFLECTOR*"

New York lawyer William Livingston felt the city needed a forum for the discussion of issues, and in 1752 he began publishing the Independent Reflector. *The publication was based on the English papers* Tatler *and* Spectator. *Both were single-subject journals, meaning they discussed only one item per week, usually the one chosen by the author of the paper. In his introduction and statement of purpose, Livingston promised impartiality on all subjects. His words, like those of many during the era, were more noble than realized. Livingston soon attacked political and religious leaders in New York, and printer James Parker refused to print the* Reflector *for Livingston one year after the publication began.*

Independent Reflector (New York), 30 November 1752

The Author being under no Attachment to any Party, thinks himself the better qualified to make impartial Remarks on the Conduct of every Party, so far as it proves injurious to the Public, and farther he is determined not to interfere with the political Controversies of his Country.

The Espousing any polemic Debate between different Sects of Christians, shall be the last Charge against him; tho' he shall be every ready to deliver his Sentiments on the Abuses and Encroachments of any, with the Freedom and Unconcernedness becoming Truth and Independency. . . .

The Author will ever be more ready to detect his Errors, than he to correct them. But on the Slander and Scurrility of his Enemies, if such it should be his Misfortune to create, he will look down with a Sovereign Contempt. . . . Z.

DANIEL FOWLE: "REMARKS ON THE ADVANTAGES OF PRINTING"

The week after issuing his prospectus for New Hampshire's first newspaper, Daniel Fowle began his second issue of the Gazette *with an essay on the advantages of printing. According to Fowle, the openness of the press was the best way to ensure the political health of the colony, and an open and fair press also ensures an informed populace.*

New-Hampshire Gazette (Portsmouth), 14 October 1756

Remarks on the Advantage of PRINTING.

IT is obvious to every one who attends to it, That the *Art of Printing*, is one of the most useful Inventions the World has ever seen. . . .

There are no Emoluments arising from it, peculiar to the Learned, the Religious, or any particular Societies: it extends to all Parts of Civil Life: all Conditions of Men, High and Low, Rich and Poor, are some way or other serv'd by it, and even those Nations which have not use of it among them receive by this Mean more certain, as well as more frequent Intelligence of Affairs greatly interesting, and of which they often avail themselves.

But among the numerous Advantages accruing from this Art, the traveling of these Weekly Mercuries is not the least. The speedy Communication of the State of Affairs, from one part of the World to another, that easy Intercourse maintain'd between the different Parts of a Kingdom, the quick Conveyance of such Advices as direct what Measures, connected with the general Good, are to be pursued, afforded by this Circulation, which like a good Circulation in the natural Body keeps the Body Politic . . . in sound Health; as well as what is relative to particular Matters in the political, commercial and active Scenes of Life, are Advantages the World never knew before Printing. 'Tis of great Consequences that the People should be informed of every Thing that concerns them; and without Printing such Knowledge could not circulate either so fast, or so easily. How barren, how rare! By this Means Knowledge is spread even among the Common People, a useful Curiosity is rais'd in their Minds, their Attention is rous'd, their Minds are enlarg'd, their Views extended, and by familiar Acquaintance with Facts, which nearly concern others, the sympathetic and social Affections are augmented; and they become more humane. . . . Or as a better Man directs, may learn, *to look not every one on his own Things, but everyone one on the Things of another*.

AN ATTENTIVE OBSERVER: "PAPERS SHOULD BE OPEN TO ALL PARTIES"

The anonymous "Attentive Observer" took objection with Purdie and Dixon's competitor, Clementina Rind, who refused to print a letter sent to her. As a result, he sent this letter praising an open and impartial press and accusing Rind of having anything but. Rind's response to this letter may be found in the readings on a partial press above.

Virginia Gazette (Williamsburg, Purdie and Dixon), 23 December 1773

To *Mr.* PURDIE.
SIR,
THE Motto of your Sister Printer's Gazette is *Open to All Parties, but influenced by none*. It is very properly descriptive of that *Freedom* which renders the Press beneficial to Mankind. But how does the fair Promise contained in this Motto consist with refusing to publish a Piece. . . . It is said, indeed, that as it descends to Particulars it is not proper for Mrs. Rind's Paper. It is agreed, that the Press should not be made a Vehicle for the Conveyance of Slander. . . . Merely *descending to Particulars* is surely no good Reason for shutting up the Press, because it is in such Instances confessedly that the Publick may receive essential Benefit from its Freedom. It is the only Method by which the guilty Great can be punished. They are, and they ought to be, amenable to the Publick through the Medium of the Press. . . .
I am, Sir, your humble Servant.
AN ATTENTIVE OBSERVER.

JAMES RIVINGTON: "A PRINTER SHOULD BE IMPARTIAL"

As the rift between the Tories and Patriots grew in America, printers faced continued pressure to support a particular side, especially that of the Patriots. Rivington, one of the printers best known for his British leanings, was constantly under attack for printing Tory letters. In a simple statement, Rivington suggests that printers not take sides, but remain neutral in all that they present to the public.

Rivington's New-York Gazetteer; or the Connecticut, New-Jersey, Hudson's-River, and Quebec Weekly Advertiser, 11 August 1774

The printer of a newspaper, ought to be neutral in all cases where his own press is employed.

THOMAS AND JOHN FLEET: "WE WILL NOT PROSTITUTE OUR PAPER"

As England and America grew farther apart and the possibility of an armed revolution seemed inevitable, printers came under increasing pressure about the material they should publish. Thomas and John Fleet, brothers who had grown up working in the print shop of their father, Thomas Sr., advocated impartiality in their printing. In this printers' note, the brothers reiterated their promise to remain neutral in all they printed and not to prostitute their Evening-Post *by selling its space to the highest bidder in the propaganda war that was taking place among American newspapers.*

Boston Evening-Post, 10 March 1775

Whereas it hath been hinted in several letters lately received from England, that one or more printers of the public newspapers in the principal towns in America are hired, or rather bribed . . . for the vile purpose of publishing pieces in their respective papers tending to favor despotism and the present arbitrary and tyrannical proceedings of the ministry relative to America; The publishers of the Boston *Evening Post* (whose papers have always been conducted with the utmost freedom and impartiality) do, for themselves, thus publicly declare, that no application has ever been made to them to prostitute their paper to such a base and mean purpose; and should they hereafter be applied to for that design, they shall despise the offer and those who make it, with the greatest contempt; not but that their paper shall, as usual, be open for the insertion of all pieces that shall tend to amuse or instruct, or to the promoting of useful knowledge and the general good of mankind, as they themselves . . . shall think prudent, profitable, or entertaining to their numerous readers.

QUESTIONS

1. After reading the selections, what do you think the printers meant when they said they operated an impartial and open press?

2. Discussing what issues seems to have most often brought charges of biased reporting?

3. According to the *Independent Reflector*, explain when printers should be impartial in their printing and when they should refuse to publish all they receive.

4. Why did printer Clementina Rind think that not printing anonymous letters did not violate her claim to an open and impartial press?

5. What were Benjamin Franklin's main reasons for advocating an open, impartial, and objective press?

6. Why do you think the printers and writers of newspapers declared themselves to be of no party when they began to publish their newspapers?

7. According to the *New-Hampshire Gazette*, what did an impartial press do for society?

8. Using your knowledge of today's media, how close do you think James Rivington was in 1774 to our current understanding of an objective media? Explain.

9. Do you think the Fleets believed what Rivington believed? Explain by using their editorial comment.

NOTES

1. *Pennsylvania Gazette* (Philadelphia), 10 June 1731, 1.

2. *New-York Gazette*, 22 January 1739 (1740), 2.

3. See, for example, *Virginia Gazette* (Williamsburg, Rind), 2 December 1773.

4. Quoted in David T. Z. Mindich, *Just the Facts: How "Objectivity" Came to Define American Journalism* (New York: New York University Press, 1998), 7.

5. Quoted in ibid., 6.

6. *New-York Gazette Revived in the Weekly Post-Boy*, 22 January 1750, 1.

7. *Boston Evening-Post*, 27 March 1741.

CHAPTER 4

Attakulakula Visits King George II, 1730: Native American–English Relations

In 1730 America's newspapers carried a series of articles from London concerning the arrival of foreign dignitaries in the British capital. The reports followed the visit of the king, princes, and generals to the sites of the capital and with the nation's political leaders, including King George II. What made the news reports unique was the fact that these leaders were not from other European countries, Africa, or Asia. From North America, specifically the colony of South Carolina, they were the leaders of the Cherokee nation.

The news accounts refer to the Cherokees as the leaders of a nation, and this element of the story is important. This delegation from the largest group of Native Americans in the British colonies of North America had not been brought to England without purpose. They were there to meet with the prime minister and king in an effort to benefit the British Empire politically and financially. As one article explained,

Sir Alexander Cummings, Bart. The Gentleman who lately arrived from South-Carolina, who brought over the Indian Chiefs from the Cherokee Nation, is now employed in drawing up a new Scheme to be laid before Sir Robert Walpole and the Board of Trade, where the Trade, Riches and Power of the British Nation, and of all his Majesty's Dominions may be increased, the Debts of the Nation paid.[1]

Before the Cherokees left England, they were treated to royal affairs of state, and they visited privately with King George at Windsor, where the king presented the Cherokees with a purse of money.[2] In order to ensure that trade could be enhanced with the Cherokees, London merchants held parties for them, and a ship belonging to the king was outfitted specially for their return.[3] The British crown and its merchants did all within their power to make sure that a strong relationship could be cemented between them and this powerful nation in North America. Their perseverance succeeded. Leaders of the two nations signed the Articles of Agreement, which regulated trade between them for the next half century. The Articles also included a pledge made by the Cherokees to fight for the English in the event any country—specifically France—should attack English settlements in America.

Among the Cherokees who traveled to England was a young leader named Attakulakula. Better known to the English settlers of North America as the Little Carpenter, Attakulakula played a vital role in South Carolina and American development through the 1760s. In 1736 he convinced Cherokees not to accept French aid following a failed fall harvest and to remain allied with the English. During the French and Indian War, the Little Carpenter organized groups of Cherokee warriors to fight with the colonists and with British regulars. Attakulakula negotiated the peace settlement between the Cherokees and South Carolina in 1761 that ended the Cherokee War (see Chapter 15).

Attakulakula's significance in America may be seen in an event of 1756. Rarely did Attakulakula refuse to help the English, but when he appeared to break his promise and did not lead an excursion against the French, it was news throughout America. Newspapers in Boston, New York, Philadelphia, and Annapolis reported the apparent breech with the valued Cherokee leader. South Carolinians, especially, wanted an explanation. That is why the *South-Carolina Gazette* happily reported to its readers on January 27, 1757, that "The *Little-Carpenter* coming to Town is now no longer a Doubt, for we can assure our Readers, that he is already arrived within a few Miles of it." Attakulakula met with the governor and council and resolved the differences.

The political ties between the Cherokees and their leaders such as the Little Carpenter represent part of the diplomacy that occurred in colonial America. Native American nations were viewed as autonomous governments capable of forming alliances with individual colonies as well as with Britain. Native Americans, as was seen with the 1730 treaty between Britain and the Cherokees, were regarded as valuable trade partners. Indians were also viewed as dangerous enemies and were for the most part feared by settlers moving into regions of colonial America sparsely settled by whites and inhabited primarily by Native Americans. This perception of Native Americans led to a dual understanding of Indians in newspapers. For colonials, Indian alliance and trade was imperative, but Indians were also bloodthirsty savages capable of the most horrific atrocities.

This chapter discusses the political relationships between the colonies and Native Americans as presented in newspapers. It includes reports by both Native American and colonial leaders. Within these news articles, one can see the significance of each group to the other. One also sees how whites viewed Native American groups as sovereign nations and how Native Americans reciprocated. What is also evident is the fact that when the colonies no longer needed Native American assistance or trade, or whenever the numbers of Native Americans within a particular colony decreased to the point they were no longer considered a threat to whites, colonial political actions toward Indians were often harsh. What was needed from Native Americans often determined how the newspaper information was expected to persuade readers.

The first section presents positive aspects of Native American–colonial relationships. It begins with a report during King George's War that the Six Nations confederacy has renewed its agreements with England and the colonies to fight the French and their Native American allies. The second entry is an eloquent speech made by a Cherokee chief that reaffirms that nation's loyalty to King George. These accounts are followed by three stories that demonstrate how the colonies attempted to protect Native Americans and their lands because of the sovereign status tribes maintained and because to do otherwise would likely lead to Native American attacks on white settlements. The first two discuss violations of Native American lands and land use. One asserts that whites are violating Indian territory by hunting illegally and must be stopped. The second warns whites not to stop Native Americans from deer hunting at any time. The third, which includes part of an official announcement made by the government of Virginia, places a £100 reward on the head of anyone who killed Indians in the colony's backcountry.

The last entries in the section on positive political relationships with Native Americans include the Anderscoggin nation's "Declaration of Independence" from all interference by whites or other Native Americans. It calls for autonomy and respect by all groups for the sovereignty of the Anderscoggin. The last two news reports deal with Native American alliances formed during the Revolution.

The negative political relationship entries in the chapter begin with a speech made by the headman of the Cape Sable Indians to the governor of Nova Scotia. In it, the Indians plead for a place that they may go that will not be taken from them by immigrating whites. It is followed by a warning from a New York resident that colonists must placate Native Americans or the Indians will destroy all whites moving westward into Indian territory. The third entry is an essay written to appear as if it is a news story. In the story, all male Native Americans on the continent obediently hang themselves so that they will no longer be a bother to whites.

The section concludes with a series of three official reports from Massachusetts Governor William Shirley that appeared in the *Boston Evening-*

Post dealing with the Penobscot tribe of New England. In the first, war is declared and bounties are announced on all tribes except the Penobscot. In the second, a bounty is placed on the lives and scalps of all Penobscot. In the third, the Penobscot are told that all of them will be hunted down and killed if they ever cause any more trouble for whites living within their territory.

POSITIVE NATIVE AMERICAN–COLONIAL RELATIONS

OFFICIAL REPORT: "THE SIX NATIONS ALLY WITH ENGLAND"

In 1744 England and France were at war. It was the third time the two European powers had declared war on each other since the two began colonization of North America. Known as King George's War, the fighting involved Native American on both sides. Because the French had better relationships with most Native Americans than did the British, gaining a fighting alliance with the Six Nations—the largest and most powerful group of Native Americans in the Middle and New England colonies— was seen as vital for the British colonists. In this official report, Massachusetts reported that the Six Nations had promised to help the British and "take up the hatchet" against the French and their Indian allies.

New-York Evening Post, 4 November 1745

Boston, Oct. 28. On the 20th Instant in the Evening the Commissioners appointed by this province, return'd from Albany; and we are inform'd that the Indians of the six Nations have very readily renew'd their Covenant with the several Governments that treated with them; that the jealousies that were raised among those nations the last Winter, are entierly [*sic*] removed: That they have taken the Hatchet against the French and Indian Enemy, and only wait till the Governor of New-York shall order them to make use of it.

AN ANONYMOUS SOUTH CAROLINA WRITER: "THE SPEECH OF CHULOCHCULLAH"

When hostilities between the French and Indians and the British colonies began in 1754, colonial leaders quickly scrambled to firm up relationships with those Native American nations closest to them. South Carolina desperately needed to make sure its alliance with the Cherokees remained intact. For that reason, an official delegation from Charleston traveled into the backcountry of the colony to meet with

Cherokee leaders in 1755. In this anonymously sent report, the speech of a Cherokee headman gracefully describes Cherokee loyalty to King George. At the end of the meeting, the two signed an agreement bound with the seal of the colony.

Virginia Gazette (Williamsburg), 19 September 1755

CHARLES-TOWN, July 31.

HIS Excellency the Governor having, by the Advice of his Majesty's Council, yeilded [*sic*] to the pressing Instances of the Cherokees, to meet them at a Place 200 Miles distant from hence, set out on that Expedition. . . .

The Head-men who were sent hither to sollicit this Favor alledged, that at the Meeting, they proposed to consult him about several Affairs, of great Importance to their Nation; that they wanted his Advice, how to secure their Towns against the Attempts of their Enemies, who were very numerous. . . .

The Cherokees have not, like some other Indian Nations or Tribes, wandered and moved from Place to Place, but inhabited the Lands where they still dwell long before the Discovery of America. They have no Tradition, that they came originally from any other Country, but affirm, that their Ancestors came out of the Ground where they now live. . . .

The Cherokees are computed to be three Times the Number of the Six Nations put together; they are a free and independent People; were never conquered, never relinquished their Possessions, never sold them, never surrendered or ceded them.

It would, no Doubt, be entertaining to our Readers, could we acquaint them with all that passed at the several Conferences betwixt the Governor and them, on this Occasion, which lasted six or seven Days, as these Conferences were not only very interesting to this Province, but all his Majesty's Colonies on this Continent: But at present, we can only lay before them the Conferences of the second of July, being the sixth Day. . . .

On Wednesday July 2d Cannacaughte the Chief, and the other Indians, arrived from their Camp . . . all the Head-men and Head-warriors were placed on Benches fronting them, the other Warriors and Indians (to the Number of 506) sitting all around the Ground under the Trees, Chulochcullah, the Speaker, rose up, and holding a Bow in one Hand, and a Shaft of Arrows in the other, he delivered himself in the following Words, with all the Distinctness imaginable, with the Dignity and graceful Action of a Roman or Grecian Orator, and with all their Ease and Eloquence.

"What I am now to speak, our Father the great King George shall hear. We are now Brothers with the People of Carolina, and one House covers us all: The Great King is our common Father. (At this Time a little Indian Child was brought to him, whom he presented to the Governor with these Words.) We, our Wives, and all our Children, are the Children of the Great King George, and his Subjects; he is our King, our Head, and Father, and we will obey him as such. I bring this litle [*sic*] Child, that, when he grows up, he may remember what is now agreed to, and that he may tell it to the next Generation, that so it may be handed down from one Generation to another for ever."

The Indian then opening a small Leather Bag, in which was contained some Earth, laid the same at his Excellency's Feet, adding, "That they gave all their Lands to the King of Great-Britain; and as a Token of it, they desired, that this Parcel of Earth might be sent to the King, for they acknowledge him to be the Owner of all their Lands and Waters." . . .

The Indian then opened another small Bag of Leather, filled with parched-Corn Flour, and said, "That as a Testimony, that they had not only delivered their Lands, but all that belonged to them, to be the King's Property, they gave the Governor what was contained in that small Bag, desiring, that it might be sent also to the Great King George." . . .

The Indian then delivering a Bow and Arrows to the Governor . . . "The Bow and Arrows which they delivered to be laid at the Great King's Feet, were all the Arms that they could make for their Defence; they therefore hoped, that he would pity the Condition of his Children, and send them Arms and Ammunition, to defend them against his and their Ene-mies. . . ."

The Indian then added, "That the new Governor of Carolina and the Head-men of Chotte were both present, he hoped, the Governor of Caro-lina would soon let the Great King know all that had passed; and that the Head-men of Chotte should let all the Cherokees know, that every Thing that had now passed must be performed, and that it must remain for ever."

His Excellency the Governor, in a Speech to the Indians . . . "That, in his Name [King George], he accepted of what they had delivered to him at this present Conference, and promised, that they should be soon sent. . . .

The Governor promised it should be done, and that he would order the Great Seal of the Province affixed to it.

AN ANONYMOUS GEORGIAN: "KILLING BEAVER IN CHEROKEE TERRITORY"

In 1765 the memory of the Cherokee War (1759–1761) was still fresh in the minds of most colonials from Virginia to Georgia (see Chapter 15). Colonies took efforts to ensure that the Cherokees would have autonomy and land. Whenever these guarantees were broken or threatened, news-paper reports alerted officials. In this news story, accounts of beaver

trapping in Cherokee lands are supplied as a warning that the Chero-
kees have been complaining about white activities on their hunting
lands.

Georgia Gazette (Savannah), 28 March 1765

CHARLESTOWN: Several white men from the western parts of this province and North-Carolina, have lately gone into the Cherokee settlements and killed beaver, which occasions some uneasiness, as it is expressly contrary to treaty; and we hear the Cherokees have complained of it; but in the same modest terms they have adopted for two or three years past.

GOVERNOR WILLIAM BULL: "AN ACT FOR THE PRESERVATION OF DEER"

Deer hunting was imperative for the Native American nations in the Southern colonies. As whites pushed farther west in South Carolina, land for hunting decreased for Native Americans. In Governor William Bull's decree, he limited the hunting of deer by South Carolinians while reminding all that Native Americans, in this case the Catawbas, had rights to hunt deer at any time. The move was a good one politically for South Carolina because it maintained friendly ties with the tribes in the colony.

South-Carolina Gazette; and Country Journal (Charleston), 3 April 1770

Charlestown: WHEREAS it has been represented unto me, that the CATAWABA INDIANS have lately been interrupted in their Deer-Hunting by sundry Persons, from a Misapprehension, that the Act passed in the last Session of the General Assembly, intitled, "An Act for the Preservation of Deer, and to prevent Mischiefs arising from hunting at unseasonable Times," extended to them, I DO therefore think fit, by and with the Advice of his Majesty's honourable Council, to publish this my Proclamation, to NOTIFY, That in and by the said, Act, it is provided, that nothing therein contained should extend, or be construed, to extend, to deprive the Indians in Amity with this Province, of any Right or Priviledge, that they are intitled to, by Virtue of any Treaty now subsisting between them and this Government; and I DO THEREFORE hereby strictly inhibit and forbid any Person or Persons whatever, to interrupt or hinder the said Catawba Indians, or any Indians in Amity with this Government, in their Deer-Hunting, for the future.
Wm. Bull.

GOVERNOR FRANCIS FAUQUIER: "SETTLERS WANTED IN THE MURDER OF CHEROKEES"

In 1759 a group of Cherokees returning to South Carolina after fighting with colonial and British troops against the French were killed for the bounties placed on Native American scalps by Virginia. The action, in part, led to an uprising of the Cherokee that lasted until 1761. When a group of Cherokees was attacked in 1765 and five were killed, Virginia Governor Fauquier placed bounties on the heads of those involved, the amount of money equal to or greater than the rewards given for Indian scalps during the French and Indian War.

New-York Mercury, 3 June 1765

WILLIAMSBURGH: WHEREAS a party of Cherokees arrived at Staunton in Augusta, and intended to proceed from thence to Winchester, having obtained a pass from Col. Lewis for that purpose, were on their way thither attacked by upwards of 20 men, and their Chief, and four more of the said Indians killed, and two others of them wounded, in violation of the treaties subsisting between that nation and us: That such villains may not escape with impunity, and that the honour of the country may be vindicated and maintained, by inflicting the severest punishment on such atrocious violators of the laws, I have thought proper, by and with the advice of his Majesty's Council, to issue this proclamation in his Majesty's name, hereby promising a reward of One Hundred Pounds for the apprehending and securing each or any two who shall be proved principal promoters of and ringleaders in the said murders, and Fifty Pounds for every one of the others who was aiding and assisting therein; and I do further offer a pardon to any person concerned in the same, and not an actual perpetrator of murder, who shall make a full discovery of the principal actors therein, so that they may be brought to Justice.

THE ANDERSCOGGIN NATION: "DECLARATION OF INDEPENDENCE"

The Anderscoggin Indians lived in New Hampshire, Maine, and Canada. Their name came from the central river of the region, now spelled Androscoggin. Their declaration of independence coincided with the beginning of the Revolution. In this declaration, the Anderscoggin acknowledge the autonomy of all groups and the right to protect one's land from encroachment. Readers should pay attention to the land rights and issues of privacy addressed by the Anderscoggin.

New Hampshire Gazette, and Historical Chronicle (Portsmouth),
5 May 1775

Portsmouth: A LETTER from the Anderscoggin Tribe to Col. SAMUEL THOMPSON of Brunswick. . . . WE allow that passive Obedience, and Non-resistance, is only due to the Laws of God, and our own Tribe.

We allow that Unanimity in our own Tribe, or among the Tribes of this Land, strengthens like the Bone of Steel, and Sinews of Brass.

We allow for the keeping up, & nourishing that Unanimity, it is necessary that the Heads of the Tribe should assemble often together.

We allow that every Sannop, Squaw, and Papposs should stand to, and abide by the Determinations and Resolutions agreed to by the Heads of the Tribes when so assembled.

We allow that Mobs and Tumults in any Tribe, relaxes their Nerves, breeds Contentions, Confusions, and every evil Work ensues.

We allow that every Indian's Wigwam, is his own Citadel of Defence, in which he has a Right to defend himself, his Squaw & Papposs.

We allow that every one's Person and Property ought to be protected by the Laws of his own Tribe.

We allow that if any Tribe or even white People with their great Canoes should attempt to stop our little Canoes from going to catch Fish, get Clams, sell our Furs and Skins, or to buy Rum, their great Canoes ought to be set on fire, as ever they come into our River Anderscoggen.

We allow that no white People or great Folks ought to endeavour to stop or hinder our Tribe from meeting together when we please.

We allow that no other Tribe of black or white Folks ought to come and build Forts on any of our Land without the Leave of the Heads of our Tribe, or buying the Land first of us.

We allow that every Tribe on this our Land ought to make their own Sagamors, Sachems and Captains, to learn & instruct their young Men in the Use of the Bow, the Tomahawke, and Scalping-Knife, & to muster them together often for that Purpose.

The above were the Sentiments of our Tribe when assembled last. We shall assemble at Scundogoda, on Anderscoggin River, the next new Moon; and after that will send you our further Sentiments on the Affairs of the present Times. Selah.

AN ANONYMOUS REPORT: "NO INDIANS FOR ENGLAND"

With the outbreak of the Revolution, America and Britain scrambled to align Native Americans as allies, just as had been done during the French and Indian War. Here, a writer from Massachusetts explains that no tribes have yet allied with England.

New-York Mercury, 14 August 1775

Cambridge: . . . We can't yet learn that a single Tribe of Savages on this continent have been persuaded to take up the Hatchet against the Colonies, notwithstanding the great Pains made use of by the vile Emissaries of a savage Ministry for that Purpose.

AN ANONYMOUS REPORT: "SIX NATIONS TO REMAIN NEUTRAL"

Every time Americans could report something positive during the Revolution, especially during the first few months of fighting, they did so. In this article from Connecticut, warriors from the Six Nations report on the nations' neutrality. Not having the Six Nations fight against Americans was good news and its appearance in newspapers no doubt helped bolster American resolve to fight.

Connecticut Journal, and New-Haven Post-Boy, 16 August 1775

NEW LONDON: We hear from Westmoreland, in the western Part of this Colony, that last Thursday se'nnight about 50 Indians of the Six Nations came to that Place, and incamped at a small Distance from the Settlement; the next Day they came in and delivered a Message, which was to this Purpose.————That they were sorry to hear of the Difference which subsisted between Great-Britain and the Colonies————That they should not take up the Hatchet on either Side————That they meant to be at Peace with the English as long as the Stream ran down the Susquehannah River————That should Difference in future arise between us and them, they would try every gentle and healing Measure to obtain Redress of the Grievance————That as Col. Guy Johnson had left his Habitation, and they were destitute of a Superintendant, they desired Col. Butler to take upon him that Trust; and that the Place for holding their future Congresses might be Westmoreland.

NEGATIVE NATIVE AMERICAN–COLONIAL RELATIONS

CAPE SABLE INDIANS: "SHOW ME WHERE I CAN GO"

In most cases, whenever colonial governments no longer felt they needed alliances with Native American tribes, hostile decrees were issued against the Indians. In this notice, the Cape Sable Indians acknowledge that there is nowhere left for them to go, that they have been driven from all that once was theirs by the whites. In a passionate plea, the

Cape Sable leaders request that the whites tell them where they can go to live in peace because all they believe that is left for them is death.

Pennsylvania Gazette (Philadelphia), 2 January 1749 (1750)

Boston: Dec 4. The place where thou art, the place thou dost lodge, the place where thou dost fortify, the place where thou thinkest to establish, the place thou desirest to make thyself master of; that place is mine.

I am sprung from this land as doth the grass, I that am a savage, am born there, and my fathers before me. This land is mine inheritance, I swear it is, the land which God has given to be my Country for ever. . . . Shew me where I an Indian can retire. 'Tis thou that chasest me; shew me where thou wilt that I take refuge. Thou hast taken possession of almost all this country, insomuch that Chebucta is my last recourse; yet thou enviest me, even that spot, thou wouldst drive me from that. . . . The worm creeping, that creeps, knows how to defend itself when attacked; surely savage as I am, am better than a worm, and must know how to defend myself when attack'd. I shall come to see thee soon; yes, trust me, I will see thee.—I hope that what I shall hear from thy own mouth will afford me some comfort.—I greet thee well. Signed, All the Savages of Isle Royal and Malkakonnock.

AN ANONYMOUS REPORT: "THE INDIANS MUST BE OUR ALLIES"

The colonial situation in 1755 was precarious. Unless colonists could thwart French attacks, British Colonial America would cease to exist under British rule. In a simple statement from Boston, an unidentified writer pleads that the colonies' governments do all in their power to make alliances with Native Americans. To do anything less, the writer intimates, will mean sure defeat.

Boston Gazette, or Weekly Advertiser, 28 January 1755

If the Indians are neglected, and nothing more done to secure them in our Interest than has been, Time will shew the great Disparity between us (be we ever so regular) and the Indians in the Woods; for we are an unequal Match to them in the Wilderness.

AN ANONYMOUS WRITER: "THE 'GRAND' INDIAN CONGRESS"

Writers to newspapers sometimes liked to present imaginary events as if they had happened. In this anonymous letter to the Maryland Gazette, *the writer speaks of a congress of Native Americans where all the men obligingly kill themselves. By 1765—in the East—the numbers of Native Americans had been reduced greatly, and most colonists no longer felt that treaties were needed with Indians or that Indians needed to be treated with any kind of equality. This vision demonstrates how Native Americans often were not considered human and their removal a blessing.*

Maryland Gazette (Annapolis), 20 June 1765

His Majesty's Agent in order effectually to prevent all farther Ravages by those barbarous Savages, had summoned all the Indians in America to meet him at a grand Congress, at which every individual adult Indian in America attended; the whole Number amounting to Three Million Five Thousand Seven Hundred and Thirty-four. At this Congress the Agent informed them . . . that they were a People whose Promises could not be relied on; and that from the immense Increase of the Whites the Country would soon be too narrow for both, if they were really determined to give the highest Evidence in their Power of their Loyalty and Affections to the Crown of Great-Britain, and of their so frequently pretended Friendship for him. . . . Upon which the whole Audience who all heard him very distinctly and easily took the Hint, unanimously rose up and immediately went and hanged themselves.————It is thought that the Subject of Ways and Means how to dispose of their Wives and Children to prevent the tragical Consequences of the Repopulation of America by such Savages, will be one of the first that will engage the Deliberation of the Parliament at their next Sitting.

GOVERNOR WILLIAM SHIRLEY: "DECLARATION OF WAR ON NATIVE AMERICANS"

Early in the French and Indian War, Native American tribes took sides with either the French or the British. In this decree from Massachusetts Governor William Shirley, all tribes in the colony except one are declared enemies of the colony. The governor offered a bounty on the scalps of Native Americans, even those of children.

Boston Evening-Post, 16 June 1755

I Have therefore thought fit to issue this Proclamation, and to Declare the Indians of the Norridgewock, Arresaguntacook, Weweenock and St. John's Tribes, and the Indians of the other Tribes now or late inhabiting in the Eastern and Northern Parts of his Majesty's Territories of New-England, and in Alliance and Confederacy with the above-recited Tribes, the Penobscots only excepted, to be Enemies, Rebels and Traitors to His Most Sacred Majesty: And I do herby [*sic*] require His Majesty's Subjects of this Province to embrace all Opportunities of pursuing, captivating, killing and destroying all and any of the aforesaid Indians, the Penobscots excepted. . . .

I have thought fit to publish the same; and I do hereby promise That there shall be paid out of the Province Treasury to all and any of the said Forces, over and above their 'bounty upon Enlistment, their Wages and Subsistence, the Premiums or bounties following, viz.

For every Male Indian Prisoner above the age of Twelve Years, that shall be taken and brought to Boston, Fifty Pounds.

For every Male Indian Scalp, brought in as Evidence of their being killed, Forty Pounds.

For every Female Indian Prisoner, taken and brought in as aforesaid, and for every Male Indian Prisoner under the Age of Twelve years, taken and brought in as aforesaid, Twenty-five Pounds.

For every Scalp of such Female Indian or Male Indian under Twelve Years, brought as Evidence of their being killed, as aforesaid, Twenty Pounds.

GOVERNOR WILLIAM SHIRLEY: "A BOUNTY ON PENOBSCOT SCALPS"

The Penobscot were considered allies of Massachusetts in June, but by November 1755, they, too, were declared enemies of the colony. In this decree, the governor offers a bounty for Penobscot scalps, just as he had on other Native Americans in June. The Penobscot no doubt had reacted to bounty hunters who did not care to what tribe an Indian belonged because an Indian scalp brought money.

Boston Evening-Post, 10 November 1755

BOSTON: . . . For every Male Penobscot Indian above the Age of Twelve Years, that shall be taken within the Time aforesaid and bro't to Boston, Fifty Pounds.

For every Scalp of a Male Penobscot Indian above the Age aforesaid, brought in as Evidence of their being killed as aforesaid, Forty Pounds.

For every Female Penobscot Indian taken and brought in as aforesaid and for every Male Indian Prisoner under the Age of Twelve Years, taken and brought in as aforesaid, Twenty-five Pounds.

For every Scalp of such Female Indian or Male Indian under the Age of Twelve Years, that shall be killed and brought in as Evidence of their being killed as aforesaid, Twenty Pounds.

GOVERNOR WILLIAM SHIRLEY: "WE TAKE POSSESSION OF PENOBSCOT LAND"

By 1760 the Americans and British had successfully driven the French and Indians from most places in the colonies. In addition, Massachusetts' war against the tribes within its borders had depleted them. As a result, Governor Shirley no longer felt that any alliances or treaties were necessary with Indian nations. In this report, the governor tells the Penobscot to either assimilate or leave the colony.

Boston Evening-Post, 12 May 1760

Boston: WHEN the Governor was at Penobscot the last spring in order to take possession of the Country and build a fort therein, he sent the following message to the Penobscot Indians by some of the tribe who had come in.——Tell your People that I am come to build a fort at Penobscot and will make the land English——I am able to do it——and I will do it; if they say I shall not, let them come and defend their land now in time of war——take this red flag to remember what I say: When I have built my fort and set down at Penobscot, if ever there be an English man killed by your Indians——you must all from that hour fly from the country, for I will send a number of men on all sides the river, sweep it from one end to the other and hunt ye all out. . . . As to the people of Penobscot, I seek not their favour nor fear them, for they can do me neither good nor harm——I am sorry for their distress and would do them good, let them become English, they and their wives and families, and come and live under the protection of the fort, and I will protect them.

QUESTIONS

1. According to the news reports, why do you think that white colonists might consider Native American tribes as independent nations?
2. Why was it important to the English to form alliances with Native tribes?
3. What kinds of allegiances did the Cherokees make with Great Britain?
4. Why might colonial governments have been so concerned about violations of Indian hunting territories and arrest any who may have committed crimes against Native Americans?
5. What is the Anderscoggin understanding of autonomy?
6. How would you describe Native Americans from the descriptions given in the readings of this chapter?
7. How would you describe white attitudes toward Native Americans from the readings?
8. Why do you think the Massachusetts government changed its position concerning the Penobscot nation?

NOTES

1. *Maryland Gazette* (Annapolis), 1 December 1730, 4.
2. For assorted stories about the Cherokees in London, see *Boston News-Letter*,

15 October 1730, 1; *Pennsylvania Gazette* (Philadelphia), 15 October 1730, 4; *Boston Gazette*, 23 November 1730, 2; *New-York Gazette*, 15 December 1730, 2; *Maryland Gazette* (Annapolis), 22 December 1730, 4.

   3. *Boston News-Letter*, 19 November 1730, 1.

CHAPTER 5

The Trial of John Peter Zenger, 1735

Americans have grown accustomed to seeing media accounts critical of government and government officials on all levels. From the presidency down to local commissioners, reporters and letter-to-the-editor writers complain about what officials do. In colonial America, objections against government occurred, but they were illegal. Americans operated under British law, under which criticism of the government or any of its officials was a crime. It did not matter if what one said was true, the statement was considered seditious libel, or criticism of the government, and it was grounds for arrest.

On November 17, 1734, New York printer John Peter Zenger discovered exactly how the seditious libel laws worked. He was arrested by the sheriff for publishing articles that criticized New York's royal officials for the way in which they were running the colony. The printer was charged with sedition, inflaming the people, and being in contempt of the government. The next day, Zenger's newspaper, the *New-York Weekly Journal*, did not appear as it had regularly for a year. Although most of New York City's approximately 7,000 residents no doubt already knew about the arrest, Zenger informed his readers of it in the next edition of the *Weekly Journal*. He also noted that the current issue was courtesy of his wife, Anna, who talked to her husband "through the Hole of the Door" in his cell.[1]

Zenger continued to talk to his wife through the hole in the door for months because his bail was set at £600, an amount too high for the immigrant printer to pay. Zenger's backers could have paid the money and had him released, but the printer was of more value in jail. He became a martyr to the cause and proof that New York's governor, William Cosby, was, indeed, crooked.

The August 1735 trial of John Peter Zenger has become central to understanding the growth of the freedom of the press in America, but it had little to do with anything other than political power in New York in the 1730s. Even though the *Weekly Journal* ran articles espousing the freedom of the press, printers used these essays as a way to protect themselves whenever political controversy became a heated subject in the newspaper.[2] Freedom of the press was not the reason for this political war in New York.

The controversy centered around Cosby, who arrived in New York in 1732. Immediately, he demanded a pay raise and half of the salary that had been paid to the interim governor Rip Van Dam who, Cosby reckoned, had been filling in for the new governor. Even though Cosby received the raise, the colony's supreme court denied the half-salary request. Cosby remedied that problem by ousting Chief Justice Lewis Morris. New York became a colony divided politically. Cosby's opposition needed a way to make known its views and a way to attack the governor. A newspaper seemed to be the perfect venue, but New York's only newspaper, the *New-York Gazette*, was "published by Authority" of the government. Its printer, William Bradford, had the contract to do all the government's printing. It was quite obvious that his paper would not be the place to launch an assault against the governor.

Zenger provided the perfect opportunity to initiate a mouthpiece opposing Cosby. Once an apprentice in Bradford's shop, Zenger now owned his own press but had little business. When the anti-Cosby group approached him about starting a newspaper, he agreed. Zenger served as the printer, but the contents of the paper were for the most part controlled by James Alexander, one of the lawyers who had defended Van Dam when Cosby sought part of the interim governor's salary. Alexander was well aware of seditious libel laws and let it appear as if Zenger, a German immigrant who wrote and spoke English poorly, was the guiding force behind the attacks on Cosby.

The *Weekly Journal* leveled several charges at Cosby via unsigned letters. In addition to calling him a French sympathizer, which was a damning charge since Britain and France had been at war off and on for decades, the paper charged that through Cosby "We see Mens Deeds destroyed, Judges arbitrarily displaced, new Courts erected with the consent of the Legislature, by which it seems to me Tryals by Juries are taken away when a Governour pleases." The week before Zenger's arrest, one writer declared, "Only the wicked Governours of Men dread what is said of them."[3]

All of the statements made in the *Weekly Journal* were libelous under law. It did not matter who wrote them; Zenger the printer was responsible for their appearance in public. Cosby had attempted to warn Zenger of his libelous actions by having copies of the *Weekly Journal* burned by the public hangman. In November 1734, all that was left to do was to arrest the printer.

Alexander and William Smith, who had also defended Van Dam, disclosed they would defend Zenger, but Cosby disbarred them immediately after their announcement. To most it appeared as if Zenger would not have legal representation, but when the trial began, Philadelphia lawyer Andrew Hamilton entered the courtroom and announced he was Zenger's attorney.

According to English law, the Zenger trial should have been simple. All that the court needed to prove was that Zenger published the materials considered libelous. The jury would affirm the fact and return a guilty verdict. Hamilton admitted that Zenger had published the tracts in question, which was all that was needed to convict the printer. Hamilton, however, did not stop there. He went on to say that lack of governmental approval did not necessarily make a publication libelous and that the jury, not the judge, should decide the libelous nature of the material. Hamilton, not Zenger or anyone else, turned the case into a free press issue when he said of the *Weekly Journal's* accusations, "They are notoriously known to be *true*."[4] The jury members disregarded precedent and the instructions given them by the judge and found Zenger not guilty of publishing the articles in question. In reality, they were affirming the fact that Zenger had the right to publish the truth.

As in most disputes that occurred during the colonial era, the names of those being accused of wrongdoing were generally omitted. For example, instead of accusing Cosby of being corrupt, a letter writer would describe a corrupt leader from the past and make references to similar actions happening in the present. Pro-Cosby writers intimated that Zenger was responsible for these attacks. The anti-Cosby faction blamed the government printer, Bradford, for similar criticism of Zenger. The printers' names were published on the newspapers anyway; therefore, they became the scapegoats for controversial articles, essays, and letters that appeared in their publications because the law stated that whoever printed the material was guilty of the libel as much as those who wrote it.

When Zenger's *New-York Weekly Journal* began its anti-Cosby campaign that led to the printer's arrest, it did so by claiming freedom of the press as its principal purpose. The attack, however, quickly moved into an explanation of what causes crooked officials. The letter was introduced with the pseudonym "Cato." Cato was the widely known pen name of John Trenchard and Thomas Gordon, English authors who wrote in the 1720s advocating libertarian philosophy and free speech. The use of the name Cato would have immediately associated the essay with the right of the people to criticize openly governmental wrongdoings.

The second anti-Cosby piece comes from one of the four *Weekly Journals* burned by the hangman. Cosby is accused of aiding the French in obtaining valuable and potentially harmful information about New York. This incident, the *Le Cæsar* affair, involved Cosby's approval for a ship from Cape Breton and the French fortress of Louisbourg to dock under pretense of obtaining supplies for hungry French settlers. Cosby's critics, however, said the governor was helping the French gain vital information about New York harbor. Alexander probably wrote this query. The third entry is from one of the burned editions. It charges that anyone that sides with the governor will eventually be betrayed by him. The final anti-Cosby essay, again appearing with the Cato pseudonym, asserts that breaches in authority by evil rulers and those who follow them ultimately lead to their downfall. This essay was probably written by Alexander.

The pro-Cosby readings, which appeared in the government-controlled *New-York Gazette*, begin with a poem that praises Cosby. The second, unsigned, letter attempts to refute the initial charges brought in the *Weekly Journal* by pointing out that Zenger has misquoted information to attack Cosby's government. The letter then outlines why the news in Zenger's newspaper is libelous and why false printing by the press must be punished. The third pro-Cosby letter, from the same February 1734 issue, anonymously accuses Zenger of lying about Cosby's social contacts and warns the printer not to spread falsehoods, especially when they involve certain members of New York's high society. Interestingly, an appended note from Bradford that appears with another letter in the same paper states about Zenger, *"I fear if he goes on at this Rate, he will print himself into a Proverb, and when any thing false and scandalous is publickly Reported, it will be call'd A ZENGER."*

ANTI-COSBY FACTION

CATO: "THE IMPORTANCE OF LIBERTY OF THE PRESS"

When New York lawyer James Alexander and his cohorts sought out Peter Zenger to print a newspaper for them in order to attack the regime of Governor William Cosby, they knew they had to establish the significance of a free press in order to justify their criticisms in light of the libel laws. In this essay, which appeared over a two-week period, the anonymous Cato sets out why press freedom is of such importance. The writer, probably Alexander, also calls upon the principle of truth in printing and upon the concept that truth always wins out when chal-

lenged by falsehood. The argument's purpose was to establish that what would be said about Cosby in the weeks ahead should be weighed against any arguments supporting the governor. Cato was certain his truth would win out if given a chance to be heard in the Weekly Journal.

New-York Weekly Journal, 12 November 1733 and 19 November 1733

Mr. *Zenger*,

Insert the following in your next, and you'll oblige your Friend, CATO.

THE Liberty of the Press is a Subject of the greatest Importance, and in which every Individual is as much concern'd as he is in any other Part of Liberty: Therefore it will not be improper to communicate to the Publick the Sentiments of a late excellent Writer upon this Point. such is the Elegance and Perspicuity of his Writings, such the inimitable Force of his Reasoning, that it will be difficult to say any Thing new that he has not said, or not to say that much worse which he has said.

There are two Sorts of Monarchies, an absolute and a limited one. In the first, the Liberty of the Press can never be maintained, it is inconsistent with it; for what absolute Monarch would suffer any Subject to animadvert on his Actions, when it is in his Power to declare the Crime, and to nominate the Punishment? . . .

But in a limited Monarchy, as *England* is, our Laws are known, fixed, and established. They are the streight [*sic*] Rule and sure Guide to direct the King, the Ministers, and other his Subjects: And therefore an Offence against the Laws is such an Offence against the Constitution as ought to receive a proper adequate Punishment. . . .

That *Might over comes Right*, or which is the same Thing, that Might preserves and defends Men from Punishment, is a Proverb established and confirmed by Time and Experience, the surest Discoverers of Truth and Certainty. It is this therefore which makes the Liberty of the Press, in a limited Monarchy, and in all its Colonies and Plantations, proper, convenient, and necessary, or indeed it is rather incorporated and interwoven with our very Constitution; for if such an over grown Criminal, or an impudent Monster in Iniquity, cannot immediately be come at by ordinary Justice, let him yet receive the Lash of Satyr, let the glaring Truths of his ill Administration, if possible, awaken his Conscience, and if he has no Conscience, rouze [*sic*] his Fear, by shewing him his Deserts, sting him with the Dread of Punishment, cover him with Shame, and render his Actions odious to all honest Minds. These Methods may in Time, and by watching and exposing his Actions, make him at least more Cautious, and perhaps at last bring down the great haughty and secure Criminal, within the Reach and Grasp of ordinary Justice. This Advantage therefore of Exposing the exorbitant Crimes of wicked Ministers under a limited Monarchy, makes the Liberty of the Press, not only consistent with, but a necessary Part of the Constitution it self.

It is indeed urged, that the Liberty of the press ought to be restrained, because not only the Actions of evil Ministers may be exposed, but the Character of good ones traduced. . . . Truth will always prevail over Falshood.

If men in Power were always Men of Integrity, we might venture to trust them with the Direction of the Press, and there would be no Occasion to plead against the Restraint of it; but as they have Vices like their Fellows, so it very often happens, that the best intended and the most valuable Writings are the Objects of their Resentment, because opposite to their own Tempers or Designs. In short, I think, every Man of common Sense will judge that he is an Enemy to his King and Country who pleads for any Restraint upon the Press; but by the Press, when Nonsense, Inconsistencies, or personal Reflections are writ, if despised, they die of Course; if Truth, solid Arguments, and elegant, just Sentiments are published, they should meet with Applause rather than Censure; if Sense and Nonsense are blended, then, by the free Use of the press, which is open to all, the Insconsistences of the Writer may be made apparent; but to grant a Liberty only for Praise, Flattery, and Panegyric, with a Restraint on every Thing which happens to be offensive and disagreeable to those who are at any Time in Power, is absurd, servile, and ridiculous.

AN ANONYMOUS WRITER: "THE *LE CÆSAR* AFFAIR"

In the fall of 1733, a French ship, the Le Cæsar, *docked in New York with the approval of Governor Cosby. The ship's captain said he needed food for hungry settlers on Cape Breton, but many New Yorkers—distrusting of any Frenchman—believed the ship was on a reconnaissance mission to learn about the fortifications of the port. In the unsigned letter, probably written by James Alexander, Cosby is charged with collusion.*

New-York Weekly Journal, 17 December 1733

It is agreed on all Hands that a Fool may ask more Questions than a wise Man can answer, or perhaps will answer if he could . . . And it will be no great Puzzle to a wise Man to answer with a *yea*, or a *nay*, which is the most that will be required in most of those Questions.

Q. 1. Is it Prudent in the French Governors not to suffer an Englishman to view their Fortifications, sound their Harbors, tarry in their Country to Discover their Strength?

Q. 2. Is it Prudent in an English Governor to suffer a Frenchman to view our Fortifications, sound our Harbors, &c.?

Q. 3. If the above Affidavits be True, had the French a bad Harvest in Canada? Or do they want Provisions?

Q. 4. Was the Letter from the Governor of Louisbourgh to our Governor True?

Q. 5. Might not our Governor as easily have discovered the Falshood of it as anybody else, if he would?

Q. 6. Ought he not to be endeavored to do it?

Q. 7. Did our Governor endeavor to do it?

Q. 8. Was it not known to the greatest Part of the Town, before the Sloop *Le Cæsar* left New York, that the French in the Sloop *Le Cæsar* had sounded and taken the Landmarks from without Sandy Hook up to New York? Had taken the View of the Town? Had been in the Fort?

Q. 9. Might not the Governor have known the same Thing, if he would?

Q. 10. Is there not great probability that he did know it? . . .

Q. 15. If a French Governor had suffered an English Sloop and Company to do what a French Sloop and Company has done here, would he not have deserved to be——?

Q. 16. Since it appears by the Affidavits there was no such Scarcity of Provisions as by the Letter from the Governor of Louisbourgh to our Governor is set forth, since the Conduct of the French to the English that happen to go to Canada shows they think it necessary to keep us Ignorant of their State and Condition as much as they can. Since the Sounding our Harbors, viewing our Fortifications, and the honorable Treatment they have received here (the Reverse of what we receive in Canada) has let them into a Perfect Knowledge of our State and Condition. And since their Voyage must appear to any Man the least Penetration to have been made with an Intent to make that Discovery, and only with that intent. Whether it would not be reasonable in us to provide as well and as soon as we can for our Defense?

Q. 17. Whether it can be done any way so well and effectually as by calling the Assembly very soon together?

Q. 18. If this be not done, and any dangerous Consequences follow after so full warning, who is blamable?

AN ANONYMOUS WRITER: "HERE TODAY, GONE TOMORROW"

James Alexander knew how to anger Governor Cosby. When he penned the statement that said governors sacrifice those who befriend them, the man behind the writings in the Weekly Journal *practically ensured the arrest of printer Peter Zenger. This statement was a great contributor to the arrest of Zenger; within a month, this issue of the* Weekly Journal *had been burned and the printer had been placed behind bars.*

New-York Weekly Journal, 7 October 1734

. . . Governors often smile one Day and frown the next; nay, they may make a Sacrifice of those that have lost all others' Friendship by courting theirs; and at best they are here Today and gone Tomorrow.

CATO: "INSTRUMENTS OF PUBLIC RUIN"

James Alexander, using the Cato pseudonym, kept the pressure on Governor Cosby with his writings. In this letter, Alexander pointed out all the ways that evil leaders oppress the law and those whom they are to govern. Such leaders, Alexander said, are instruments of public ruin and ultimately are crushed by those they subject to their evil policies.

New-York Weekly Journal, 28 January 1733 (1734)[5]

SIR,

MEN in a Torrent of Prosperity seldom think of a Day of distress, or Great Men that their greatness will ever Cease . . . as if their Reign were never to End, and they were for ever secure against all After-reckonings, all casualties and disgrace. From whence else comes it, but from such blind Security in the permanence of their Condition, and in the impunity of their Actions, that ministers have sometimes concerted SCHEMES OF GENERAL OPPRESSION AND PILLAGE, SCHEMES TO DEPRECIATE OR EVADE THE LAWs, RESTRAINTS UPON LIBERTY AND PROJECTS FOR ARBITRARY WILL? Had they thought that ever they themselves should suffer in the common Oppression would they have advised *Methods of Oppressing*? Should they have been for *Weakning* or *abrogating the Laws*, had they Dreamed that they should come to want THE PROTECTION OF THE LAW? Would they have aimed at *Abolishing Liberty*, had they apprehended that they were at any time to fall from Power; or at establishing *despotick Rule*, but for the Sake of *having the Direction of it* against others, without seeing ITS Weight and Terrors in their own Particulars? . . .

The INSTRUMENTS OF PUBLICK RUIN have generally at once intailed misery upon their Country and their own Race. Those who were the Instruments and Ministers of *Cæsar* and *Augustus*, and put the Common Wealth under their Feet AND THEM ABOVE THE LAWS, did not consider that they were not only forging Chains for their Country, but whetting Swords against their own Families. . . .

[T]hese wicked Men, who raise up an enormous *Power* in their Country, because they wear its Livery, and are for some Time indulged by it in their Pride and Oppression! And so ungrateful is THAT POWER when it is raised; even to the Props and Instruments that raised it! they themselves are often crush'd to Death by it, and their Posterity certainly are.

This may serve among other Arguments, to prove, that Men ought to be Virtuous, Just, and Good, for their own sake and that of their Families; and especially great Men, *whos* [*sic*] LASTING SECURITY *is best found in the* GENERAL SECURITY, and *in Preserving the* CONSTITUTION *and* LAWS, *and in Banishing all* ARBITRA[R]Y *and* LAWLESS POWER *and sensing against the Return of it.*

I am, &c.

CATO

PRO-COSBY FACTION

AN ANONYMOUS WRITER: "COSBY THE GREAT"

Not all New Yorkers despised Governor Cosby. In fact, printer William Bradford's New-York Gazette *became a source of praise and support for the governor. In this unsigned poem, a New Yorker praises Cosby while considering James Alexander and those who are attacking the governor as nothing more than hot air.*

New-York Gazette, 7 January 1733 (1734)

COSBY *the Mild, the happy, good and great,*
The strongest Guard of our little State;
Let Malecontents in crabbed Language write,
And the D—b H—s, belch, tho' they cannot bite:
He unconcern'd will let the Wretches roar,
And govern Just, as others did before.

AN ANONYMOUS WRITER: "ABUSING CATO"

The pseudonym Cato was greatly admired by Americans. Cato's letters, from London in the 1720s, espoused the rights of freedom of expression and freedom from authoritarianism. Written by John Trenchard and Thomas Gordon, Cato's letter advocated that truth in publication was always acceptable and never punishable. The writer of this letter believed James Alexander's use of the Cato pseudonym was libelous because the letters signed Cato in the Weekly Journal *were filled with lies. Interestingly, the writer puts the blame for these falsehoods on the printer, not on the writer. This may help to explain why printers were sometimes hesitant to print controversial essays and letters since they, not the writer, would probably be charged with libel, which is exactly what happened in the Zenger case.*

New-York Gazette, 4 February 1733 (1734)

Mr. *Bradford*,

UPON reading a Letter in *Zenger*'s late Journal . . . I could not but re-gret to see one of the Greatest Names in Antiquity prostituted to a Pla-giary. . . . And I cannot help thinking, that every Expression in those Discourses . . . are now swoln into a Gigantick Size, and have undergone an Alteration by *Peter Zenger*'s Types at *New-York*. For Mr. *Gordon*'s Re-flections are founded upon Truth, and the Reason of Things, and will recommend themselves, with their just Force, by their agreeableness to the Reason of Things, to all Men of Sense and Integrity at all Times, and be esteem'd worthy of that great Author. . . . For my part, I can compare them to nothing more justly, than to so many very rich Piece of Embroi-dery tacked together with very course [*sic*] Pack-thread, and Cobler's Ends. However, I must do *Zenger*————Justice, and say, he is so far of a piece and consistent with himself, that rather than he will be guilty of dealing ingeniously, he attempts to deceive, even when he publishes Truth, and would impose, not only the Thoughts, but Words of others on the Word, for his own. . . .

So much for *Cato's Letter*, the *best* Part wrote by Mr. *Gordon*, and miserably abused by *Zenger*.

As I pass'd on to the Title, DOMESTIC AFFAIRS, I could not enough admire the consumate Vanity therein exprest, surely, thought I this Man is *strangely* crept into the Hearts and Affections of the People of this *City* and *Province*, That he dares so boldly affirm what they *Think*; says he *'They think as Matters now stand, That their Libertys and Properties are precarious, and that Slavery is like to be entailed on them and their Posterity, if some Things past be not amended, and this they called from many past Proceedings.'*

Now give me leave to say, what I have reason to believe some of the People of this City and Province think in relation to that Paragraph in *Zenger*'s Paper, *They think*, that it is an *aggravated Libel*; and they are so ingenious to say, that if Serjant *Hawkis*, who writes on the Pleas of the Crown; be an Author of that undoubted Credit, as he is universally esteem'd to be; 'tis he that induc'd them to this way of thinking; for he says . . . All Contempts against the Kings [*sic*] Person or *Government* are very highly Criminal, &c. and then gives an Instance in what particular . . . 'The charging the *Government* with Oppression or weak Administra-tion. . . . To confirm this . . . He has these Words; 'Nor can there be any Doubt, but that a Writing which defames private persons only, is as much a *Libel* as that which defames Persons intrusted with a public Capacity, insomuch as it manifestly tends to create ill Blood, and to cause a Dis-turbance of the public Peace. However it is certain, That it is a very high *Aggrevation of a Libel* that it leads to *Scandalize the Government*, by reflecting on those who are intrusted with the Administration of public Affairs, which doth not only endanger the public Peace, as all other *Libels* do, stiring up the Parties immediately concern'd in it, to Acts of Revenge; but also has a direct Tendency to breed in the People, a Dislike of their *Governours*, and incline them to *Faction* and *Sedition*. . . .

This is all the Answer, that Scrap of *Zenger*'s Paper deserves, till he can make the reasonable Part of the World believe that the People of this City and Province, have plac'd so great a Confidence in him, as to trust him with their Thoughts, if they have, I doubt not but they will indulge him with a List of their Names; if they have not, 'tis superlative Assurance in him to say so; besides, as this is a general Proposition in *Zenger*'s Journal, it lies upon him first to prove in what Particular the People's Liberties and Properties are precarious, and how they collect this from many past Proceedings.

A little lower, in the same Paper, he advances for a Truth, that 'The *Liberty of the Press* is now struck at, which is the Safeguard of all our other Liberties.' How that comes to, I know not, I always thought the *Magna Carta* and such other wholesome Laws wisely introduc'd and en-forc'd by our Legislature, from Time to Time, were rather the Bulwark and Safeguard of our Liberties and Properties: Will *Zenger* make any body in that their Senses believe . . . That the *Liberty of the Press* is now struck at? Who told him so? How is he warranted to publish this as a Truth? As a Truth, I believe just the Contrary; for every body that I hear speak of the Press is highly delighted with it, and wish that it may be always open, to defend the Innocent, and shame the Guilty. But here is the Fallacy, here lies the Imposition upon the People of this City and Province; it would here be insinuated, That to punish the Licentiousness of the Press, would be to take away the Liberty of the Press; but alas, this false Gloss will serve no longer, Men of Sense have discovered the Mistake, & disdain the Construction; and a few familiar Instances will obviate it: Is the Art of Printing less criminal than Natural Speaking? Nature has given us the Liberty of Speech, but that will not protect a Man from Having his Head broke, if he gives ill Language: Does not an Action lye for Defamatory Words? Will not a Jury give Damages proportion'd to the Heniousness [*sic*] of the Expression; and was it ever known that a Judgment was given, that the Descendant shall be depriv'd of the Liberty of Talking for the future? No, 'tis the Abuse not the Use of the press that is Criminal, and ought to be punished. . . .

'*These*', says *Zenger* (alluding I suppose to the above cited libellous Paragraph) *are the Sentiment of many of this City and Province*.' I know not what they were, but they appear much otherwise now, and I believe few in the End will thank *Zenger* for publishing these supposed Senti-ments of their's; when the Cobweb Disguise comes to be pull'd off, and Things appear in their natural Colours and true Light: 'Twas never know

but a deceived Populace, were as justly ready to turn against their De-
ceivers, as they were imprudently drawn in to be led by them. . . .

Mr. *Bradford*,

I have read *Zenger*'s Journal of this Day, and find, that he has verify'd
the odd Proverb, *That busty Bitches bring forth blind Puppies*. He has
been so impetuous to deliver himself of his Abortion, that he begins
with——I know not what, and ends with a Mistake. The Governour was
not at the *Hum-drum-Club* of this City on *Friday* Night last; but was
pleased to Honour the worthy Gentlemen of that Club with his Company
on *Saturday* was Sevenight, and last Saturday Night; therefore, as I an
old Member of that Club, and a Friend of my Country, I thought it necessary to give *Zenger* a Caution against publishing false News, especially
of that Society.

QUESTIONS

1. What is the difference in liberty of the press in a limited monarchy and an
   absolute monarchy?
2. Why do you think the charges that Governor Cosby allowed the French to
   enter New York harbor were so serious?
3. Why might Zenger's statements of January 28 and October 7, 1734, be considered seditious libels according to Cosby supporters?
4. How was politics involved in the trial of Zenger?

NOTES

1. *New-York Weekly Journal*, 25 November 1734, 1.
2. Margaret A. Blanchard, "Freedom of the Press 1600–1804," in *The Media in
America: A History*, ed. Wm. David Sloan and James D. Startt, 3d ed. (Northport,
Ala.: Vision Press, 1996), 131.
3. *New York Weekly Journal*, 11 November 1734, 1.
4. James Alexander, *A Brief Narrative of the Case and Tryal of John Peter
Zenger* (1736).
5. The newspaper is dated January 1733 but should be known as a January
1734 issue. England and its colonies, unlike most of Europe, followed the Julian
calendar at this time. The Julian calendar, established by Julius Caesar, changed
years on March 25 instead of January 1. Most Americans talked of January 1 as
the beginning of the new year after the Gregorian calendar established by Pope
Gregory XIII in 1582. Nevertheless, some American printers continued to use to
the Julian calendar to date their papers until England officially switched in 1752.
The switch was made in September, and England had to drop days from the year
to come in line with the Gregorian system, going from September 2 to September 14.

CHAPTER 6

Women's Rights, 1738

In December 1738, the unthinkable happened to Elizabeth Timothy. Her husband, Lewis, died, leaving her pregnant and with six children aged 14 and younger. He also left her with a printing house and a massive debt to Benjamin Franklin for the publishing business he had financed for the Timothies in Charleston, South Carolina.

Lewis and Elizabeth Timothy and their children had moved to Charleston in 1733 so that Lewis could assume the role of printer for South Carolina. The family had emigrated from Holland to Philadelphia in 1731, and Lewis found work as a journeyman printer for Franklin. When South Carolina's printer, Thomas Whitmarsh, died, Franklin arranged for Lewis to assume the position. The Philadelphia printer provided him with a press and type. In return, Franklin was to receive one-third of the profits until the debt for the press was paid. After six years, the Timothies had the option of buying Franklin out of the partnership.[1] Now, with Lewis dead, how would that be possible?

Elizabeth Timothy expected the printing business to continue and for the business to become totally owned by the Timothies. She explained her plans in her newspaper, the *South-Carolina Gazette*, on January 4, 1739:

Whereas the late Printer of this Gazette hath been deprived of life . . . I take this Opportunity of informing the Publick, that I shall contain the said paper as usual. . . . Wherefore, I flatter myself, that all those Persons, who, by Subscription or otherwise, assisted my late Husband, on the prosecution of the Said Undertaking, will be kindly pleased to continue their Favours and good Offices to this poor afflicted Widow and six small children and another hourly expected.

Timothy turned out to be a good printer and a good businesswoman. She paid back the debt to Franklin "with the greatest Regularity and Exactitude every Quarter," purchased the business outright for her family, and eventually turned it over to her oldest son, Peter, in 1746.[2]

Elizabeth Timothy's success as a printer was rare but not uncommon in the eighteenth century. Printing was a family affair. Wives and children helped in the print shops, and women sometimes took over printing businesses when their husbands were unable to work. Because wives had to do the same work that their husbands did in print shops, they were able to continue the businesses and produce newspapers.

Finding a job outside the home, however, was not easy for women during the era. Women comprised less than 10 percent of the colonial workforce and the occupations available to women were few.[3] Women who supported themselves were most often seamstresses. Less often, they were teachers, shopkeepers, or tavern keepers. Women could also work in the medical field as midwives and healers. Prostitution, a part of life in colonial America, afforded women one more manner of financial self-sufficiency.

Regardless of the station of women in eighteenth-century America— indentured servants, planters' wives, widows, backcountry settlers' wives, or women in cities—their expected roles remained fairly constant. Women were expected to exist within the sphere of the home. Within this environment, women were to assume all sorts of roles. They might be cooks, educators, ministers, or anything else that was needed. Even though they were expected to assume these tasks, they were also expected to defer to their husbands in all situations. Most males thought that the very nature of females made them incapable of doing the work that society required of men.

Even though the percentage of women in the American workforce was small, women increasingly found they could support themselves with jobs in larger towns, especially in the second half of the eighteenth century. Many times, women's outside work was deemed essential to the success of families. Still, women were expected to serve in domesticity, just as they had done in the seventeenth century and would continue to do in the nineteenth. As one French observer of America noted:

The women every where possess, in the highest degree, the domestic virtures, and all others. . . . Good wives, and good mothers, their husbands and their children engage their whole attention; and their household affairs occupy all their time and all their cares; destined by the manners of their country to this domestic life.[4]

Women were expected to work at home and remain subservient to men, but they increasingly looked for ways to escape the confines of the female world and gain some autonomy over their own lives in the eighteenth century. Women discussed their business abilities, called for equality in the marriage relationship, and even filed for divorces, according to newspapers.

The first set of readings below discusses independence and equality for women. It begins with a letter, written by an unknown woman to the *New-York Weekly Journal*. The letter claims that women—if given the opportunity—would be superior in educational endeavors to men. The second letter, also written by an unknown female, claims the same for business. The third entry, a poem, claims equality for women in marriage. It says that women abused or neglected by their husbands have the right to be free of the spouse. The fourth piece, an obituary notice, describes Sarah Goddard, who served as printer of the *Providence Gazette*.

The final account of women's move to equality and independence is the story of Hannah Snell. Snell's story was told in many newspapers in 1750. She disguised her sex and served in the British army and navy and completed her service as a hero, a term changed to heroine when she petitioned the king for a pension for her military service.

The second section of the chapter discusses women's role in domesticity and service. It begins with "Rules and Maxims for promoting Matrimonial Happiness," which was addressed to women in Philadelphia in 1730. The same essay, with additional paragraphs of instruction, appeared in the *Providence Gazette* forty years later. It serves as the second entry in this section with its additional admonitions to women.

The third article on domesticity is an obituary that describes what made the woman who died worth remembering. It is followed by a gruesome news story of a woman who literally cut out her tongue at her husband's request. The printer of the story reckoned that what she did was exactly what a woman who knew how to serve her husband should do. In the final letter of this section, a man complains because his wife is too pious, virtuous, and religious—the very traits most men sought in wives.

IN FAVOR OF INDEPENDENCE AND EQUALITY
FOR WOMEN

AN ANONYMOUS WRITER: "SPECIES, NOT SEX"

In the eighteenth century, American women began to question their roles of subservience in society. In this letter written by an unknown female, women's ability to learn is compared to that of men. The writer declares that learning is more adapted to the female world than the male and explains why. Women no doubt read newspapers in the eighteenth century, and the fact that women wrote letters such as this means they were questioning their traditional societal positions.

New-York Weekly Journal, 19 May 1735

I have often wondered that Learning is not thought a proper Ingredient in the Education of a Woman of Quality or Fortune. Since they have the same improveable Minds as the male part of the Species, why should they not be cultivated by the same method?

There are Reasons why learning seems more adapted to the female World, than to the male. As in the first Place, because they have more spare Time upon their Hands and lead a more sedentary Life. Their Employments are of a domestic nature, and not like those of the other Sex. . . . A second Reason why Women should apply themselves to useful Knowledge rather than Men is because they have that natural Gift of Speech in greater Perfection. . . . There is another Reason why those especially who are Women of Quality, should apply themselves to Letters, because their Husbands are generally Strangers to them. . . . If we look into the Histories of famous Women, we find many eminent philosophers of this Sex. . . . Learning and Knowledge are Perfections in us, not as we are Men, but as we are reasonable Creatures, in which Order, of Beings the Female World is upon the same Level with the Male. We ought to consider in this Particular, not what is the Sex, but what is the Species to which they belong.

A LADY: "WOMEN IN BUSINESS: BETTER THAN MEN?"

An anonymous Boston woman wrote to the Boston Gazette *to explain how women were just as capable as men to run businesses, perhaps even more so. The writer called for equality in education for males and females, saying that if placed on a level playing field, women would be superior to men.*

Boston Gazette, 24 March 1740

A new method for making Women as useful and as capable of maintaining themselves, as the men are, and consequently preventing their becoming old Maids, or taking ill Courses. By a LADY. . . .

There are few Trades in which Women cannot weigh and measure as well as Men, and are as capable of selling as they, and I am sure will buy as cheap, and perhaps cheaper: For they can go to the wholesale Merchant's House, and purchase their Goods; whereas the Men generally transact all Business of this kind in Taverns and Coffee houses, at a great additional Expence, and the loss of much Time, so as even frequently to neglect their Affairs at Home, whilst Women, upon the Conclusion of a Bargain, have no Inducement to make a longer Stay, but go directly Home, and follow their Affairs.

By this means a single Woman may get a handsome and reputable Living, and not be forc'd to a disagreeable Match, or even to marry at all. . . . If Women were train'd up to Business from their early Years 'tis highly probable they would in general be more industrious, and get more Money, than Men; and if so, what Woman of Spirit would submit to be a Slave, and fling herself away, as many are forc'd to do, merely for a Maintenance, because she cannot stoop to be a Servant, and can find no reputable Business to go into?

AN ANONYMOUS WRITER: "THO' HUSBANDS ARE TYRANTS, THEIR WIVES WILL BE FREE"

As America moved toward independence from Great Britain, a number of women believed they needed to be freed from the tyranny practiced by husbands. The number of divorces in America grew during this period, and this poem advocates such if a woman finds herself harshly and unfairly dominated by a husband. Note in the poem the use of terms such as tyrant and liberty, terms in vogue in the Patriot political rhetoric of the day.

New-York Journal; or the General Advertiser, 25 October 1770

POET'S CORNER: A New Favourite Song for the Ladies.

Though man has long boasted an absolute sway,
While woman's hard fate was, love, honour, obey;
At length over wedlock fair liberty dawns,
And the Lords of Creation, must put in their horns;
For Hymen among ye proclaims his decree
When husbands are tyrants, their wives may be free.
Away with your doubts, your surmises and fears,
'Tis Venus beats up for her gay volunteers;
Inlist at her banner, you'll vanquish with ease,
And make of your husbands what creatures you please;
To arms then ye fair ones, and let the world see,
When husbands are tyrants, their wives will be free.
The rights of your sex wou'd ye e'er see restor'd,
Your tongues shou'd be us'd as a two-edged sword;
That ear piercing weapon each husband must dread,
Who thinks of the marks you may place on his head:
Then wisely waite, till the men all agree,
That woman, dear woman, shall ever be free.

Nor more shall the wife, all as meek as a lamb,
Be subject to "Zounds do you know who I am."
Domestic politeness shall flourish again,
When women take courage to govern the men;
Then stand to your charter, and let the world see,
Tho' husbands are tyrants, their wives will be free.

JOHN CARTER: "TRIBUTE TO SARAH GODDARD"

Sarah Goddard became a newspaper printer at about the age of sixty-five when she took over operation of the Providence Gazette; and Country Journal *from her son, William. William began the* Gazette *in 1762, but the publication continually lost money or barely broke even under his guidance. In May 1765, William left the paper under his mother's supervision, and she turned it into a profitable business and sold it to John Carter in 1768. Goddard moved to Philadelphia where she assumed part control of her son's printing business there. This obituary extols her business sense and reinforces the idea that women in colonial society were capable at business.*

Providence Gazette; and Country Journal, 10 February 1770

IN the last New-York Gazette, under the Philadelphia head, I find the following article, dated the 8th instant: "Last Friday morning died, in an advanced age, Mrs. SARAH GODDARD, late of Providence, in Rhode-Island; and yesterday her remains were decently interred in Christ Church burying-ground, in this city, attended by a number of respectable inhabitants. She was widow of Dr. GILES GODDARD, formerly of New-London, in Connecticut.

This is so very short and simple an account of the decease of a very amiable person, who was really an ornament and honour to her sex, that in justice to her character I think myself obliged, though no relation to the family, nor very intimately acquainted, to mention the following particulars, which have come to my knowledge. . . . Having taken a liking to the Printing business, through her means her son was instructed in it, and settled in a Printing-House in the town of Providence, to which place she soon after removed, and became a partner with him in the business, which was carried on several years to general acceptance, the two last years under more immediate joint management and direction; the credit of the paper was greatly promoted by her virtue, ingenuity and abilities.

AN ANONYMOUS WRITER: "THE STORY OF HANNAH SNELL"

One way for women to gain independence in a male-dominated society was to assume the role of a man. While few chose to do so, one who did was Hannah Snell, and her story became one of the most widely publicized of 1750. Snell became a Marine and served seven years; her gender was never detected. For her bravery, Snell received a lifetime pension from the British government.

South-Carolina Gazette (Charleston), 8 October 1750

Last week one Hannah Snell, born at Worcester, who was seven years in a Marine Regiment by the name of James Gray, went to the East-Indies in Adm. Boscawen's Squadron, and was at the Siege of Pond-cherry, presented a Petition to his Royal Highness the Duke of Cumberland, praying some Provision might be made for her now she is discharged the Service. His Royal Highness referred her Petition to General Frazer, to report it to him, and make her a suitable Provision, according to her Merit. It seems her sweetheart being impressed into the Marine Service, she put on mens Cloaths and entered in the same Regiment, went to the East-Indies in the same Ship with him, and was his mesmate [*sic*] while he lived (he dying in his voyage) and was a Servant to one of the Lieutenants. She behaved with great intrepidty as a Sailor and Soldier, and her sex was never discovered by either her Sweetheart or any of her Comrades, 'till she made the Discovery of herself by the above mention'd Petition.

WOMEN SHOULD BE LIMITED TO DOMESTICITY AND SERVICE

AN ANONYMOUS WRITER: "MAXIMS FOR PROMOTING MATRIMONIAL HAPPINESS"

One way that males sought to keep women in a position of servitude and domesticity during the eighteenth century was through writings that described the proper way for women to act. Almost always, these rules or maxims stressed service to husband and family for women. In the set provided here, the rules applied to all women married or not.

Pennsylvania Gazette (Philadelphia), 8 October 1730

RULES and MAXIMS for promoting Matrimonial Happiness. Address'd to all Widows, Wives, and Spinsters.

THE likeliest Way, either to obtain a good Husband, or to keep one so, is to be Good yourself.

Never use a Lover ill whom you design to make your Husband, lest he either upbraid you with it, or return it afterwards: and if you find, at any Time, an Inclination to play the Tyrant, remember these two Lines of Truth and Justice.

Gently shall those be rul'd, who gently sway'd;
Abject shall those obey, who haughty were obey'd.

Avoid, both before and after Marriage, all Thoughts of managing your Husband. Never endeavour to deceive or impose on his Understanding: nor give him Uneasiness . . . but treat him always beforehand with Sincerity, and afterwards with Affection and Respect. . . . Always wear your Wedding Ring, for therein lies more Virtue than usually is imagined. . . . Let the Tenderness of your conjugal Love be expressed with such Decency, Delicacy and Prudence, as that it may appear plainly and throwly [*sic*] distinct from the designing Fondness of an Harlot.

AN ANONYMOUS WRITER: "THE LIKELIEST WAY TO OBTAIN A GOOD HUSBAND"

Forty years passed between the above essay and the one below, but men were still telling women what was needed to ensure marriage and marital happiness. In this essay, the word obey is stressed as vital to women's role in society.

Providence Gazette; and Country Journal, 6 January 1770

RULES and PRECEPTS for promoting Matrimonial Happiness, addressed, by Way of New-Year Gift, to the Virgins, Wives, and Widows, of New-England.

THE likeliest way to obtain a good husband, or keep one so, is to be good yourself. Never use a lover ill, whom you design to make your husband, lest he should either upbraid you with it, or return it afterwards. . . . Be assured a woman's power, as well as happiness, has no other foundation but her husband's esteem and love, which consequently it is her undoubted interest, by all means possible, to preserve and increase.—Do you therefore study his temper, and command your own; enjoy his satisfactions with him; share and sooth his cares, and with the utmost diligence conceal his infirmities.—Read frequently, with due attention, the matrimonial service; and take care in doing so not to overlook the work OBEY. . . . Let not many days pass together without a serious examination how you have behaved as a wife; and if, upon reflection, you find yourself guilty of any foibles or omissions, the best atonement is to be exactly careful of your future conduct. . . .

OBITUARY: "MRS. REBECCAH FISK"

Obituaries in the first half of the eighteenth century were generally reserved for the famous. Listings of all who died in a community would come later in the century. Women's obituaries, with notable exceptions such as the one of Sarah Goddard in the readings on independence and equality, generally were dependent upon the significance of the husband. The obituary of Rebeccah Fisk is typical. Her husband and lineage are of prime importance. After that, she is described in terms of her service to society and how well she fit into the role of domesticity.

Boston Evening-Post, 1 October 1750

On the 13th Instant, died, and this Day was decently interred here, Mrs. Rebeccah Fisk, Consort of Capt. Thomas Fisk, late of Wenham, and Daughter of the Rev. Mr. Perkins of Topsfield; a Woman of good Education, uncommon Courtesy and Civility, a sincere hearty Friend, given to hospitality, a lover of good Men, the Ministers of Christ particularly, and of a blameless Christian Life and Conversation. Having acted her Part upon the Stage agreeable to such noble and divine Principles, she is gone off with Approbation from her Acquaintance, and to the Grief of her particular Friends, who while they lament her Death, should carefully imitate the Vertues of her Life.

AN ANONYMOUS WRITER WITH AN EDITORIAL NOTE BY THOMAS FLEET: "AN OBLIGING WIFE"

This news article relates how a wife cut off her tongue after her husband said he wished it cut out. The story demonstrates how women were expected to do as men said. The printer's note by Thomas Fleet praises the woman for performing such a selfless act for her husband.

Boston Evening-Post, 8 October 1750

We hear from Westchester, that last Week one of the Inhabitants receiving a Curtain Lecture from his Wife, he wish'd her Tongue was cut out; whereupon the good obedient Woman snatched up a Razor, and immediately cut off great Part of that unruly Member, and had not the great Effusion of Blood put her Life a little in Danger, doubtless it would hereafter be found a grateful, as well as unprecedented Sacrifice. [Happy Man! How rare a Thing is it to find a Wife so good natured and obliging, in these Parts!]

AN ANONYMOUS WRITER: "A POOR AND UNHAPPY RASCAL"

As much as men wrote to newspapers describing what virtues they wanted in wives, too much piety was not one of those traits. In this anonymous letter, the writer laments the fact that his wife—a paragon of virtue—tends to overlook some of his needs. The writer wants to know how he can keep his wife subservient but a bit less religious.

Providence Gazette; and Country Journal, 2 March 1765

I AM an unhappy poor Rascal, and have, to my unspeakable Mortification, been married these three Years, to a Woman of extraordinary Piety and Virtue.—Don't be surprised—I am neither angry with her Piety, nor offended with her Virtue: on the Contrary, I revere her for both the Qualifications; but they are attended with Consequences. . . . Sir, her Sanctity renders her commons as cross as the very Devil, and if I say a single Syllable, I am sure to hear a Volley of charitable Ejaculations for the Welfare of my poor Soul, and to be treated the Remainder of the whole Day like a down right Reprobate. . . . Is there no Way, Mr. Printer, of curing this unaccountable Malady of being Righteous overmuch? Is there no Way of convincing these narrow-minded Women, that a Moroseness of Temper, or a Disregard of rational Enjoyments, are in no Manner encouraged by the Sentiments of Religion; but that on the Contrary, a Sweetness of Dispositon, and an Endeavour to discharge the necessary Duties of Wife and Mother, are particularly some of its most beautiful Characteristics.—I don't think this Subject would be unworthy the Pen of our most eminent Divines.—Suffer me, through your Paper, to beg some of them will consider it, since it is more likely that a Lesson on this Matter will come with more Weight from the Pulpit than any other Quarter.

QUESTIONS

1. How do the writers of the articles on education and business explain why women could be equal or superior to men in these areas? Why have women not been regarded so, according to the writers?

2. In one poem, the writer maintains, "When husbands are tyrants, their wives may be free." What does this statement tell you about marital relations in the eighteenth century and how they may have been changing?

3. Where were women to work and what were the chief characteristics that were expected of them, according to the essays, letters, poems, and obituaries included in the domesticity section?

4. Why do you think printers—who were usually men—repeatedly inserted articles telling women what was expected of them in marriage and society?

NOTES

1. Benjamin Franklin, *Autobiography*, ed. J. A. Leo Lemay and P. M. Zall (New York: W. W. Norton, 1986), 81, 91.

2. Ibid.

3. Mary Beth Norton, *Liberty's Daughters: The Revolutionary Experience of American Women, 1750–1800* (Boston: Little, Brown, 1980), 137.

4. From the travels of Duc de la Rochefoucauld, in Mary Sumner Benson, *Women in the Eighteenth Century America* (New York: Columbia University Press, 1935), reprinted in Barbara Welter, *The Woman Question in American History* (Hinsdale, Ill.: Dryden Press, 1973), 23.

CHAPTER 7

The Stono Rebellion, 1739

In September 1739, an event greatly feared by most white colonials took place twenty miles from Charleston, South Carolina: the slaves in the region revolted. A small group of them broke into a store, stole the store's supply of guns and ammunition, and murdered the store's owner. The severed head of the slain merchant was left on the steps of his store.

The slaves, now equipped with a deadly arsenal, headed south toward Florida. The slaves no doubt thought that if they could move through South Carolina and Georgia and into Spanish-controlled territory, they would be free of the shackles of slavery. As the rebellious slaves traveled, they were joined by like-minded slaves who were willing to fight for freedom. They killed more whites. Soon, the rebellious slaves numbered between sixty and one hundred.

Even though white South Carolinians were always apprehensive about slaves, the size of this slave revolt, which was called the Stono Rebellion, called for a collective response from plantation owners. About one hundred of them moved south to head off the slaves and to keep them from increasing the size of their forces. When the white planters encountered the main body of slaves, a battle ensued between the two groups, and the whites successfully halted most of the rebellious slaves. More than twenty whites and forty slaves were left dead. Even though small groups of slaves continued the rebellion and the quest to reach Florida, the insurrection was doomed.

When the fighting and revolt ended, the South Carolina legislature quickly enacted a harsh slave code and granted total immunity to anyone who may have committed atrocities against slaves in suppressing the insurrection. The code stated that slaves were the personal property of their owners who had the legal right to do with them as they pleased. In addition, the law required slaves to undergo examination by any white person, and if the slave reacted violently to such requests, "such slave may be lawfully killed."[1]

The Stono Rebellion of 1739 was the largest slave revolt to occur in colonial America. That it took place in South Carolina was probably no accident. Even though revolts had occurred in at least seven colonies, according to newspapers before the Revolution, South Carolina's white population was the minority in the 1730s. One writer from Charleston, at the beginning of the decade, estimated that for "the whole Province we have about 28 thousand negros to 3 thousand Whites."[2] In 1740 the calculated population of South Carolina was 45,000; 30,000 of that number was projected to be slaves of African origin.[3] With two-thirds of the colony's population in bondage, revolts by those enslaved were inevitable, and it was also inescapable that the minority in power would pass restrictive laws against those they controlled.

African slaves were introduced to America in 1619. As the size of plantations in the South grew, the need for slaves to work them increased. Southern planters invested profits to purchase more slaves, which increased revenue and produced a spiraling cycle of bondage for blacks. The same was true in other parts of America but not to the extent of the Southern colonies. The Massachusetts slave population, for example, doubled from 1700 to 1750; 8 percent of Boston's residents in 1755 were slaves.[4]

News of slave insurrections and slave crimes was some of the most repeated information in newspapers. Repetition of news suggests its importance to readers, and in the case of news about slaves, it implies a fear on the part of whites of those blacks in servitude. In 1755, for example, a slave in Kittery—now in Maine but then a part of Massachusetts—murdered the child of his master because the owner had admonished the slave in public. The news of the tragedy was reported in eight newspapers.[5] Newspapers printed all sorts of reports of brutal crimes by slaves, attempted crimes, revolts, and attempted revolts. Innuendo about slave activity was sometimes all that was needed to produce a news story that created panic among the white population. Often the activities of blacks were referred to in newspapers as "The Proceedings of the Rebellious Negroes."

This chapter looks at the way in which newspapers fostered an atmosphere of fear and distrust of African slaves. It could be done through reports of governmental decree, through letters and essays, or through basic news stories. Usually, these pieces were short, but length does not determine effectiveness. Rarely was much printed that intimated that blacks deserved to be treated equally, but some reports were issued.

The section advocating harsh treatment of rebelling slaves begins with a news report from New York in 1712. It tells of a defeated slave revolt and the punishments meted out to the rebellious slaves. At the time, only one newspaper existed in America. The fact that the *Boston News-Letter* chose to run it suggests that such rebellions were considered a possibility in the Boston area. The second selection describes a foiled slave rebellion in Charleston. The third discusses a foiled slave revolt in the Caribbean.

The next selections illustrate how fear of slaves led to governmental decrees restricting the movement and congregation of slaves. The first was issued by New York Governor James De Lancey. The second was passed through the Massachusetts assembly. Both laws were approved, at least in part, to keep slaves from joining with the French and Indians in attacking British colonists. If government actions were not enough, as another article demonstrates, citizens organized watches to control slaves. The final newspaper articles in this section describe crimes committed by slaves against their masters or court decisions handed down against slaves.

The second set of readings focuses upon equal treatment for slaves. It begins with two news reports dealing with slaves and the American legal system. In the first, the court refuses to convict slaves on a number of counts. In the second, a slave owner is bound over on murder charges for having killed his servant. The third selection, an excerpt from a Cambridge, Massachusetts, sermon, postulates that white Americans, who are demanding freedom from England's political shackles, have no right to insist on their own independence until they can grant the same to blacks in slavery. The final reading in this section is a poem, which speaks to the dignity, equality, and humanity of those of African origin.

ADVOCATING HARSH TREATMENT OF SLAVES

AN ANONYMOUS REPORT: "A NEW YORK SLAVE REVOLT"

In 1712 a number of fires destroyed homes and businesses in New York. After investigation, town leaders discovered arson as the cause and determined that slaves were the culprits. The fires, along with an April slave conspiracy to murder whites, produced a volatile time for the city as the growing number of Africans introduced to servitude in the port reacted to their involuntary situation. America's only newspaper in 1712, the Boston News-Letter, *reported the conspiracy, which is signifi-*

cant. The possibility of slave rebellions existed in all parts of America, and the News-Letter's report—the first in the paper about a slave revolt in America—signaled a new era when slave owners and other whites had to be cautious about the movement and activities of slaves.

Boston News-Letter, 12 April 1712

New York, April 14. We have about 70 Negro's in Custody, and 'tis fear'd that most of the Negro's here (who are very numerous) knew of the Late Conspiracy to Murder the Christians; six of them have been their own Executioners by Shooting and cutting their own Throats; Three have been Executed according to Law; one burnt, a second broke upon the wheel, and a third hung up alive, and nine more of the murdering Negro's are to be Executed to morrow.

AN ANONYMOUS WRITER: "AN AVERTED UPRISING"

The possibility for slave revolts was real for any place in America with slaves, but South Carolina may have offered slaves the best opportunity to rebel and succeed. This letter, written by an unknown Charleston resident to a friend in Boston, tells of a plot by slaves that was uncovered. Even more, however, the letter reveals something about the composition of South Carolina's population, which the letter writer said favored Africans to whites by more than nine to one.

Boston News-Letter, 22 October 1730

Charlestown. I Shall give an Account of a bloody Tragedy which was to have been executed here last Saturday Night (the 15th Inst.) by the Negroes, who had conspired to Rise and destroy us, and had almost bro't it to pass: but it pleased GOD to appear for us, and confound their Councils. For some of them propos'd that the Negroes of every Plantation should destroy their own Masters; but others were for Rising in a Body, and giving the blow at one in surprize; and thus they differ'd. The soon made a great Body at the back of the Town, and had a great Dance, and expected the Country Negroes to come & join them; and had not an ever-ruling Providence discovered their Intrigue, we had been all in blood. For take the whole Province, we have about 28 thousand Negros to 3 thousand Whites. The Chief of them, with some others, is apprehended and in irons, in order to a Tryal; and we are in Hopes to find out the whole Affair.

AN ANONYMOUS WRITER: "WEST INDIAN SLAVE REVOLT"

Slave rebellions anywhere in the New World and on board ships were news in eighteenth-century America. In this letter, a West Indies writer

*describes what was done to slaves who revolted there. The graphic de-
scription of the punishment may have been included for the purpose of
reading to slaves in America, but the harshness and severity of it indicate the fear that whites had of slaves. There can be little doubt that
many slaves had to view these executions as a preventative measure for
more uprisings.*

Pennsylvania Gazette (Philadelphia), 9 August 1750

We have for these three Weeks past had Nothing done in our Island
but Racking and executing a parcel of New Negroes, who had plotted to
destroy all the Whites and Creole Negroes in the Island, which they began
on a Plantation belonging to the West India Company . . . thank God they
were soon repulsed, taken, destroy'd, and scatter'd . . . 38 of the Negroes
had been executed, most of whom were rack'd, cut open, and their hearts
taken out and dash'd in their faces.

GOVERNOR JAMES DE LANCEY: "SLAVE ANTI-ASSEMBLY BILL"

*In 1755 many Americans worried that discontented slaves might join
with the French and Indians and attack American settlements. Just as
bad, slaves might decide to undertake their own rebellions against
whites who were preoccupied with French hostilities. As a result, New
York passed a law making it unlawful for more than three slaves to
congregate together at any time.*

New-York Gazette; or, the Weekly Post-Boy, 10 February 1755

It is among other Things enacted, That it shall not be lawful for above
Three Slaves to meet together at any Time, nor at any other Place, than
when it shall happen they meet in some servile Employment, for their
Masters or Mistresses Profit, and by their Masters or Mistresses Consent,
upon Penalty of being whipt upon the naked Back, at the Discretion of
any one Justice of the Peace, not exceeding Forty Lashes for each Offense.
And whereas it is well known, that, contrary to the good Intention and
Meaning of the said Act, the Negroes in the City of New-York, and in
other Parts of this Province, have assembled, and do assemble themselves
together, as well in private as in publick: And, as it hath been represented
unto me, have uttered very insolent Expressions, and otherways misbe-
haved themselves, in Defiance of the Laws in such Cases made and provided, a Mischief which may greatly endanger the Peace of the Province
if not timely prevented. I have therefore, by and with the Advice of his
Majesty's Council, thought fit to issue this Proclamation, hereby strictly
enjoyning and requiring, all Magistrates and Justices of the Peace, to see
the Laws against Negroes duly and punctually executed, suffering no unlawful Meetings of them within their several Districts. And the more ef-

fectually to answer this End, the said Magistrates and Justices are directed to charge all the Constables and other Officers to be diligent in their Duty, and to apprehend and bring before them, or some one of the, all and every Negro or other Slave or Slaves so offending as also, all and every such Person and Persons as shall be found to harbour, conceal, entertain or sell Strong Liquors to such Slaves, that they may be punished according to Law.

MASSACHUSETTS ASSEMBLY: "THE RIGHT TO DESTROY SLAVES"

Massachusetts, like New York, also passed restrictive laws against slaves early in the French and Indian War. The Massachusetts law, however, went beyond that of New York in the actions whites could take against slaves. The Massachusetts law allowed any slave to be killed if he or she were farther than one mile from home without any repercussions for the murderer. As in the decree above, this radical law speaks to the situation at the time and the fear that must have existed in Massachusetts of slave backlash to servitude and to French and Indian invasion.

Boston Evening-Post, 10 March 1755

If one or more Negro, Indian, or Mulato Slave or Slaves, above the Age of fourteen Years within this Colony, shall, in the Time of Alarm or Invasion, be found at the Distance of one Mile or more from the Habitation or Plantation of their respective Owners, without a Certificate from their respective Owners, signifying the Errand or Business they are sent upon, it shall be adjudged Felony without Benefit of Clergy in such Slave or Slaves; and it shall and may be lawful for the Person or Persons finding such Slave or Slaves, at or beyond the said Distance or Limits, to shoot or otherwise destroy such Slave or Slaves, without being impeached, censured or prosecuted for the same; any Law, Usage or Custom to the contrary notwithstanding.

AN ANONYMOUS WRITER: "DISORDERS COMMITTED BY NEGROES"

Newspapers often detailed criminal slave activity. In this anonymous report and the four that follow, writers to newspapers describe crimes committed by slaves or disorderly slave activity. In this letter, slaves have been roaming the streets of Boston committing various acts of vandalism, and a "community watch" is being set up to stop them.

Boston Evening-Post, 14 July 1740

BOSTON: The great Disorders committed by Negroes, who are permitted by their imprudent Masters, &c. to be out late at Night, has determined several sober and substantial Housekeepers to walk about the Town in the sore part of the Night, to see the Law made in that Behalf vigourously put in Execution; and it is hoped that all lovers of Peace and good Order, will join their endeavours for preventing the like Disorders for the future.

AN ANONYMOUS REPORT: "MURDER ON LONG ISLAND"

Early in the eighteenth century, fewer restrictions existed concerning slave activities. This report reveals how some slaves reacted when what freedoms they did have were curtailed.

Boston News-Letter, 9 February 1707 (1708)

On Saturday night Last Mr. William Hallet junior of Newtown on Long-Island, his Wife who was big with Child, and five Children were all inhumanely murdered by . . . their own Slaves, who are Apprehended and have confest the Fact; Tis said they committed this Murder, because they were restrained from going abroad on the Sabbath days.

AN ANONYMOUS REPORT: "ARSENIC AND CHOCOLATE"

Slaves were often given responsibility over the mundane but important duties in a household. They cooked, and they bought supplies. When a Boston slave bought rat poison and put it in the family breakfast, many Bostonians received a wake-up call of their own. This letter describes the crime and suggests how a similar incident might be kept from occurring.

Weekly Rehearsal (Boston), 4 August 1735

Tuesday Morning last the Town was greatly surprized with an Account, That Mr. Humphry Scarlet, Victualler, together with his Wife and 2 Children, were poisoned by their Negroes. The Fact is as follows, viz/ Mr. Scarlet, his Wife and children had eaten chocolate for Breakfast, and another Person who had not Time to eat at the same Time with the Family, in pouring hers out of the Skillet, found 3 white hard Lumps, which while she was viewing, the young Child began to vomit, as did quickly after the others who had eaten Chocolate, Upon this a Physician was presently sent for, who found that the Lumps taken out of the Skillet were Arsenick, or Rats-bane. . . . Mr. Scarlet had 3 Negroes, one of which was suppos'd to have made this horrid Attempt upon the Lives of so many Innocent Persons. . . .

It would doubtless be well for the Publick, if some more Care were taken than is at present, of the Shops where this pernicious Drug is sold; for if we are rightly informed, some of them are looked after chiefly by

Blacks, and even Boys of that Colour. Some are of Opinion, that this deadly drug should be kept lock'd up, and sold by none but the Masters of Shops, and even then to take down the Names of the Buyers. If this Method had been observed, or any other proper Caution heretofore used, 'tis more than probable that Mr. Scarlet's Negroes would not have had such a Stock of Arsenick by them.

AN ANONYMOUS WRITER: "THE MURDER OF JOHN CEDMAN"

John Cedman was not as fortunate as the Scarlet family, who escaped with their lives when a slave put rat poison in their breakfast chocolate. Cedman died from poisoning. A pair of Boston Evening-Post *stories described the crime and the execution of the two slaves convicted of the murder.*

Boston Evening-Post, 7 July 1755; 25 August 1755

Last Tuesday died at Charlestown, after a few Days Illness, capt, John Cedman of that Town, strongly suspected to have been poisoned by a Negro Fellow of his own. After taking the poisonous Potion, he was seized with most exquisite Pain in his Bowels, and when dead, all his lower Parts turned as black as a Coal, and being opened, some of the deadly Drug was found undissolved in his Body, which . . . we hear, was found in the Negro's Chest. He is committed to Goal [*sic*] and 'tis hoped will meet with his just Desert.

Last Tuesday in the Afternoon, at the Assizes held at Cambridge, in the County of Middlesex, Phillis, a Negro Woman, and Mark, a Negro Man, Servants to the late Capt. Cedman of Charlestown, deceased, who were found Guilty of poisoning their Master, received Sentence of Death:— The said Phillis to be drawn to the Place of Execution, and there burnt to Death; and the said Mark, to be drawn to the Place of Execution, and there to be hanged by the Neck 'till he be dead.

AN ANONYMOUS REPORT: "MURDER IN THE WOODS"

As more and more slaves were needed to work fields, control of them became harder. Outside Annapolis, a Maryland overseer, seeking to keep control of the slaves under his direction, mistakenly walked into the woods with them. There, the slaves beat him and slit his throat. Stories such as this one hastened closer and greater supervision of slaves.

Massachusetts Gazette (Boston), 19 July 1770

Annapolis: We are informed . . . a most horrid murder committed in Prince George's County—Mr. William Elson, who was overseer for Mr. Stephen West, walking with some of his negroes in the woods, and having before threatened to chastise one of them for an offence, was struck with a club, which occasioned him to fall. After this, supposing him dead, they carried him some distance, and covered him with leaves, but soon discovered that he had crept out of the place where they had put him; they then notwithstanding he begged his life, cut his throat from ear to ear with a broad axe, and buried him near the threshold of a tobacco-house door.

ADVOCATING EQUAL TREATMENT FOR SLAVES

AN ANONYMOUS REPORT: "SLAVES ACQUITTED"

Despite the fact that slaves usually received harsher and more severe punishment than whites, a day in court was taken seriously in colonial America. Slaves were not automatically guilty just because charges were leveled against them as this brief report confirms.

New-England Weekly Journal (Boston), 24 February 1735

BOSTON: On Wednesday and Thursday last at the Superiour Court holden here two Negros were Tryed, one for Burglary, and the other for setting on Fire his Master House &c. but the Evidences on the part of the King not being strong enough to convict them in the apprehension of the Jury, they were both acquitted.

AN ANONYMOUS REPORT: "CHARGED WITH SLAVE MURDER"

Even though colonies passed a number of harsh laws against slaves during the French and Indian War era, whites did not have license to do with slaves as they pleased. In this Pennsylvania account, a slave owner was charged with murder after an autopsy revealed the slave had been abused by his owner. The master was subsequently charged with the crime and taken into custody.

Pennsylvania Journal, or Weekly Advertiser (Philadelphia), 21 January 1755

A Servant Man belonging to one Mattias Auble, died. . . . And a Jury being called, and his Body opened by the Physicians, it was judg'd his Death was occasioned by the Cruelty of his Master a few Days before in chastising him for some Misdemeanour; and Auble was immediately taken up and secured in the Country Goal [*sic*] in order to be brought to Trial for the same.

A FREE AMERICAN: "A SERMON ON THE CAUSE OF THE AFRICAN SLAVES"

As early as 1700, Americans were writing about the rights of slaves to be free, but it was not until the second half of the eighteenth century that a sizable manumission movement appeared. In this letter from the unknown Free American, the sermon of a minister named Cook is excerpted. The sermon compares the rights of slaves to liberty with that of Americans demanding the same from England. The sermon also does something that usually happened in the abolition literature of the period: it conceded the inequality of Africans and whites.

Essex Gazette (Salem, Massachusetts), 19 June 1770

From a FREE AMERICAN, this is an extract of a sermon by Rev'd Mr. Cook preached in Cambridge.

"I Trust, on this occasion, I may, without offence—plead the cause of our African slaves; and humbly propose the pursuit of some effectual measures, at least, to prevent the future importation of them. . . .

When God ariseth, and when he visiteth, what shall we answer! . . ." We have said,—we repeat it,—that our liberty—our rights as Men and as Englishmen—are dearer to us than our lives—The Africans also are Men: —but men, I confess, debased—miserably debased—with ignorance and bondage.—I fear that "insuperable difficulties prevent an adequate remedy for what is past."—The poor Africans already in the province must perhaps remain in servitude, thro' necessity.—Ignorant and dejected,—unskilful and improvident in the ways of life,—their freedom might subject them to greater inconveneinces than they now endure: not to mention the manifest hazard to the province from persons of such a character, if suffered to live at their own hand. But under this hard necessity—may we not hope, with the highest reason, that their masters, who themselves feel and enjoy the blessings of liberty, will avoid imperious domineering,—treat them with humanity,—and make their lives as easy to them as their circumstances will admit. . . .

They who regard liberty, merely as it procures freedom of thinking and acting, for themselves, are no better than the veriest Tyrants: for these also are extravagantly fond of liberty—for themselves—that they may have it in their power to make slaves of others.

He whose breast is warmed, whose mind is enlarged, with true, genuine notions of liberty, would delight in giving freedom & happiness to all mankind. But the man—rather shall I say—the wretch—who for "sordid gain,"—to increase his heap of shining dirt,—unfeeling and unrelenting at the distress of human nature,—can, with heart and hand, impose slavery on his fellow men, the miserable Africans,—himself deserves,—richly deserves,—to wear the galling chain for life.

AN ANONYMOUS WRITER: "PUNISH THE MASTER"

In New England in the 1770s, abolition became an important issue in a number of newspapers. In Connecticut, many papers supported freedom for slaves. In this short statement, the writer chastises Christian slave owners for not giving slaves the freedom they are naturally due.

New-London Gazette, 1 May 1772

It is esteemed very laudable to us to contend for Liberty, and to 'value our freedom more than our Lives,' but should one of these poor Blacks assert that he was naturally free, and that it was unjust (as in truth it is) to enslave him, what might he expect from his Christian Master but to be severely punished?

THE POET'S CORNER: "TAKEN FROM THE LYBIAN SHORES"

The Poet's Corner was a regular feature in many newspapers in the second half of the eighteenth century. Often its content was aimed at women, but poetry was also used to address controversial subjects. In this anonymous poem, the virtues of Africans are extolled, and their inhumane treatment is described.

Pennsylvania Ledger: Or the Virginia, Maryland, Pennsylvania, & New-Jersey Weekly Advertiser (Philadelphia), 28 January 1775

SEE the poor native [a Negroe-from page's footnote] quit the
    Lybian shores,
    Ah? not in love's delightful fetters bound?
No radiant smile his dying peace restores,
    Nor love, nor fame, nor friendship heals his wound.
On the wild beach in mournful guise he stood,
    E'er the shrill boatswain gave the hated sign;
He dropped a tear, unseen in the flood;
    He stole one secret moment to repine———
"Why am I ravish'd from my native strand?
    What savage race protects this impious gain?
Shall foreign plagues infest this teeming land,
    And, more than sea-born monsters, plough the main?
Ye prouling wolves pursue my latest cries!
    Thou hungry tyger leave thy reeking den!
Ye sand wastes in rapid eddies rise!
    O tear me from the whips and scorn of men!
Yet in their face superior beauty glows'
    Are smiles the mein of rapine and of wrong?

Yet from their lips the voice of mercy flows,
   And e'en religion dwells upon their tongue.
Of blissful haunts they tell, and brighter climes,
   Where gentle minds, convey'd by death, repair;
But stain'd with blood, and crimson'd o'er with crimes,
   Say, shall they merit what they paint so fair?
No, careless, hopeless, of those fertile plains,
   Rich by our toils, and by our sorrows gay,
They ply our labours and enhance our pains,
   And feign these distant regions to repay.
For them our tusky elephant expires;
   For them we drain the mine's embowell'd gold;
Where rove the brutal nation's wild desires;
   Our limbs are purchas'd, and our life is sold!
Yet, shores there are, blest shores for us remain,
   And favour'd isles with golden fruitage crown'd,
Where tufted flow'rets paint the verdant plain,
   Where ev'ry breeze shall med'cine ev'ry wound.
There the stern tyrant that embitters life,
   Shall, vainly, suppliant, spread his asking hand;
There, shall we view the billows raging strife,
   Aid the kind breast, and waft his boat to land."

QUESTIONS

1. Why do you think some of the laws passed in America were so harsh for slaves and so lenient for those who may have abused or even killed slaves?
2. What was the likely result of all the stories about revolts, murders, and crimes committed by slaves?
3. Why do you think the execution of slaves was turned into large public events?
4. Why would the poisoning of whites, such as the Scarlets and John Cedman, by household slaves be considered such horrific crimes?
5. What reasons are given for treating slaves with a measure of equality to whites?
6. Even though the Reverend Cook preached about freedom for slaves, what were his opinions about the true equality of blacks and whites?
7. In the poem from the *Pennsylvania Ledger*, the description of slaves' treatment seems romanticized. In reality, is it? Would a poem such as this increase sympathy for slaves and decrease the slave trade? Explain.

NOTES

1. *Statutes at Large of South Carolina*, vol. 7, 397, 399, 386, quoted in A. Leon Higginbotham, *In the Matter of Color: Race and the American Legal System* (New York: Oxford University Press, 1978), 193–95.

2. *Boston News-Letter*, 22 October 1730, 2.

3. *Historical Statistics of the United States: Colonial Times to 1970* (Washington, D.C., 1975), 1168.

4. Higginbotham, *In the Matter of Color*, 81.

5. See David A. Copeland, " 'The Proceedings of the Rebellious Negroes': News of Slave Insurrections and Crimes in Colonial Newspapers," *American Journalism* 12 (Spring 1995): 1–23.

The Great Awakening and George Whitefield, 1739–1745

Understanding the role played by religion in colonial America is difficult for most Americans today. Many of the first settlers made the hazardous journey across the Atlantic Ocean for religious reasons. The Bible was the one book owned by almost every colonist, and parents insisted that children learn to read, if for no other reason than that they could understand the Bible. America's educational system was established to train ministers. Political assemblies passed laws that affected religious practices and decreed days of public prayer. Religion was, as historian Patricia Bonomi has declared, so much a part of eighteenth-century America that it influenced all aspects of life.[1]

If religion was so important in American life, why, then, did a religious revival take place? The answer is complex, but it is based partly in the growth of America's population and subsequently the number of churches in existence in the eighteenth century. In 1660 the estimated American population of nonindigenous people was slightly more than 75,000. By 1740 that number had swelled to nearly 906,000, an increase of nearly 1,200 percent.[2] Similarly, in 1660, there were an estimated 154 churches in America, and 75 percent of them were either Congregational or Anglican, which meant that the religious practices of most churches within a region were similar. By 1740, 1,176 churches were in operation, but the percentage of churches that were Congregational or Anglican had dropped to slightly more than 55 percent.[3] The increased number of people and churches meant that not as much control could be main-

tained by church leaders. The growth of denominations created a proliferation of beliefs and worship practices.

Another reason for the revival was the preaching of a number of powerful ministers, including Theodore J. Frelinghuysen, Gilbert Tennent, and
Jonathan Edwards. But it was not until 1739, when a 26-year-old Anglican
itinerant preacher from England came to America, that religious revival
occurred in all parts of the colonies. This minister was George Whitefield,
and the man called the "Son of Thunder," because of his powerful voice,
ushered in the period that came to be known as the Great Awakening.

Whitefield conducted seven preaching tours of America from 1739 until
his death in New England in 1770. His preaching style drew thousands,
and the volume of his voice allowed all to hear him while he preached.
Newspapers in 1740 put the numbers in attendance at Whitefield sermons at four, six, ten, and sometimes fifteen thousand or more at a time.
Skeptics doubted such congregations were possible, but Benjamin Franklin, calculating the number of people who could fit into the area in which
Whitefield's voice could be heard, estimated more than thirty thousand
would be able to hear the preacher at any one time.[4]

Whitefield's message revolved around the concept that humankind, because of original sin, could never know or reach God. Using this concept,
known as total depravity, Whitefield constructed his messages to elicit
the question, "What must I do to be saved?" from those who heard him.
Whitefield's answer was to receive God's grace through Jesus, and he
always preached as one who asked the same question of himself and had
found the same answer.

Whitefield was able to preach the same message over and over because
he never tied himself to any one church. He preferred to spread the
gospel as a traveling evangelist, which earned him another nickname, the
"Grand Itinerant," and the revival became known as the Great Awakening
because it touched all colonies and all people in one way or another.

Whitefield did more, however, than initiate a revival. He changed communication in America. He became a media sensation, and during his
first preaching tour from 1739 to 1741 and during the second in 1745,
newspapers focused upon everything the Grand Itinerant did and said.
According to Isaiah Thomas, one of America's colonial printers, "This
celebrated itinerant preacher, when he visited America, like a comet drew
the attention of all classes of people . . . and he became the common
topic of conversation from Georgia to New Hampshire. All the newspapers were filled with paragraphs of information respecting him, or with
pieces of animated disputation pro or con."[5]

Many ministers adopted Whitefield's call and began to preach in the
same manner. Others, notably Boston's Charles Chauncy and Charleston's Alexander Garden, consistently denounced Whitefield's preaching

style and his message. The results were divisions among denominations, increases in colleges to train ministers, and a growth in church membership—something that had declined in America during the eighteenth century despite the role of religion in daily life.

The readings in this chapter look at the reactions to Whitefield and to his revivalism. Despite the fact that he was universally praised at the time of his death, Whitefield received no such unanimous acclamation during his first two preaching tours. In fact, in 1745, a number of colonies passed anti-itinerant laws to prevent Whitefield and his apostles from preaching from the pulpits of churches with regular ministers. Most of the newspaper attacks on Whitefield were also attacks on revivalism, even if they did not directly say so.

The section containing attacks on Whitefield and revivalism begins with a London letter reprinted in America concerning the Anglican church's efforts to silence Whitefield. It is followed by unsigned comments on Whitefield's style of preaching and his type of revivalism. The letter charges that Whitefield preaches with "enthusiastick Ravings" when the Gospel message needed to be presented rationally. In addition to being an attack on Whitefield, the letter is an example of the Enlightenment controversy that was taking place in America during the middle of the eighteenth century.

The next selection opposing Whitefield is an unsigned letter from Philadelphia to Boston warning of the ill effects Whitefield has had on the people of Pennsylvania. This *Boston Weekly Post-Boy* letter was one of two in the same issue. The other, which is included in the pro-Whitefield section, praises the itinerant's preaching.

Whitefield and the revival spurred controversy, and the next entry deals with one of the larger tragedies of Whitefield's first preaching tour. The article, from printer Thomas Fleet's *Boston Evening-Post*, describes how five people who had gathered to hear Whitefield preach in a church were trampled to death when the overflowing congregation panicked. Fleet, who disliked itinerants, added an editorial comment to the news story, which garnered a response in Boston. The response is included in the pro-Whitefield selections. It is important to know that Fleet was a devout Anglican and detested Whitefield. He directly blamed the itinerant for the meetinghouse deaths and for many of Boston's other problems. His paper was a voice of opposition to Whitefield until the printer's death in 1758. The meetinghouse story is followed by two 1745 *Evening-Post* polemics against Whitefield and enthusiasm. They are followed by a Fleet-printed essay against Whitefield in 1754. While America's other newspapers were warning of imminent French and Indian attacks on the colonies, Fleet was railing against Whitefield.

The last selection in the anti-Whitefield part of the chapter attacks itinerants in general and at the same time shows how widespread revivalism was in America in the 1740s.

The Pro-Whitefield and revival section begins with a poem, which may have also been a song, printed only a month after Whitefield arrived in America in 1739. The next entry, a letter, speaks of Whitefield's virtue and his efforts to close concert and dance halls in America. The unknown writer of this South Carolina letter is appalled that the colony has called for a ball, rather than public days of prayer, to celebrate the end of a smallpox epidemic, a fact uncovered in other parts of the *South-Carolina Gazette*.

The next two selections are part of the Whitefield promotional literature written by the itinerant's traveling companion, William Seward, and sent to and printed by newspapers throughout America. These public relations press releases—some of the first ever used in America—told of the money Whitefield raised for his Georgia orphan house, the numbers in attendance at his sermons, and where the itinerant would speak next. The press releases are followed by the *Boston Weekly Post-Boy* letter praising Whitefield that was described in the anti-Whitefield section, as well as the letter that responds to Fleet's negative comments on Whitefield following the meetinghouse accident.

The pro-Whitefield section closes with the *Boston Evening-Post*'s description of Whitefield's funeral followed by a eulogy of the preacher. Ironically, the same newspaper that had been Whitefield's nemesis during its entire tenure under Thomas Fleet, praised Whitefield's efforts in 1770 when the paper was printed by Fleet's sons, John and Thomas Jr.

ANTI-WHITEFIELD AND REVIVALISM

AN UNKNOWN LONDON WRITER: "SILENCING WHITEFIELD"

George Whitefield's reputation as a fiery orator grew from his preaching in England prior to his first American tour in 1739. In 1738 Whitefield visited Georgia with John and Charles Wesley. He promised to return to America to preach and raise money for an orphan house. Before his return, however, he was encouraged to try outdoor preaching to capitalize upon his powerful voice. It was Whitefield's message at these "trial" sermons that offended the Anglican clergy and motivated this letter.

Virginia Gazette (Williamsburg), 18 January 1739 (1740)

The Rev. Mr. Whitefield's Preaching is become so very offensive to the Clergy of this Kingdom, that 'tis said one of my Lords the Bishops a few

Days since, went to the King to desire his Majesty to silence him: Upon which his Majesty enquired, whether he preach'd Treason, Sedition, &c. but none of these things being alledg'd against him, his Majesty seem'd at a Loss how to satisfy the Bishop; which a Noble Duke present observing, humbly proposed, that in order to prevent Mr. Whitefield's preaching for the future, his Majesty would be graciously pleased to make him a Bishop.

AN ANONYMOUS WRITER: "ENTHUSIASTICK RAVINGS"

Part of the controversy surrounding George Whitefield and the Great Awakening centered on presentation. A logical exposition of the Gospel with a deliberate and usually read sermon was the standard of the time, favoring the rationalism of the Enlightenment. Whitefield, however, introduced excitement into his presentation. Benjamin Franklin remarked on the way in which Whitefield used a cadence to present his material and the oration improved and grew stronger with each preaching of the sermon. The writer of this letter objected to Whitefield's emotional appeal, considering it nonsense and not of God.

Pennsylvania Gazette (Philadelphia), 24 July 1740

I am not against Preaching of Terror, in order to convince prophane, impenitent Sinners of their awful and tremendous Danger, provided it be prudently managed; but such Preaching as we have lately been entertained with, I do now openly profess my Abhorrence of it: It was unbecoming a Minister of the Gospel, and a Reproach to that sacred Character. . . . What Spirit such Enthusiastick Ravings proceed from, I shall not attempt to determine; but this I am very sure of, that they proceed not from the Spirit of God; for our God is a God of Order, and not of such Confusion: Such whining, roaring Harangues, big with affected Nonsense, have no other Tendency, but to operate upon the softer Passions, and work them up to a warm Pitch of Enthusiasm, which when the Preacher has gone, he has fully gain'd his End, and goes away rejoicing in his triumphant Conquests over weak Minds. . . . The Effects of such Preaching are very notorious in this Town; and Religion is sufficiently disgraced by it.

AN ANONYMOUS WRITER: "THE DANGERS OF WHITEFIELD'S PREACHING"

Many members of the established denominations of America felt that Whitefield's preaching threatened the groups' existence. Indeed, many denominations split during the Great Awakening with the new branch more closely aligned with Whitefield's brand of religion than with the old standing order. In this unsigned letter, a Philadelphian writes to a friend in Boston warning him to be wary of Whitefield and his Gospel message.

Boston Weekly Post-Boy, 23 June 1740

Mr. Whitefield and his Adherent Ministers have infatuated the common People with the Doctrines of Regeneration, free Grace, Conversion, &c. after their peculiar Way of thinking. . . . I have inform'd you of this, because Mr. Whitefield intends for Boston in the Fall or Autumn, where I understand he is impatiently waited for; I wish his Ministry there may not be attended with the same bad Effects as here, by diverting and distracting the Labouring People, who are generally too much inclined to Novelties, especially in point of Religion: He is the more to be guarded against because I can assure you, He is qualified to sway and keep the Affections of the Multitude.

THOMAS FLEET: "THE CHECKLEY MEETING-HOUSE ACCIDENT"

Even though people argued about the exact numbers, no one denied the fact that whenever Whitefield preached, large numbers of people congregated. At one sermon scheduled at the Reverend Samuel Checkley's New South church, the numbers filling the church quickly surpassed capacity. When a board in the balcony broke, people, assuming the balcony was falling, panicked. The resulting stampede for the door left five people dead. Printer Thomas Fleet, who never liked Whitefield or any of the other enthusiastic preachers, wrote up the event, appending his editorial note on the state of Boston upon Whitefield's departure. The note drew criticism, and Fleet, in the next Evening-Post, *attempted to explain that the comment was not really directed at the itinerant preacher but at Boston's overall condition.*

Boston Evening-Post, 29 September 1740

Boston: Last Monday at Four o'Clock after Noon, a most melancholy and surprising Accident happened here, viz. The Rev. Mr. Whitefield being to preach in the Rev. Mr. Checkley's Meeting-House, the People crowded so thick into it, that before the Time of Mr. Whitefield's coming, the Galleries were so thronged, that many People apprehended some Danger of their falling; and being thus pre-possess'd with Fear, and a Board on which several People stood, breaking, the Word was soon given by some ignorant and disorderly Persons, that the Galleries gave Way; upon which the whole Congregation was immediately thrown into the utmost Confusion and Disorder, and each one being desirous to save themselves, some jump'd from the Galleries into the Pews and Allies below, others threw themselves out at the Windows and those below pressing hard to get out at the Porch Doors, many (especially Women) were thrown down and trod upon by those that were crowding out, no Regard being had to the terrible Screeches and outcries of those in Danger of their Lives, or other; so that a great Number were sore wounded and bruised, and many had their Bones broke: Two married Women, viz. Mrs Storey and Mrs. Ingersole, and a Servant Lad were so crush'd that they died a few Minutes after; and on Tuesday Mrs. Shepard, a Widow of good repute in Town, and Mrs. Ruggles, a married Woman, died also of their Wounds and Bruises; and some others we hear are so much hurt, that 'tis to be feared they cannot recover. . . .

And this Morning the Rev. Mr. Whitefield set out on his Progress to the Eastward, so that the Town is in a hopeful Way of being restor'd to its former State of Order, Peace and Industry. . . .

NATH. BELLS AND RUSTICUS: "NOT UNDER GOD"

The religious controversy that began in 1739 increased in New England. Ministers copied Whitefield's message and style. A magazine called The Christian History *was even begun to chronicle the activities of Whitefield and the Great Awakening. As a result, when Whitefield returned for a second preaching tour in 1745, the controversy surrounding his first preaching tour was rekindled, and he again became a center of dissension. In light of all the controversy surrounding Whitefield, two writers question Whitefield's claim to be a man of God in the* Boston Evening-Post.

Boston Evening-Post, 4 February 1745

BOSTON; IT has been for some Time a Difficulty in my Mind, to reconcile the Rev. Mr. Whitefield's Conduct with a due regard to his Subscriptions and solemn Promises, as a Minister of the Church of England. . . .

I have been, and still am of the Opinion, that there hath been in several Towns in New-England, within a few Years past, a great revival of Religion; But never was of the Opinion that Mr. Whitefield was under God, the principal Means of reviving it. . . . Nath. Bells

To the Reverend Gentlemen in Boston, who set the grand Itinerant a strolling and propagating his Errors in this Land.

'TIS exceeding surprising, that Gentlemen of your Sagacity and Penetration, shou'd set on going again that Engine of Enthusiasm and Error, who did so much Mischief (if setting this whole Land together by the Ears, in quarrellings and Disputes, and dividing of Families and Churches, and in setting People against their Pastors and Teachers, may be call'd so) among us about four Years ago, without letting us know, what Satisfaction he gave you respecting the many Abuses and scandalous Libels he publish'd in his vain, empty, nonsensical Journals, and other Writings against our Clergy in general, and our Colleges in particular, and the false Doctrines he has endeavour'd (with too much success) to propagate among us. . . . What can be expected from a Man that would betray and destroy, as far as in him lies, the Church he was bred up in, and from which he had his Ordination. . . . And therefore what trust can be put in such a Man? Could it be ever thought that after such Treatment, a Man who ever had heard what Modesty means, or had the least Show of it in him, should have the Front ever to shew himself in this Country again. . . . Whether this Man be of such Consequence to us, as that the Honour of the Religion of JESUS, the Prince of Peace, the Quiet and Peace of this Land, should continue to be disturb'd, rather than this Man should be drove out from among us? (in a proper Manner) I pray you will not any longer make an Affair of this Importance a Matter of Indifferency among you. . . . Rusticus

AN ANONYMOUS WRITER: "WHITEFIELD, GET YOU GONE"

Whitefield's return to America in 1754 marked his fifth trip to the colonies to preach. This trip coincided with the hostilities between France and the colonies that led to the French and Indian War. In this unsigned letter, the writer belittles all that Whitefield preaches and requests that he leave the colonies. What makes this letter and others that appeared in the Boston Evening-Post *during this period unique is the fact that other Boston newspapers concentrated upon the growing possibility of war with the French and Indians. Thomas Fleet continued to attack Whitefield.*

Boston Evening-Post, 23 September 1754

An Epistle to the Rev. Mr. *G——W——*
Master of Arts Indeed! . . .

Hail *Itinerant Stroller*, who have found your Way by a pretended Message and counterfeit Zeal, who daily draw together your turbulent popular Assemblies, and there so tickle the itching Ears of silly Women with a frothy Chime of Phrases, that they think nothing devoutly gone about, but where Mr. *W——*, the Mr. *W——* is present, to thunder with open Mount, distorted Looks, and admirable Volubility of Speech, tho' at the same Time . . . all for ready Cash. . . .

Who has seduced Shepherds from their Sheep, and the Sheep from their Shepherds? *W——*. Who has enticed Wives from their Husbands, Mothers from their Children, Children from their Parents, Servants from their Masters? *W——*. Who has diverted People of all Ranks from looking after their proper Business? *W——*. Who has exacted Rewards for Flattery, or a Price for their Prayers and that even from the Poor? The same *W——*. . . .

Forbear your enthusiastick Agitations, and stuttering thus insolently about: Forbear your vain Boast of Celestial Riches, while you thus lust after, or gape for Ours. Keep what is your own, and let us peaceably possess what we have. Get you gone, in the Name of Goodness, from this Country with Disgrace.

AN ANONYMOUS WRITER: "AN ATTACK ON ITINERANTS"

Because Whitefield's message was so popular, many preachers copied his style and method of presentation. As a result, the colonies saw a dramatic increase in the number of ministers who moved freely about preaching rather than accepting the call to the pulpit in a single church. In this unsigned letter from South Carolina, the writer complains about the damage itinerants are doing to the religion of the region.

South-Carolina Gazette (Charleston), 25 May 1745

It is not easy to conceive how this poor Country is pester'd with Itinerants and strolling Preachers: They pour in upon us like Egyptian Caterpillars. They sow Discord and Dissentions wherever they come, by exclaiming against the settled Ministers whatever Denomination they are of. They ask us what sort of Preachers can be expected from our Nurseries of Learning, which they say are covered with Darkness, yea Darkness that may be felt, tho' they themselves are Men of no Education. . . . They are always crying out stink, shewing putrified Sores, raw Bones, Infants wallowing in their Blood, flowing Corruptions, and boggy Sepulchers, all in a Quag-Mire. These Things they frequently discharge at our Tables as well as in the Pulpit.

Such Nastiness, such lucious, such greasy, such bawdy Allusions, such spiritualizing of carnal Things, such displaying of filthy Rags, such exposing of bloody . . . Issues, and the like. I believe the very Dregs of the common Bunters would blush.

PRO-WHITEFIELD AND REVIVALISM

JUVENTUS: "COMMISSIONED FROM ON HIGH"

Few people in America remained ambivalent about George Whitefield. They either despised his message, or they loved it. In this poem written

*by the anonymous Juventus, the glories and wonders of Whitefield and
his preaching are extolled in verse.*

New-York Weekly Journal, 26 November 1739

Mr. Zenger, Please to give the following Lines on the Reverend Mr.
WHITEFIELD, a Place in your Journal; and you'll oblige many of your
Readers, as well as your Humble Servant, &C.

> WHITEFIELD! That Great, that pleasing Name
>   Has all my Soul possessest:
> For sure some Seraph from above
>   Inspires his Godlike Breast.
> He comes commission'd from on High,
>   The Gospel to proclaim;
> And thro' the wide extended World
>   To spread the Saviour's Name.
> See! See! He comes, the Heav'nly Sound
>   Flows from his charming Tongue;
> Rebellious Men are seiz'd with Fear,
>   With deep Conviction stung.
> List'ning we stand with vast Surprize,
>   While Rapture chains our Powers,
> Charm'd with the Musick of his Voice;
>   Not know the passing Hours.
> Blasphemers hear the dreadful Sound,
>   Inspir'd with trembling Awe;
> While he declares their crimson Guilt,
>   And loud proclaims the Law.
> While, WHITEFIELD, to thy sacred Strain,
>   Surpriz'd we listen still,
> Immortal Heights we seem to reach,
>   Celestial Transports feel.
> Approach ye Mortals here below,
>   And flock around the Song;
> With Pleasure hear the Saviour's Name
>   Sound from a Mortal Tongue.
>   Juventus.

AN ANONYMOUS WRITER: "AGAINST BALLS AND PUBLIC DANCING"

*In his preaching, Whitefield emphasized that people needed to spend
more time in prayer and fasting than at public performances and
dances. In this letter to the* South-Carolina Gazette, *an anonymous*

writer laments the fact that colonists continue to dance and attend the theater, instead of spending time in prayer. Whitefield's pronouncements against theaters and dance halls ultimately got him into trouble in Philadelphia in May 1740. The preacher's publicist, William Seward, requested and got a story inserted into the Pennsylvania Gazette *that the dance hall and theater there had been nailed shut with none attending because of Whitefield's preaching. The story, however, was challenged, and Benjamin Franklin admitted that the story had been submitted and that all of its statements were not true.*

South-Carolina Gazette (Charleston), 19 January 1740

Mr. Timothy, As the Publick will naturally expect some Account of Mr. WHITEFIELD, in Imitation of other Places where he has preach'd for publick Service in this Week's Gazette: Sir, your Compliance will oblige many of your Subscribers. . . . I Presume, you can be no stranger to the Name of the famous *Son of Thunder*, the Rev. Mr. GEORGE WHITEFIELD; since there is no Speech nor Language, I may almost say, where his Sound is not hear'd. It has often enter'd into the Subjects of Conversation, as it has given Rise to many Debates and Speculations in the publick Prints.— Some of the People saying: He is a good Man; others, Nay; but he deceiveth the People.— . . . the Pulpit seem'd almost to be the Tribunal, and the Preacher himself, if the Comparison may be pardon', the Great Judge, cloathed in Flames, and adjudging a guilty world to penal Fire. . . . I can't conclude, without wishing Success to Mr. WHITEFIELD'S publick and repeated Censures upon our BALLS, and MID-NIGHT ASSEMBLIES; especially the present Scituation [*sic*] of our Province. To bid such open Defiance to Heaven, to turn such a Season of Mourning, under its Judgments, into publick Dancing, has such a Mixture of Impiety and Infatuation, that I can't see, how any Minister of Christ who desires to be found faithful, dare to shew any Indifference to it; nor will I ever believe, that Religion and Virtue can thrive under the Shadow of a Theatre.

WILLIAM SEWARD: "THOUSANDS ATTEND WHITEFIELD SERMONS"

William Seward was one of Whitefield's traveling partners. He wrote up news stories and sent them to newspapers in towns where Whitefield would soon be and to other papers to promote Whitefield's preaching. In this press release, the place and numbers attending the itinerant's sermons are listed. In addition, Seward tells the number of sermons preached and the amount of money raised for the orphan house in Georgia.

Pennsylvania Gazette (Philadelphia), 17 April 1740

The middle of last Month the Rev. Mr. WHITEFIELD was at Charles-town, and preached there five Times, and collected at one Sermon Seventy Pounds Sterling, for the Benefit of the Orphan-House in Georgia: And on Sunday last . . . he landed at New-Castle, where he preached Morning and Evening. On Monday Morning he preach'd to about 3000 at Wilmington, and in the Evening arrived in this City; on Tuesday Evening he preach'd to about 8000 on Society-Hill; and preach'd at the same Place yesterday Morning and Evening: This Morning he preaches at Abingdon, and in the Evening again at Society-Hill in this City: Tomorrow Morning he preaches at Whitemarsh, and in the Evening at Germantown; on Saturday Morning and Evening in this City; On Sunday the same, when Collections are to be made for the Benefit of the Orphan-House above-mentioned: On Monday he is to Preach and Salem, &c. in the Jerseys: On Tuesday in this City; and on Wednesday he sets out for New-Brunswick, New-York, &c. On Wednesday Evening he is to Preach at Heshaminy. On Thursday Morning the 24th Instant at Skippack, and in the Evening at Henry Antis's Plantation in Frederick Township. On Friday Evening the 25th at Amwell. On Saturday Evening the 26th at New-Brunswick; and at the same Place on Sunday the 27th. On Monday the 28th at Elizabeth-Town; And on Tuesday the 29th at New-York.

WILLIAM SEWARD: "THE FAREWELL SERMON"

Whitefield may have run into more dissension in New England than in any other region of America during his first preaching tour. In this press release written by Seward, Whitefield's grand work in Boston is detailed. Note that twenty thousand people saw Whitefield off as he headed for Connecticut, according to Seward.

Pennsylvania Gazette (Philadelphia), 23 October 1740

Boston Oct 13: Yesterday in the Afternoon the Rev. Mr. WHITEFIELD preach'd his Farewell Sermon in the Audience of 20,000 People, assembled on the common; and this Morning he sets out on his Journey towards Connecticut, New-York, &c. He has been in and about this Town for this three Weeks last past: In all he has preach'd Forty-eight Times in Publick, besides expounding and exhorting in private. Vast Bodies of People have crowded every where to hear him; and great and remarkable, and we hope saving Impressions have been made on great Numbers. . . . He purposes, GOD willing, to go to Philadelphia by Land, and there embark for Georgia. His Health seems perfectly restored, and in Spring he intends, GOD willing, to return to England.

AN ANONYMOUS WRITER: "GROWING PIETY AND DEVOTION"

The Great Awakening increased church attendance and religious devotion in America. In this anonymous letter, those traits are attributed directly to the work of Whitefield.

Boston Weekly Post-Boy, 23 June 1740

Never did People show so great a Willingness to attend Sermons, not the Preachers greater Zeal and Diligence in performing the Duties of their Function. Religion is become the Subject of most Conversations. No Books are in Request but those of Piety and Devotion; and instead of idle Songs and Ballads, the People are every where entertaining themselves with Psalms, Hymns and Spiritual Songs. All which under God is owing to the Successful Labours of the Rev. Mr. Whitefield.

AN ANONYMOUS WRITER: "A RESPONSE TO MR. FLEET"

Not everyone in Boston understood the Checkley Meetinghouse Accident in the same way as printer Thomas Fleet. This unsigned letter from the Boston News-Letter *attacks Fleet's comments surrounding the accident in the New South church, which are included in the anti-Whitefield section of the chapter.*

Boston Weekly News-Letter, 2 October 1740

In the Evening-Post of Monday last, we find the following Article of News:

THIS Morning the Revd Mr. Whitefield set out on his progress to the Eastward; so that the Town is in a hopeful way of being restor'd to its former State of Order, Peace and Industry.

What is Insinuated in this Article, is by no means esteem'd the Sense of the Town; For we are very certain, that the Generality of sober and serious Persons, of all Denominations among us, (who perhaps are as much for maintaining Order, Peace, & Industry, as Mr. Evening-Post and Company,) have been greatly Affected with Mr. Whitefield's Plain, Powerful and Awakening Preaching.—And as for those Comparitively few, who appear to Oppose, and speak Evil of Mr. Whitefield and his Preaching, we hope it will be thought no breach of Charity, if we say,—That they discover too much of the Spirit of those Jews, who, when the Apostle Preach'd at Antioch, were filled with Envy, and spoke against those things which were spoken by Paul, Contradicting and Blaspheming.—And of the Spirit of the Gadereens; who when Christ had Preached and wrought Miracles among them,—Desired Him to depart out of their Coasts.

AN ANONYMOUS REPORT: "THE FUNERAL OF GEORGE WHITEFIELD"

At age sixty-five, Whitefield returned to America for his seventh preaching tour. This time, however, the asthma that had plagued him his entire life overcame him, and the Grand Itinerant died after preaching a sermon in Newburyport, Massachusetts. Thousands attended the funeral, but just as numbers in attendance at his sermons had been questioned throughout his career, the numbers reported in attendance at his funeral also varied. The news story here says six thousand attended, but the Connecticut Journal *recounted fifteen thousand in attendance.*

Boston Evening-Post, 8 October 1770

BOSTON; Early on Monday Morning last a Number of Gentlemen set out from hence for Newbury Port, in order to convey the Corps of the Reverend Mr. WHITEFIELD, to this Town, to be here interred: But the People at Newbury-Port would not allow the Corps to be brought away, they having prepared a Brick Tomb under the Presbyterian Meeting-House: His Funeral was attended by a great Concourse of People on Tuesday Afternoon.—Mr WHITEFIELD, the Day before his Death, preached in an open Field at Salisbury, and arrived at Newbury-Port in the Evening;—about Two o'Clock he got up and dressed himself, complained of his Illness, and went to Prayer with the Gentleman who accompanies him:—then lay on the Bed with his Cloaths on, and at Four o'Clock, rose again, said his Asthma was coming on—opened the Windows—found himself greatly distress'd for Breath—walk'd two or three times across the Chamber—went into the Entry-way, and threw up the Window there, but could get no Relief—said to his Companion, He was just a going—who then took hold of him, led him to, and seated him in a Chair, and about Six o'clock he fainted and died without saying any Thing more. . . . It may be said, that he has for a long course of years astonished the world as a prodigy of eloquence and devotion! it is questionable whether any one since the days of the Apostles, or even they, had more hearers, he having delivered above seventeen thousand Discourses, to five, ten, fifteen, & twenty thousand persons at a time, both in Europe & America.—He kept up his zeal and popularity to the last discourse, which he delivered the day before his death to an audience of at least six thousand in open air, and tho' he was then much troubled with the Asthma, yet the charms of his rhetoric & oratory were surprizing. . . . He seem'd to have a clear view of the entertainments of another life; and would commonly converse so familiarly of death, as tho' he was a kind friend he was waiting for, and even long'd to receive the summons; and was unwilling to tarry here any longer than he could be serviceable to mankind.—Such was the character of the Person whose departure we lament.—

QUESTIONS

1. Why do you think many Anglicans and other members of established religious groups may have opposed Whitefield's preaching, itinerants, and revivalism?
2. Why might people who believed in solving problems through rational thought have disliked Whitefield's emotional approach to religion?
3. Support or refute Thomas Fleet's position on Whitefield following the meetinghouse tragedy.
4. What were the arguments in opposition to itinerant preaching?
5. Many people claimed that William Seward's press releases on Whitefield contained inflated figures. Why do you think news articles were written about Whitefield? Do you think they enhanced or detracted from his mission? Explain.
6. Why do you think, from all that you have read in this chapter and perhaps elsewhere, a great religious awakening occurred in America in the 1740s?

NOTES

1. Patricia U. Bonomi, *Under the Cope of Heaven: Religion, Society, and Politics in the Colonial Era* (New York: Oxford University Press, 1986), 3.

2. *Historical Statistics of the United States: Colonial Times to 1970* (Washington, D.C., 1975), 1168.

3. Mark A. Noll et al., eds., *Christianity in America* (Grand Rapids, Mich.: William B. Eerdmans, 1983), 96.

4. Benjamin Franklin, *Autobiography*, ed. J. A. Leo Lemay and P. M. Zall (New York: W. W. Norton, 1986), 89.

5. Isaiah Thomas, *The History of Printing in America* (1810; reprint, New York: Weathervane Books, 1970), 568.

CHAPTER 9

Religious Divisions, 1740–1745

When most people think of religion in colonial America, they envision Puritans in New England, Anglicans in the South, Quakers in Pennsylvania, Catholics in Maryland, and religious dissenters in Rhode Island. Religious groups in America never broke down that simply, however, especially with the influx of immigrants with more varied religious traditions in the late seventeenth and early eighteenth centuries.

Even though America was home to various religious groups, political power often rested in the hands of the larger and more powerful groups. That is why many smaller groups, such as Baptists, advocated religious freedom for Americans during the colonial period, especially in the ten to fifteen years prior to the Revolution (see Chapter 22). It is also why many of those in positions of authority in both the church and government opposed new religious groups and the denominational schisms that occurred during the 1730s and 1740s. Others opposed the splits for theological reasons. Primarily, they did not agree with the emotional response to the Gospel message as presented by George Whitefield (see Chapter 8) and ministers who adopted his style of loud, rhythmic preaching that humankind was hopelessly lost in sin and needed personally to experience God during the Great Awakening.

As a direct result of religious revival, denominations divided, particularly the Presbyterians and Puritans. For Presbyterians, the division produced two groups, the Old Sides and the New Sides. The Old Side Presbyterians opposed revivalism and the emotionalism it introduced into worship. They also insisted that ministers hold degrees from major universities. If ministers did not, they would have to be examined by a committee of the synod, the organization of Presbyterian churches in a particular region, to determine their ability to preach the Gospel message. Old Sides tended to favor a more formalistic worship with adherence to confessions and rational preaching.

New Side Presbyterianism grew out of revivalism and its pietism. Pietism, which was referred to by eighteenth-century newspaper writers as "enthusiasm," called for people to experience God personally. It worried less about formal worship, confessions, and catechisms and more about what its followers saw as a right relation with God, an imitation of Jesus, and, consequently, a transformation of life. This transformation was to take place not only within an individual but also within church and society. Presbyterian Jacob Frelinghuysen had preached this basic message as early as 1720, but Whitefield's preaching tour, which began in 1739, provided the catalyst for widespread adoption of these concepts among Presbyterians. The New Sides had a readily available source of ministers to preach this personal message in the graduates of "The Log College" in Neshaminy, Pennsylvania. The graduates of this seminary, which became Princeton College in 1746, actively followed the Whitefield message.

Because of their differing views, Old Sides and New Sides increasingly grew apart. In 1741, when the Synod of Philadelphia convened, the parties split after the synod voted to exclude "Hot Gospelers," a derisive name given to the graduates of the Log College, from preaching in the churches of the synod. The New Sides formed a new synod based in New Brunswick, New Jersey. The two groups rejoined in 1758, but at that time New Side Presbyterians held the upper hand: its ministers had increased by more than 227 percent, while the number of Old Side ministers had steadily decreased since 1741. Presbyterians throughout America faced similar splits.

Americans discussed these religious issues in newspapers. In the mid-1730s, some people began to call for the dissolution of denominations. These people felt that it would be in America's best interest to operate under one religious umbrella, much like America operated under one form of government based on the English constitution. Those who proposed religious union, however, considered including only Protestants; never would Roman Catholicism or Judaism be considered as acceptable religions.

Hopes of any religious union were lost with the Great Awakening and the beginning of such new religious sects as the Methodists. Now, instead of calling for a unity of denominations, people began to attack the new groups and the divisiveness of preachers such as George Whitefield. Others saw the proliferation of religious groups as a valuable asset to society and God's work on earth. They praised the Methodists and the preaching of the enthusiasts such as Whitefield for changing the focus of Americans to praise and worship of God, and they attacked established churches such as the Church of England for becoming steeped in traditionalism, not in Christian principles.

In this chapter, the calls for religious union are grouped with the attacks on new religious sects. After the proposals for unity of denominations failed, many, instead, sought to preserve the status quo among religious groups. That is, they sought to maintain the Congregational hold on New England and the Church of England's dominance in the South, for example. In opposition to these views are writings that support denominationalism and new sects.

The readings supporting denominational union and opposition to new sects begins with an unsigned letter from a Presbyterian that explains why and how denominations should and could be united in America. It is followed by letters that attack the splits caused by Whitefield, one signed by a minister from Lynn, Massachusetts. These letters are followed by one written by Thomas Prince. Prince, considered one of the most learned ministers in New England, began the magazine *The Christian History* to follow the work of Whitefield. His letter establishes that groups such as the New Side Presbyterians are correct and in the majority and must now fight heresy. These letters are followed by a series of letters from all across America attacking Methodism. These letters demonstrate how much people despised new sects that threatened the religious status quo.

The entries supporting new denominations and religious sect begin with one of the many replies both in support of and in opposition to the *Boston Gazette* letter writer whose call for unity of denominations is the first selection in the above section. The next selection is a call to allow all to interpret scripture and worship as they please. Even though this unsigned letter is an excellent example of a call for religious liberty, it, nonetheless, supports the concept that people had the right to have denominations to achieve personal satisfaction in religious worship. It is followed by an attack on the Church of England, the established church of the British Empire, as a perverter of true religion. It tacitly supports the rise of new forms of worship.

The next selection in this section praises Methodists. It is followed by a letter that praises the way religion has changed in America following the preaching of revivalists. The chapter closes with a letter from the Revolutionary period that notes that Americans are of many religious persuasions. All, however, have been able to put any religious differences behind them to unite in opposition to British invasion.

FOR RELIGIOUS UNION AND AGAINST NEW RELIGIOUS SECTS

P.N.C.: "A PROPOSAL FOR A UNION OF DENOMINATIONS"

In New England, Congregationalists were the largest religious group, and taxes supported their churches and ministers. Other denominations, however, continued to spring up. Quakers, Baptists, Anglicans, and others, although small in number, were making inroads into New England society. This fact, coupled with the preaching of Jonathan Edwards on subjects such as justification by faith, which declared that divine acceptance, freedom from the guilt of sin, and righteousness unite all believers, helped initiate a movement to unite all denominations into one. In this proposal from the anonymous P.N.C., just how such a union could be accomplished is laid out. Note that Roman Catholics were never included in any plans of unity or toleration by most Americans.

Boston Gazette, 23 December 1734

To the Publisher of the BOSTON GAZETTE. . . . Your most humble Servant, P. N. C. . . .

It is but too obvious that loose Principles, and even Infidelity itself, are gradually coming in among us: It therefore deeply concerns all that love Christianity and their Country, to be seriously engaged to unite against the Common Enemy, and laying aside all Party Matters, and the study of those Things wherein the different Perswasions divide, jointly to conspire in being chiefly concerned to secure our common Christianity. For if we look into the Fate of Christianity in other Times and Countrys, we shall find, that running into different Sects and Communions, and thereby weakening and enervating the Discipline of each, has been the chief Occasion of Licentiousness. . . . Happy will it be for us, if, from the misfortunes of others, we learn to secure our selves, and provide against so great a mischief, by uniting into one. . . .

I would also be very happy if we could be all united in the same Method of publick Worship, all jointly conspiring to approach our common Father and Lord in the same Address both as to the Matter and Manner of it. . . .

Suppose therefore that different Worshipping Assemblies in the Country, should continue to have different Modes of Worship as to the external Circumstances of Language, Habit, Gesture, and the like; why might we not all notwithstanding these, be united into one Communion, since this being of different Communions, is a Thin of such pernicious Tendency to disunite our Hearts and Interests, and enervate our common Christianity. . . .

However, in order to our being of one Communion, it is necessary in the Nature of the Thing, that we all come under one Polity as to the method of Church Government. . . . But as to this, if we would come to the consideration of it with true Brotherly Love, and the joint study of Peace and the publick Good, I cannot see why we should long differ.

For,

I. The generality of us call our selves *Presbyterians and Congregationalists*, and of one or other of these Denominations this Country mainly consists: Now these two Opinons are so near one another, that I should think we might easily agree. And as to our Brethren the *Anabaptists*, their difference from us is not worth mentioning, save in the business of denying Baptism to Infants, and dipping or plunging in Baptism: As to both which, it were better they should be indulged in Unity, than that they should continue of a separate Communion. . . .

As to the *Quakers*, he is a Creature of so peculiar a make, and a Man so much by himself, that I know of no way to accomodate [*sic*] him, so that I can see no hope but that he must still stand by himself, however I would have him tolerated and tenderly used.

2. As to the *Church of England*, tho' the face of the Things between them and us is considerably different, yet I am not willing to dispair but that they and we might be brought into one Communion. In order to do this indeed, there must be some Compliances on both sides, but they might be such as I should hope no reasonable and good Man would be against making in order to such a happy Union, and the publick Good of the Country. The Difference between our Brethren of the Church and us, consists only in these two points, *viz.* That they insist upon worshiping GOD by publick Forms of Devotion, according to the Method in *England*, and that they hold the necessity of Episcopal Government. . . .

And this leads to . . . the business of *Episcopacy*. And as to this, I think it is their main Scruple, which if it were removed, they and we might be reduced all into one Communion. Now tho' we think they are wrong in insisting on the absolute necessity of . . . Divine Appointment; yet why might not we admit of such an Episcopacy as they would submit to, as a good prudential? . . .

Surely, methinks reducing us all into one Communion, without imposing any thing peculiar to each, would be so great a publick Good, both for ourselves and for all Posterities forevermore, that it were worth while, seriously to consider, whether it were not infinitely better for us to come into such a Modell, than to continue thus severed and disjointed in Communions, Interests, and Affections. . . .

Such a mixed limited Government, centering in Unity, is generally allowed to be most excellent in the Nature of the Thing. It is what we glory in as to the Constitution of the *English* Monarchy that it is the best Government in the World: And all our Provinces in Secular Matters, are constituted after this Manner, according to the Modell of the Mother Country, and why would it not be most eligible and amiable that our Ecclesiastical Government should be constituted after the same Manner with our Civil? Which is most truely *English*, and I think it cannot be denied that it would be then most truely primitive: for whether such an Episcopacy as I have been speaking of was established at first by the Apostles and primitive Christians as Necessary and Divine, or not; may possibly be a Question, but I must own I think it can be none, whether it was, in Fact every where established by them, at least as a good prudential?—I would therefore humbly submit it to the serious Consideration of my Country, and those of all Denominations in it, whether something of this kind might not be done towards an Accomodation [*sic*], earnestly wishing we may all unanimously endeavour on all Accounts and especially with respect to this of Religion, our most important common Interest, to promote what may in the best Manner tend to the greatest Good, both of ourselves and our latest Posterity.

TWO ANONYMOUS WRITERS: "AN INSTRUMENT OF DIVISIONS"

George Whitefield's emphasis on an emotional response in his preaching conflicted with the rationalism and logic of the era. Since most church services were based on rationalism, those who found Whitefield's preaching appealing often left their established churches to form new ones. In these two letters, anonymous Boston writers attack this movement and blame the Grand Itinerant for the splits.

Boston Evening-Post, 11 March 1745

ALTHO' it is abundantly evident to all unprejudiced Persons, who are acquainted with our religious Affairs, that Mr. Whitefield has been the great Instrument of causing the Divisions and Separations which have disturbed and rent in Pieces so many of the Churches in this Land; yet his zealous Friends have taken vast Pains, and used a variety of Arts, that if possible they might free him from the Imputation. . . . Mr. Whitefield by his preaching and writing has procured the unhappy Separations among us, so it is no less clear and certain, that several of the Ministers of Boston have been building on the same Foundation, and carrying on the same Work ever since Mr. Whitefield left New-England before. . . .

The important Question [is], whether Mr. W——d be a true Christian, or a Child of the D——. . . . But what Pleasure must the Thought afford to all (except the infatuated Followers of Mr. W——d) that the Reign of Enthusiasm will not last always!——that a Time will come, when New-

Light shall be no more!——when Men shall no longer be ashamed to own themselves reasonable Creatures!——or value themselves upon being Beasts and D——s!

NATHANAEL HENCHMAN: "SEEDS OF SEPARATION"

Nathanael Henchman, according to this letter, was a minister in Lynn, Massachusetts. In it, he blames Whitefield directly for all of the divisions of the New England churches. Many ministers viewed Whitefield and itinerant preachers as threats to their congregations, and numerous New England ministers banded together in 1744 and 1745 to keep Whitefield out of community pulpits. They thought that if he had no place to preach, Whitefield could not further divide the churches and denominations.

Boston Evening-Post, 15 July 1745

To George Whitefield

It is beyond Dispute, that you have sown the pernicious Seeds of Separation, Contention and Disorder among us; and by cherishing the Separatists, and your injurious Insinuations respecting Ministers as unacquainted with Christ, you have greatly impeded the Success of the Gospel, and struck boldly, not only at the Peace and good Order, but the very Being of these Churches.—Viewing you in this Light, in Faithfulness to Christ, and the Souls of my Flock; I desire you not to preach in this Parish, but rather to hasten to your own Charge, if any you have. . . .

I have little Expectation, that you will pay any Regard to what I have wrote; but leaving the Event, I choose thus to declare against your Services with us, as a dangerous Man, and greatly injurious to the Interest of the undefiled Religion of Jesus Christ. . . .

Nathanael Henchman, Pastor of the first Church in Lynn.

THOMAS PRINCE: "A CALL FOR A MEETING"

Thomas Prince was one of Boston's leading ministers. He believed in the work of George Whitefield and began The Christian History *in 1743 to support Whitefield's activities. In this letter, Prince calls for all New Side Presbyterians—those who now practiced the enthusiasm of Whitefield's revivalism—to unite to fight heresy.*

Boston Gazette, or Weekly Journal, 16 July 1745

WHEREAS a considerable Number of Ministers, lately met at Boston, taking into their erroneous Consideration the late gracious Visitation of GOD by reviving Religion in many Places of our Land, together with the present unhappy Decay thereof, and the Report of the spreading of some dangerous Doctrines and Divisions; judged it highly seasonable that all those Ministers in this Country, who rejoice in the said Revival, lament the said Decays, dangerous Doctrines and Divisions, and who cordially approved of the well-known Confession of Faith, agreed to and recommended by our excellent Fathers in their venerable Synod in 1680; should have a Meeting together in September next, at Boston, in order to declare their united Approbation of, and Adherence to the great Truths of the Gospel, as exhibited in the said Confession. . . . Thomas Prince

AN ANONYMOUS WRITER: "METHODISTS AND THE SCARLET WHORE"

John Wesley, who advocated a new method of worship and on whose practices Methodism was founded, never left the Church of England. His followers, however, did, and they attacked the Anglican Church continually. This story from London describes how one Methodist minister described England's state church as the "Scarlet Whore," meaning it was not a true church and was covered in sin.

Boston Evening-Post, 10 November 1740

As the Methodists still continue their Meetings both in London and in other Parts of the Kingdom, the following Passage may be of good Use in order to apprize well-meaning People of the real Intentions of these Enthusiasts, and to shew the Reason why the Dissenters have favoured them. Mr. Hooker, YOU have, no doubt on't, seen an Account in the public Prints of the Riot we had in this Country. It took its Rise at Dewsbury, where Mr. Ingham has propagated Methodism. . . . A Gentleman of Leeds who was one of Mr. Ingham's Followers, ask'd him, what Difference there was between the Church of England, and his Way of Worship? To which Mr. Ingham reply'd, 'the Church of England is the Scarlet Whore, prophesied of in the Revelations; and there will be no true Christianity as long as the Church subsists.'

AN ANONYMOUS REPORT: "A PLOT AGAINST SOUTH CAROLINA"

New religious groups, including the Methodists, are often the target of established ones. Here, a Methodist minister was jailed in Charleston, South Carolina, charged with plots against the colony. In reality, the minister probably attacked the Anglican Church's control there.

South-Carolina Gazette (Charleston), 13 May 1745

Charlestown: Here is a Methodist Parson in our Goal [*sic*], who is charg'd with having laid dangerous Plots against this Province. He goes by the Names of Ebenezer Vinces and Theobald Roche.

AN ANONYMOUS REPORT: "AN ATTACK ON METHODISTS"

As Methodism drew larger numbers of converts in England and its ministers made comments such as the one in the report above that referred to the Church of England as the Scarlet Whore, outrage against them grew. In this news report from England, an attack upon Methodists is described in detail. While the action done to the Methodists is the principal focus of the report, the number in attendance to witness the abuse should not be omitted. It supports the dislike of Methodists in their formative years.

Maryland Gazette (Annapolis), 16 August 1745

We hear from Exeter, that on Monday Evening, as the Methodists were assembled together in a House which they had taken behind the Guild-hall, large a Mob was got together at the Door, who pelted them as they went in, and daubed them with Dung, Potatoes, Mud, &c. Before they came out, the Mob was increased to some Thousands, with the Spectators, who as the Methodists came out, threw them in the Dirt, trampled on them, and beat all without Exception; so that many fled from them without their Hats and Wigs, others without their Coats, or with half of them tore off; and the Women they used most inhumanly, some they lamed, stripp'd others almost naked, and rolled them indecently in the Kennel, besmearing all their Faces with Lampblack, Flour, and Mud; thus they continued 'til near 12 at Night, when they thought fit to disperse.

AN ANONYMOUS REPORT: "DR. WHIMWHAM"

One way to attack a new denomination was to show how foolish its leaders were. Consequently, anyone who joined such a movement must either be foolish or misled. In this report, a Methodist preacher, derogatorily referred to as Dr. Whimwham, leads his followers as sheep to slaughter. Trying to avoid an earthquake he predicted in a sermon, the minister leads his followers onto a hill where many are struck by lightning.

Maryland Gazette (Annapolis), 22 August 1750

A methodist teacher, known in these parts by the name of Dr. Whimwham, a word he makes use of in his sermons having foretold there would be an earthquake hereabouts, several deluded people assembled at a place of safety, and out of the reach of the shock, when he enthusiastically preached to them, that he could ensure the lives of those who followed his wholesome advice, to the age of threescore and ten; but instead of an earthquake, a violent storm of thunder and lightning ensued; one Daniel Field was kill'd on the spot, one woman had her arm blasted, and another, whose name was Lovat, miscarried, and died on the spot. After the storm was over, the enraged people set the false prophet on an ass, and led him, in derision, thro' the whole town: This poor ignorant fellow, (who was formerly a journeyman carpenter) was held in esteem by the common people, not more for his preaching than his odd dress and food; he lived chiefly on milk, snails, &c.

AN ANONYMOUS REPORT: "LOST WITS"

The idea that anyone other than ignorant commoners would join a religious movement such as Methodism was considered impossible by members of the Church of England. In this brief note from London, an aged nobleman turns to Methodism. His move, the writer insinuates, must be because of advanced age and the loss of mental ability.

Essex Gazette (Salem, Massachusetts), 6 February 1770

London: A celebrated Nobleman of this kingdom greatly advanced in years, but formerly esteemed one of the prime wits of the age, is now so far changed from what he was, that falling into the hands of the Methodists, he is become one of that sect.

IN SUPPORT OF DENOMINATIONS AND RELIGIOUS SECTS

AN ANONYMOUS WRITER: "ONE COMMUNION NOT ADAPTED TO HUMAN NATURE"

The letter by P.N.C., which begins the first section of this chapter, initiated numerous replies to his call for one communion among Protestant Christians. In this letter, the anonymous writer explains how various methods of worshiping are best adapted to human nature. Christians all believe in the same things, the writer says, but they profess them in different ways.

Boston Gazette, 15 September 1735

I must tell you that the Project among Christians in these Parts, and the uniting of them into one Communion, by each of the different Denominations making some Abatements; is not at all adapted to the Condition of humane Nature, nor to the Tendency and Design of the Gospel. There is no need, in order to bring Disciples of Christ, and fellow Members of the Body, to alter our Way of Thinking in respect to Things of an indifferent Nature; much less to pretend that we do, when we do not. Truth is an inflexible and stubborn Thing. . . . And as we all ought to act with

the utmost Sincerity, especially in those Things that relate more immediately to God, and the eternal Concerns of our own Souls; so we must
be content . . . to have different Sentiments, in religious Things, as well
as in Things of less Concernment in Life. And if our Thoughts are different, there must be different Professions.

AN ANONYMOUS WRITER: "THE RIGHT TO INTERPRET SCRIPTURE"

*In many places in America, the concepts espoused by the writer of this
essay would not be accepted for decades. But in Philadelphia in 1730,
one writer stated that all people should be able to read and interpret
scripture for themselves. In this dramatic call for religious liberty, the
writer acknowledges the right of people to assemble in as many religious
groups as they choose, and no one has the right to stop such assemblies.
It is likely that the abuses suffered by many members of the Society of
Friends, or Quakers, who founded Pennsylvania, may have stimulated
the writing of this letter.*

Pennsylvania Gazette (Philadelphia), 30 July 1730

Every Man has a Right, a divine Right to interpret for himself; and there
can be no Reason why an Inquisition should not be set up, if universal
Liberty of Speculation should not be allowed; for the shortest Way is the
best. But if Mens Minds cannot be forced, the shortest Way to destroy
Heresy, is to be less fond of Orthodoxy: And this you will certainly be, if
you consider what terrible Work the different Sentiments about the Meaning of certain texts have occasioned; how piously Christians, as they have
affected to call themselves, have cut one anothers Throats by Turns, about
hard Words, and Sounds without Sense; if you consider, for how many
Ages the most absurd Tenets have been forced upon Mankind, and all
who could not believe, or were not wicked enough to say they believed,
were burnt here, and doomed to eternal Flames hereafter. Not only the
Papists, who, like Master Workmen, lay their Foundation in Infallibility:
but Protestants, who solemnly renounce, upon Oath all Pretences to it,
have, to their eternal Shame, dealt plentifully in Imprisonments, Fines,
Whippings, cruel Mockings, and Scourgings, Confiscations, Banishments
and Death too. . . . A Spirit of Liberty is growing amongst us; and not
only many of the Clergy of the Church of England, but some among the
Dissenting Teachers, and one entire Sect of Dissenters, the Quakers, do
as thoroughly abhor these Diabolical Practices, as the most generous spirited among the Laity. . . . Blessed Time! Then will Men be distinguished,
not by their Opinions, but by what alone they ought to be, their Actions;
and then, shall we have few Evils left, but those which arise from our
own ill Conduct; our Imprudence, or Immoralities.

AN ANONYMOUS WRITER: "AN ATTACK ON THE CHURCH OF ENGLAND"

The Great Awakening caused many Americans to reevaluate their religious beliefs. In this anonymous letter, one Philadelphian writes that the Church of England has left behind the Reformation principles of scripture and faith alone for human creations. In attacking the Anglican Church, the writer is conceding that new denominations are needed that are closer to the principles established by the Reformers of the sixteenth century.

American Weekly Mercury (Philadelphia), 26 June 1740

PHILADELPHIA—THAT the Generality of the Clergy of the Church of England have departed from the Doctrines of the Reformation, is a Truth too notorious to be deny'd. . . . The Doctrine of original Sin, and the Imputation of Adams Transgression to his posterity, is cast by with a Sneer, and reckon'd too grating to the Ears of a polite modern Auditor; whilst the Dignity of Perfection of human Nature are extoll'd, and painted in lovely Colours. . . . The Necessity and Irresistibility of divine Grace in Conversion is treated with Contempt. . . . And what is the present Corruption of Practice and Manners but the Result of loose principles? How does Iniquity abound in the midst of us! The Name of God is openly profan'd, and taken in vain by leud and filthy Jesters and Pretenders to Wit. The Lord's Day is broken, and made a Day of Pleasure to serve the Lusts of the Flesh. Publick Worship is forsaken, and the private Duties of the Family and the Closet are too frequently neglected. . . . And what must all this be owing to, but a too general Defection from the Doctrines of Christianity; Such is the melancholy State of Affairs in our Day, and it becomes us all to lay it seriously to Heart, and say, Lord! How much have I contributed towards this Decay of Religion? and at the same Time to entreat and beg the Presence and longer Stay of a departing God.

AN ANONYMOUS WRITER: "THE CHARACTER OF METHODISTS"

Even though many news reports in the first section of this chapter derided Methodists, many Americans and British admired this new form of worship and the piety of its members. In this poem, the unknown writer describes the character of Methodists in a poem of praise.

Pennsylvania Gazette (Philadelphia), 7 February 1739 (1740)

A Character of the METHODISTS.
SEE! how those holy, self-abasing souls,
Whom the Blest Spirit with his influence rules,

See! with what watchful industry and care
They labour in salvation's great affair:
Their bodies with what abstinence they tame,
   To quench Concupiscence's raging flame;
In their just bounds the passions to restrain,
And give to Reason's hand to guide the Rein;
Their souls to ev'ry duty to prepare,
And chiefly, on which all depends, for pray'r
Pray'r the sweet exercise of heav'nly Minds,
   Ever at heav'n's high throne acceptance finds;
To the light regions of eternal day,
On the pure flame of love it wings it's [*sic*] way.
Pray'r (how important should we pray'r esteem!)
Seeks our re-union to our good supreme;
With sweet composure aims at lasting rest,
And in it's [*sic*] longing to be blest, is blest.
The deeper is the soul's devout desire,
And loftier soars, the eucharistic fire;
The praying breast, when holy transports raise,
Burns, brightens, triumphs, and exults with praise,
Contemplating it's [*sic*] sov'reign bliss above,
Bursts forth in rev'rence, and adoring love:
Enraptur'd (oh exalted them!) to sing—
The praises of the world's eternal king:
With angels and arch-angels to rejoice,
And with all heav'n to join the hymning voice.

AN ANONYMOUS WRITER: "THE ALTERATION OF THE FACE OF RELIGION"

The change that the Great Awakening caused in religious habits in America was noted by many writers. In this letter, which refers to what has happened because of George Whitefield's preaching, a writer praises the way new worship patterns and groups have altered for the better the religious climate of America.

Pennsylvania Gazette (Philadelphia), 12 June 1740

The Alteration in the Face of Religion here is altogether surprizing. Never did the People show so great a Willingness to attend Sermons, nor the Preachers greater Zeal and Diligence in performing the Duties of their Function. Religion is become the Subject of most Conversations. No Books are in Request but those of Piety and Devotion; and instead of idle Songs and Ballads, the People are every where entertaining themselves with Psalms, Hymns and Spiritual Songs. All which, under God, is owing to the successful Labours of the Reverend Mr. Whitefield. . . .

AN ANONYMOUS WRITER: "OF MANY PERSUASIONS BUT STILL IN UNITY"

The fact that America was a country of many religious groups by the time of the Revolution was undisputed, but this letter writer notes that even though Americans were diverse in their religious practices, they were unified in belief. Playing upon the word concord for this union and for the site of the shots that began the Revolution, the writer uses religious rhetoric to support the language of unity against England. Note that in this letter even Catholics are included, a necessity to demonstrate total unity of Americans against Great Britain.

Constitutional Gazette (New York), 9 September 1775

An American Anecdote. When the emigrants and adventurers first went to America, they met on their arrival with Calvinists, Hugonots, Papists and Protestants; such a medley of people of different tenets and persuasions promised much discord; however, good sense prevailed, and they unanimously agreed that no difference in opinion should disturb the public tranquility, but that they would live in all brotherly love with each other, and then named the first founded spot and town CONCORD; is it not whimsical, that upon this spot, they should first draw blood, and gallantly contend for the rights and liberties of America.

QUESTIONS

1. Why did the writer to the *Boston Gazette* in 1734 believe denominations needed to unite under one communion?
2. Why do you suppose there was such opposition to Whitefield, revivalism, and new religious groups?
3. What inferences can be made from the readings about what many people thought about Methodists?
4. Why should religious divisions and denominations be supported, according to the *Pennsylvania Gazette* essay of 1730?
5. The Church of England was the official religion of all Britain, but what reasons existed, according to one Philadelphia writer, to remove it and make other forms of Protestantism acceptable?
6. How and why were various religious groups in America drawn together in concord?

CHAPTER 10

Massachusetts Legalizes Lotteries, 1744

These names or similar ones are familiar to almost everyone: Lotto, Power Ball, bingo, Publishers' Clearing House Sweepstakes, church raffle. No matter the name, these games of chance, contests, or lotteries offer participants the opportunity to invest a small amount in hopes of a large return. Lotteries usually offer the greatest return on the investment, but they also have the greatest odds against being a winner.

Lotteries were not a creation of the twentieth century. In fact, lotteries have been a part of America since the first settlement in Jamestown. In 1612 the Virginia Company, which backed financially the New World settlement, held a lottery in England to give away prizes—presumably land in Virginia—and to raise money for more colonization. In fact, lottery funds were seen as vital to Jamestown's success, and in 1620 and 1621 the Virginia Company estimated that about 45 percent of the operating expenses of £17,800 for the settlement would come from lotteries.[1]

In 1744 Massachusetts held its first government-sanctioned lottery to raise money to protect the colony's large coastline, which included the present states of Massachusetts and Maine.[2] England and France were engaged in the third war the two European powers had fought that involved their New World settlements. Known as King George's War, the majority of the fighting in North America took place in New England and nearby French-controlled Cape Breton or in the waters off both.

The lottery was the first of twenty-two government-sponsored ones held by Massachusetts through 1765. Even though most of the colony's inhabitants no doubt saw the protection of trade and shipping as vital to their interests and the lottery, therefore, a good way to raise money, it was not without controversy. Lotteries had been outlawed in Massachusetts since 1719 because their number had grown, and the colony had no means of regulating these privately run contests. Corruption among many of those sponsoring lotteries ran rampant, so the colony passed a law that stated, "Whereas there have been lately set up within this Province certain mischievous and unlawful Games called Lotteries, whereby the Children and Servants of several Gentlemen, Merchants and Traders, and other unwary People have been drawn into a vain and foolish Expence of Money . . . all such Lotteries, and all other Lotteries are common publick Nusances."[3] The colony reinforced this law in 1733, adding fines up to £500 for running illegal lotteries with a £100 fine for publishing information about them.[4]

Massachusetts was not the only colony to outlaw lotteries in the first third of the eighteenth century nor was it the only colony to reinstitute legalized, government-authorized lotteries as a way to raise revenue to pay for government affairs. Connecticut and New York, for example, followed the Massachusetts lead and outlawed the chance drawings. In Pennsylvania, however, the Quaker-dominated government had consistently denounced lotteries almost from the moment of settlement. Four times in the late seventeenth and early eighteenth centuries, the Pennsylvania government passed antilottery legislation. Each time, however, the laws were repealed by the British government, which held final authority over all colonial laws, because lawmakers felt that the Pennsylvania laws provided too much regulation.[5]

Wars with France in the middle of the eighteenth century signaled the return of lotteries to favorable status in most colonies. Virginia sanctioned a lottery to pay for protection of its western lands from the French in 1754. New York did likewise four years later. But colonial governments viewed lotteries as a means of making numerous internal capital improvements as well. Bridges, roads, and public buildings were financed with lotteries. Governments also sanctioned lotteries for numerous private endeavors, education and religion being the chief benefactors (see Chapter 13). Denominations and individual congregations within a colony often petitioned the government for permission to hold a lottery to pay for a new sanctuary, something Rhode Island Baptists did in 1774. The Providence newspaper carried the "List of the fortunate Numbers" of winners.[6] Colonies also used or approved lotteries to pay for colleges such as the "College Academy and Charitable School of Philadelphia," which received much of its initial funding from a series of lotteries in 1755.[7]

From 1749 to 1751, Massachusetts used the lottery to raise money to pay back war debts from King George's War and to finance a series of capital improvements in the colony. Printer Thomas Fleet disliked gambling in general and lotteries specifically. Fleet, who had come to America in 1712 as a printer and began printing a newspaper in Boston in 1731, used the *Evening-Post* to rail against all forms of gambling in the first issue of 1750. He charged that lotteries were a culmination of the worst kind of gambling.

Some Americans viewed gambling of any kind as immoral and wrong. In some cases, colonial governments passed laws against gaming. Even though such laws were sometimes passed and gambling of any kind was deemed immoral, lotteries and other games of chance flourished in colonial America as ways to start schools, churches, and even colonies.

The pro-lottery section of this chapter begins with an announcement of the lottery scheme to be used to raise money for the Academy at Philadelphia, today the University of Pennsylvania. It is followed by a similar notice that money for New-Jersey College, or Princeton, will be raised through a wheeled lottery. The third selection describes a lottery that will be used to help foster the English settlement attempts in Nova Scotia. The fourth entry is a proposal to use lotteries to lower the British national debt and to pay for the Seven Years' War, the American part of which is known as the French and Indian War.

The antilottery section begins with Fleet's essay opposing lotteries and gaming. It is followed by a similar moral attack upon games of dice and is presented as a letter from a father to his son. It includes a poem on the evils of rolling dice. The third moral exhortation against gaming expands the attack to cock fighting and horse racing, two of the more popular pastimes of the colonial period. The final selection of the chapter is a recommendation to the Continental Congress to ban all games of chance during a time of crisis for the colonies.

PRO-LOTTERY

AN OFFICIAL ANNOUNCEMENT: "A LOTTERY FOR THE ACADEMY OF PHILADELPHIA"

Pennsylvania decided to establish a college in 1754, and the best way that the colony found to raise the funds to build it was through a lottery. In this official announcement, the nature of the lottery, its purpose, and the number of tickets and prizes to be awarded are explained to the citizens of Philadelphia.

Pennsylvania Gazette (Philadelphia), 3 October 1754

SCHEME Of a LOTTERY, for raising 3000 Pieces of Eight, for the Use of the ACADEMY at Philadelphia.

THE Purchase of Ground and Buildings for the Academy, the Alterations and Improvements that were necessary to accommodate the Scholars, and the furnishing of the several Schools, having, all together, prov'd an Expence far beyond their first Expectation, the Trustees, desirous as soon as possible to compleat their Plan, for the Good of the Publick and of Posterity, find themselves under a Necessity of obtaining some Assistance by way of Lottery: And as several Lotteries have, since the Founding of this Academy by Subscription, been carried on and encouraged here, for the Benefit of Schools and Colleges in the neighbouring provinces, 'tis hoped it will not be thought less reasonable that we should at length have one for the Benefit of our own. Those who in this way have lately contributed liberally to Matters of *mere external Ornament* to the City, will doubtless more chearfully encourage the Academy; an Undertaking which aims at *adorning* Minds of our Youth with every Excellence, and rendering them really useful and serviceable Members of Society.

Prizes		Dollars		Dollars
3	of	1000 each,	are	3000
6	of	500	are	3000
12	of	250	are	3000
24	of	125	are	3000
48	of	62 & a half	are	3000
1000	of	5	are	5000

1093 Prizes,

3907 Blanks,

5000 Tickets, at Four Dollars each, are 20,000

The Monday to be paid to the Possessors of Prizes as soon as the Drawing is finished, *Twenty per Cent*, being first deducted from the larger Prizes; but the 1000 small Prizes to be paid without any Deduction, which reduces the Deduction on the whole to *Fifteen per Cent*.

The Drawing to begin punctually on Monday the 20th next, or sooner if sooner full. The Prizes to be published in this Gazette. . . .

Prize Money not demanded within six Months after the Drawing is finished to be deemed as generously given to the Academy, as applied accordingly.

AN ANONYMOUS REPORT: "TICKETS STILL AVAILABLE FOR NEW JERSEY LOTTERY"

Lotteries were considered credible ways to raise money to support any new venture, including churches and schools. In this story, the people who have set up the lottery for the New Jersey College are advertising that tickets are still left. Probably not enough tickets have been sold to pay off the lottery when winners are drawn, and the sponsors are hoping to attract more ticket purchasers.

Pennsylvania Journal (Philadelphia), 24 May 1750

Philadelphia: As the drawing of the Lottery, set up in Philadelphia, for the benefit of the New-Jersey College, will certainly begin on Monday the 28 Instant, at Mr. Samuel Hazard's, this is therefore to inform the Adverturers that the Ticketts are now putting into the Wheels, such as chuse to be present may give their Attendants. . . . A few Tickets still remain unsold which the Managers will continue to sell till Saturday Night.

AN ANONYMOUS WRITER: "MONEY FOR NOVA SCOTIA"

Even though Nova Scotia is today a part of Canada, it was considered an integral place for English colonization before the French and Indian War. Here, a lottery is proposed that will help establish a British colony there along with the fishing industry.

Maryland Gazette (Annapolis), 4 April 1750

We hear the lottery for Nova Scotia this year will be on the same footing as that for the charitable corporation, which was 500000l. of which 100000l. was for the benefit of the proprietors: This is to be for 600000l. and 125000l. to go for the establishing the colony of Nova-Scotia, on the plan formed by the right hon. joint-managers of the Scotch fishery.

AN ANONYMOUS REPORT: "A LOTTERY TO REDUCE THE NATIONAL DEBT"

The fact that England proposed a lottery in 1765 to lessen the national debt would have been of great interest to Americans. Americans had heard that Parliament might place a stamp tax on the colonies to help reduce the debt incurred by England during the Seven Years' War (French and Indian War in America). The fact that an English lottery was proposed for the same purpose might mean that America could avoid the Stamp Act, which in reality was passed (see Chapter 16).

Massachusetts Gazette (and Boston News-Letter), 31 January 1765

London: It is said, that a Scheme is now under Consideration for lessening the National Debt by an Annuity Lottery. The Tickets are to be l00l. each, to be purchased at Par at the Bank for a limited Time, thereby to hinder the evil Effects of Ally-Jobbing: The Blanks are to be an Annuity of Three per Cent for the Life of the Owner. Eight per Cent. Interest to be allowed upon the whole Sum to be raised.

ANTI-LOTTERY

THOMAS FLEET: "THE MOST EXTENSIVELY MISCHIEVOUS SORT OF A GAME"

Boston printer Thomas Fleet was one of that city's most vocal opponents of lotteries and gambling in general. As a printer of a newspaper, he had the perfect way to voice his opinions. After the 1744 lottery to raise funds for the protection of the colony's coast, Massachusetts voted numerous lotteries to finance public projects. This antigambling, antilottery essay by Fleet was a reaction to one of those lotteries.

Boston Evening-Post, 1 January 1750

In short, a Gaming-Table is the School of Iniquity, where all the Vices of the Age are taught and practic'd; the Temple of Lucifer, in which Immorality and Prophaness, Drunkeness and Debauchery, Cheating and Lying, Rapine and Murder, have their Place of Residence; nor can any Man enter without great Danger of infection: But what is still worse, the Distemper is of such malignant Nature, that whoever has the Misfortune to catch it, remains uncurable; for there is not one in a Thousand that ever recovers. Age and Experience, Time and Reflection, have in some Cases reform'd Numbers and turn'd them aside from their favourite Vices. The Debauchee, enfeebled and emitiated in the Service of Bacchus and Venus, is very apt, on Retrospection to censure his past Conduct, and will often retire to repent of his Folly; but the gamester's years increase his Malady, Age adds to his Avarice. . . . [Quere, Whether a LOTTERY is not the most extensively mischievous Sort of a Game? It is certain the General Assembly of this Province were of this Opinion, when they passed an Act for suppressing of Lotteries, in the Year 1719, the Preamble of which is as follows: Whereas there have been lately set up within this Province certain mischievous and unlawful Games called Lotteries, whereby the Children and Servants of several Gentlemen, Merchants, and Traders, and other unwary people have been drawn into a vain and foolish Expence of Money; Which tends to the utter Ruin and Impoverishment of many Families, and is to the Reproach of this Government, and against the common Good, Trade, Welfare and Peace of the Province. And the first Clause in that Act declares, 'That all such Lotteries, and all other Lotteries are common and publick Nusances.'

AN ANONYMOUS FATHER: "BEWITCHING DICE"

In a letter from an unnamed father to his son, the father explains how gambling ruined not only himself but his family. The letter warns the son to avoid the temptations of the dice and other games of chance where betting occurs.

New-York Evening Post, 29 April 1744 (1745)

SOME Years ago, the bewitching Dice tempted me then, as they do you now: First, to look on others at play then to play myself; whereby I often empty'd my Purse, then ran upon Tick; which fill'd my Breast full of Anger, my Mouth full of Oaths. . . . I impoverish'd my Family, not by my Mis-fortunes but Faults; which grieved my Friends and Relations, and oft made your dear Mother shed Tears.

Lastly, I lavish'd away a great Part of my Time, which might have been far better spent; I often omitted both my publick and private Devotions, and caused some others to do the same. Thus in many Respects, I stained my Character, wounded my Soul, and by All, highly offended my Maker. Therefore' by God's Assistance, I then did, and now do, and hope always shall, renounce immodrate [*sic*] Gaming: And your renouncing it too, before it does you those Evils, would much oblige.

> Your sorrowful Father.
> Dice keep some Men from Home, some from their Works;
> Who simply lose their Cash, then rage like Turks:
> Not only so, but lost the good Respect.
> Of those whose urgent Business they neglect. . . .
> Those Mischiefs Dice have done, with divers more;
> And of each Sex, still hurt both Rich and Poor:
> In short, they spread among Mankind such Evil,
> As greatly offend God, and please the Devil!

AN ANONYMOUS WRITER: "THE UNPROFITABLE FRATERNITY OF GAMESTERS"

American society by the middle of the 1700s had progressed to the point where many had ample free time. Many members of society used that time to gamble. In this anonymous letter written in Williamsburg, the author advises that those with so much free time that allows them to become experts with cards and dice should instead learn how to use a musket. At the time, the colonies were involved in warfare with the French and Indians, and Virginia's western territory was at the center of the fighting.

Virginia Gazette (Williamsburg), 12 September 1755

Among the many useless Members of Society, there are none so unprofitable as the Fraternity of Gamesters. I therefore, think, that they (especially this Summer) would be much better employed in handling a

Musket, than in shuffling a Pack of Cards, attending Cock Pits and Horse Races, or shaking the Dice Box. As to the Gamblers and Sharpers, it is a Pity that the same Dexterity which enables them to palm an Ace or cog a Dice, is not used by them in going thro' the manual Exercise in the military Way. These latter might, indeed, be employed as Marines.

PUBLIC NOTICE: "AN ORDER TO DISCONTINUE GAMING"

Gambling obviously must have been considered a problem in many parts of America throughout the colonial era. In this New Hampshire recommendation, which was based on a similar one made by the Continental Congress, citizens are requested to refrain from gambling and instead focus their attention upon the troubles with England.

New Hampshire Gazette and Historical Chronicle (Portsmouth), 10 February 1775

Portsmouth: THE COMMITTEE for carrying the ASSOCIATION Recommended by the Continental Congress into Execution, have taken under their serious Consideration, the Practice of GAMING, more especially that at CARDS & BILLIARDS, which there is great Reason to think, still prevails in this Town: They therefore do earnestly recommend it, to all those who furnish the Accomodations [*sic*] for those Purposes, to discontinue their unjustifiable Proceedings at this Time, when all the Colonies are involved in deep Distress and Danger; otherwise they may depend upon seeing their Names in the publick Papers, as recommended in the Association.

QUESTIONS

1. Why might governments have sanctioned lotteries for schools and churches even though they may have felt lotteries were immoral?

2. According to the laws passed by Massachusetts, what part did education and station in society play in restricting lotteries?

3. How might government-sanctioned lotteries in the eighteenth century be compared with state lotteries today?

4. People such as Thomas Fleet in the eighteenth century felt lotteries were morally wrong and a corrupting influence on society. Some people feel that way today about lotteries. What is their rationale for opposing lotteries?

5. A New Hampshire group petitioned the Continental Congress to ban games of chance. Is it possible for governments to legislate morality? Explain.

NOTES

1. George Sullivan, *By Chance a Winner: The History of Lotteries* (New York: Dodd, Mead, 1972), 13.

2. John Samuel Ezell, *Fortune's Merry Wheel: The Lottery in America* (Cambridge: Harvard University Press, 1960), 32.

3. Quoted in David A. Copeland, *Colonial American Newspapers: Character and Content* (Newark: University of Delaware Press, 1997), 245–46.

4. Province of Massachusetts Bay, *The Acts and Resolves, Public and Private* (Boston, 1874), II: 663–64. See also Ezell, *Fortune's Merry Wheel*, 21.

5. Ezell, *Fortune's Merry Wheel*, 19.

6. *Providence Gazette; and Country Journal*, 7 January 1775, 4.

7. See, for example, *Pennsylvania Gazette* (Philadelphia), 25 March 1755, 1.

CHAPTER 11

Medical Discoveries and the Amazing "Chinese Stones," 1745

When people get sick, they take medicine to make them better. In colonial America, however, doctors were not numerous, most of them had no medical education, and many of the diseases that no longer affect us today were deadly then (see Chapter 2 on smallpox). Because there were so few university-trained physicians and because there were few known cures for diseases, Americans often treated themselves at home by using handbooks prescribing various remedies that were claimed to cure an illness. The authors of these texts, which resembled current medical encyclopedias, often had little or no medical background. John Wesley, the man responsible for the religious movement of Methodism, for example, published one of the most popular of these books called *Primitive Physick*. It was used by people to cure everything from the slightest illness to cancer.

Because so little was known about the nature of disease, Americans often believed in any cure that was made known to them. They believed, for example, that rabies could be cured by using liverwort, pepper, and warm cow's milk and that a toothache could be cured with a magnet.[1] Real medical breakthroughs did occur during the eighteenth century: physicians perfected methods of removing cataracts and gallstones. They also discovered that electricity could help with some problems such as muscle stimulation, which assisted in the use of injured arms and legs. John Wesley claimed that electricity was "the nearest of an universal medicine as any yet know in the world."[2] Despite Wesley's, or anyone else's, claim, electricity could not cure smallpox or dislocated joints.

Newspapers were important for spreading information about medical advancement. Books such as that written by Wesley and the yearly almanacs contained cures, but these publications could not be produced as easily or as often as newspapers. People, therefore, depended upon their weekly newspapers to let them know about the latest discoveries in the fight against disease and other health-related problems. People also used newspapers to warn others about the dangers of cures. Just such a controversy arose in 1745 over a newly reported medical breakthrough called "Chinese Stones," a "Cheymical Composition" that was said to cure everything from cancer to foot pain. Benjamin Franklin ran a full page in one issue of the *Pennsylvania Gazette* that discussed just what Chinese Stones could cure with affidavits from those cured throughout the colonies. Two weeks later, he printed a letter that refuted the properties of Chinese Stones.

Discussions of the virtues and dangers of medical discoveries in America led more and more doctors to test the cures before prescribing them. By the close of the eighteenth century, doctors began standardizing medical treatments, a practice not totally embraced in America until early in the nineteenth century.[3]

The first set of readings in this chapter discusses what would be termed medical quackery—cures that have no practical application to fighting the source of an illness or medical problem. The first is a testimonial to the cures provided by the Chinese Stones. The second is a news report that tells how a self-trained eye doctor blinded his patient instead of curing his visual problems. The story also demonstrates the physician problem that existed in America in the eighteenth century. Anyone could be considered a doctor; medical credentials were unnecessary. The third piece, an essay by the Irish bishop George Berkeley, is similar to the Chinese Stones report, except this time a well-known and educated person is endorsing a product with little medical value.

The second set of readings attacks quackeries or points to medical discoveries that were of value. The first letter, a refutation of the Chinese Stones, is signed by an unknown writer calling himself "Acidus," Latin for sour. The second letter attacks the use of tobacco products, claiming they are filled with poisonous additives. The third is an essay written by the university-trained Philadelphia physician Benjamin Rush. Rush attempts to explain the causes and cures of hives. His report points out how little even the best of doctors in the eighteenth century knew or understood of illnesses. The last piece, a news story, tells of a successful operation in New Hampshire to remove stones from the bladder.

MEDICAL QUACKERY

ANONYMOUS REPORTS: "THE AMAZING CHINESE STONES"

Because so little was understood about the nature of disease in the eighteenth century, almost anyone and anything were considered potential cures for medical problems. Many natural and herbal remedies were used with success, but the fact that they worked made the likelihood that other things found naturally might do the same. In 1745 a Mr. Torres toured America offering what he called Chinese Stones as a remedy for almost all ailments. In this reading from the Pennsylvania Gazette, *affidavits supporting the healing power of the stones are compiled into one long story. In all probability, Torres provided these testimonials himself and probably paid Benjamin Franklin to run them in his newspaper.*

Pennsylvania Gazette (Philadelphia), 17 October 1745

RHODE ISLAND. We do hereby certify, that Mr. Torres has a Chymical Composition, called Chinese Stones, which effectually cure the Bites of All venomous or poisonous Creatures; as Rattle (and other) Snakes, Scorpions, mad Dogs, &c. The Experiment has been made in the Bay of Honduras, on the bodies of two white Men, and four Negroes, who were bit by Rattle-snakes, the said Stones being applied to the Wound, and the Persons cured immediately. . . .

CHARLES-TOWN. Col George Pawley certifies, that William Poole, a Neighbour of his, told him, that he had a Dog so bit by a Snake that he seemed dead; but applying one of the Chinese Stones he bought of Mr. Torres, to the Wound, the Dog immediately recovered. . . .

This is to certify, that I was in the greatest Extremity of Pain in my Feet for six Days, so that I could not rest Night or Day; and Mr. Torres applied a chymical Composition to the Part, and the next Morning my Foot was intirely well, and I felt no Pain. . . . The Daughter of Col. Moore, who had her Face very much swelled with the Tooth-ach, having applied one of these Bags of Powder to her Cheek, the next Morning she was well. . . . the Minister's Wife of this Place having very sore Eyes, so that she could not see, for the violent Humour which ran from them; and having applied a small bag of this Powder to them, in 24 Hours she was perfectly well. . . . This is to certify, that I was in the greatest Extremity of Rheumatic Pains in my Right-shoulder and Arm, so that I could not rest Night or Day; and Mr. Torres applied a chymical Powser to the Parts, and in 3 Minutes the Pains began to cease, and by the next Morning my Shoulder and Arm were intirely well, and I felt no Pain in them. . . . William Corington having a Negro burnt in the Foot for 3 Years, which was turned to a Cancer, was cured with one Bag of this Powder. . . . This is to certify, that William Usher was in the greatest Extremity of Pain with the Toothach; and having applied one of these Bags of Powder to his Cheek, in three Minutes he was perfectly well. . . .

DIRECTIONS for using the Chinese Stones and Powder. WHEN any Person has been bit by a Snake, or other venomous Creature, the Stone must be immediately applied to the Wound . . . and draw out the Venom. . . . Then put the Stone about two Minutes in a Glass of warm Water, it will purge itself; afterwards dry it in warm Ashes, wrap it up carefully, and so continuing to do every time it is used, it may serve an hundred times. For Gout and Reumatic Pains, Pleurisie, Pain in the Back, and all the Accidents before mentioned, the Patient must apply one of the small Bags of four Ounces of Powder, to the Place most affected, which will in a Night's time suck out and dry up the Humour. . . . To purge the Powder from the Venom or ill Humours which it hath drawn from the affected Places, and to make it fit for Use again, lay the Bag before the Fire for a small Space of Time. . . . It cures the Hemmorrhoides, is good for a weak Stomach; if the Bag is laid on the Pit of the Stomach, it creates an Appetite, and promotes Digestion. The Stones will heal Biles, and the Bite of a Horn-snake, as well on Cattle, Horses, and other Beasts, as on Men. . . . The Price is Twenty-five Shillings Currency, for one Stone and one Bag, containing four Ounces of this Powder, which is enough for one Family, to cure all these Distempers before mentioned for many Years. The Stones are also good for the bloody Flux.

AN ANONYMOUS REPORT: "THE BLIND OCCULIST"

A license to practice medicine was not required in colonial America. Anyone people trusted who offered cures had patients. In New Jersey, a man who thought he could cure eye problems, instead, caused blindness. This report, probably written by Samuel Kneeland or Timothy Green, Jr., printers of the New-England Weekly Journal, *served as a warning to Boston residents to be cautious in their choices of doctors in treating medical problems.*

New-England Weekly Journal (Boston), 21 October 1735

We are inform'd from Prince Town in the jerseys, that a certain Person . . . has lately turn'd Occulist, and tried his Skill upon several in that Place; but his Success has not as yet gain'd him any Credit: It seems his Operations have turn'd out contrary to the Desire of his Patients, for instead of restoring their Sight, he intirely takes it away. This Effect his Experiments have had in particular on Mr. Benjamin Randolph, who before this blind Occulist had any thing to do with his Eyes, could See, but now he is quite Blind and in great Pain. *It's to be hop'd People will take Caution by this who they suffer to meddle with their Sight; and not employ those who will put out both their Eyes to make them see clearly.*

BISHOP GEORGE BERKELEY: "TREATISE ON TAR WATER"

George Berkeley, a philosopher of the early eighteenth century and an Anglican bishop of Cloyne in Ireland, visited America in 1728 and assisted in the development of a number of colleges including Yale. When he wrote about a medical discovery, people paid more attention to what he had to say than to an unknown. His Treatise on Tar Water appeared in four installments in the Virginia Gazette, *from May 9 through May 30, 1745. Excerpts from the first two weeks are included here where Berkeley explains how to make tar water and delineates some of its uses.*

Virginia Gazette (Williamsburg), 9 May–16 May 1745

An Abstract from Dr. BERKLEY's *Treatise on* Tar-Water; *with some Reflections therein, adapted to Diseases frequent in* America.

IN certain Parts of *America* . . . Tar-Water is made, by putting a Quart of cold Water to a Quart of Tar, and stirring them well together in a Vessel, which is left standing 'til the Tar sinks to the Bottom. . . .

This cold Infusion of Tar hath been used in some of our Colonies, as a Preservative or Preparative against Small-pox, which foreign Practice induced me to try it in my own Neighbourhood, when the Small-pox raged with great Violence. And the Trial fully answered my Expectation: All those within my Knowledge, who took the Tar-Water either escaped that Distemper, or had it very favourably. . . .

It seemed probable, that a Medicine of such Efficacy in a Distemper attended with so many purulent Ulcers, might also be useful in other Foulnesses of the Blood; accordingly I tried it on several Persons infected with cutaneous Eruptions and Ulcers, who were soon relieved, and soon after cured. . . .

Having tried it in a great Variety of Cases, I found it succeed beyond my Hopes; in a tedious and painful Ulceration of the Bowels, in a consumptive Cough and . . . in a Pleurisy and Peripneumony. . . .

I have never known any Thing so good for the Stomach as Tar-Water; it cures Indigestion, and gives a good Appetite. It is an excellent Medicine in an Asthma. . . . As it is both healing and diuretic, it is very good for the Gravel. I believe it to be of great Use in a Dropsey. . . .

It seems that Tar and Turpentine may be had more or less from all Sorts of Pines and Firrs whatsoever, and that the Nature, Spirits and essential Salts of those Vegetables are the same in Turpentine and common Tar. . . .

[S]ome Gentlemen of the Faculty have declared, that Tar-Water must inflame, and that they would never visit any Patient in a Fever who been a Drinker of it. . . . To me it seems, that its singular and surprizing Use in Fevers of all Kinds, were there nothing else, would be alone sufficient to recommend it to the Publick.

I found all this confirmed by my own Experience in the late sickly Season of the Year 1741; having had 25 Fevers in my own Family cured by this Medicinal Water, drank copiously. . . . And it was remarkable, that such as were cured by this comfortable Cordial, received Health and Spirits at once, while those who had been cured by Evacuations often languished long, even after the Fever had left them, before they could recover of their Medicines, and regain their Strength. . . .

I have known a Bloody Flux of long Continuance, after diverse Medicines had been tried in vain, cured by Tar-Water. . . .

Nothing that I know corrobates the Stomach so much as Tar-Water. . . . I do verily believe it the best and safest Medicine either to prevent the Gout, or so to strengthen Nature against the Fit. . . .

The great Force of Tar-Water . . . appears in nothing more than in the Cure of A Gangrene from an internal Cause. . . .

From what I have observed, Tar-Water appears to me an useful Preservative in all epidemical Disorders, and against all other Infection whatsoever, as well as that of the Small-pox. . . .

I have found by my own Experience, and that of many others, that Tar-Water raiseth the Spirts, and is an excellent Antihysteric, no less innocent than potent in all hysterical and hypochondriacal Disorders. . . .

After having said so much of the Uses of Tar, I must add, that being rubbed on them, it is an excellent Preservative of the Teeth and Gums; that it sweetens the Breath and that it clears and strengthens the Voice.

REFUTING MEDICAL QUACKERY/PROMOTING
MEDICAL DISCOVERIES

ACIDUS: "A REFUTATION OF CHINESE STONES"

Even though medical cures of questionable reliability were accepted by some in America, not everyone believed all the fanciful stories about miracle cures. This letter written by the anonymous Acidus refutes the attributes of the Chinese Stones, whose reported curing properties are discussed above. Acidus reveals that the Chinese Stones are nothing more than deer antlers ground or cut into shapes with no healing power other than that of a placebo.

Pennsylvania Gazette (Philadelphia), 31 October 1745

Mr. FRANKLIN,

SINCE Monsr. Torres, a Native of FRANCE, and lately an Inhabitant of NEW-SPAIN, out of mere Christian Love to his Enemies, daily hazards himself in long Journeys thro' their Territories, to cure all their Distempers by means of his Chinese Stones and Bags of Powder, at the Price of Twenty five Shillings per Stone and Bag; how much ought I to be ashamed, if, knowing how to make these wonderful Stones and Bags at the Rate of four pence per Dozen, I should not, in Compassion to the Poor among my Countrymen, divulge the important Secret. If therefore you cannot afford 25s. to the good Mr. Torres, go to a Cutler's Shop, there you'll find a Remnant of Buckshorn, cut off probably from a Piece that was too long for a Knife Handle, saw and rasp it into what shape you please, and then burn it in hot Embers; and you will have Mons. Torres's Chinese Stone, which will stick to a wet Finger, a fresh Sore, &c. &c. and have all the Virtures of—a new Tobacco Pipe. Your Sawdust, and Raspings and Chips of the same Horn, burnt in the same Manner, and put into a little Linnen Rag, makes the miraculous Chymical or Comical Powder. This is the whole Affair, which please to communicate to your Readers.

I am yours. &c.
ACIDUS

AN ANONYMOUS REPORT: "SUCCESSFUL CATARACT REMOVAL"

Cataracts were a problem for people in the eighteenth century just as they are today. With cataracts, the lens of the eye loses its transparency and often leads to blindness. In this report from London, the procedure is described. It stresses little danger to the eye and the restoration of sight. As opposed to the report of the "blind occulist" above, this story discusses the number of successful operations the doctor has performed, a way to ensure readers that when the procedure is available in America, it will be safe.

American Weekly Mercury (Philadelphia), 18 December 1735

Amongst a great Number of Operations which Dr. Taylor made on Saturday last for the Disorders of Sight, there was that of his new method of removing a Cataract, & 'tis said that this Gentleman declares himself capable to demonstrate, that by his method there is no Necessity of waiting for what the Vulgar call the Maturity of the Cataract, nor having any Regard to certain Species of them. . . . That it is impossible this Operation should endanger any Part of the Eye immediately necessary to Sight. That this Operation requires little or no Confinement, and cannot be attended or succeeded by any Pain.—That it is almost impossible the Cataract should return to its former Situation, so as to require a second Operation, or that the Patient should be from any other Reason disappointed of Success, and that the Operation of itself is every way as simple and less painful or dangerous than that of a common Bleeding. . . . The Success of this Operation has so evidently appear'd since his Arrival in England, to the Satisfaction of the most eminent of the Profession, who have been often present on these Occasions, that notwithstanding the Variety of Operations that he has almost duly made in this manner, he flatters himself that not one Example can be produced who has been disappointed of this Success.

AN ANONYMOUS WRITER: "THE DANGERS OF SNUFF"

Tobacco was a principal cash crop in the Southern colonies, and the plant was used for a time as money in some colonies. Its use became the rage in England, and colonial archaeological digs often date sites by looking at the shape and designs of smoking pipes. Not all Americans, however, believed in the use of tobacco. Some who wrote to newspapers called tobacco the "stinking weed" and advocated the elimination of its use. In this anonymous letter, the writer warns that the use of snuff was potentially deadly for some because of the chemicals and plants added to the mixture.

Essex Gazette (Salem, Massachusetts), 2 January 1770

A very intelligent person assures that by a chymical analysis lately made by him of a great many sorts of snuff he has found them all adulterated in a manner the most destructive to health, some mixed with vitriol, and also with alum: others with rotten hemlock, and rind of tan, a dissolution of sublimate, or mercurial water. He observes that all these different ingredients may affect the brain, the stomach and breast; that the most obstinate chronical disorders owe their origin to causes of this nature; and insalubrious, for the use of persons who are subject to that unwholesome, expensive, and uncleanly custom of taking snuff, which ought to be avoided or dismissed by all sensible, cleanly, rational, and delicate persons. All parents, preceptors, &c. should be attentive not to permit youth that dirty, prejudicial habit. The present of a snuff-box is the most useless and detrimental gift that can be made to a child, for many young persons have been induced to take snuff from the vanity to show their boxes.

DR. BENJAMIN RUSH: "OBSERVATIONS ON THE CAUSE AND CURE OF THE HIVES"

Benjamin Rush was professor at the College of Philadelphia. He received medical training in Edinburgh, London, and Paris. This treatise on hives demonstrates the lack of knowledge that existed about the causes of medical problems in the era. It also illustrates how university-trained physicians undertook inquiry into the causes and cures of ailments. Rush went about his study of hives in a methodical manner not by randomly creating concoctions and trying them.

New-York Gazette: or the Weekly Post-Boy, 15 January 1770

Observations on the Cause and Cure of the HIVES: by Dr. Benjamin Rush: I am entirely ignorant of the derivation of this word. It was first given to the disorder by the Irish people, from a resemblance it bears to a disorder which prevails in Ireland of that name. We understand by it a DIFFI-CULTY OF BREATHING, joined with Hoarseness and other symptoms of Oppression and Disorder in the Lungs. This Disorder appears to have been little known by the Antients. . . . Many of the Symptoms of the Hives indicate it to be rather of the nervous or spasmodic, than of the pitutitous kind. . . . My principal reason for supposing that this Disorder is entirely spasmodic, is founded upon a Dissection which I had the good fortune to be present at a few Days ago.—A Child of three years old was seized early in the Morning with all the Symptoms of Hives. She breathed with difficulty, insomuch that her abdominal Muscles were brought into much greater actions than are natural to them in Respiration. Her Pulse was quick and her Fever pretty considerable.—Her Face appeared of that pale livid colour which above all things characterizes this Disorder. She had lost several ounces of Blood before I was called to her. . . . I treated her in the usual way with antinomial emettics, squill mixtures, blisters, warm bath, &c. but all to no purpose. She died the next day about five o'clock in the afternoon.

AN ANONYMOUS REPORT: "SUCCESSFUL SURGERY FOR STONES"

Gallstones and kidney stones were as painful in the eighteenth century as today, and surgery for them was no doubt more serious because doctors lacked anesthesia and other modern medical tools. In this report, however, a doctor in Portsmouth, New Hampshire, successfully removed a stone from a minister. The story does not tell the kind of stone, though some reports from the era did.

Essex Gazette (Salem, Massachusetts), 16 January 1770

Last Monday Morning, the Rev. Mr. Samuel Drowne, pastor of one of the Churches at Portsmouth, New-Hampshire went thro' the dangerous Operation of being cut for the Stone, a Disorder he has for some years past been severely exercised with; and a very large rough one was taken out of his Bladder: He is now in a fair Way of Recovery. . . . We hear this ingenious and difficult Operation was performed by Dr. Hall Jackson of that Place.

QUESTIONS

1. Looking at the opposing pieces on the Chinese Stones, what is the chief argument for not using them?
2. Why might the testimonials for Chinese Stones have been persuasive in eighteenth-century America?
3. How can you explain Dr. Berkeley's affidavit that claims tar water cured smallpox and a host of other ailments and diseases?
4. What are the correlations between today's arguments against tobacco use and those of the eighteenth century?
5. If Dr. Benjamin Rush's medical cures for hives represented the best for America in the eighteenth century, what conclusions can you draw about medicine, disease, and chances for recovery for patients?

NOTES

1. See David A. Copeland, " 'A Receipt Against the Plague': Medical Reporting in Colonial America," *American Journalism* 11 (1994): 229–30.

2. John Wesley, *Diary of John Wesley*, quoted in Maurice Bear Gordon, *Æsculapius Comes to the Colonies* (Ventnor, N.J.: Ventnor Publishers, 1949), 498.

3. Richard Harrison Shryock, *Medicine and Society in America, 1660–1860* (New York: New York University Press, 1960), 117–66.

CHAPTER 12

Paper Money and the Currency Act, 1751

In colonial America, money—especially currency or coins—was scarce. Despite what many in England had hoped, the first settlers discovered no gold or silver, and, consequently, there was none to mine to send to England or to use to make coins during the colonial period. In addition, many Americans were poor and had little or no cash when they came to America. As a result, much business in colonial America was done through bartering or on credit. In some places, such as Virginia, cash crops such as tobacco were so valuable that the crop itself became the currency. People bought what they needed with tobacco leaves.

Starting around 1690, colonial governments began issuing paper money or bills of credit that had no backing in gold or silver. The issue of paper money coincided with the beginning of a series of wars fought between Britain and France. During King William's War (1689–1697) and Queen Anne's War (1702–1713), seven of the twelve colonies issued paper money to help defray war costs and pay debts. Two more wars between the two European powers that were fought in North America, King George's War (1740–1748) and the Seven Years' or French and Indian War (1754–1763), firmly established the need for paper currency in America. The two wars also firmed English resolve not to allow American paper money to be used to pay debts owed to England. This refusal to accept American paper bills of credit helped widen the rift between the colonies and the mother country that ultimately ended in revolution.

Because specie, or currency, was so rare in America and because paper money was controversial, newspaper articles and advertisements of the era discussed payment for services and products in various forms of currency. In addition to the English unit of pound sterling, payment was accepted in Spanish coinage—pieces of eight and pistols—along with any number of other European coins. Using so many different types of money for payment created problems in America because the value of each specie usually changed from region to region. As a result, Parliament passed "An Act for Ascertaining the Rates of Foreign Coins in her Majesty's Plantations in America" in 1708. Called the Currency Act by Americans, the act was largely ignored until 1740 when colonial governors were threatened with removal from office if the act was not enforced. Not even royal decree, however, could make Americans accept a common exchange rate for foreign currency.

The monetary problem in colonial America was further compounded by counterfeiters who regularly worked the colonies. They reproduced paper money easily as well as coins. South Carolina, for example, called in all of its £10 notes in 1735 because the colony had been flooded with bogus ones. The only way to ensure that the counterfeit ones would not be used was to cease use of all £10 paper bills.[1] Counterfeiting was considered one of the more serious crimes of the period. Those convicted of it were fined heavily, forced to stand in pillories, whipped, and often had their ears cropped. In some colonies like New York and Pennsylvania, counterfeiting became such a problem that it was deemed a capital offense punishable by death.[2]

Even though paper money was easily counterfeited, authorization of it was a way of ensuring that there was currency for circulation in a colony. A plentiful amount of money was needed to make sure commerce continued and grew. *"There is a certain proportionate Quantity of Money requisite to carry on the Trade of a Country freely and currently,"* Benjamin Franklin said in a 1729 pamphlet, adding, "It will be an Advantage to every industrious Tradesman, &c. Because his Business will be carried on more freely, and Trade be universally enlivened by it."[3]

Despite such arguments, English merchants balked at payment with American paper money, wanting, instead, debts paid with English currency. In response to their objections, Parliament passed the Currency Act of 1751. Aimed specifically at New England, the act declared that paper money could not be used to pay private obligations. This effort to curtail paper money usage was temporary, however. With the outbreak of the French and Indian War in 1754, all colonies printed paper money to pay for the war effort. When the colonies used the same money to repay England as the mother country attempted to recoup its losses from years of fighting in America, Parliament passed the Currency Act of 1764, which stated that any money issued by a colonial government was not acceptable as payment to England.

Even though colonial governments issued paper money, Americans did not universally accept its use, and many of those who supported its use did so only as a method of last resort since specie was not readily obtainable in America. This chapter looks at the debates concerning paper money that took place in the newspapers.

The first letter opposing paper currency is a reply to an earlier letter written by a New Yorker calling himself "John Farmer" that asked for the assembly to put paper money into circulation. This letter warns of the dangers of introducing bills of credit. The second entry, an essay probably written by William Livingston, a New York lawyer and writer, warns that the more paper currency used in a colony, the more likely the economy and trade of the colony will be harmed. The third selection, from 1773, warns that paper money will devalue what specie exists. Just as the other writers in this section, the unknown "A Virginian" believes that paper money will drive any gold and silver money from the colony.

The selections supporting paper money begin with two pieces written by Benjamin Franklin who believed properly managed paper currency could hold its value comparably to gold and silver. The first entry is part of Franklin's "Busy-Body" essays written for Andrew Bradford's *American Weekly Mercury*. The second appeared in Franklin's *General Magazine*. In a pamphlet that never appeared in any of his periodicals, the Pennsylvania printer outlined in detail the arguments for and against paper currency, supporting the former.

The next entry is the Massachusetts assembly's response to Governor Jonathan Belcher's refusal to approve the issuing of any more bills of credit for the colony. In trouble for most of the eighteenth century because of a lack of specie, Massachusetts had authorized numerous paper money printings. In 1737 the colony ordered more paper money. Some was to be in the older form of bills of credit, known as "old tenor." The remainder was to be "new tenor." Taxes paid in old tenor were to be assessed three to one compared to new tenor.[4] Citizens strongly opposed this action, and the legislature's response here is a continuation of the problem. They threaten nonsupport of Belcher's government and predict a collapse of the colony's economy.

The final entry in support of paper currency is a response to "A Virginian" in the section above. The writer, Ro. C. Nicholas, reminds readers that paper money properly managed will retain its value and is needed by colonials. He also provides a brief history of paper currency since the French and Indian War.

OPPOSING PAPER MONEY

AN ANONYMOUS WRITER: "AGAINST PAPER MONEY"

Americans argued over whether individual colonies should produce bills of credit—often referred to as paper money—in order to ensure that the colonies had enough money to carry on trade successfully. This anonymous New York letter discusses this problem, and the writer concludes that paper money would simply devalue any currency currently in circulation in the colony. The writer also asked the readers to think about the situations in Boston and North Carolina, two places where bills of credit had reduced the value of existing money and driven prices upward.

New-York Weekly Journal, 27 May 1734

Mr. Zenger; . . .

I am of an Opinion that we want a good deal of Cash in the Province. That it is absolutely necessary to carry on a Trade, and that it is at present the only Return we have to make to Great Britain *for the Goods we receive from thence, but how to obtain a competent Stock of current Cash seems to be the Difficulty the Province labours under at present, and in my poor Opinion nothing can so well remedy the Evil as extending our Trade and Manufactures, if we can by our Industry make the Ballance of Trade in our favour, it is so much clear gain, which will soon give us a competent Stock of currant Cash.*

I know many People are fond of striking Bills of Credit, and think that will add to our currant Cash. I believe every Man when he comes seriously to consider the Nature of Paper Money, the terrible Condition it has reduced some of our Neighbours to, he will think it will daily add to our Misfortunes and not to our Cash; one plain Consequence of it will be this, just so much Paper Money as you make, just so much less Specie you will retain in the Country; and had we Paper enough for a Currency for the Province, Silver and Gold would soon become as scarce here as it is Boston *or* Carolina.

WILLIAM LIVINGSTON: "THE PROBLEM WITH BILLS OF CREDIT"

In 1753 New York issued its sixth round of paper money since 1709. Lawyer William Livingston, or perhaps one of his partners, William Smith, Jr., or John Morin Scott, felt the continuing issuance of bills of credit meant that New York's trade with Europe would ultimately suffer. Livingston believed that while paper money might hold its value for a time, ultimately it would lose value and necessitate the printing of more, which would devalue New Yorkers' assets and decrease their potential for trade.

Independent Reflector (New York), 24 May 1753

Thy Silver is become Dross. Prophet JEREMIAH[5]

THAT whenever a base Currency, or Medium of Trade, be admitted in a mercantile Country, it will in Proportion banish from it every better Currency, is a Truth capable of the clearest Demonstration. . . . It is not so in those inland Countries, whose Commerce is entirely confined within their own Limits: For among themselves they may agree to put what Value they please on what they please. They may make Leather, or what would otherwise be but waste Paper, pass for Money. . . . But that will only answer as far as such mutual Agreement reaches; for in a Country that carries on any foreign Trade, this kind of Currency will soon lose its Credit, and become of little or no Value. Experience will teach them that the Estimate set on it arose entirely from their own Consent, and that the Rest of the World will desire to be excused from receiving for their valuable Commodities, what has no intrinsic Value. . . . Paper Money is emitted to be ever so good, yet if the Quantity made, be so large as to be nearly equal to what the Currency was before in Gold and Silver, it must inevitably fall; and as more is struck, will gradually sink to its true Value. . . .

Another grand Evil resulting from a Paper Currency, is its promoting amongst us a Spirit of Extravagance, and a greater Consumption of *European* Goods than the Province will be able to pay for. With this imaginary Money we go to Market, and buy freely what we might often as well be without; and tho' the Merchant be paid, yet if Gold and Silver, or Bills of Exchange, happen to be scarce, he is obliged to give an extraordinary Price for Remittances, and then down goes the Value of Paper Money, and that of all Specialties regulated by it.

On a little Reflection, it will evidently appear to every thinking Person, that the Inhabitants of a Province must be impoverished as they increase the Quantity of their Bills, or at least prevented from becoming so rich as they otherwise would . . . as our Paper Bills are cancelled, our Exchange of Money with *Europe*, must necessarily fall; and the People of this Province grown more frugal and wealthy.

A VIRGINIAN: "THE MANIFOLD EVILS OF PAPER MONEY"

The fact that Americans wrote about the dangers of paper money and bills of credit throughout the colonial era attests to the monetary problems of America in the eighteenth century. The anonymous Virginian regarded the danger of paper money as one that might reduce a person's financial value simply through the issuance of more money. Legislatures could not ensure the stability of the paper money's value, he asserted. In addition, any community could also print money. The whole situation, Virginian noted, had the potential financially to ruin anyone who dealt in paper currency.

Virginia Gazette (Williamsburg, Purdie and Dixon), 16 September 1773

To Mess. PURDIE & DIXON. . . .

TO profit from Experience is the Business of Wisdom, and happy is he who can derive this Advantage from the Good or Ill that has attended the Conduct of others. . . . But very unhappy must they be, who, inattentive to the Injuries that other People have received, and insensible of the Mischiefs which past Transactions amongst themselves have produced, continue still to pursue Systems which such united Experience joins in condemning. I am led into these Reflections from considering the manifold Evils that many Communities, as well as this my native Country, have sustained from the Admission of Paper Money. To consider this Subject in Theory, it will appear reasonable to conclude that the Price of Provisions and Labour must increase in Proportion to the Increase of Money; . . . there appears no Reason for . . . counterfeit Money which Foreigners will not accept, which any great Disorder in the State will reduce to nothing, and which, instead of being the Effect of Wealth, is here supposed to be the Offspring of publick Distress, and general poverty. . . . A farther Attention to this Subject will show it not only hurtful to our Virtue, but to our Interest also. Although the Causes are certainly many which contribute to the Rise and Fall of Exchange, yet I suppose it will not be denied that our Paper Money was the Cause of Exchange rising in this Country, in the Manner it did some Years ago. As little, I imagine, will it be denied that a Price was put on imported Goods proportionate to the increased Exchange. . . . A still farther Objection, and a very weighty one, to these Paper Emissions, is, that they have driven, and with too much Certainty will continue to banish Gold and Silver from among us. So that, although our Assembly cannot make their Paper a legal Tender, yet the Countenance of an Act of the Legislature, with Want of Thought, and the Absence of other Money, together operating, occasion its general Reception among the People; and yet 1000 *l.* of this Money is not a Security to its Possessor that he shall not go to Jail for a Debt of 20 *l.* I am not without Authority for this Assertion, having lately met with an Instance; where a Gentleman of affluent Fortune, good Credit in England, and possessed of the Paper Money, was daily in Terrour of a Jail, because his Creditor insisted on Gold or Silver. From this Distress he could not be relieved (as he told me) on Application to the Treasury, where he hoped to get his Paper exchanged for Specie. . . . This is a Subject, Mr. Printer, of momentous Concern to the Publick; and I earnestly wish my Countrymen would apply their most serious Attention to it, that we may, before it is too late, depart from a Plan so fatally pregnant with Ruin to the Community. The learned Montesquieu, treating of Money, says: "Nothing ought to be so exempt from Variation as that which is the common Measure of all." Yet under our Paper System the Man who to-day is possessed of as much Treasury Money as entitles him to 100 *l.* Sterling may to-morrow, by a sudden Irruption of 30 or 40,000*l.* from our Printing office, find his Sterling Capital many per Cents reduced in Value.

A VIRGINIAN.

IN FAVOR OF PAPER MONEY

BENJAMIN FRANKLIN: "THE BUSY-BODY, NO. 8"

Benjamin Franklin wrote under numerous pseudonyms. The Busy-Body was the one he used to introduce his ideas to Philadelphia when he wrote for Andrew Bradford's American Weekly Mercury. *Pennsylvania in 1729 faced a financial crisis, and Franklin believed that a well-managed system of paper currency was the only practical short-term solution.*

American Weekly Mercury (Philadelphia), 27 March 1729

I have received Letters lately from several considerable Men, earnestly urging me to write on the Subject of *Paper-Money*; . . . The Subject of *Paper Currency* is in it self very intricate, and I believe, understood by Few; I mean as to its Consequences *in Futurum*; . . .

I am not satisfied that it is for our Advantage to rest contented with *Paper-Money* for ever, without endeavouring to recover our Silver and Gold; which may be done without so much Difficulty . . . if those who have the Management of Publick Affairs should have no Interests to pursue separate from those of their Country. Yet at this Time it seems absolutely necessary to have a large Additional Sum struck for the Relief of the People in their present miserable Circumstances, and until such Methods of Trade are thought on, and put in Practice, as will make that Currency needless; which I hope the Legislature will as soon as possible take into their Consideration. . . .

The whole Country is at this Instant filled with the greatest Heat and Animosity; and if there are yet among us any Opposers of a *Paper-Currency*, it is probably the Resentments of the People point at them. . . .

I cannot but think it would be highly prudent in those Gentlemen with all Expedition to publish such Vindications of themselves and their Actions, as will sufficiently clear them in the Eyes of all reasonable Men. . . . And such a Vindication is the more necessary at this Time, because if the People are once convinced there is no such Scheme on Foot, (and Truth without Doubt will prevail) it may exceedingly tend to the Settlement of their Minds, the Abatement of their Heats, and the Establishment of Peace, Love, and Unity, and all the Social Virtues.

BENJAMIN FRANKLIN: "FIXING VALUE TO PAPER MONEY"

In his first, unsuccessful attempt at producing a magazine, Franklin addressed the continuing paper currency problem. British merchants and traders complained about being paid with American bills of credit, but Americans had so little minted British money that they had little choice but to issue the bills. Franklin proposed that England set a value on American paper money that would be accepted by all. In this way, he felt, Americans would still be able to obtain goods from England, and English merchants would be able to receive fair payment.

The General Magazine (Philadelphia), February 1741

To the Author of the GENERAL MAGAZINE.

It appears by the Resolutions of the Honourable the House of Commons of *Great Britain*, that it is their Opinion, that the Issuing Paper Currencies in the *American* Colonies hath been prejudicial to the Trade of *Great Britain*, by causing a Confusion in Dealings, and lessening of Credit in those Parts; and that there is Reason to apprehend, that some Measures will be fallen upon, to hinder or restrain any future Emmissions of such Currencies, when those that are now extant shall be called in and sunk. But if any Scheme could be formed, for fixing and ascertaining the Value of Paper Bills of Credit, in all future Emissions, it may be presumed such Restraints will be taken off, as the Confusion complained of in Dealings would thereby be avoided.

MASSACHUSETTS HOUSE OF REPRESENTATIVES: "REACTION TO A VETO OF BILLS OF CREDIT"

In an effort to ease Massachusetts' financial crisis concerning lack of currency, the legislature passed a bill authorizing £60,000 in bills of credit be issued. The bills would be redeemable for gold or silver coin. Governor Jonathan Belcher, however, effectively killed it refusing to sign the bill. Here, the legislature responds to the governor asking him to reconsider as the representatives explain why the new issue of paper money is needed.

Boston Gazette, 22 January 1739

May it please your Excellency,

HIS Majesty's Council and the House of Representatives in General Court assembled, in Consideration of the near Approach of the Periods when all the Bills of Credit now passing will be sunk, have agreed on a Bill for the Emission of *Sixty Thousand Pounds*, redeemable by Silver and gold; which Bill your Excellency was pleased in your SPEECH of Yesterday, to inform us you could not consent to, consistent with His Majesty's Instructions.

Wherefore we His Majesty's loyal and dutiful Subjects, crave Leave to observe to your Excellency, the great and distressing Difficulties His Majesty's good Subjects of this Province will be under in supporting the Government, and in carrying on their common Affairs and Business if the said Bill or some of that Nature shall not take Effect.

Your Excellency cannot but be sensible that for many Years past the publick Taxes for the Support of Government have been wholly paid in Bills of Credit, by which Bills also the Trade and Commerce have been for near thirty Years almost wholly managed, and that the whole of these Bills of Credit must be intirely sunk by the End of the year 1741, and that it will bring great Distress, if not an intire Stagnation of all Trade, if about two hundred and fifty thousand Pounds, computed in Bills of the old Tenor, the Sum now extant, should be in that short Time intirely taken away, and nothing substituted in its Room, and especially since this Court have in their present Session for supporting the Credit of their own Bills, found it necessary to discountenance those of the neighbouring Governments, as being not well founded.

We would therefore pray your Excellency favourable Consideration of the important Affair, and how much the Safety Interest and Quiet of His Majesty's good Subjects under your Excellency's Care depend on its Success, and do Intreat your Endeavours that your Excellency may give your Consent to this Bill, or a Bill of this Nature.

RO. C. NICHOLAS: "REPLY TO A VIRGINIAN ON THE SUBJECT
OF PAPER MONEY"

In the colonies, arguments made for or against issuing paper money generally drew a reply because Americans were divided concerning the necessity of bills of credit. In this letter, Nicholas refutes the arguments made by A Virginian and points out why paper money is a necessity for the colony. The author traces the use of paper currency back to the French and Indian War to prove its necessity.

Virginia Gazette (Williamsburg, Purdie and Dixon), 30 September
1773

To Mess. PURDIE & DIXON. . . .

THE very earnest Address of your Correspondent, "A Virginian," on the
Subject of Paper Money unquestionably demands our most serious Attention; especially as it comes warmly recommended by so respectable a
Number of Your readers. . . . The Author's extreme Aversion to every kind
of Paper Currency may be, in his own Opinion, well founded, and he has
displayed too large a Share of good Sense to admit a Suspicion that he
could have wished to depreciate what Paper Money we have now remaining in Circulation, but yet it is to be feared that his Observations
may have this Tendency. I will, for a Moment, suppose the original Evil
in first admitting it amongst us to have been, even as great as he would
represent it; but surely we are now called upon by every Principle of
Justice, by every Dictate of political Wisdom, to support its Credit; should
this fail, the Confusion the Country may be thrown into and the Losses,
which may be sustained by Individuals, the present Possessors of the
Money, are more easily to be conceived than described. . . .

I should now leave the Author's Observations. . . . That other Countries, as well as Virginia, have sustained Inconveniencies and, perhaps,
Losses from a Paper Currency, I am not at all concerned to deny; what I
undertake to maintain is that these have not arisen from Paper Money,
merely, as *such*, but that they have been chiefly, if not totally owing,
either to these Bills of Credit not being established upon proper Funds,
or to a Superabundance of them, or to some Mismanagements. . . .

I take the Liberty . . . once more to remind your Readers of the Circumstances we were in, when our Paper Money was first introduced. Attacked, as we were in all Quarters by a most powerful, in Conjunction
with a most savage and barbarous Enemy; when our Country was in the
most imminent Danger and we had to contend for all that was dear and
valuable, could we possibly have looked supinely on and suffered every
Thing to go to Destruction? . . . Under these Circumstances, what was to
be done? Money, the acknowledged Sinews of War, was necessary, *immediately necessary*; Troops could not be levied and supported without
it; of Gold and Silver, there was indeed some, what Quantity I do not
know, in the Hands of Individuals, but the Publick could not command
it. Did there not result from hence a Necessity, an *absolute* Necessity of
our having Recourse to a Paper Currency, as the only Resource, from
which we could draw Relief? . . . Not being able to procure Specie in
Time, it was resolved to issue Treasury Notes, which were to pass current
according to the Value of their Denomination expressed in each Note.
. . . The Quantity of Paper Money issued, in the Course of the late War

was very considerable, having exceeded Half a Million, which perhaps was more than this Country could have conveniently borne, if it could have been avoided; it may point out one of the Inconveniencies I have mentioned, arising from a *Superabundance* of such Sort of Money, but cannot, as I conceive, militate against a Paper Currency altogether. That so large a Quantity of Paper Money contributed to raise Exchange, I will freely own as my Opinion; though, at the same Time, I am thoroughly persuaded that the Balance of Trade being so much against us was the chief governing Cause of it. That, as a necessary Consequence of a high Exchange, the Prices of foreign Goods were enhanced, I will not deny. . . . Who were the few Individuals alluded to, as alone reaping "temporary Advantages" from this Paper Money, I do not know. . . . I suppose particular Men, in the Course of Circulation, might have made the same Advantages with it, as they would have done with any other Sort of Money. . . .

I am not and never was an Advocate for Paper Money. . . . The present Object of my Concern is to support the Credit of what we have left and I must own it gives me Pain to see any Thing done, however undesignedly, that has a Tendency to depreciate it. If a Doubt remains with any one as to the Sufficiency of the Security, which the Holders of our Paper have for its Redemption, I flatter myself that I can, with great Ease, give the utmost Satisfaction upon this Head. . . .

I am apt to think that some have not fully considered how very necessary a sufficient Quantity of Money is in every Community to transact their internal Affairs, to promote Industry and employ the Inhabitants of every Class to Advantage; let them consult the Police of the best regulated and most thrifty Countries in the World and they may be thoroughly informed; but, if they should not be satisfied from thence, let them exercise a little Patience, till our Paper Money is quite gone, and then, without pretending to the Gifts of Prophecy, I will venture to believe that they will feel the Loss of it. . . .

The Gentleman speaks of an "Irruption of thirty or forty Thousand Pounds from our Printing Office" . . . but surely he would not insinuate that nothing more hath been thought necessary, that barely sending an Order to the Printer to strike off such a Number of Treasury Notes, as if they were no more than many simple Advertisements, he must know that there never has been an Emission voted, but upon the maturest Deliberation and then only, on the most pressing Emergency; he must also acknowledge that, *in every Instance*, the most competent Funds have been established for the Redemption of the Money.

RO. C. NICHOLAS.

QUESTIONS

1. What were the principal concerns for providing paper money in colonial America?

2. What were the principal reasons given not to issue paper money?

3. What, according to Franklin, were England's chief reasons for opposing paper currency?

4. According to Ro. C. Nicholas, why was paper currency necessary during the French and Indian War?

5. How could paper money retain its value?

NOTES

1. *South-Carolina Gazette* (Charleston), 26 July 1735, 2.

2. David A. Copeland, *Colonial American Newspapers: Character and Content* (Newark: University of Delaware Press, 1997), 108.

3. Benjamin Franklin, *A Modest Enquiry into the Nature and Necessity of a Paper-Currency* (Philadelphia, 1729).

4. *The Acts and Resolves, Public and Private of the Province of the Massachusetts Bay* (Boston: Wright and Potter, 1886), II: 845.

5. The scripture reference actually is Isaiah 1.

CHAPTER 13

The New York Public Education Controversy, 1753–1755

In 1746 the colonists of New York began to discuss the formation of a college. The idea was not new in America. Massachusetts Bay had founded Harvard in 1636, Virginia had established William and Mary in 1693, and Connecticut had started Yale in 1701. What was unique about these institutions from a contemporary view was the fact that they were all run by religious denominations but received government financing. The pattern of establishing religious institutions of learning with government funding continued throughout most of the colonial era.

The central purpose of these colleges, then, was to train ministers and instruct students in Christianity. "The chief Thing that is aimed at," a New York writer said, "is, to teach and engage the Children to *know God in Jesus Christ*, and to love and serve him in all *Sobriety, Godliness* and *Righteousness* of Life *with a perfect Heart and a willing Mind*."[1] But education, others such as Benjamin Franklin said, was the best foundation for creating stable governments and informed citizenry. Schools did not necessarily have to have religious backing. "The good Education of Youth has been esteemed by wise Men of all Ages, as the surest Foundation of the Happiness both of private Families and of Commonwealths," Franklin wrote in a pamphlet on education.[2]

The issue in America surrounding education, then, did not focus on the necessity of education, but on the religious affiliation of the institution. These differences were exacerbated in American society in the 1740s following the Great Awakening and the religious divisions it caused (see Chapters 8 and 9). Denominations and Americans in general wanted an

educated clergy, but, in reality, the schools begun in America more resembled liberal arts colleges than seminaries. Religious affiliation was
never a prerequisite for admission, and by the end of the eighteenth
century, about 80 percent of college graduates did not enter the ministry.[3]

Even though denominational colleges accepted students of any Christian denomination, many people in New York feared that if its college
operated under the auspices of one group—in this case the Anglican
Church (Church of England)—Anglicans would proselytize all students.
In turn, the sudden increase in Anglicans, who would assume positions
of importance in government and community, would work to establish
Anglicanism as the state church (one supported by taxes collected by the
government) and limit free worship for non-Anglicans. As part of the
proof for this, opponents pointed to the recently established Log College
of New Jersey, which would later become Princeton. They said the strong
Presbyterian ties at the institution had influenced the direction of that
colony. Similarly, Congregationalism was the established church of Connecticut, not ironically the denomination that operated Yale.

As a result of all the above concerns, New York swirled in controversy
from 1753 to 1755 over the establishment of a publicly supported college
with religious ties. King's College opened in July 1754 as an Anglican
institution, but during this three-year span, opponents of Anglican ties
for the school used the press constantly. William Livingston, a lawyer of
the city, led the charge against Anglican ties to the New York college. Late
in 1752, he began the *Independent Reflector* as a commentary on politics
and life in the colony. By March 1753, the *Reflector* turned its attention
to the college and subsequently so, too, did the other newspapers of the
town. After a year of stirring controversy, printer James Parker refused to
publish the *Reflector* any longer. Livingston and his partners, William
Smith, Jr., and John Morin Scott, turned to printer Hugh Gaine, who
agreed to give the trio space in his paper for them to publish essays under
the title "The Watch-Tower." For another year, the three attacked any
denominational ties to the college. Their attacks were successful in keeping the school from obtaining lottery funds that New York had originally
intended to use to support the college.[4]

In 1756 the school did obtain part of the lottery money raised by the
colony, but Livingston, writing in the last "Watch-Tower," said his effort
to keep King's College from receiving state support had succeeded.[5] This
chapter, then, looks at the debate that took place in New York over the
establishment of a state-funded, religiously controlled college, a discussion that took place in many colonies in America.

The readings begin with those opposed to church affiliation with public
colleges. The first entry and the one that follows are the first two essays
opposing Anglican control of the proposed New York college that ap-

peared in the *Independent Reflector*. The publication's chief aim was to present editorial opinion, not news, and its principal author, William Livingston, did just that during the *Reflector*'s one-year existence. A six-week series by the New York lawyer railed against affiliation of the college with the Church of England. In these two editorials, the *Reflector*'s author explains why religious affiliation for the college would be dangerous for New York.

The next readings come from "The Watch-Tower" series. The fifty-two essays ran for a year, from November 1754 to November 1755, and reiterated the basic arguments expounded against church control of the school that had appeared in the *Reflector*. In number five, Livingston argues that an established state religion does not necessarily mean the state should sponsor religious schools. In his last, number fifty-two, Livingston says that his mission is complete. While King's College opened as an Episcopal school, it did not initially receive public funding, and Livingston credited that fact to his continual newspaper campaign.

In the last essay in the chapter's first set of readings, Livingston enumerates the advantages of establishing schools throughout the colony. It is included to demonstrate how serious many in the eighteenth century were about establishing universal education.

Religious control of the proposed New York college was the point of contention, not the establishment of a school. For that reason many writers focused on the establishment of a state religion. In the first reading in the section supporting church relations with the college, the anonymous X.Z &. explains why religious establishment provides advantages for a government. The second reading, an unsigned letter, was written to an unnamed member of the New York Assembly. Like nearly all correspondence that favored a church-related institution, this one attacked the arguments against such affiliation as made by Livingston in the *Independent Reflector* or "The Watch-Tower" series. In this particular letter, the writer responds to Livingston's argument that a sect college will affect the general religion of New York in years to come.

AGAINST ESTABLISHING A CHURCH-AFFILIATED COLLEGE

WILLIAM LIVINGSTON: "THE PROPOSED COLLEGE FOR NEW YORK"

Lawyer William Livingston started the Independent Reflector *as a medium for addressing what he and his associates viewed as New York's problems. Because the colony began discussions of a public college with religious affiliation as early as 1747, the school was one of the principal issues Livingston discussed. For Livingston, Anglican control of the college would lead to more Anglican influence in New York government, perhaps even an establishment of the Church of England as the colony's official religion. To support his beliefs, Livingston offered examples from other colonies.*

Independent Reflector (New York), 29 March 1753

THE Design of erecting a College in this Province, is a Matter of such grand and general Importance, that I have frequently made it the Topic of my serious Meditation. Nor can I better employ my Time than by devoting a Course of Papers to so interesting a Subject. A Subject of universal Concernment, and in a peculiar Manner involving in it, the Happiness and Well-being of our Posterity! . . .

The Consequences of a liberal Education will soon be visible throughout the whole Province. They will appear on the Bench, at the Bar, in the Pulpit, and in the Senate, and unavoidably affect our civil and religious Principles. . . .

The Principles or Doctrines implanted in the Minds of Youth grow up and gather Strength with them. In Time they take deep Root, pass from the Memory and Understanding to the Heart, and at length become a second Nature, which it is almost impossible to change. While the Mind is tender and flexible, it may be moulded and managed at Pleasure: But when once the Impressions are by Practice and Habit, as it were incorporated with the intellectual Substance, they are obliterated with the greatest Difficulty. . . .

At *Harvard* College in the *Massachusetts-Bay*, and at *Yale* College in *Connecticut*, the Presbyterian Profession is in some sort established. It is in these Colonies the commendable Practice of all who can afford it, to give their Sons an Education at their respective Seminaries of Learning. While they are in the Course of their Education, they are sure to be instructed in the Arts of maintaining the Religion of the College, which is always that of their immediate Instructors; and of combating the Principles of all other Christians whatever. When the young Gentlemen, have run thro' the Course of their Education, they enter into the Ministry, or some Offices of the Government, and acting in them under the Influence of the Doctrines espoused in the Morning of Life, the Spirit of the College is transfused thro' the Colony, and tinctures the Genius and Policy of the public. Administration, from the Governor down to the Constable. Hence the Episcopalians cannot acquire an equal Strength among them, till some new Regulations, in Matters of Religion, prevail in their Colleges, which perpetually produce Adversaries to the hierarchical System. . . .

[T]he extensive Influence of a College so manifestly appears, it is of the last Importance, that ours be so constituted, that the Fountain being pure, the Streams (to use the Language of Scripture) may make glad the City of our GOD.   Z.

WILLIAM LIVINGSTON: "WHY MUST A COLLEGE BE AFFILIATED WITH A RELIGIOUS GROUP?"

Part of Livingston's argument for nonaffiliation of a college in New York centered around how the lawyer understood the religious breakdown of New Yorkers. He believed that the great majority of those in the colony were not Anglican. A "Party-College," as Livingston referred to it, would alter the religious and political structure of the colony. An Anglican school would, he reckoned, teach Anglican tenets, accept a preponderance of Anglicans, and train the majority of the colony's political leaders. The result would mean a lessening of the roles of other religious groups in New York.

Independent Reflector (New York), 29 March 1753

I HAVE in my last Paper shewn, from Reason, Experience and History, the vast Influence of a College, upon the civil and religious Principles of the Community in which it is erected and supported. I shall now proceed to offer a few Arguments, which I submit to the Consideration of my Countrymen, to evince the Necessity and Importance of constituting *our* College upon a Basis the most catholic, generous and free.

It is in the first Place observable, that unless its Constitution and Government, be such as will admit Persons of all protestant Denominations, upon a perfect Parity as to Privileges, it will itself be greatly prejudiced, and prove a Nursery of Animosity, Dissention and Disorder.... Should our College, therefore, unhappily thro' our own bad Policy, fall into the Hands of any one religious Sect in the Province: Should that Sect, which is more than probable, establish its religion in the College, shew favour to its votaries, and cast Contempt upon others; 'tis easy to foresee that Christians of all other Denominations amongst us, instead of encouraging its Prosperity, will, from the same Principles, rather conspire to oppose and oppress it.... Which-soever of these [denominations] has the sole Government of the College, will kindle the Jealousy of the Rest, not only against the Persuasion so preferred, but the College itself. Nor can any Thing less be expected, than a general Discontent and Tumult; which, affecting all Ranks of People, will naturally tend to disturb the Tranquility and Peace of the Province.

In such a State of Things, we must not expect the Children of any, but of that Sect which prevails in the Academy will ever be sent to it: For should they, the established Tenets must either be implicitly received, or a perpetual religious War necessarily maintained....

A Party-College, in less than half a Century, will put a new Face upon the Religion, and in Consequence thereof affect the Politics of the Country. Let us suppose what may, if the College should be entirely managed by one Sect, probably be supposed. Would not all possible Care be bestowed in tincturing the Minds of the Students with the Doctrines and Sentiments of that Sect? Would not the Students of the College, after the Course of their Education, exclusive of any others, fill all the Offices of the Government? . . . Can it be imagined that all other Christians would continue peaceable under, and unenvious of, the Power of that Church which was rising to so exalted a Pre-eminence above them? . . . I am convinced, that under the Management of any particular Persuasion, it will necessarily prove destructive to the civil and religious Rights of the People. . . .

Argument against suffering the College to fall into the Hands of a Party, may be deduced from the Design of its Erection, and Support to the Public.

The Legislature to whom it owes its Origin, and under whose Care the Affair has hitherto been conducted, could never have intended it as an Engine to be exercised for the Purposes of a Party. . . . No, it was set on Foot, and I hope will be constituted for general Use, for the public Benefit, for the Education of all who can afford such Education: And to suppose it intended for any other less public-spirited Uses, is ungratefully to reflect upon all who have hitherto, had any Agency in an Undertaking so glorious to the Province, so necessary, so important and beneficial.

At present, it is but in Embryo, yet the Money hitherto collected is public Money; and till it is able to support itself, the Aids given to it will be public Aids. . . . Can it, therefore, be supposed, that all shall contribute for the Uses, the ignominious Uses of a few? . . .

It is farther to be remarked, that a public Academy is, or ought to be a mere civil Institution, and cannot with any tolerable Propriety be monopolized by any religious Sect. . . .

For such is our Capacity of endowing an Academy; that if it be founded on the Plan of a general Toleration, it must, naturally, eclipse any other on the Continent, and draw many Pupils from those Provinces, the Constitution of whose Colleges is partial and contracted. . . .   A.

WILLIAM LIVINGSTON: "WATCH-TOWER, NO. 5"

In all the controversy surrounding the public college, Livingston acknowledged that the possibility of a state religion for any colony was possible given the nature of church-state relations in England. Although that possibility existed, Livingston did not believe that the colony's public schools had to reflect that fact.

New-York Mercury, 23 December 1754

Ecclesiastical Establishment . . . *extends* to the American Plantations; and . . . such Establishment does *confer a Right* upon that Church, to the Direction and Government of a *Provincial* Academy, which is not an *ecclesiastical*, but a *civil* Institution. When those two Points are clearly settled in their Favour, I am verily persuaded, the Inhabitants of the Province, who are loyal Subjects to the best of Kings, and firmly attached to the Constitution of their Country, will readily acquiesce in a *legal* Right. But till this Right be evinced, by *grave* and *solid* Arguments . . . the People who are, and ought to be equally tenacious of *their* Privileges, must justly esteem an Attempt, in any one Denomination, to erect a *sovereign Dictatorship* over the public Education of their Youth, to be an Instance of bold and harden'd Effrontery.

WILLIAM LIVINGSTON: "WATCH-TOWER, NO. 52"

In the last of the Watch-Tower series, Livingston explains what has happened in New York with its public school. The school opened under Anglican direction, but the colony did not use public funds to support the endeavor.

New-York Mercury, 17 November 1755

Dark as was the Design of appropriating the Public Monies to private and sinister Purposes; yet such was the general Inattention to our provincial Concerns; that had I not sounded the Alarm, Bigotry would e'er now, have triumphed over the natural Rights of *British* Subjects; and a Party-College been erected, to serve the Interests of one particular Sect, and reflect Dishonour on all the other Denominations in the Province. . . . The highest hopes of my Antagonists are entirely blasted, and our Representatives ever tender of the Liberty and Privileges of their Constituents, have sufficiently demonstrated their Aversion to a Party-College.

WILLIAM LIVINGSTON: "THE IMPORTANCE OF PUBLIC EDUCATION"

The nineteenth century is known more for the push for public education than the eighteenth, but in this essay, Livingston outlines the advantages of such a system and why one should be founded.

Independent Reflector (New York), 8 November 1753

To enumerate all the Advantages accruing to a Country, from a due Attention to the Encouragement of the Means of Education, is impossible.

The happy Streams issuing from that inexhaustible Source, are number-less and unceasing. Knowledge among a People makes them free, enter-prizing and dauntless; but Ignorance enslaves, emasculates and depresses them. When Men know their Rights, they will at all Hazards defend them, as well against the insidious Designs of domestic Politicians, as the un-disguised Attacks of a foreign Enemy: But while the Mind remains in-volved in its native Obscurity, it becomes pliable, abject, dastardly, and tame: It swallows the grossest Absurdities, submits to the vilest Im-positions, and follows wherever it is led. In short, irrefragable Arguments in favour of Knowledge, may be drawn from the Consideration of its Nature. But it is sufficient barely to observe its Effects. He must be a Stranger to History and the World, who has not observed, that the Pros-perity, Happiness, Grandeur, and even the Strength of a People, have always been the Consequences of the Improvement and Cultivation of their Minds. And indeed, where this has been in any considerable Degree neglected, triumphant Ignorance hath open'd its Sluices, and the Country been overflowed with Tyranny, Barbarism, ecclesiastical Domination, Su-perstition, Enthusiasm, corrupt Manners, and an irresistible confederate Host of Evils, to its utter Ruin and Destruction. . . .

It is with joy I observe the present Disposition of our Legislature, to remove the Scandal of our former Indolence, about the Means of Edu-cation, in the Measures we are pursuing for the Establishment of a Col-lege. That important Design must flourish under the Care of the Public. Our Province is growing and opulent, and we are able to endow an Uni-versity in the most splendid Manner, without any Burden upon the Peo-ple. Scarce any Thing at present but the Nature of its Constitution demands the Study of the several Branches of the Legislature. And that alone is a Subject worthy of their utmost Vigilance and Attention. A Col-lege in a new Country, and especially in a Province of such scanty Limits as ours, will necessarily make a vast Alteration in our Affairs and Condi-tion, civil and religious. It will, more or less, influence every Individual amongst us, and diffuse its Spirit thro' all Ranks, Parties and Denomina-tions. If it be established upon a generous and catholic Foundation, agreeable to the true Nature and End of a Seminary for the Instruction of Youth in useful Knowledge, we and our Posterity will have Reason to bless its Founders, and long will it continue the Fountain of Felicity to the Province. But should it unhappily be made the Engine of a Party in Church or State—should it be constituted with any Badge of religious Discrimination or Preference, we have no Reason either to believe or wish its Prosperity. Such an impure Source must necessarily poison us with its infected Streams endanger our precious Liberties, discourage our Growth, and be obstructive to the public Emolument.   A.

FOR ESTABLISHING A CHURCH-AFFILIATED COLLEGE

X.Z.&.: "RELIGIOUS AFFILIATION WILL NOT ESTABLISH A RELIGION"

William Livingston's writings concerning the college for New York produced numerous replies. In this anonymous piece, the writer discounts Livingston's argument that religious affiliation in the college will ensure the establishment of Anglicanism as the religion of New York.

New-York Mercury, 23 July 1753

I think little need be said to shew that *national Establishments* can alone diffuse, thro' a Country, the full social Advantages arising from Religion and Men set aside to explain and inculcate it. If, according to the *Reflector*'s Scheme, all Religions were equally favor'd by the Civil Power, none establish'd, and every Man left at Liberty to preach and practise what he thought proper, what a Scene of Confusion would a Country, in such a Situation, undergo! What Strugglings, what incessant Heart-Beatings would there be among the various Sects! What Means could the Civil Power make use of to controul them . . . for we suppose full unbridled Liberty of Conscience by the Constitution. But if the Wisdom of a country has established one Religion, and that the best they could frame or devise, we are sure to have this one Religion flow down thro' Ages, as pure and uncorrupted, as the Flux of Human Affairs permits.

AN ANONYMOUS WRITER: "NO RELIGIOUS EFFECT IN COMING YEARS"

Every time Livingston offered a new rationale for keeping New York's college from religious affiliation, a writer found reasons to refute him. In this unsigned letter, the writer, addressing his words to an assemblyman, denies any effect that a church college would have on the colony's religion in the future. The writer also offers reasons why the college should be affiliated with the Church of England.

New-York Mercury, 30 July 1753

If a College will prove of the most lasting Influence on the Genius of this People, it highly imports us to concert the Government of it in such a Manner, that it do not clash with our civil Government and Constitution.—But if the Nature of the Constitution of an *English* Colony or Province is enquired into, it will appear that the *Reflector*'s republican Scheme for the Government of our College is repugnant to it.

The Government of our College, as well as every other Branch of civil Government, if constitutional, should be partly in the Crown, and partly in the People. . . . The *Reflector*'s Scheme then for founding a College without deriving its Privileges immediately from the Crown, seems to me entirely calculated to hinder our College. . . .

With Regard to what the *Reflector* has wrote against establishing the Prayers of any particular Denomination of Christians for our College, I cannot but laugh at it, however serious the Subject is in its own Nature.— Why did he not as well, out of his great Sagacity, enter a *Proviso* against employing a Mason or Carpenter to undertake the Edifice, until he should first declare upon Oath that he is of no Religion at all, and consequently cannot excite the Envy of any one Sect by the Preference given him in the Erection of the Building?—How inconsistent is this Writer upon himself! One While he tells us, that to use the Prayers of any one Church in our College, particularly the *Church of England*, however excellent, would do a Preference and Badge of Distinction, that would excite the Envy of all other Churches and Sects. . . . The necessity of giving the Preference to some one Denomination among us in the religious Establishment of our College, has been shewn. . . . He tells us that, in half a Century, the Religion of our College will become the Religion of the Country; and consequently if no Religion at all is established in the College, this Country, in half a Century, must either have no Appearance of Religion, or a new One patch'd up from the Ruins of all those we have at present.—But, O Heavens! What dreadful Convulsions must this poor Country undergo, before such a Change could be effected in it; or how are we certain that this new Religion, if we should have any, would not be a thousand Degrees farther remov'd from *Orthodoxy*, than the most erroneous of those now subsisting among us? Who would establish a College upon such a Bottom, more inconstant than the Winds—more undulating than the Waves? Our future Safety, Security and Happiness then, greatly depends [*sic*] upon making the Establishment in Favor of the Church established here, and in the Mother Country, by the ablest Heads and best Hearts she ever boasted of. For, as the Constitution of this Church is invariably fix'd, and her Government naturally mild, we are sure, half a Century hence, to be as orthodox, as happy, and as far removed from a Country of *Infidels* on the one Hand, and *Fanatics* on the other, as were are at this Day. Nor is there a religious Sect in the Province, but had rather see the *Church of England* uppermost, than any Denomination. . . .

It is hop'd what is said, will help to convince every thinking Person, that as the *Church of England* is established here, we neither can, nor ought to establish any Religion in our College, but what is already establish'd in the Province.—And indeed the Moment we attempt such a Thing, we at once give up that Superiority which our College would have over every other on the Continent.

QUESTIONS

1. How does Livingston support his argument that religious instruction will produce religious favoritism in society? How valid is this argument?

2. Why do you think that writers such as Livingston ignored the fact that all colleges in America allowed students of any Christian denomination to enter the school and focused instead on the potential for the indoctrination of students?

3. How could Livingston reconcile an established church for a colony but no religious ties to a state-supported college?

4. The First Amendment separates church and state. How do the arguments presented in these readings foreshadow that guarantee for Americans?

5. What advantages do national establishments and church relatedness for colleges give people, according to the readings in the section supporting church colleges?

6. Which side in this controversy presents the best arguments to support its cause? Explain.

NOTES

1. *New-York Mercury*, 3 June 1754, 1.

2. Benjamin Franklin, *Proposals Relating to the Education of Youth in Pensilvania* (Philadelphia, 1749), in *Benjamin Franklin: Writings*, ed. J. A. Leo Lemay (New York: The Library of America, 1987), 324.

3. Richard Hofstadter and Walter P. Metzer, *The Development of Academic Freedom in the United States* (New York: Columbia University Press, 1955), 116.

4. *New-York Mercury*, 3 June 1754, supplement. The paper lists the winning lottery numbers and the fact that the game's earnings were to be used to open the college.

5. Ibid., 17 November 1755, 1.

CHAPTER 14

The Albany Congress, the Plan of Union, and the French and Indian War, 1754–1763

In the spring of 1754, many Americans believed that life in the colonies was in danger. From the western boundaries of the colonies, reports were trickling in of groups of French and Native Americans gathering military forces, especially in the Ohio Valley. There, the French had built a number of forts, and that did not sit well with colonials hoping to settle west of the Appalachian Mountains.

In 1754 France controlled most of the territory in North America. French jurisdiction of Canada prevented expansion by British colonials northward, and France's claim to the lands west of the Appalachians effectively limited the territory of the American colonies. Colonists, however, disputed French claims to the Ohio Valley, and settlers from Virginia began moving past the Appalachian Mountains to construct settlements after the British government approved land grants there.

The fact that these settlers reported Frenchmen with Indians was significant. Hostilities between English and French settlers in the New World started almost immediately after colonization began in 1607–1608. The English captured Quebec in 1629, and the two nations had fought three wars since 1689, the last—called King George's War—officially ended in 1748. While most Native American nations may have wanted nothing to do with either English or French colonists, a century of exchange and warfare led most Native Americans to view the French as militarily superior and the better of the two groups with which to align. The fact that the French and Indians were massing troops surely meant trouble for the colonists.

In order to discover exactly what was happening in the Ohio Valley, Virginia Governor Robert Dinwiddie sent out a young soldier named George Washington to scout the region. Washington's reports were not encouraging, and when newspapers published the accounts of his personal confrontations with the French, beginning in March 1754, concern grew in all parts of America. At the same time, news reports of attacks in the backcountry reported that the French were encouraging Native Americans "to take up the Hatchet against the English." In addition, increased French privateer activity in the Atlantic and Caribbean led to the conclusion that the French were laying "a solid and lasting Foundation, for making themselves in Time Masters of all *North-America.*"[1]

Colonial and British officials realized that the activity of the French, especially among the Indians, had to be curtailed. For that reason, colonial leaders requested a meeting between their representatives and those of the Six Nations, a confederation of tribes still in alliance with England, for June 1754. The meeting was to be held in Albany, New York, with representatives from all the colonies from Virginia northward invited to attend. The Indians arrived late. Newspaper accounts of the meeting put a positive spin on the congress, but the Native Americans left without promising to fight with the English in the event of war with the French. The leaders of the Six Nations had already seen the French forts and other war preparations in the area around the Great Lakes and in the Ohio Valley and found the English woefully unprepared.

The American representatives at the Albany Congress realized that colonial welfare would be jeopardized without Native American assistance, and one of those representatives, Benjamin Franklin, was prepared to offer another solution. As he traveled from Philadelphia to Albany, Franklin formulated a plan for a union of the colonies. He presented it to the twenty-three other representatives at the beginning of the congress. By the meeting's conclusion, the delegates agreed that the times called for such a union, which would have a president general and a grand council elected by the colonial assemblies. The union would have power over all Native American relations, including war declarations, peace treaties, and land acquisitions. The union could raise an army and navy for common colonial defense, and it could levy taxes to pay for these things. Franklin said the union of colonies was "for their Mutual Defence and Security, and for Extending the British Settlements in North America."[2] With the congress completed and the plan of union approved, the representatives returned home with hopes that Franklin's proposal and their discussions with the Native Americans would be enough to halt France's quest to control all of North America.

This chapter examines newspaper reports on the Albany congress, the Plan of Union that grew out of it, and the colonies' preparations to wage war against the French and Indians. The French and Indian War lasted from 1754 to 1763. From the newspapers, it appears that most printers supported the idea of a union, but most colonial assemblies viewed the plan, which would usurp some of their powers, as unnecessary and either voted it down or ignored it, even though all the assemblies, which controlled each colony's purse strings, voted funding for the war and raised troops. Because the Plan of Union proposed central control of land expansion, individual colonies would not be able to make treaties with Native American nations to acquire territory.[3] As for the war itself, English colonists universally detested the French, and newspapers never questioned the fact that all Americans needed to join together to fight against the French and their Indian allies.

The documents supporting the Albany Congress and the Plan of Union begin with Massachusetts Governor William Shirley's address to the colony's assembly on the importance of securing a treaty of alliance with the Six Nations. It is followed by an anonymous letter, which appeared in the *Pennsylvania Gazette*, that called for a union of colonies. The wording in the letter sounds very much like that which appeared in the *Gazette*'s editorial the following week, which was written by Franklin.

Franklin's editorial was perhaps the most significant newspaper piece written before the Stamp Act crisis of 1765 (see Chapter 16) because it introduced the editorial cartoon to America. The woodcut, the famous "JOIN, or DIE," depicts a dismembered rattlesnake, which represented the American colonies. The editorial was reprinted by most American newspapers. The printers of these newspapers also recreated the disjointed snake woodcut. The JOIN, or DIE snake would also become the symbol of resistance during the Stamp Act crisis and the Revolution.

The JOIN, or DIE essay and cartoon are followed by pleas in Massachusetts and New York for ratification of the Plan of Union. A sermon preached by Boston Congregational minister Jonathan Mayhew is the next selection. Mayhew claims that a union of colonies is the only miracle that can save America. The next entry in support of the congress and union is an editorial note made by New York printer Hugh Gaine, which is appended to an essay, "*the* PRESENT STATE *of this Continent*." The last selection is a one-line prayer that appeared in the *Maryland Gazette*.

The opposition writings to the congress and union begin with an address made by South Carolina Governor James Glen, which questions how the Plan of Union will be implemented. It is followed by an attack, by an unknown writer calling himself Philopatris, on alliances with any Native Americans, even those considered friendly to the colonists. The next readings include the New Jersey assembly's rejection of the Plan of Union and Virginia Governor Robert Dinwiddie's chastisement of the Virginia legislatures for refusing to vote to raise money for intercolonial protection.

FOR THE ALBANY CONGRESS AND PLAN OF UNION

WILLIAM SHIRLEY: "THE IMPORTANCE OF AN ALLIANCE WITH THE SIX NATIONS"

Massachusetts Governor William Shirley understood how valuable Native American support could be to the colonies if war broke out with the French, and he strongly supported the proposed Albany Congress. In this speech, published in the Boston Weekly News-Letter, *the governor pleads with the Massachusetts assembly to send representation to the meeting.*

Boston Weekly News-Letter, 25 April 1754

His Excellency the Governor was pleased to make the following SPEECH to the Great and General Court or Assembly of the Province of the *Massachusetts-Bay.* . . .

I am persuaded, *Gentlemen*, I need not use Arguments to convince you, that it is of very great Consequence to the Interest of His Majesty's Colonies upon this Continent at all Times, that as many of the Tribes of Indians inhabiting it, as may be (those of the Six Nations more especially) should be kept in Friendship with the English, and a Dependance upon the Crown of *Great-Britain*; and that as free a Commerce and Intercourse should be maintained with them as is possible. . . .

You must be sensible, *Gentlemen*, what frequent Attempts, the *French* have made from Time to Time to draw off the Six Nations from the *English* Interest into their own; and from the repeated Advices, we have received from His Majesty's Southern Colonies on this Continent, what Efforts they have lately exerted to win over their Allies, together with the other numerous Tribes inhabiting the vast Country lying along the great Lakes and Rivers, and to the Westward of the *Apalachean*-Mountains, (all of which may be reckon'd to exceed double the Number of the Indians of the Six Nations and those in their Alliance); as also what Measures the *French* are taking to exclude the *English* from all Trade and Commerce with those Indians. . . .

They have committed Hostilities against some of the Tribes in Friendship with the *English*, engag'd others to take up the Hatchet against them, and threatened those with Destruction, who shall interfere with their avow'd Design to drive the *English* out of that Country.

Should the *Indians* of the *Six Nations*, at this critical Conjuncture, desert our Alliance, and go over to the *French*, how fatal an Influence must such an Event have upon the *British* Interest? On the other Hand, should proper Measures be taken to attach them firmly to it, how greatly would it disappoint and check the present Scheme and Enterprizes of our dangerous Neighbours? . . .

Nothing could at this Time so effectually reclaim them to their old Alliance with us, as the Measures directed to by the Lordships of the Board of Trade; *One general League of Friendship comprizing all his Majesty's Colonies, to be made with them in his Majesty's Name*. . . .

Such a Coalition of the Colonies for their Defence would be a convincing Proof to them, that they might safely depend upon his Majesty for Protection, and confirm them in their antient Alliance with the *English*; and how necessary such a Confederacy of the Colonies for their Safeguard. . . .

I would therefore earnestly recommend to you, *Gentlemen of the House of Representatives*, to make suitable Provision for sending Commissioners on the Part of this Government, to join in the approaching Interview at *Albany*. . . .

Such an Union of Councils, besides the happy Effect it will probably have upon the Indians of the Six Nations, may lay a Foundation for a general One among all His Majesty's Colonies, for the mutual Support and Defence against the present dangerous Enterprizes of the *French* on every Side of them.

AN ANONYMOUS WRITER: "WE NEED A UNION OF COLONIES"

Although this letter is unsigned, its wording sounds similar to that used by Benjamin Franklin to support a colonial union. The letter paves the way for Franklin's "JOIN, or DIE" editorial and woodcut which appeared in the next Pennsylvania Gazette.

Pennsylvania Gazette (Philadelphia), 2 May 1754

To the Printers of the GAZETTE.

I am extremely sorry to hear that the Governments of Pennsylvania, and Maryland, have not view'd the Encroachments of the French in their proper light. . . . Unarm'd, and disunited as you are, will you be able to repel the Invaders, or prevent their ravaging & laying waste your Country, or hinder them from committing their too well known Barbarities on such of your Inhabitants as may fall within their Power? The evil Day may a while be put off, but sooner or later it will surely come, unless you rouse from the Lethargy you seem at present in, and make Use of those Means to protect yourselves which the Almighty has put in your Power; the most proper way of doing which is, to obstruct those Incendiaries, the French and their Indians, from settling your Frontiers. By a hearty Union of the Colonies, and proper Management, we might, with little Assistance from our Mother Country, not only dislodge the French from

Ohio, but from Quebeck itself. But to send three or four Hundred Men against five times their Number, can answer no other End than to expose us to the Contempt of our Indian Allies, who will think themselves obliged to quit the Interest of those that seem unable to protect them.

BENJAMIN FRANKLIN: "JOIN, OR DIE"

Benjamin Franklin used the news of George Washington's surrender of Fort Necessity, built where the Monongahela and Allegheny rivers join in western Pennsylvania, to issue a call for unity among colonies. To emphasize his point, Franklin added a woodcut of a disjointed rattle-snake to his essay. Each part of the snake represented a different section or colony. The message, "JOIN, or DIE," was simple and easy to understand. The French and Indians could easily defeat individual colonies or regions, but united the colonies were dangerous and could stop an invasion. Franklin's woodcut was the first use in America of the editorial cartoon, and its symbolism was quickly copied by other printers in America. Printers used the same disjointed snake cartoon to protest the Stamp Act in 1765 and English taxes, troop quartering, and trade embargoes prior to the Revolution.

Pennsylvania Gazette (Philadelphia), 9 May 1754

Friday last an Express arrived here from Major Washington, with Advice, that Mr. Ward, Ensign of Capt. Trent's Company, was compelled to surrender his small Fort in the Forks of Monogahela to the French, on the 17th past; who fell down from Venango with a Fleet of 360 Battoes and Canoes, upwards of 1000 Men, and 18 Pieces of Artillery, which they planted against the Fort; and Mr. Ward having but 44 Men, and no Cannon to make a proper Defence, was obliged to surrender on Summons, capitulating to march out with their Arms, &c. And they had accordingly joined Major Washington, who was advanced with three Companies of the Virginia Forces, as far as the New Store near the Allegheny Mountains, where the Men were employed in clearing a Road for the Cannon, which were every Day expected with Col. Fry, and the Remainder of the Regiment.—We hear farther, that some few of the English Traders on the Ohio escaped, but 'tis supposed the greatest Part are taken, with all their Goods, and Skins, to the Amount of near 20,000£. The Indian Chiefs, however, have dispatch'd Messages to Pennsylvania, and Virginia, desiring that the English would not be discouraged, but send out their Warriors to join them, and drive the French out of the Country before their fortify; otherwise the Trade will be lost, and, to their great Grief, an eternal Separation made between the Indians and their Brethren the English. 'Tis farther said, that besides the French that came down from Venango, another Body of near 400, is coming up the Ohio; and that 600 French

JOIN, or DIE. America's first editorial cartoon appeared in Benjamin Franklin's *Pennsylvania Gazette* on May 9, 1754. The woodcut of a rattlesnake cut into pieces that represented the American colonies warned Americans that if they did not join together to fight the French and their Indian allies, the colonists would die separately. Americans readily accepted the concept and used Franklin's snake again as a symbol of resistance to the Stamp Act in 1765 and as an emblem of resistance against Great Britain in the months before the start of the Revolution.

Indians, of the Chippaways and Ottaways, are coming down Siota River, from the Lake, to join them; and many more French are expected from Canada; the Design being to establish themselves, settle their Indians, build Forts just on the Back of our Settlements in all our Colonies; from which Forts, as they did from Crown-Point, they may send out their Parties to kill and scalp the Inhabitants, and ruin the Frontier Counties. Accordingly we hear, that the Back Settlers in Virginia, are so terrify'd by the Murdering and Scalping of the Family last Winter, and the Taking of this Fort, that they begin already to abandon their Plantations, and remove to Places of more Safety.—The Confidence of the French in this Undertaking seems well-grounded on the present disunited State of the British Colonies, and the extreme Difficulty of bringing so many different Governments and Assemblies to agree in any speedy and effectual Measures for our common Defence and Security; while our Enemies have the very great Advantage of being under one Direction, with one Council, and one Purse. Hence, and from the great Distance of Britain, they pre-

sume that they may with Impunity violate the most solemn Treaties subsisting between the two Crowns, kill, seize and imprison our Traders,
and confiscate their Effects at Pleasures (as they have done for several
Years past) murder and scalp our Farmers, with their Wives and Children,
and take an easy Possession of such Parts of the British Territory as they
find most convenient for them; which if they are permitted to do, must
end in the Destruction of the British Interest, Trade and Plantations in
America.

AN ANONYMOUS REPORT: "GOOD NEWS FROM ALBANY"

*Even though the leaders of the Six Nations arrived in Albany late and
left without promising support for the colonies, newspaper reports from
the Albany Congress generally placed a positive spin on negotiations
that had taken place there. In this account, the writer focuses on the
plan of union, not the Indian talks.*

New-York Mercury, 29 July 1754

BOSTON, *July 22*.

On Tuesday Evening came to Town, the Hon. Thomas Hutchinson,
Esq; Judge of Probate for this County, and one of the Commissioners at
the late Convention at Albany.—We are informed, That the Indians had
all left that City in a good Temper, but that a much smaller Number
attended the Interview, than heretofore has been usual:—That the Commissioners from the several Governments were unanimously of Opinion,
That an Union of the Colonies was absolutely necessary in order to defeat
the Schemes of the French.—That a Representation of the State of the
British Interest on this Continent, as it stands related to the French and
Indians, has been drawn up and approved of: And that a Plan of Union
has likewise been projected, and will, by the said Commissioners, be laid
before their respective Constituents.—All the Commissioners left Albany
the 12th Instant.

JAMES DE LANCEY: "WHY WE NEED A PLAN OF UNION"

*Most colonial governors, like most printers, favored a plan of union for
the colonies. In this speech, New York Governor James De Lancey explains to the New York assembly why such a plan is necessary and tells
the assemblymen that the Six Nations have pledged support, something
that was not completely truthful.*

New-York Mercury, 26 August 1754

The SPEECH of the Honourable JAMES DE LANCEY. . . .
   Gentlemen of the Council and General Assembly, . . .

It is evident, and needs no Arguments to prove, how conducive it must be to his Majesty's Service, and the general Welfare of all the Colonies, that we should be aiding and assisting to each other in Case of any Invasion. In this Situation, it is incumbent on all the Provinces to give the *Virginians* the Aid they stand in Need of. . . .

In Case of a War, we may expect great Assistance from the Six Nations of Indians: I left them in a very good Disposition at the late Treaty; but unless we put ourselves in a proper Posture of Defence, they will be unwilling to expose themselves to the Resentment of the Enemy. If we will protect them they will be ready to fight for us. The building of a Fort, and making a Settlement in the *Senecas* Country, is a Matter of great Consequences. . . .

The Things I have recommended to you, highly concern his Majesty's Honour, and the Interest and Safety of the Province. We may learn from the Relations published by the *French*, that they have long had a Design upon this Province. . . . They would gladly be Masters of a Country that must soon put it in their Power to reduce the Six Nations, and their numerous Allies, to an entire Dependence on them. By preventing this, you will go a great Length in defeating their Views, to subject the whole Continent to the *French* Yoke. . . .

When I was at *Albany*, I proposed to the Commissioners of the several Governments met there, the building Forts in proper Places, to cover the Northern Frontiers . . . that they were unwilling to enter upon the Consideration of these Matters, and formed a Plan for a general Union of all the Colonies, to be enforced by Act of Parliament; which, together with a Representation they prepared of the State of the Colonies, I shall order laid before you.

Gentlemen, I need not recommend Unanimity to you; the Matters laid before you are of such Importance, that they will naturally lead you to unite your utmost Endeavours to bring them to a happy Conclusion. It will give me the highest Satisfaction, if, while I have the Honour of Administration, something effectual be done to assist our Neighbours and to strengthen and secure ourselves. You will ever find me ready to give my Assent to any Bills for his Majesty's Service, and the Good of this Country.

JAMES DE LANCEY.

JONATHAN MAYHEW: "YE CANNOT BE SAVED FROM THE
STORM EXCEPT YE ARE AT UNION AMONGST YOURSELVES"

The fact that Jonathan Mayhew, a Congregational minister in Boston, preached this sermon with the governor in attendance affirms that Mayhew had some influence in Boston. The reverend, who emphasizes in his sermon the importance of friendly relations with Native Americans, considers a union of colonies the only miracle that can save America.

Pennsylvania Gazette (Philadelphia), 29 August 1754

EXTRACTS from Doctor MAYHEW's SERMON, *preach'd in the Audience of his Excellency* WILLIAM SHIRLEY, *Esq: Captain General, Governor and Commander in Chief . . . of the Province of Massachusetts-Bay. . . .*

THAT which seems, at present, chiefly to engage the Attention of the Publick, is the *British* Settlements on the Continent being now, in a Manner, encompassed by the *French.* And this is a Matter of much more serious Importance than it would be, were it not for the numerous Tribes of warlike Natives on our Back; who, it is to be fear'd, are more generally disposed to fall in with that Interest, than with ours. . . . Indeed, whoever has the Friendship of most of all, of these Natives, may probably, in Time, become Masters of this Part of the Continent. Whether we, or they who are now making such a resolute Push for it, Heaven knows! . . .

Their late Conduct may well alarm us; especially considering our Disunion, or at least Want of a sufficient Bond of Union, amongst ourselves: An Inconvenience, which, it is to be hop'd, we shall not always labour under. And whenever all our scatter'd Rays shall be drawn to a Point and proper Focus, they can scarce fail to consume and burn up these Enemies of our Peace, how faintly soever they may strike at present. What UNION can do, we need only look towards those Provinces, which are distinguished by the Name of THE UNITED, to know. But, in the mean time, each Government that considers its own true Interest, will undoubtedly concur in such Measures as are necessary and practicable for the common Safety. . . .

Ye cannot be saved from the Storm you are now threatened with, yea, which is already begun, except ye are at UNION AMONGST YOURSELVES; and exert your Strength together, for your common Interest. Upon this Condition, you are safe, even without a Miracle; otherwise, nothing short of one can save you.

HUGH GAINE: "THE PRESENT STATE OF THIS CONTINENT"

Printer Hugh Gaine published an essay on the state of North America describing the precarious situation facing America. At the end of the essay, Gaine appended the italicized comment included below. It urges unity of the colonies. Much of its language, which speaks of the blessings of liberty, foreshadows the revolutionary language of the 1770s and the Declaration of Independence.

New-York Mercury, 23 September 1754

I hope, and pray the Almighty, That the British Colonies on this continent, may cease impolitically and ungenerously to consider themselves as distinct States, with narrow, separate and independent Views, pursue temporary and ineffectual Expedients, and sink their public Wealth into private Emoluments;—that they will unite like Brother Protestants, and Brother Subjects . . . and secure to themselves and their Posterity, to the Ends of Time, the inestimable Blessings of Civil and Religious Liberty, and the Possession and Settlement of a great Country, rich in all the Fountains of human Liberty.

AN ANONYMOUS WRITER: "GOD'S BLESSING ON UNION"

Letters, essays, and comments of various sizes found their way into newspapers. This one-line prayer summed up many people's sentiments on the success of the Albany Plan of Union.

Maryland Gazette (Annapolis), 10 October 1754

May God of Heaven grant success for the plan for an union of the British Colonies on the Continent of America.

AGAINST THE ALBANY CONGRESS AND PLAN OF UNION

JAMES GLEN: "ASSESS YOUR OWN STRENGTH"

In the summer of 1754, South Carolina had yet to face the threat of French and Indian invasion as had Virginia and colonies to the north. To a certain extent, Governor James Glen and others in the colony felt that their alliance with the Cherokee would protect them. That is why the governor, in this speech, recommended that South Carolina allow all the colonies to calculate their military and monetary strength before committing to a union of the colonies.

South-Carolina Gazette (Charleston), 20 June 1754

CHARLES-TOWN, June 20.
   Mr. Speaker and Gentlemen, . . .
   Before the united Strength of these Colonies can be properly applied, it is absolutely necessary that the particular Force of each respective Colony should be known and ascertained: By the Force of a Colony I understand, their Ability to defend themselves, and to contribute to the common Defence, or to the Offence of the common Enemy. The Strength of a Colony is chiefly to be computed from its Numbers and Wealth, Men and Money being now the Nerves and Sinews of War in all Countries; and therefore, before a mutual Agreement can be entered into by the

Colonies, for their common Defence, or, in other Words, before such a League can rightly be formed, these capital Points must first be fixed; otherwise any Succours that may be occasionally sent from any particular Province, will be of little Service, and we shall gradually consume ourselves in vain, and waste our Strength.

James Glen

PHILOPATRIS: "OUR OWN DEFENSE"

Not everyone believed a plan of union was needed to stop the French. The anonymous Philopatris was one writer who thought that New York could better muster money, ammunition, and militia to protect itself than depend on the same from all the colonies.

New-York Mercury, 16 September 1754, Supplement

Mr. Gaine,
Please to give the inclosed a Place in your Paper, and you'll oblige your constant Reader, and a Lover of his Country.
PHILOPATRIS.

THERE never perhaps was a Time, when it more concern'd this Province to be active in its own Defence, than the Present: and yet, perhaps, it never was less so than now: While the *French*, those persidious and implacable Enemies off ours, are, for aught we know, aiming at the Empire of *North-America*, and contriving Schemes for the Destruction of this and the neighbouring Provinces, we sit indolent and careless, or rather lie asleep, in an inglorious Security. . . . Are not the Encroachments of the *French* and *Indians* on our Frontiers, sufficient to awaken our Apprehensions? and especially as there is Reason to believe the *French* use those very Nations of *Indians* as willing Instruments in their Designs of Darkness, which are hir'd by the Province from Time to Time, at so great an Expence, to wear a Mask of pretended Amity and Friendship, which they may put off at Pleasure. The frequent Conferences with them necessary to prevent their throwing off the Mask, and acting as professed Enemies, is a sufficient Evidence, that their highest Principle of Action is Interest, and that they will act for those in whose Service they see the greatest Prospect of Advantage. . . . So wretchedly are we over-reach'd and abus'd in our Treaties with them, by their deceitful Pretences of Friendship, and so far are the *Indians* initiated in the hidden Mysteries of *French* and infernal Perfidy! Are these Allies, *My Countrymen*, that deserve so much Respect as we show them, or so much Expence as we throw away upon them? No, *My Friends*, they are Enemies we caress, and Serpents we nourish in our Bosom. Should I hire a Man from whom I was under Apprehensions for my Life, if he killed me, at least to do it privately, lest I should be capable of Self-defence; surely I should act a very ridiculous and imprudent Part: Yet imprudent as it would be, it is the Part we have long, in some Sort, been acting, as tho' faithless Allies were better than none at all. What we spend upon those persidious Wretches, would be perhaps sufficient to defend us against all their Attempts; whereas now it promotes them: Thus we put a Rod into the Hands of others, and like Fools, receive the Blows, a just Punishment for our Credulity! Why then should we value their fallicious Friendship at so high a Rate? Why should we be so fearful, least they should declare against us? For however friendly they may sometimes appear, they are but Enemies in Disguise, and therefore more dangerous than the *French* themselves. . . .

In short, whatever others may think, for my part, I am under no less Apprehensions from the *Friend Indians*, than from the *French* themselves; and hope some effectual Measures will be taken by the Government, to defend the Province from both; and I think the least that ought to be done, with respect to the *Indians*, is to be upon our Guard and keep a watchful and jealous Eye upon them. . . . PHILOPATRIS.

NEW JERSEY GENERAL ASSEMBLY: "NO PLAN OF UNION"

New Jersey Governor Jonathan Belcher had presented the plan of union to the assembly and requested passage of the proposal. Here, the assembly responds to the governor after voting down the plan. The response is typical of colonial assemblies in the reasoning given for not supporting the union plan.

Boston Gazette, or Weekly Advertiser, 5 November 1754

NEW-JERSEY,
To His Excellency JONATAAN [*sic*] BELCHER, *Esq; Captain General Governour and Commander in Chief in and over His Majesty's Province of* New-Jersey, *and Territories thereon depending in* America, *Chancellor and Vice Admiral in the same, &c.*

The Humble ADDRESS of the Representatives of said Province, in General Assembly met.

May it please your Excellency,

WE his Majesty's most dutiful and loyal Subjects, the Representatives of the Colony of *New-Jersey*, in General Assembly met, beg Leave to acquaint your Excellency, that we have taken the Incroachments of the *French* (with the Indians) upon His Majesty's Territories, into our most serious Consideration.

We can truly say, we want not Arguments to convince us of the absolute Necessity of the strictest Union among all his Majesty's Provinces and Colonies for the Preservation of the Whole; and on our Part have endeavoured to cultivate such an Union, by contributing our Endeavours in the best Manner the Circumstances of this Colony will admit. Your Excellency must be sensible, that the Scarcity of a Currency in this Colony at this Time, makes it very difficult for the Inhabitants to exert themselves as fully as the Exigency of the Times seems to require: And therefore, we cannot doubt, but the Measures we have fallen upon, not only to give a handsome Sum to the King's Use at present, but to provide a Fund to do it hereafter, in Case of a like Necessity, will prove agreeable to your Excellency, and all concerned. . . .

We have also taken into Consideration the Plan for the Union of the *British* Colonies on the Continent of *America*, as agreed on in the late Congress at *Albany*; and are sorry to say, that we find Things in it, which, if carried into Practice, would affect our Constitution in its very Vitals; and for the Reason we hope and believe they will never be countenanced by a *British* Legislature.

ROBERT DINWIDDIE: "YOU LEAVE YOUR COUNTRY IN DISTRESS"

Virginia Governor Robert Dinwiddie initiated warnings about French and Indian encroachment in 1753. His speeches were filled with imagery of brutality and death for Virginians at the hands of the enemy. In this speech, he responds to the Virginia assembly's rejection of the Plan of Union, intimating that Virginia was leaving its fellow countrymen—all Americans from New England to Georgia—in distress.

South-Carolina Gazette (Charleston), 19 December 1754

The Council of Virginia *having rejected a bill, on the 4th of September last, intitled, an act for raising the sum of* 10,000 *l. for the protection of his majesty's subjects.* . . .

His honour the governor was pleased to prorogue the assembly by the following speech.

Gentlemen of the Council, Mr. Speaker, and Gentlemen of the House of Burgesses,

THE impending danger . . . of the French; their threats and depredations, were the only motives of calling you together at this time. And as the lives, liberties and properties of your constituents are in such imminent hazard, I did not in the least doubt, but that you would, before this, have strengthened my hands with proper supply, to frustrate their malicious intentions: and especially, when I receiv'd from you such strong and repeated assurances, that you *were determin'd, on your parts, to withstand the impending danger, and to pursue every measure in your power, to defeat these pernicious attempts of your enemies.* I though I might readily admit pleasing hopes, that *you would effectually provide for your country's preservation, and convince the world, that you had nothing more at heart, than a zealous discharge of your duty to the best of kings, and the sincerest regard for your country's welfare.*

How great then, Gentlemen, must be my surprise, and with what amazement must that country and the world see such high expectations cast down so low! See you called upon in the day of your country's distress; hear you declaring your knowledge of her danger, and professing the most ardent zeal for her service; yet find these declarations only an unavailing flourish of words; and that, inconsistent with them, and the purposes of your meeting, you withhold your aid, and thereby leave the enemy at full liberty to perpetrate their destructive and unjust designs. . . .

QUESTIONS

1. What reasons did Americans give for wanting alliances with Native Americans?
2. How did supporters of the Albany Congress and Plan of Union use fear to persuade?
3. Why do you think the commissioners who attended the Albany Congress and printers supported the Plan of Union while most colonial legislatures opposed it?
4. What do you think made Franklin's woodcut editorial cartoon, "JOIN, or DIE," so powerful for colonial Americans?
5. What reasons did South Carolina's governor and the New Jersey assembly give for opposing the Plan of Union?
6. Why did Philopatris think the Albany Congress or any such meetings or treaties with Native Americans were futile?
7. Knowing that most of the early French and Indian attacks had taken place either in Virginia or in territories claimed by the colony, what valid reasons could the colony's assembly have had for refusing to allocate funds for the defense of all colonies?

NOTES

1. *New-York Mercury*, 8 April 1754, 3; and *Pennsylvania Gazette* (Philadelphia), 11 April 1754, 2.

2. Benjamin Franklin, "The Albany Plan of Union," in *Benjamin Franklin, Writings*, ed. J. A. Leo Lemay (New York: Library of America, 1987), 378.

3. Franklin, writing thirty-four years later in his autobiography, asserted that the Plan of Union was not permitted by the British government, which feared American military growth. His comment, however, may have been clouded by the Revolution, and it ignores the fact that it was first rejected by the assemblies.

CHAPTER 15

The Cherokee War, 1759–1761

The environment provided many advantages as well as hardships to the colonists who came to America. Sometimes, both were found in the same source. That is exactly how many whites viewed the Native Americans who inhabited North America before the arrival of Europeans and who in the eighteenth century lived in a precarious relationship with whites.

In 1759 the Cherokees, long the allies of the colonists, entered into war with colonists of South Carolina. This war, known as the Cherokee War, lasted from the fall of 1759 to the fall of 1761. The war was the largest single concerted effort made by an individual Indian nation against white colonists during the eighteenth century; the Cherokees were the largest single group of Native Americans not bound together in a confederation of tribes. In fact, one writer to newspapers estimated that the Cherokee nation had three times the members of the famous Six Nations confederacy of New York.[1]

Cherokee sovereignty, along with that of the Six Nations, had been unmatched in the colonial era. When the French and Indian War began in 1754 (see Chapter 14), Southern colonists had been quick to point out that the Cherokees were their best defense against invasion. As one Virginian said, "[C]ould we secure the Friendship . . . of the *Cherokees* alone . . . they would undoubtedly prove the best Defence of our Frontiers." Yet the same writer also pointed out that the Cherokees could be the most dangerous of adversaries. "Suppose the *Cherokees*, break down upon us like a Torrent," he warned, "how terrible would be the Consequences! what Horror and Consternation, what inhuman Murders, Tortures and Streams of Blood, would fill our Land!"[2]

This view of Cherokees as a group to fear and a group with which to seek peaceful relations forms the foundation for understanding the colonial–Native American relationship. Colonists used Indians for protection and trade, but most often, whites viewed Native peoples as "the Sculking Indian Enemy," an often-used phrase to describe Indians in newspapers. The Cherokees and the Cherokee War demonstrate how whites could view Native Americans as both.

The reasons for the Cherokee War were complicated. The Cherokees represented one of many sovereign Native American nations in America. Each carried on political relations with individual British colonies and other Native tribes. Old animosities between the Cherokee and Creek may have helped precipitate the war, but it was mainly the relationship between whites and Cherokees that led to the war. The British quickly sought Cherokee assistance at the beginning of the French and Indian War in 1754, and groups of Cherokees fought for the British through the capitulation of Canada in 1760.

In 1758 and 1759, however, a number of atrocities occurred to Cherokees returning from fighting the French and their Native American allies in the middle colonies and in the Ohio Valley. In one, about forty Cherokees returning to South Carolina were ambushed and scalped by whites in Virginia. The Indians were killed for the bounties placed on "French Indian" scalps by the colony. No repercussions were taken against the offending whites nor apologies offered. The Cherokees also came to believe they were fighting and dying in vain to preserve the colonial frontier from the French. The Cherokee had been successful in their efforts. Now they were losing their hunting grounds to the same colonists they had protected. Whites were moving into Cherokee territory and claiming the land for themselves.[3]

A peace treaty between the Cherokees and South Carolina was signed in November 1761. Central to the peace effort was the work of a Cherokee leader known to colonials as the Little Carpenter (see Chapter 4). With the war over, many Cherokees worked to assimilate the ways of Europeans and to live in harmony with white Americans. While their efforts were probably more successful than many other Native Americans, almost all Cherokees and other Southern native nations were forced into American territory west of the Mississippi River in the 1830s under the policies of President Andrew Jackson.

The readings in this chapter look not only at the Cherokee War but at the fear of Native Americans that existed throughout the colonial era. It contrasts this fear with positive newspaper accounts of Indians. As one might expect, negative articles, letters, and essays greatly outnumbered those that portrayed Indians in a positive way. Usually, when Native Americans were seen positively, it was because Indians could be of use to whites.

The first selection that depicts Native Americans as a group to be feared is part of a body of literature that developed in America in the late seventeenth century known as captivity literature. These writings, usually first-person accounts of people kidnaped by Indians who later escaped, evoked brutality and horror. Captivity literature, as well as most accounts of Indian atrocities that appeared in newspapers, was graphic and described torture in vivid terms. The letter describing the torture was written by an unknown trader who was allowed to view it and leave.

The second selection is a speech made by Virginia Governor Robert Dinwiddie. It describes what white settlers in the backcountry of the colonies could expect if Native Americans went to war against them. This speech appeared in newspapers throughout America. The third is a description of capture and torture of South Carolina soldiers during the Cherokee War.

In the fourth selection, a description of brutal attacks and murders in Massachusetts is described. Whites moved onto lands previously reserved for Indians even while France and England were going to war and tribes were choosing sides. In the next reading, Massachusetts Lieutenant Governor Spencer Phips places a bounty of up to £100 on scalps of Native Americans. Such bounties were posted by most colonial governments at some time during the era in a effort to eradicate Native people within the area of colonial jurisdiction. These decrees demonstrate how the fear of Indians could lead to calls for genocide of entire tribes. The remaining selections on fear of Native Americans offer news stories and commentary on white perceptions of Indians and how fear of their activities was increased by newspapers.

The section on friendship and positive accounts of Native Americans begins with two reports on Cherokee assistance to colonials. The first comes from the Tuscarora War, which began in 1711 in North Carolina, and tells how 1,200 Cherokees enlisted to fight with the whites. The second account, from South Carolina, again describes how the Cherokee fought other Native Americans to protect white settlers. The third selection, a speech made by South Carolina Governor James Glen, addresses the significance of peaceful relationships with Native nations. The fourth selection, from the Revolutionary War era, relates how Native tribes in New England were prepared to join Americans to fight the British. The final two selections discuss Native Americans in relationship to their inclination to accept Christianity.

FEAR OF NATIVE AMERICANS

AN ANONYMOUS WRITER: "TORTURE BY SHAWNEE INDIANS"

Trade between Native Americans and whites was important from the beginning of the European colonization of North America. This account of Shawnees torturing to death a prisoner was witnessed by a white trader. Benjamin Franklin did not omit any of the brutality of the encounter, passing on all the details to readers, which no doubt only increased fear of Native Americans as whites moved farther west into areas principally inhabited by Indians.

Pennsylvania Gazette (Philadephia), 24 February 1729 (1730)

PHILADELPHIA: The Shawana Indians . . . had taken three Prisoners: One of them was an old Man, whom they knock'd on the Head because he was not able to Travel as fast they; another made his Escape from them in their Return; the third they brought home; and on the 16th of January past, about 3 Hours before Day, they made the Prisoner Sing and Dance for some Time, while six Gun Barrels were heating red hot in the Fire; after which they fastned him to a Post in the Cabin, and with these Gun Barrels they began to burn the Soals of the poor Wretches Feet until the Bones appeared, and continued burning him by slow Degrees up to his Privites, where they took much Pains; then they proceeded to burn him up to his Arm-pits after the same Manner. This Barbarity they continued about six Hours, and then, notwithstanding his Feet were in such a Condition, they drove him to a Stake about 20 Perches off the Cabin beforementioned, to which they fastned him standing, and stuck Splinters of Pine all over his Body, and put Fire to them. Upon this one of our Traders ask'd if he might give him a Dram, which being granted, he brought him half a Pint of Rum, and the poor Creature drank it off greedily. In the next Place they scalp'd him and threw hot Embers on his Head. Then they loosed him from the Post, and threw him into a great Fire made for the Purpose, and instantly hall'd him out again, and threw Water on him. Thus they served him several Times. At last they ran two Gun Barrels, one after the other, red hot up his Fundament, upon which he expired. . . .

This Account I had from a Spectator, in whose Relation there are several Circumstances worth Notice, which I must omit at present, having scarce Time to write this. I am, Sir, Yours, &c.

P.S. They cut off his Thumbs and offer'd them him to eat, and pluck'd off all his Nails.

ROBERT DINWIDDIE: "THE WELFARE OF ALL THE COLONIES ON THIS CONTINENT"

As confrontations with the French and Indians increased in 1754, Virginia Governor Robert Dinwiddie felt he had to rouse Virginians and other Americans to action. In a speech reprinted throughout America, the governor described what was happening as the French turned hostile Native Americans loose on colonists in the backcountry. While Dinwiddie uses some graphic language, he prefers to sketch the outline of Indian brutality and let the hearer or reader imagine what else might happen.

New-York Mercury, 25 March 1754

NOTHING less than a very important Concern could have induced me to call you together again . . . but the Dignity of the Crown of Great-Britain, the Welfare of all the Colonies on this Continent, and more especially of this Dominion, engage me to have your Advice and Assistance in an Affair of the greatest Consequences. . . .

Think you see the Infant torn from the unavailing Struggles of the distracted Mother, the Daughters ravished before the Eyes of their wretched Parents; and then, with Cruelty and Insult, butchered and scalped. Suppose the horrid Scene compleated, and the whole Family, Man, Wife, and Children (as they were) murdered and scalped by these relentless Savages, and then torn in Pieces, and in Part devoured by wild Beasts, for whom they were left a Prey by their more brutal Enemies. . . .

Consider the bloody Villains, thievishly lurking about a Man's Plantation, and where they dare not attack like Men, basely, like Vermin, stealing and carrying away, the helpless Infant, that happened to wander, though but a little Distance from his Father's Threshold.

I assure you, Gentlemen, these Insults, on our Sovereign's Protection, and Barbarities on our Fellow Subjects, make deep Impressions on my Heart; and I doubt not, as you must hear them with Horror and Resentment, but you will enable me, by a full and sufficient Supply, to exert the most vigorous Dignity of our Sovereign; to drive away these cruel and treacherous Invaders of your Properties, and Destroyers of your Families.

AN ANONYMOUS REPORT: "THE TORTURE AND DEATH OF CAPTAIN DEMERÉ"

Raymond Demeré was in charge of South Carolina forces at Fort Loudon, in the colony's backcountry. Since the war had begun, whites and Native Americans had committed numerous atrocities in the region surrounding the fort. Indians watched as their dead were chopped up and fed to dogs, their scalps run up the flag pole. Cherokees, likewise, per-

formed similar acts designed to hurt their enemy psychologically. When Demeré's party was surprised outside the fort, the outnumbered whites fought but were no match for the Cherokees. Demeré suffered for his leadership role, and his execution was described for readers of the South-Carolina Gazette.

South-Carolina Gazette (Charleston), 4 October 1760

Charlestown: On the 10th of August in the morning, as a serjeant and 12 men were beginning to march and the rest were packing up their bundles to follow, a soldier from the advance guard discovered many Indians and gave the alarm; upon this capt. Stuart ran towards the river or brook, and called to the men to stand to their arms; the Indians in the grass immediately fired within 60 yards, and put our men, who were unprepared for such a piece of treachery, into the utmost confusion.— Capt. Demeré received two wounds the first volley, was directly scalped, and the Indians made him dance about for their diversion some time, after which they chopped off one hand or arm, than the other, and so his legs, &c. using the most shocking barbarities on the bodies of others of our people.

AN ANONYMOUS REPORT: "CANNIBALISM"

Most Americans probably never grew accustomed to newspaper reports or books published about Native American cruelty. When Indians killed a captain, drank his blood, and ate from his body, readers no doubt cringed; however, the Indians probably regarded the act as a means of gaining the strength of a brave warrior. Massachusetts reacted to such acts with the decree found in the entry following this one.

Boston Evening-Post, 29 July 1745

Boston: The Enemies had 2 kill'd and as many wounded in the Engagement, which being over, the Indians cut open Capt. Donahew's Breast, and suck'd his Blood, and hack'd and mangled his Body in a most inhuman and barbarous Manner, and then eat a great part of his Flesh. They also suck'd the Blood and mangled the Bodies of the other Slain, after which they carried their Prisoners to Menis, where they were about to kill and eat Mr. Picket, but he being acquainted with some of the French Inhabitants, they so far stood his Friend . . . as to procure his Liberty for a Sum of Money.

SPENCER PHIPS: "£100 FOR AN INDIAN SCALP"

Massachusetts Lieutenant Governor Spencer Phips and the Massachusetts legislature approved offering money for scalps of all Native Americans twelve years of age and older during King George's War and after acts such as the one described in the previous reading. Fighting in America started in 1740 between the French and English with Native Americans fighting as well. In this announcement, Phips essentially declares war on Indians in Massachusetts.

Boston Evening-Post, 26 August 1745

WHEREAS the Indians of the Penobscot and Norridgewack Tribes, and other Eastern Indians, as also the Indians inhabiting the French Territories, and Parts adjacent thereto, have by their Violation of their solemn Treaties, and by open Hostilities committed against His Majesty's Subjects of this Province, oblig'd Me, with the Advice of His Majesty's Council, to declare War against them;

And whereas the General Assembly in their last Session, have Voted, For the Encouragement of any Company, Party, or Person singly, of His Majesty's Subjects belonging to and residing within this Province, who shall voluntarily, and at their own proper Cost and Charge, go out and kill a Male Indian of the Age of twelve Years or upwards of such Eastern Indians, or such others as may be found with them at any Time so long as the War may continue, and produce the Scalp in Evidence of his Death, the Sum of One hundred Pounds, in Bills of Credit on this Province of the new Tenor; and the Sum of One hundred and five Pounds in said Bills for any Male of like Age who shall be taken Captive, and deliver'd to the Order of the Captain General, to be at the Disposal and for the Use of the Government; and the Sum of Fifty Pounds in said Bills for each Woman, the like Sum for Children under the Age of twelve Years kill'd in Fight, and Fifty five Pounds in said Bills for such when taken Prisoners, and the Plunder; And to such Person or Persons this Province shall provide Ammunition and Provisions.

AN ANONYMOUS REPORT: "THE SCULKING INDIAN ENEMY"

One way that newspapers described Native Americans was with the phrase "Sculking Indian Enemy." This 1707 account is a straightforward and typical description of what many colonists faced daily as they continued to move into Indian lands to live.

Boston News-Letter, 6 October 1707

Piscataqua, Octob. 2. We are still infested with the Sculking Indian Enemy, who on Sabbath Day Evening attacked a group of men. They scalped two. Four of the Inhabitants well knowing the Enemys walk, waylaid them.

AN ANONYMOUS REPORT: "THE MEYER FAMILY ATTACKED"

The family of Frederick Meyer was a typical one in colonial America— father, mother, and children. The attack on the family from the Reading area of Pennsylvania was also typical for the French and Indian pe-riod—women were taken, men killed, and babies destroyed.

Pennsylvania Gazette (Philadelphia), 7 July 1757

Extract of another Letter from Reading, July 3.

"Last Wednesday Morning, Frederick Meyer, of Bern Township . . . was killed and scalped by 3 or 4 Indians. He had his Son, of about 10 Years, in his Arms running away from them, when he received a Ball through his Body, which lodged in one of the Child's Hands. His Wife was scalped, and three of his Children taken away. The Son shot in the Hand was left, and is safe. His Baby, at the Mother's Breast, was thrown into a Creek. . . . Last Friday, three Women and four Children were killed and scalped in Tulpehocken, and were this Day buried.

AN ANONYMOUS REPORT: "INDIANS DROWN"

Even after most Native American–colonial fighting ended in the sea-board regions of America, the eradication of Indians was still consid-ered a good thing by many. In this brief statement, one can see the attitude of most whites concerning what should happen to Indians.

Green & Russell's Boston Post-Boy & Advertiser, 15 July 1765

We hear from Albany that 6 Indians in a bark canoe, attempting to cross the ferry at Green Bush, were overset, & four of them *happily* drowned.

AN ANONYMOUS REPORT: "FEAR OF INDIAN TROUBLE"

In 1770 the memory of the French and Indian and Cherokee wars was still fresh in most Americans' minds. When unconfirmed reports of In-dian uprisings in Virginia reached colonial capitals, reactions were sim-ilar to this report; people would prefer a war with a European nation to war with Native Americans.

Boston Evening-Post, 20 August 1770

WILMINGTON: An express went thro' this province a few days ago, with dispatches from the Governor of Virginia to our Governor, and the Lieut. Governor of South Carolina, to notify them that a number of In-dians had destroyed 20 or 30 families on the back parts of Virginia. If this is fact we shall soon have employment for our province. It would have given us more pleasure to have heard of a war with France and Spain, than with those Savages.

AN ANONYMOUS REPORT: "CHEROKEE PRISONERS"

During the Cherokee War, South Carolina and the Cherokees sometimes exchanged prisoners. In this case, Raymond Demeré paid to get a woman and children from the Indians. The comment on treatment of prisoners here made such activities all the more urgent.

South-Carolina Gazette (Charleston), 7 June 1760

CHARLESTOWN: LAST Saturday Night the Negro Abram, arrived in Town with the Dispatches he brought from Fort Loudoun and Fort Prince-George. . . . Capt. Demeré had ransomed a Woman and three Children from the Indians, but the poor Woman had been so cruelly used that she died soon after: . . . The Indians burn all their Men Prisoners; they had lately burnt Six at Conasatchee (the Sugar-Town) amongst them John Downing, whose Arms and Legs they first cut off, and otherwise tortured him.

FRIENDSHIP AND POSITIVE ACCOUNTS OF NATIVE AMERICANS

AN ANONYMOUS REPORT: "CHEROKEES ASSIST COLONISTS"

When more and more whites moved into North Carolina early in the eighteenth century, the largest eastern tribe of Indians there, the Tuscaroras, fought back. Despite the fact that the Cherokees went to war with whites in 1759, this Native American nation generally sought peaceful relations with whites and often fought with and for colonials. Here, the Cherokees help defeat the Tuscaroras by sending 1,200 warriors to protect the North Carolinians.

Boston News-Letter, 11 May 1713

South Carolina, April the 16th. W are informed that col. James Moore, who went from hence some time past against the Indian Enemy with a few white Men and about 1200 Indians, made an attack upon the above-said Fort, which the Indian Enemy had best fortified and man'd, having drain'd all their other Forts but one, on purpose to try our Courage and Resolution: at which place he had a long and bloody brush with the Enemy, which continued without Intermission from the 20th of the said March at ten of the Clock till the 22d in the Morning, during which attack Col. Moore had 22 white Men kill'd of which Capt. Canty was one, and 26 wounded, none of the English that are alive but had shot through their Cloaths and others in their Bodies, he had also 36 Indians kill'd and 58 wounded. And on the Enemies side there were 640 kill'd, and we have taken 160 Prisoners and the Fort, so that we hope the heart of the Tuskeraro war is broken; The Indians have got a great many slaves, but the white Men none."

AN ANONYMOUS REPORT: "MORE CHEROKEE HELP"

In 1716 only one newspaper existed in America. The fact that the Boston News-Letter *shared information such as that below and above with readers is important in understanding how whites viewed Native Americans and needed their assistance, especially in the first part of the century.*

Boston News-Letter, 5 November 1716

South Carolina, October 4th. Three thousand men of the Charaky Indians are going to War with our Enemy Indians and about six week agoe, we sent them Ammunition in Pereaugers [a type of boat], but do not yet hear of its being arriv'd.

JAMES GLEN: "THE IMPORTANCE OF CHEROKEE FRIENDSHIP"

When the French and Indians began attacking colonial settlements in the Ohio Valley in 1754, South Carolina Governor James Glen realized the important role the Cherokees had played in what happened to his colony. Here, Glen proclaims friendship with them in an effort to ensure continued peace for South Carolina.

South-Carolina Gazette (Charleston), 22 January 1754

The SPEECH *of His Excellency* JAMES GLEN, *Esq; Governor in Chief, and Captain-General in and over His Majesty's Province of South-Carolina. . . .*

The Friendship of the *Indian* Nations around us is of the greatest Importance, and therefore to be cultivated with the greatest Care; and I can assure you, that the Attention given by the Governor and Council, to all *Indian* Affairs in general, is equal to the Importance of them.

The *Cherokee Indians* have, for many Years past, earnestly prayed to have Forts built in their Country, and the Governor, in the Presence, and at the Desire, of both Houses of Assembly, has promised that a Fort should be built there. . . .

At the same Time I acquaint you, that the Accounts I have from all our other *Indians*, are very agreeable, and breathe nothing but Peace and Friendship.

AN ANONYMOUS REPORT: "MOHAWKS JOIN AMERICA AGAINST ENGLAND"

War with Native Americans east of the Appalachian Mountains may have nearly disappeared after the French and Indian War, but Indians still lived there. When the Revolution began, the colonies sought Native American assistance just as they had done during the French and Indian War.

Massachusetts Gazette (and Boston Post-Boy), 25 May 1775

The Indian King at Stockbridge, was lately at Col. Easton's of this Town, and said there, that the Mohawks had not only gave Liberty to the Stockbridge Indians to join us, but had sent them a Belt, denoting that they would hold 500 Men in Readiness to join us immediately on the first Notice; and that the said Solomons hold an Indian Post in actual Readiness to run with the News as soon as they shall be wanted. Those Indians would be of great Service to you should the King's Troops march out of Boston, as some think they undoubtedly will, upon the Arrival of their Recruits, and give us Battle.

BENJAMIN HARRIS: "A DAY OF THANKSGIVING"

The fact that Native Americans accepted Christianity was important, especially in the seventeenth and early eighteenth centuries. In this story published in Benjamin Harris' Publick Occurrences, *"Christianized Indians" praise God for good crops. Converting Indians to Christianity was seen as one important part of colonization. Christianity did not work well with the Native American lifestyle, however. If the Indians could not be converted, many whites came to believe that perhaps they should be destroyed.*

Publick Occurrences Both Forreign and Domestick (Boston), 25 September 1690

Christianized Indians in some parts of Plimouth, have newly appointed a day of Thanksgiving to God for his Mercy in supplying their extream and pinching Necessities under their late want of Corn, & for His giving them now a prospect of a very Comfortable Harvest. Their Example is worth Mentioning.

AN ANONYMOUS REPORT: "NATIVE AMERICAN PREACHES IN BOSTON"

Acceptance of the Gospel, as mentioned above, was seen as central to relationships between Native Americans and whites by some colonists.

Here, an Indian who preached in Boston is ready to join missionaries as they visit tribes, and the success of the mission was no doubt greatly enhanced by the presence of the preaching Native American.

Boston Evening-Post, 17 June 1765

BOSTON: Since our last the Rev'd Mr. Samson Occum, an Indian educated at the Rev. Mr. Wheelock's School, preached twice at the Reve. Mr. Moorhead's Meeting House in this town, to the general Acceptance of the Hearers; at the last of which a handsome Collection was made for the Benefit of the School, and to assist several Missionaries now ready to go among the Indians of the Six Nations, who appear well disposed to be instructed in Christianity.—Several private Donations have also been given by some Gentlemen here, to help forward that good design.

QUESTIONS

1. How could Native Americans be both feared and seen as a necessity to survival by the colonials?
2. If you were a colonist considering moving from a town on the Atlantic seaboard into the backcountry of a colony, how might newspaper stories that described in exact details atrocities committed by Native Americans affect you?
3. What role do you think Christianity played in white Americans' perceptions of Native Americans?
4. From the readings, how likely do you think it is that colonials could have defeated enemies during and before the French and Indian War without Native American assistance? Explain.
5. On what political agendas and hidden agendas may Virginia Governor Dinwiddie and Massachusetts Lieutenant Governor Phips have based their speeches and decrees?
6. Do you think the perceptions of Native Americans in the eighteenth century affect our concepts of Native peoples today?

NOTES

1. *South-Carolina Gazette* (Charleston), 31 July 1755, 1.
2. *Pennsylvania Gazette* (Philadelphia), 17 March 1757, 1.
3. *South-Carolina Gazette* (Charleston), 22 September 1759, 3.

CHAPTER 16

The Stamp Act Crisis, 1765–1766

In 1764 Great Britain faced a massive debt. For years, it had been involved in the Seven Years' War, a world war with France, but the Peace of Paris in 1763 officially ended the confrontation. Fighting had taken place on every continent or adjacent body of water except Antarctica and Australia. Now it was time to pay the war's expenses. Most of the fighting in the war took place in Great Britain's colonial possessions, and many governmental leaders believed that those who were protected by British troops and sailors should now pay for the expense of that protection.

America's part in the Seven Years' War, known as the French and Indian War, began in 1754, two years before the official beginning of the Seven Years' War. American colonies, before the end of that year, had already pledged thousands of pounds to protect the colonies. New York, for example, passed an act to raise £5,000 to protect the colonies of Pennsylvania and Virginia,[1] and North Carolina's assembly voted to spend £12,000 to protect colonial interests in the Ohio Valley.[2] Even earlier, Maryland had levied a tax on tobacco to create a stockpile of weapons and ammunition because its leaders believed war with France was imminent.[3] Similar acts for raising money and assessing taxes took place in nearly all the colonies.

By 1763, the colonies had spent hundreds of thousands of pounds on the war and these debts had to be paid. But the British Lord of the Treasury, George Grenville, also wanted Americans to pay their fair share in reducing Great Britain's debt, which had doubled since 1754. Americans felt that Grenville's proposed taxes represented a double burden on them because they were already responsible for the debts incurred by the colonies. Despite colonial objections, Parliament approved Grenville's taxation proposal and passed the Sugar Act of 1764, which placed a duty on sugar but lowered the tax on Americans' other sweetener, molasses.

The Lord of the Treasury was not finished. He wanted to levy another tax, one which he thought the colonists would not object to strenuously. After all, they, themselves, had passed similar taxes in 1755 and 1757 to raise revenue for military expenditures. Grenville set out to find out how the stamp tax had been handled in the colonies, when New York and Massachusetts had placed temporary taxes on paper goods during the French and Indian War. He asked one of his deputies to write to a Boston official and ask, "What difficulties have occurr'd in executing it? What objections may be made to it, and what additional provisions must be made to those in force here?"[4]

On March 22, 1765, Parliament passed the Stamp Act. It placed a tax "upon every paper, commonly called a pamphlet, and upon every newspaper." It taxed "every advertisement to be contained in any gazette, news paper, or other paper." And, it taxed almanacs with the tax on each printed item based on its size and number of pages.[5] The Stamp Act was to become law in America on November 1, and each colony was to have a stamp official, appointed by Britain, to oversee the sale, distribution, and use of the stamps.

While the Stamp Act would have an effect upon whoever bought a printed item, the direct burden of the tax was placed on printers. Newspapers had grown in numbers and popularity because of the need to know about the French and Indian War. Now, printers used their increased circulation numbers and their publications to fight the tax. Opposition to the Stamp Act by printers was universal. It was one of the few times when all printers agreed, and the language of the opposition took on a new sound. No longer were most printers referring to those living in America as British citizens; they spoke of themselves as Americans, or free born sons of America.

Following the example of printers, civic leaders joined in the protests against the Stamp Act. Ministers preached against the tax. Merchants organized boycotts of British imports. Ordinary citizens hanged effigies of stamp sellers in the streets. Legislatures called the act an affront to liberty. Printers used all of these in their newspapers to arouse opposition to the Stamp Act.

As November 1 approached, printers proposed bolder actions. As a result, stamp sellers were forced to resign. Some were tarred and feathered. Printers talked of suspending publication or going out of business. Some Philadelphia printers hit upon another idea. They decided to publish their newspapers with thick, black borders surrounding the stories.

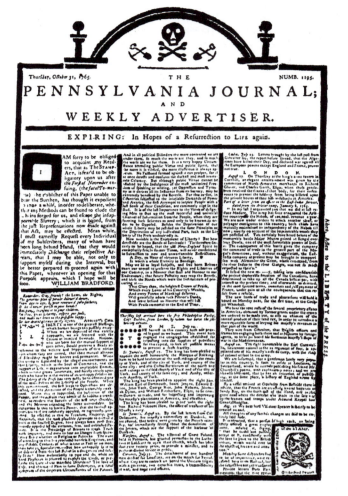

In Mourning. On the day before the Stamp Act was to go into effect in America, Philadelphia printer William Bradford published the *Pennsylvania Journal* with black borders surrounding all of the stories. Black borders were used when noting the death of important people. For Bradford and others, American freedom was dying. Britain had passed taxes on all paper to help pay for its debts from the French and Indian War. To represent the stamp, Bradford used a skull and crossbones, which was placed in the lower right corner where a real stamp would go the next week. Bradford and many other printers vowed not to print newspapers if the paper carried a tax.

Black borders in newspapers were used to signify the death of an important person. Printer William Bradford III added a skull and crossbones with the words, "the fatal Stamp," to his October 31 *Pennsylvania Journal and Weekly Advertiser* in the bottom right corner where the tax stamp was to have been placed. Below the name of the paper were the words, "EXPIRING: In Hopes of a Resurrection to LIFE again."

The date for the Stamp Act's enactment passed. Papers that suspended publication soon began printing again, and many printers noted in their papers, "No Stamped Paper to be had," Even though England passed the law, its stamped paper—that is, paper that had already been taxed and had a stamp affixed to it—never made it to America. The vehement American opposition to the Stamp Act made its mark, and in March 1766, Parliament repealed the Stamp Act. British leaders had realized the law was unenforceable in America, and no American newspaper printed on paper with an affixed British tax stamp.

This chapter looks at the way in which newspapers swayed opinion during the Stamp Act crisis. Because printers were united in opposition to the act, little appeared in print opposing the act. As has been said, printers used any information available to fight the Stamp Act and encouraged public opposition to it.

Opposition to the Stamp Act in colonial newspapers begins with letters, essays, and a public notice that appeared in the *Boston Gazette*. The *Gazette* was owned by printers Benjamin Edes and John Gill. Working with their close friend, Samuel Adams, the pair published one of the strongest papers advocating separation from England prior to the Revolution. The first, signed by the anonymous B. W., argues that acceptance of the Stamp Act is analogous to submitting to slavery. The next two articles come from the same *Gazette*. The first is a petition from the town of Marblehead asking for the repeal of the act. It is followed by a paragraph estimating the monetary loss Boston retailers and traders can expect to incur from the Stamp Act.

The next essay against the Stamp Act speaks to its ill-timed adoption for America. Philadelphia printer William Bradford's note to his readers on October 31 follows. This is the newspaper Bradford bordered in black and placed these words under the nameplate: "EXPIRING: In Hopes of a Resurrection to LIFE again." In the next selection, a mock news story portrays the fictional trial and execution of the stamp.

The final entry in this section is an attack or threat on those Americans who had agreed to be stamp agents. In addition to showing the strong feelings many had toward the stamp men, the unsigned letter demonstrates how all Americans were not united against Britain's taxing of Americans. The letter is a forerunner of the Patriot-Tory split that would occur in America from this time up to and through the Revolution. It is signed with the name Cato, the pen name used in England and America as a symbol of freedom from governmental tyranny.

The letters and essays supporting the Stamp Act begin with excerpts from a *Boston Gazette* essay that pretended to support the Stamp Act, but its last paragraph reveals it was meant to be a parody. It is included as an example of the Stamp Act's support because its arguments mirror those made in English newspapers to support the taxing of the colonies. These newspapers circulated in America. The anonymous letter is signed Judæus Apella. The next selection is a letter that originally appeared in a London paper but was reprinted in Boston. It questions why colonists complained so much about a tax on paper, a commodity whose use, the writer says, affects only the wealthy in society.

OPPOSITION TO THE STAMP ACT

B. W.: "AWAKE! SAVE YOUR LIBERTY"

Most American newspapers railed against the Stamp Act. Benjamin Edes and John Gill, the Boston Gazette*'s printers, worked closely with one of America's chief agitators for independence, Samuel Adams. Whether he wrote this letter or someone else did, the* Gazette *printed dozens of anti–Stamp Act pieces both before and after the November 1, 1765, date when the Stamp Act was to go into effect. B. W. called for Americans to save their liberty by rejecting the Stamp Act.*

Boston-Gazette, and Country Journal, 7 October 1765

To the Inhabitants of the Province of the *Massachusetts-Bay*.

MY DEAR COUNTRYMEN,

AWAKE!—Awake, my Countrymen, and, by a regular & legal Opposition, defeat the Designs of those who enslave us and our Posterity. Nothing is wanting but your own Resolution—For great is the Authority, exalted the Dignity, and powerful the Majesty of the People.—And shall you, the Descendents of Britain, born in a Land of Light, and reared in the Bosom of Liberty—shall you commence Cowards, at a Time when Reason calls so loud for your Magnanimity? I know you scorn such an injurious aspersion—I know you disdain the Thought of so opprobious a Servility—Some of you perhaps imagine all Endeavours unavailable—Banish so groundless a Fear—Truth is omnipotent, and Reason must be finally victorious. Be Men, and make the Experiment. This is your Duty, your burden, your indispensable Duty. Ages remote, Mortals yet unborn, will bless your generous Efforts, and revere the Memory of the Saviours of their Country.

The Love of Liberty is natural to our Species and interwoven with the human Frame. Inflamed with this Love, do not countenance an Act so detrimental to your Privileges. . . .

PAUSE, therefore, my Countrymen, and consider;—Revolve the Consequences in a dispassionate Mind—Weigh them in the Scale of Reason—in the Balance of cool deliberate Reflection: If any of you have been till this Time insensible of your Danger, awake now out of your Lethargy—Start, O start from your Trance! By the inconquerable Spirit of the ancient BRITONS;—by the Genius of that CONSTITUTION which abhors every Species of Vassallage;—by the August Title of ENGLISHMEN;—by the grand Preogatives of HUMAN NATURE; the lovely Image of the INFINITE DEITY;—and what is more than all, by the LIBERTY wherewith CHRIST *has made you free*; I exhort you to instruct your Representatives against promoting by any Ways of Means whatsoever, the Operation of this grievous and burdensome Law. Acquaint them *fully* with your Sentiments of the Matter; that they may be inexcuseable if they should act contrary to your declared Minds. They are cloathed with Power, not to sport with the Interests of human Nature, but to be faithful Guardians of the Liberties of their Country. . . . Happy, thrice happy should I be, to have it in my Power to congratulate my Countrymen, on so memorable a Deliverance; whilst I left the Enemies of Truth and Liberty to humble themselves in Sackcloth and Ashes.

B. W.

CITIZENS OF MARBLEHEAD: "REMOVE THIS BURDEN"
AN ANONYMOUS WRITER: "WHAT WILL BECOME OF TRADE?"

As the date for the Stamp Act legislation to take effect approached, landowners in towns across America met in hopes of influencing the repeal of the act. The residents of Marblehead, Massachusetts, were no different; they petitioned for repeal. Newspapers were filled with these announcements, which created a feeling of solidarity among Americans.

In a second letter in this issue of the Boston Gazette, *the writer estimates that payment of the stamp tax will exceed the currency available in America and ruin trade.*

Boston-Gazette, and Country Journal, 14 October 1765

To JACOBE FOWLE *and* WILLIAM BOURN, *Esq'rs. The present Representatives of the Town of* MARBLEHEAD.

GENTLEMEN,

WE the Freeholders and other Inhabitants of the said Town of *Marblehead*, in Town Meeting assembled, the Twenty fourth Day of *September*, A.D. 1765, professing the greatest Loyalty to our most gracious Sovereign, and our sincere Regard and profound Reverence for the *British* Parliament as the most powerful and respectable Body of Men of Earth, yet, at the same time, being deeply sensible of the Difficulties and Distresses, to which that August Assembly's late Exertion of their Power, in and by the *Stamp-Act*, must necessarily expose us, think it proper, in the present critical Conjuncture of Affairs, to give you the following INSTRUCTION, *viz.*

THAT you promote, and readily join in, such dutiful Remonstrances and humble Petitions to the King and Parliament, and other decent Measures, as may have a Tendency to obtain a Repeal of the *Stamp-Act*, or Alleviation of the heavy Burdens thereby imposed on the *American British* Colonies. . . .

Other Matters we leave to your Prudence, trusting you will act, as we apprehend you have ever done, consistent with the Honor and Justice to your Constituents and with due Regard to the publick Welfare.

Attest, *Benja. Boden*, Town-Clerk.

By a Computation made, it appears that if the Stamp Act should take Place, the retailers and Tavernkeepers must pay about £40 000, which is more than double what the common Charges of Government ought to be in Time of Peace, and is perhaps a larger Sum than the current Cash of the Country—What then must become of the Trade?

AN ANONYMOUS WRITER: "THE BROKEN HEART OF THE PATRIOT"

The Stamp Act was designed to help pay off Britain's huge debt in fighting France during the French and Indian War in America and the Seven Years' War in the rest of the world. The American colonies, however, had spent great sums of money themselves to fight the war. Now they felt they were being forced to pay twice as much as necessary through local taxes and the new British stamp tax. This letter addresses this problem as it refers to Americans as Patriots who will soon be placed in financial shackles by Great Britain.

New-York Mercury, 21 October 1765

It is enough to melt a stone, or even harder heart of a villain, when he views this wretched land, sinking under the merciless and ill-timed persecutions of those who should have been its upholders and protectors.

It is enough to break the heart of the Patriot, who would joyfully pour out his blood, to extricate his beloved country from destruction, to find her fainting and despairing, hourly expecting to be utterly crush'd by the iron rod of power.

At this most critical conjuncture of affairs; while we are exerting every nerve, to free ourselves from the wretched condition, to which our debts to Great-Britain have reduc'd us; and reasonably fearing that our utmost endeavours will be ineffectual;—to what can we impute the infatuation of our mother country; by whose baneful advice has she been deluded, encouraged, advised! To overwhelm a numerous and well-affected people, to plunge them deep in ruin,—never to rise again.—Ye ruthless crew! Ye infernal corrupted, detested incendiaries! . . . Come and see how well we are able to bear additional taxes! See our poor starving! Our liberties expiring! Our trade declining! Our countrymen dispairing! . . . Write again to your former correspondents; congratulate them on the good effects of their severity; bid them lay on new taxes, and spare not, for we cannot be rendered more wretched than we are.—Who that has the least spark of affection left for his native clime, can calmly think of its destroyers? Methinks the guardian angel of America, rises to my view! Indignation and the most poignant grief clouds his lovely face.—How art thou fallen! Thou envy of Europe! He cries. How art thou fallen, murder'd America! Murder'd by those for whom thou has incessantly toil'd, dismember'd, mangled and torn! Even thy own sons have joined to *stamp* on thy bowels.—Think not, whoever you are, that have been instrumental in ruining your country, that you will escape with impunity.—Misery, even in this life, shall be your portion.—The present generation shall never mention your names, but with succeeding ages, inform'd by the faithful historian, to whom they owe their shackles, shall load your accursed memory with everlasting infamy.

WILLIAM BRADFORD: "THE FATAL TOMORROW"

Printer William Bradford went to great lengths to make sure that all who saw his Pennsylvania Journal *of October 31, 1765, would know that something serious was about to happen. He lined the columns with black borders, a symbol of death, and he placed a skull and crossbones above the paper's name. In the first column of the front page, Bradford penned this apology to his readers, saying that the Stamp Act, which was to take effect the next day—"the* fatal *To-morrow"—was ending his paper's life.*

Pennsylvania Journal; and Weekly Advertiser (Philadelphia), 31 October 1765

I am sorry to be obliged to acquaint my readers, that, as the Stamp act is feared to be obligatory upon us after the *First of November* evening, (the *fatal* To-morrow,) the Publisher, unable to bear the Burthen, has thought it expedient to STOP awhile, in order to deliberate, whether any methods can be found to elude the chains forged for us, and escape the insupportable Slavery; which, it is hoped, from the just representations now made against this Act, may be effected. Meanwhile I must earnestly request every individual of my Subscribers, that they would immediately

discharge their respective arrears, that I may be able, not only to support myself during the Interval, but be the better prepared to proceed again with the paper, whenever an opening for that purpose appears, which I hope will be soon. WILLIAM BRADFORD
PHILADELPHIA, Oct, 31, 1765.

AN ANONYMOUS WRITER: "THE TRIAL OF THE STAMP ACT"

Essay writers sometimes liked taking real-life situations and placing them into imaginary scenarios. In this story, the stamp is placed on trial by the Sons of Liberty. This group, which organized in the summer of 1765, quickly assumed a role of leadership in Stamp Act protests. Here, the Stamp Act is tried, convicted, and burned in public to the delight of thousands.

Boston-Gazette, and Country Journal, 24 February 1766

Last Week was taken up and commited to the Custody of the SONS OF LIBERTY in this Town, a most *detestable* Object, lately transported to *America*—Notice being given, a jury was summon'd, and a Bill found, setting forth that said Prisoner did on the first of November last, endeavour to make its Appearance in a forcible Manner, and in Defiance of the known and establish'd Laws of the British Constitution, to deprive the Subject of his Rights and Privileges, &c.—They then proceeded Tryal, which lasted, two Hours, and after many learned Debates, the Evidence was so clear, that the Jury without going out of Court found the said Prisoner Guilty of a Breach of Magna Charta, and Design to subvert the British Constitution, and alienate the Affections of His Majesty's most loyal and dutiful Subjects in *America* from his Person and Government— Sentence was immediately past [*sic*] by the honourable Judge of the said Court, and accordingly executed. . . . Previous to this Execution on Thursday Morning last Notifications were found posted up in several Parts of the Town, on which the following is a Copy:
HANOVER SQUARE.
Boston, THURSDAY *20th February 1766*
THE Committee of the true born Sons of Liberty having in the Possession a Piece of Paper mark'd with America's Oppression*—Do hereby Notify their Brethren, that they are determin'd to make a public Exhibition of it under the TREE OF LIBERTY This Morning, where it will hang till XII o'Clock, and then be taken down, and committed to the Flames— together with the Effigies of the Authors of this Oppression.

Between two and three Thousand People assembled on this Occasion, and at the Time appointed the Effigies were taken down, and three Cheers given.

* A Crown Stamp.

CATO: "THE RUIN OF MY COUNTRY"

The pseudonym Cato was one of the most popular in America and England for writers to use when discussing the rights of citizens. In this anonymous letter, Cato discusses how the Stamp Act is set to ruin America. American tempers flared during this month over the Stamp Act. Riots occurred in some places, principally Boston, because of the impending duty on paper.

Connecticut Courant (Hartford), 26 August 1765

Since the late Impositions on the American Colonies by the Parliament of Great-Britain, our Papers have been filled with Exclamations against Slavery and arbitrary Power. One would have thought by this mighty outcry, that all America, to a Man, had a noble Sense of Freedom, and would risque their Lives and Fortunes in the Defence of it. . . .

Nothing can fill a generous Breast with greater Indignation than to see a free, brave and virtuous People unjustly sunk and debased by Tyranny and Oppression. But who can pity the heartless Wretches whose only Fortitude is in their Tongue and Pen? If we may judge the Whole by those who have been already tampered with, the Colonies are now ripe for Slavery, and incapable of Freedom. . . . Those who lately set themselves up for Patriots and boasted a generous Love for their Country, are they now saying (O Disgrace to Humanity!) Are THEY now creeping after the Profits of collecting the unrighteous *American* Stamp-Duty! If this is credible, what may we not believe? Where are the mercenary Publicans who delight in Nothing so much as the dearest Blood of their Country? Will the Cries of your despairing, dying Brethren be Musick pleasing to your Ears? If so, go on! Bend the Knee to your Master Horseleach, and beg a Share in the Pillage of your Country—*No*, you'll say, *I don't delight in the Ruin of my Country, but, since 'tis decreed she must fall, who can blame me for taking a Part in the Plunder?* Tenderly said! Why did you not rather say—*If my Father must die, who can accuse me as defective in filial Duty, in becoming his Executioner, that so much of the Estate, at least, as goes to the Hangman, may be retained in the Family?*

Never pretend, whoever you are, that freely undertake to put in Execution a Law prejudicial to your Country, that you have the least Spark of affection for her. Rather own you would gladly see her in Flames, if you might be allowed to pillage with Impunity.

You are to look for Nothing but the Hatred and Detestation of all the Good and Virtuous. And as you live on the Distresses, you will inherit the Curses of Widows and Orphans. The present Generation will treat you as the Authors of their Misery, and Posterity will pursue your Memory with the most terrible Imprecations.

CATO

SUPPORT FOR THE STAMP ACT

JUDÆUS APELLA: "OUR OBLIGATION TO GREAT BRITAIN"

Few essays or letters appeared in American newspapers in support of the Stamp Act. In this anonymous letter, the writer feigns support for the Stamp Act by offering the standard rationale used by British sympathizers. In reality, the letter turns on its arguments at the end. This letter is included here, however, because it represents a standard pro–Stamp Act argument of the time and because so little exists in support of the act.

Boston-Gazette, and Country Journal, 9 December 1765

Boston, December 6, 1765

To the PRINTERS,

AMIDST the Multiplicity of excellent Pieces which your Press has handed to the Publick, I do not recollect that any great Notice has been taken of one very popular Argument, which has been much insisted on by the ministerial Writers, to justify the present hard Treatment, the Colonies so unanimously and justly complain of. This is that as Great-Britain has expended large Sums to preserve us from Destruction, it is highly fit and reasonable she should be reimbursed the Expence contracted on *our* Account. . . .

Must we not determine ourselves under infinite Obligations to Great Britain, for the Aid and Assistance she so kindly afforded these Colonies, when surrounded by *their* French and Indian Enemies? Is it not the highest Ingratitude, to refuse to sacrifice the most invaluable Rights and Privileges, at the Call of those, who so generously took up Arms in *our* Defence? So generously, I say, as not possible Advantage could accrue to themselves. . . . Let us no longer refuse to submit to the Stamp Act, no longer grumble at what is usually stiled the Sugar Act; such Refusal, and such Discontent, being totally repugnant to that grateful Spirit by which it surely becomes us to be animated towards our tender Mother Country. . . .

Judæus Apella

AN ANONYMOUS WRITER: "THE TAX ON NEWSPAPERS CONCERNS ONLY A FEW"

As Americans fumed over the Stamp Act, the British wondered why. In this letter, taken from a London newspaper and reprinted in Boston, the writer questions why Bostonians are rioting over an act that affects only those who can afford to buy a newspaper. The tax, after all, was not upon beer or ale, which would affect the commoner in the colonies.

Boston-Gazette Supplement, 27 January 1766
From a late London Paper.

THERE was an article lately in the news-papers, which well merits your utmost attention, and loudly calls for the interposition of government; I mean the insurrection at Boston in America to prevent the execution of the Stamp-Act. . . .

The occasion of the riotous behaviour of the Bostonites is peculiarly remarkable: Had the Parliament taxed their small beer an half penny a quart, the tax would then have been most severely felt; they would naturally murmured; and an improper conduct on such an occasion had been less a matter of surprise; and perhaps ought left so have roused the Indignation of government: But in the present case, *the tax to be levied affects none of the necessaries of life; will never fall upon many of the poor; and will touch very gently and very seldom such of them will light upon*: Even a very poor person cannot be much hurt by paying a shilling or eighteen pence when he is married, puts his son for apprentice to a trade, or when he makes his will. The tax on News-papers concerns only a very few—the common people don't purchase news-papers. Is it not surprising then that the mob should be so much alarmed by the apprehension of a tax by which they are to be so little affected as to be guilty of such dreadful enormicies [*sic*], as the Bostonites have been, even before the tax is begun to be levied.

QUESTIONS

1. According to the Americans, what are the reasons that the Stamp Act should be repealed?
2. According to the British, what are the reasons that the Stamp Act should be enforced?
3. What will the Stamp Act do to America, according to the *New-York Mercury* letter writer?
4. What repercussions for the people of Philadelphia does William Bradford's notice represent?
5. What can you tell about what was happening in America politically and socially from the *Connecticut Courant* letter?

NOTES

1. *Maryland Gazette* (Annapolis), 19 September 1754, 2.
2. *Pennsylvania Gazette* (Philadelphia), 18 April 1754, 2.

3. Ibid., 13 December 1753, 1.

4. Massachusetts Historical Society, *Collections*, 6th series, 9 (1897), 22.

5. "The Stamp Act," reprinted in David A. Copeland, "The Early American Press, 1690–1783," in *The Age of Mass Communication*, ed. Wm. David Sloan (Northport, Ala.: Vision Press, 1998), 111.

CHAPTER 17

"No Taxation without Representation," 1765–1766

Before the Stamp Act crisis of 1765 (see Chapter 16), Americans in the thirteen colonies shared similar interests and concerns on many issues. All had been attentive, for example, to newspaper reports about the French and Indian War and the effect a French victory would have had on America. The Stamp Act was regarded as an attack on them by their own government. It led to the formation of a protest group known as the Sons of Liberty, and of the Liberty Tree, a place within towns where people joined together to protest and to post complaints.

The Stamp Act launched American objections to taxes and to the way colonists were represented in Parliament. Each colony had its own assembly made up of representatives from all over the colony, but any law passed by those assemblies ultimately had to be approved by Britain. If Americans were not truly represented in Parliament by delegates chosen by Americans, many colonists reasoned, Parliament had no right to pass laws that affected the colonies or to enforce those laws.

The English concept of representation for the people of Great Britain was called virtual representation, and its merits—or lack thereof—became a point of contention in 1765. The debate continued to the Revolution. In both America and England, people argued about the validity of virtual representation. George Grenville, Lord of the Treasury and the Stamp Act's chief proponent, used a pamphlet written by one of his secretaries, Thomas Whately, to explain how virtual representation worked in relation to the American colonies.

For the Fact is, that the Inhabitants of the Colonies are represented in Parliament:
they do not indeed chuse the Members of that Assembly; neither are Nine Tenths
of the People of *Britain* Electors; . . . The Colonies are in exactly the same Situation: All *British* Subjects are really in the same: none are actually, all are virtually
represented in Parliament; for every Member of Parliament sits in the House not
as Representative of his own Constituents, but as one of that August Assembly by
which all the Commons of *Great Britain* are represented. Their Rights and their
Interests, however his own Borough may be affected by general Dispositions,
ought to be the great Objects of his Attention, and the only Rules for his Conduct.[1]

To American colonists, the concept that taxes could be levied by Parliament without American-elected representation present was unacceptable. The British system maintained that the interests of all Britons—no
matter where they lived in the Empire—were represented by those
elected to Parliament because those elected to Parliament had only the
best interests of all in mind. Each county in England had two representatives, which meant, according to virtual representation, that members
of Parliament had some connection to all landowners even if those
elected did not live in that particular region of England. Americans, however, had no elected officials. They had to depend on Members of Parliament with no connection to them. In England, landowners could contact
their representatives and could, if needed, vote them out of office. How
could Americans, many writers argued, speak to representatives who lived
3,000 miles away and on the other side of the Atlantic Ocean? How could
Americans vote anyone out of parliamentary office when they elected no
representative? America's objection to virtual representation, which continued until the Revolution, was reflected in the call of "no taxation without representation."

Once again, American newspaper printers were universal in their
opposition to virtual representation in 1765 and 1766. A few British comments in support of virtual representation did make their way into newspapers, but printers chose selectively what they wanted to appear in
order to gain support for their particular causes.

The selections on America's attack on virtual representation and the
demand the colonies not be taxed without representation begin with a
long letter/essay that outlines why virtual representation is wrong. The
letter's introductory paragraph states that it was written by a "plain yeoman in New-England." As a sidelight, the letter also provides eighteenth-
century reasoning for why women do not vote.

The yeoman's letter is followed by the *Maryland Gazette* version of
the Virginia Resolves, a set of statements adopted by the colony's assembly, the House of Burgesses, on taxation by and representation in Parliament for the colony. The Virginia Resolves were the first made by a
colony. Virginia's action was followed by those of other colonies. Several

versions of the Resolves exist; those published in the *Maryland Gazette* differ from those that appeared in other newspapers. These are more confrontational and more hostile, saying that Parliament's actions would "Destroy AMERICAN FREEDOM." The Virginia Resolves, as well as those adopted by several other colonies, preceded similar resolves written by representatives of nine of the thirteen colonies at the Stamp Act Congress, which met in New York in October 1765. The Virginia Resolves are followed by those of South Carolina, which passed its petition to Parliament after the Stamp Act Congress.

The next three selections are taken from the *Boston Gazette*, one of America's more hostile papers in its attacks on Great Britain in the decade before the Revolution. Taken from the October issues leading up to the Stamp Act's November 1 enaction, the first are unsigned essays. The third is an excerpt from John Locke's *Treatise on Government*.

The Stamp Act also spurred members of Parliament into debate over representation. The final selection against virtual representation is part of that debate. The article presents William Pitt's debate on virtual representation with George Grenville, the author of the Stamp Act. Pitt, the British prime minister during the pivotal years of the French and Indian War, was considered a hero by many Americans, and he was a staunch opponent of the Stamp Act. Grenville's rationale for virtual representation is included in the section supporting virtual representation. It is worth noting that Pitt predicted Parliament's current course of action toward America would lead to revolution in the colonies.

The selections that support virtual representation begin with a letter taken from a London newspaper and written by the anonymous Pacificus. The letter states that allowing inferior Americans a place in Parliament would place the British government in jeopardy. The letter is followed by Grenville's reply to Pitt in Parliament in support of the English representational system.

AGAINST VIRTUAL REPRESENTATION

A PLAIN YEOMAN: "AMERICA VIRTUALLY REPRESENTED: A PIECE OF MOCKERY"

The Stamp Act opened a gap between England and America that could never be closed as long as America remained England's colonial possession. Closely tied to the Stamp Act was the American concept that Americans could not be taxed by England because they were not represented in Parliament. In this letter, the unknown plain yeoman explains virtual representation: British subjects are represented by those in Parliament even if the people do not vote. Americans used the concept of no taxation without representation to oppose the Stamp Act and numerous other British taxes that were levied in the years leading up to the Revolution.

Providence Gazette; and Country Journal, 11 May 1765

The following is said to be a copy of a letter, sent by a plain yeoman in New-England, to a certain great personage in Old-England.

At a time when the respective legislatures of *Great-Britain*, and of these his majesty's dominions in *America*, are as wide apart in sentiment of each one's extent of power in point of legislation, as they are east and west of each other in point of situation . . . an appeal to your lordship from a plain *American*, who never was among the great, in regard to parliamentary resolutions for taxing us, and otherwise abridging such privileges as we have long enjoyed, and humbly conceive have a right to, may be thought highly presumptuous. However . . . the matters contained in the following address are founded on the known principles of the *British* government, and managed with decency. . . .

It is very hard, my lord, that so large a portion of the king's subjects, as are contained in *North-America*, and who have ever been distinguished for their loyalty, cannot be heard on a subject, in which they are so deeply interested. Can it come within possibility, that all the individuals in the northern colonies should, without previous conference, minutely concur in sentiment, that the *British* parliament cannot, agreeable with the inherent privileges of the colonists, tax them without a representation on their part. . . . But to our infinite regret and disappointment, we have not only been deprived in a great measure of some of our ancient and invaluable rights, but virtually forbid the liberty of even complaining! . . .

A right of election is annexed to a certain species of property, franchises, &c. And every man in *England*, who falls under these descriptions, hath a right to vote, either for knights, citizens, or burgesses; but can any man in the colonies be admitted to a voice, let him come under what description he will? Every person in *England* is not qualified to be an elector, yet the country is represented;—but doth it follow that the colonies too are therefore represented, who give not a single voice, although multitudes here have as much freehold estate as serves to qualify their fellow subjects in *England*? But it is said that persons under age, women and children are not electors, but yet are represented. I wonder these subtle had not hewn, that ideots, madmen, and cattle were not electors, and from thence infer that we are represented. Women have not a share in government, but yet by their strict connexion with the other sex, all their liberties are as amply secured as those of the men, and it is impossible to represent one sex, without the other. . . .

To infer, my lord, that the *British* member actually represent the colonies, who are not permitted to do the least act towards their appointment, because *Britain* is unequally represented, although every man in the kingdom, who hath certain legal qualifications can vote for some one to represent him, is such a piece of sophistry that I had half a mind to pass by the cobweb without blowing it to pieces. . . . A right of election hath its origin from having property of freehold estate, and such only have a right to a share in government. Mens estates are represented, and such as have great and noble estates actually sit in parliament for their own estates. All how have freehold in *England* to a small value, share in the administration; but in *America*, where almost every head of a family and most other men have freehold, and very many are owners of great landed estates, they can have no share in government; and those estates are not represented, because the owners cannot elect. Suppose none of the 558 members [of Parliament] were chosen by the people, but enjoyed the right of the sitting on parliament by hereditary descent; could the common people be said to share in the national councils? How trifling then is the supposition, that we in *America* virtually have such share in the national councils, by those members whom we never chose? If we are not their constituents, they are not our representatives. . . . [I]t is really a piece of mockery to tell us that a country, detached from *Britain*, by an ocean of immense breadth, and which is so extensive and populous, should be represented by *British* members, or that we can have any interest in the house of commons.

It therefore remains fully disproved, that the inhabitants of the colonies are in *fact* represented in parliament; and therefore our most darling privilege, namely an immunity from taxes without our own consent, hath been nullified.

VIRGINIA HOUSE OF BURGESSES: "VIRGINIA RESOLVES"

Most colonial assemblies reacted to the issue of taxation, but Virginia was the first with a set of resolves opposing taxation. Several different versions of the Resolves appeared in newspapers. The Maryland Gazette *version adds a statement on American freedom. The Virginia Resolves helped shape America's collective response to the Stamp Act at the Stamp Act Congress.*

Maryland Gazette (Annapolis), 4 July 1765

RESOLVES of the House of Burgesses in VIRGINIA, *June* 1765. That the first Adventurers and Settlers of this his Majesty's Colony and Dominion of *Virginia*, brought with them, and transmitted to their Posterity, and all inhabiting in this his Majesty's Colony, all the Liberties, Privileges, Franchises, and Immunities, that at any Time have been held, enjoyed, and possessed, by the People of *Great Britain*.

That by Two Royal Charters, granted by King *James* the First, the Colonies aforesaid are Declared Entitled, to all Liberties, Privileges and Immunities, of Denizens and all Natural Subjects (to all Intents and Purposes) as if they had been Abiding and Born within the Realm of *England*.

That the Taxation of the People by Themselves, or by Persons Chosen by Themselves to Represent them, who can only know what Taxes the People are able to bear, or the easiest Method of Raising them, and must themselves be affected by every Tax laid upon the People, is the only Security against a Burthensome Taxation; and the Distinguishing Characteristic of *British* FREEDOM; and, without which, the antient Constitution cannot exist.

That his Majesty's Liege People of this his most Ancient and Loyal Colony, have, without Interruption, the inestimable Right of being governed by such Laws, respecting their internal Polity and Taxation, as are derived from their own consent, with the Approbation of their own Sovereign, or his Substitute; which Right hath never been Forfeited, or Yielded up; but hath been constantly recognized by the Kings and People of *Great Britain*.

Resolved therefore, That the General Assembly of this Colony, with the Consent of his Majesty, or his Substitute, HAVE the Sole Right and Authority to lay Taxes and Impositions upon It's [*sic*] Inhabitants: And that every Attempt to vest such Authority in any other Person or Persons whatsoever, has a Manifest Tendency to Destroy AMERICAN FREEDOM.

That his Majesty's Liege People, Inhabitants of this Colony, are not bound to yield Obedience to any Law or Ordinance whatsoever, designed to impose Taxation upon them, other than the Laws or Ordinances of the General Assembly aforesaid.

That any Person who shall, by Speaking, or Writing, assert or maintain, That any Person or Persons, other than the General Assembly of this Colony, with such Consent as aforesaid, have any Right or Authority to lay or impose any Tax whatever on the Inhabitants thereof, shall be Deemed, An Enemy to this his Majesty's Colony.

SOUTH CAROLINA ASSEMBLY: "SOUTH CAROLINA RESOLVES"

Colonial legislatures responded at different times to England's taxation schemes for America. South Carolina's response came more than two months after the Stamp Act went into effect. The colony's representatives acknowledged the king's sovereignty over them but also declared that only taxes levied by the South Carolina legislature would be recognized in the colony.

Boston-Gazette, and Country Journal, 6 January 1766

SOUTH-CAROLINA

In the Commons House *of* Assembly, the *29th Day of* November 1765.

I. RESOLVED, That his Majesty's Subjects in this Province owe the same Allegiance to the Crown of *Great Britain* that is due from his Subjects born there. . . .

IV. That is inseparably essential to the Freedom of a People, and the undoubted Right of ENGLISHMEN, that no Taxes be imposed on them but with their own Consent given personally, or by their Representatives.

V. That the People of this Province are not, and, from their local Circumstances, cannot be, represented in the House of Commons of *Great-Britain.* And further, That, in the Opinion of this House, the several Powers of Legislation in *America* were constituted in some Measure, upon the Apprehension of this impracticability.

VI. That the only Representatives of the People of this Province are Persons chosen therein by themselves; and that no Taxes ever have been, or can be, constitutionally imposed on them, but by the Legislature of this Province.

AN ANONYMOUS WRITER: "TAXATION IS BY CONSENT"

In the three weeks before the Stamp Act became law, newspapers ran dozens of letters and essays explaining why taxing Americans was illegal. In this anonymous letter, the writer goes so far as to say that taxation could be carried out only with the consent of those being taxed.

Boston-Gazette, and Country Journal, 7 October 1765

MY DEAR COUNTRYMEN,

It is a standing Maxim of *English Liberty* "That no Man shall be taxed but with his own consent," and you very well know we were not, in any *sober* sense, represented in Parliament, when this Tax was imposed. When the Legislature decree a Tax, as they represent the Community, such Tax ought to be considered as the voluntary Gift of the People to be applied to such Uses, as they, by their Representatives, shall expedient.

AN ANONYMOUS WRITER: "FREEMEN AND TAXES"

Just as the writer the week before in the Boston Gazette *had insisted a government had no right to tax people without their consent, the unknown author of the letter below insisted that freemen, according to the*

British Constitution, had an inalienable right not to be separated from their property. To represent people virtually in effect did just that— made it possible for taxes to be voted on people without their having a representative from their part of the empire.

Boston-Gazette, and Country Journal, 14 October 1765

We have always understood it to be a grand and fundamental Principle of the Constitution, that no Freeman should be subjected to any Tax, to which he has not given his own Consent, in Person or by Proxy. And the Maxim of the Law as we have constantly received them are to the same Effect, that no Freeman can be separated from his Property, but by his own Act of Fault—We take it clearly, therefore, to be inconsistent with the Spirit of the Common Law, and of the essential fundamental Principles of the British Constitution, that we should be subjected to any Tax, imposed by the British Parliament: because we are not represented in that Assembly in any Sense, unless it be by a Fiction of Law, as insensible in Theory as it would be injurious in Practice, if such a Taxation should be grounded on it.

JOHN LOCKE: "SECOND TREATISE ON GOVERNMENT"

Americans loved to quote the great minds of the age in support of their causes. Here, an anonymous writer sent in a portion of Locke's second treatise as an argument against virtual representation.

Boston-Gazette, and Country Journal, 18 November 1765

NO government can have a RIGHT to obedience from a people, who have not *freely consented* to it; which they can never be supposed to do, til either they are put in a full state of *liberty* to chuse their government and governors or at least, till they have such standing laws to which they have by *themselves* or their *representatives given their consent.*
John Locke.

WILLIAM PITT: "BY WHOM IS AN AMERICAN REPRESENTED HERE?"

William Pitt, the earl of Chatham, earned a place of honor among Americans during the French and Indian War with his strong military support against the French and Indians. He gained even greater stature in the colonies when he opposed the Stamp Act. In this news report from London, Pitt's argument with George Grenville, the author of the Stamp Act, concerning the fallacies of virtual representation, is presented.

Boston-Gazette, and Country Journal, 12 May 1766

This house represents those commons, the proprietors of the lands, and those proprietors virtually represent the rest of the inhabitants; then, therefore, in this house, we give and grant what is our own. But in an *American* tax, what do we do? We, your Majesty's commons of *Great-Britain*, give and grant to your Majesty, What? Our own property? No; we give and grant to your Majesty the property of your Majesty's commons of *America*. It is an absurdity in terms. . . .

There is an idea in some, that the colonies are virtually represented in this house. I would fain know by whom an *American* is represented here. Is he represented by a Knight of a Shire of any county in this kingdom? Would to God that respectable representation were augmented to a greater number! Or, will you tell him he is represented by a representative of a Borough, which perhaps was never seen by its representative? A Borough, perhaps, which no Man ever saw. This has been called, *The Rotten Part of the Constitution*. It cannot now endure out the century; if it does not drop of itself, it must be amputated. But the idea of the virtual representation of *America* in this house, is the most contemptible notion that ever entered into the head of man; it does not deserve a serious refutation.

They [Americans] are now grown to Disturbances, to Tumults and Riots; I doubt they border upon *open Rebellion*; and if the Doctrine I hear To-Day be confirmed, I fear they will lose that Name, to take that of a Revolution; this Government over them being dissolved, a Revolution will take Place in *America*.

IN SUPPORT OF VIRTUAL REPRESENTATION

PACIFICUS: "THE VERIEST BEGGARS IN THE WORLD"

The Maryland Gazette *reprinted this letter written by the anonymous Pacificus of London. Pacificus called Americans idiots and unworthy to sit in Parliament. Virtual representation was necessary; keeping Americans and other inferiors out of positions of importance would preserve the empire.*

Maryland Gazette (Annapolis), 20 March 1766

Our numerous and rich Islands give no Evidences of an ungovernable Temper; nor have the ceded Provinces afforded us any Cause to suspect their Loyalty. . . .

They are not so distracted as to spend much of their Blood in so idle a Cause; in which indeed no Man, above the Degree of an Ideot, would risque his Life, Property, and all that he holds dear in this World. He must have little Sense, who would become liable to be treated as a Rebel for the Sake of shunning Payment of a Shilling or Eighteen Pence for a Sheet of stamped Paper. Our Colonies must be the veriest Beggars in the World, if such inconsiderable Duties appear to be intolerable Burthens in their Eyes: And if they are in such a State of Poverty, where can they find Cannon, Ammunition, and all the other Implements of War, together with MONEY, the Sinews of Mars.—It is impossible. . . .

The Idea of a Rebellion in America, in Consequence of such an unimportant Subject of Dispute, is merely Chimerical. . . .

What Subject of this great Republic, in his right Senses, would agree that our Constitution, so vigorous and so well proportioned, should be broke up at the Pleasure of such Opponents, by the Introduction of Representatives from Virginia or New-England in our House of Commons? Would our Morals be safe under Virginian Legislatures, or would our Church be in no Danger from Pumkin Senators? Shall we live to see the Spawn of our Transports occupy the highest Seats in our Common Wealth? Dengenerate Britons! How can ye entertain the humiliating Thoughts! Remember that Mr. Pitt, and all our real Patriots, have approved of this Tax. After mentioning these great Names, all further Arguments ought to cease: So here I drop my Pen, and leave the Disapprovers of this Law to Blush for their ill-timed Disapprobation.
PACIFICUS

GEORGE GRENVILLE: "UNGRATEFUL PEOPLE OF AMERICA"

George Grenville, Britain's secretary of the treasury, regarded the colonies as a drain upon the British coffers. The French and Indian War, the American customs service, and the colonial currency shortages all added up to expenses for Britain that Grenville felt should be shouldered by the Americans. As a result, he came up with numerous taxes, including the Stamp Act. Grenville and William Pitt never saw eye to eye on the American situation. Below is Grenville's argument concerning virtual representation as he and Pitt debated on the subject in Parliament.

Boston-Gazette, and Country Journal, 12 May 1766

I cannot understand the Difference between internal and external Taxes; they are the same in Effect, and only differ in Name. That this Kingdom is the sovereign, the supreme legislative Power over *America*, is granted, it cannot be denied; and Taxation is a Part of that sovereign Power; it is one Branch of Legislation; it is, it has been exercised over those who are not, who were not represented. It is exercised over the

East-India Company, the Merchants of *London*, the Proprietors of the Stocks, and over great manufacturing Towns. . . .

When I proposed to tax *America*, I asked the House, whether any Gentleman would object to the Right; I repeatedly asked it, and no Man would attempt to deny it. Protection and Obedience are reciprocal; *Great-Britain* protects *America, America* is bound to yield Obedience; if not, tell me when the *Americans* were emancipated. When they want the Protection of this Kingdom, they are very ready to ask it; that Protection has always been afforded them in the most full and ample Manner; the Nation has run itself into an immediate Debt to give them that Protection; and now they are called upon to contribute a small Share towards the Public Expence, an Expence arising from themselves, they renounce your Authority, insult your Officers and break out, I might almost say, into Acts of *open Rebellion*. . . .

Ungrateful People of *America*!

QUESTIONS

1. According to the "plain yeoman," who is allowed to vote in England and how should that apply to America?
2. What is the Americans' chief argument against virtual representation?
3. What are the basic differences in the Virginia Resolves and South Carolina Resolves?
4. According to the newspaper articles, what do Americans mean by "no taxation without representation"?
5. Why does William Pitt believe that the issue of representation will lead to revolution in America?
6. What are the main points of Pitt and Grenville in their argument over taxation and representation for America?
7. What does Pacificus believe is really the root of America's objection to English taxes and scheme of representation? Knowing what you do of American history, do you believe he was correct?

NOTE

1. Thomas Whately, *The Regulations Lately Made concerning the Colonies and the Taxes Imposed upon Them, considered* (London, 1765), 104–9.

CHAPTER 18

The Sons of Liberty, 1765–1776

In the summer of 1765, *Boston Gazette* printer Benjamin Edes and eight merchant friends, who called themselves the Loyal Nine, met in Boston. They regarded the Stamp Act (see Chapter 16), which was to go into effect in America on November 1, 1765, as a direct threat to their livelihoods as well as those of many others. The printer knew his weekly newspaper afforded the group the perfect mouthpiece to criticize the British tax which would require all paper used in the colones to be affixed with a stamp purchased from a British agent or stamp man. Edes and fellow printer John Gill filled the *Boston Gazette* with attacks against the tax and England.

The Loyal Nine were not finished, however. They organized a series of protests in Boston, including the hanging in effigy of Boston's stamp man, Andrew Oliver. Before August ended, riots broke out in Boston as citizens rallied against the new British tax. Oliver subsequently resigned, and no one in Boston wanted to assume the job.

About the same time Edes and his associates were organizing in Boston, a similar group was doing the same in New York City. In fact, comparable bands sprang up throughout America. While they sometimes used various names for themselves, these groups quickly became known collectively to all as the Sons of Liberty, and they led America's united effort against the Stamp Act.

The Sons of Liberty soon opened their secret meetings to any who wanted to attend. They met in public places, such as the liberty poles or trees found in many towns. Well-known Americans such as John and Samuel Adams met with the Sons of Liberty, and the group, which died down briefly following the Stamp Act's repeal, organized again to protest the Townshend Acts (See Chapter 20) and the tea tax with the Boston Tea Party (See Chapter 24). Some Americans blamed the Sons of Liberty for the Boston Massacre of 1770 (See Chapter 21).

As America moved closer to confrontation and separation from England, the Sons of Liberty organized committees of correspondence, or groups in most towns designed to keep all Americans apprised of what was happening in the controversy with the mother country. The name Sons of Liberty became nearly synonymous with any effort of protest against England, so that it became difficult from about 1774 to distinguish the acts of the Sons of Liberty from those of other Patriots. Still, the merchants, artisans, and mechanics who organized into the groups known as the Sons of Liberty in 1765 were vital to America's initial steps toward independence from Britain. That all those who opposed tyranny were loosely known by the name is a tribute to the impact of the Sons of Liberty on American independence.

The readings in this chapter reveal how the Sons of Liberty were portrayed in newspapers from the Stamp Act crisis through the Revolution. Because opposition to the Stamp Act was nearly universal, comments opposing the Sons of Liberty rarely appeared during that tax crisis. After the Stamp Act's repeal, however, Americans no longer agreed over whether British taxation or legislation concerning the colonies was legal or should be followed. In this atmosphere, opinions about the Sons of Liberty varied.

The readings supporting the Sons of Liberty begin with a 1765 letter from Charleston, South Carolina. It is typical of the letters and stories that appeared in the newspapers following the Stamp Act showing how the Sons of Liberty operated within a community. In this case, they kept the peace when British sailors attempted to collect tax money from citizens. The next selection, which appeared in the *Boston Gazette* as a news story accompanied by a woodcut of a Son of Liberty taking a stamp commissioner prisoner and placing him in irons, portrays the Sons of Liberty as the protectors of the rights granted by the Magna Carta and the protectors of the widows and orphans throughout America. The account explains the use of the Liberty Tree by the Sons of Liberty as a rallying place against any activities seen as threats to the well-being of America. It also equates the Stamp Act with the work of the devil.

The next entry, by the anonymous New-York Satyrist, is a response to the first Dougliad essay, which is included with the selections that attack the Sons of Liberty. The Satyrist defends New York Sons of Liberty leader Alexander McDougall who had been arrested for seditious libel (See

Chapter 5). At the same time, the essay attacks the Tories of the city. The next selection is a card of thanks to the Sons of Liberty for fighting against the tea tax.

The chapter entries attacking the Sons of Liberty begin with an unsigned reply to a letter written by the anonymous Mucius Scævola which appeared in the *Massachusetts Spy* and attacked the government of Governor Thomas Hutchinson. The next essay pokes fun at the Sons of Liberty as the author pretends to be an Irish "White boy" who wants to earn his way into Parliament by serving as a Sons of Liberty thug. The letter is signed, PATRICK MCADAM O'FLAGHARTY, Esq.

The next selection is the first Dougliad essay to appear in the *New-York Gazette*. This series of essays was written to attack the Sons of Liberty, specifically their New York leader Alexander McDougall, who had written and published a handbill assailing the colony's assembly. McDougall was arrested and charged with seditious libel. McDougall became a hero of the Patriots and an enemy of the Tories. The writer of the Dougliad series was unknown, but he supported the assembly and attacked the Sons of Liberty. The writer did distinguish between the Sons of Liberty who fought against the Stamp Act and those who were currently in operation in America. The writer of the Dougliad admitted that America had been done wrong by Parliament but believed the actions of McDougall and the other Sons of Liberty were putting America in jeopardy. The last reading of the chapter is an unsigned Tory letter that attacks the Sons of Liberty as preachers of subversion and revolution.

IN SUPPORT OF THE SONS OF LIBERTY

AN ANONYMOUS WRITER: "LIBERTY BOYS KEEP THE PEACE"

Groups known as the Sons of Liberty, or by variations such as Liberty Boys, operated in most American ports in 1765 to ensure no stamped paper or any tax stamps might be sold or even promoted. This typical description of the activities of the Sons of Liberty comes from Charleston, but it could just as easily have been written about the group's activities in any other American port town.

Boston Gazette, and Country Journal, 27 January 1766
Supplement

Extract of a letter from Charlestown, South Carolina, Dec. 2, 1765.

The Petitions which were drawn up at the Congress were agreed to, without any Altercation, and signed afterwards by our Assembly. The Members who attended at New York, have received the Thanks of the

House, and are re elected again. At present every thing is very quiet here; our Liberty Boys being content to keep out the Stamps, do not injure, but protect, the Town; for some Time ago a Parcel of Sailors, having a Mind to make the most of this Suspension of Law, formed a Mob, to collect Money of the People in the Streets; but these Sons of Liberty suppressed them instantly, and committed the Ring-leaders to Goal [*sic*] While they act thus cooly and determinately we have little Reason to fear they will give up the Point, especially as the Country People are all unanimous in it.

AN ANONYMOUS WRITER: "THE CAPTURE AND TRIAL OF A TRAITOR"

During the Stamp Act crisis of 1765, many Americans transformed the Sons of Liberty into heroes. In this imaginary news account, the Sons of Liberty arrest and place the stamp tax on trial. The accompanying woodcut showed the stamp, portrayed as a stamp man, chained to the gallows with the devil above him.

Boston Gazette, and Country Journal, 24 February 1766

LAST Week was taken up and committed to the Custody of the SONS OF LIBERTY in this Town, a most *detestable* Object, lately transported to *America*—Notice being given, a Jury was summon'd, and a Bill found, setting forth that the said Prisoner did on the first of November last, endeavour to make its Appearance in forcible Manner, and in Defiance of the known and establish'd Laws of the British Constitution. . . . They then proceeded to Tryal, which lasted two Hours, . . . the Evidence was so clear, that the Jury without going out of Court found the said Prisoner guilty of a Breach of Magna Charta, and a Design to subvert the British Constitution. . . . A Stage having two Effigies thereon was erected . . . over whom was a Gallow, on which the Devil appeared with a Stamp Act, and a Stamp Paper in one Hand, and a Chain in the other hanging over the Gallows. . . . Upon the Stamp Paper were these Words, *For the Oppression of the* WIDOW *and* FATHERLESS.—Previous to this Execution on Thursday Morning last Notifications were found posted up in several Parts of the Town, of which the following is a Copy: . . .

THE Committee of the true born Sons of Liberty having in their Possession a Piece of Paper shark'd with America's Oppression—DO hereby Notify the Brethren, that they are determin'd to strike a public Exhibition of it under the TREE OF LIBERTY This Morning, where it will hang till XII o'Clock, and then be taken down and committed to the Flames—together with the Effigies of the Authors of Oppression.

Between two and three Thousand People assembled on this Occasion, and at the Time appointed the Effigies were taken down, and three

Cheers given. . . . The Sons of Liberty afterwards repair'd to their own Apartment in Hanover Square. . . .

The Friday preceeding the TREE OF LIBERTY was prun'd after the best Manner, agreeable to a Vote pass'd by the Committee of the true-born SONS of LIBERTY at their last Meeting in Hanover Square, when a Number of Carpenters were appointed for Purpose. . . . Since which a large Plate has been affix'd to the Tree with the following Inscription, *viz*. "This Tree was planted in the Year 1646, and prun'd by Order of the SONS OF LIBERTY, February 14, 1766: So that the Tree is now become a great Ornament to the Square.—*And we doubt not but the TREE of LIBERTY will thrive and flourish when all the Friends to the Stamp Act will decay and perish*.

THE NEW-YORK SATYRIST: "DEFENSE OF ALEXANDER MCDOUGALL"

In 1770 New York Sons of Liberty leader Alexander McDougall was charged with seditious libel after being named the author of a handbill titled "To the Betrayed Inhabitants of New York." According to the flier, New Yorkers' liberty and property had not been properly protected by the assembly. While McDougall was considered a hero to some, others viewed him as the traitor, not the assembly. This letter was written to answer the first in series called the Dougliad, which appeared in the New-York Gazette *from April 9 through June 25, 1770. The first Dougliad essay is included below in the section opposing the Sons of Liberty.*

New-York Gazette; and the Weekly Mercury, 16 April 1770

The NEW-YORK SATYRIST. . . .

THE *ungenteel* and inhuman Treatment of our *Patriot Prisoner*, CAPTAIN MCDOUGALL, appears beyond the Power of Description;—The rude and malicious Writings and Publications *of some of the New-York Tories against him* (particularly that of the Dougliad, No. 1.) are scarce to be equalled in all the Volumes of History.—[The Dougliad is an amazing *Stab* indeed;—we may certainly conclude that Piece was *intended as one of the deepest Stabs to the* LIBERTIES; *to the* SONS OF LIBERTY *in* AMERICA, &c. that ever was published from any Press on the Continent.]—is it *possible* that any Person . . . under the *British Jurisdiction*, will endeavour to *insure* and PUBLICKLY *vilify a Prisoner* OF AN UNBLEMISHED REPUTATION, and that before he is legally adjudged by his Peers; Guilty, or not Guilty?—*Shame.—Shame to common Honesty.*—SHAME TO EVERY THING THAT IS GOOD.

"TORY, *stand forth*,—I dare thee to be tried
In that great *Court*, where *Conscience* must preside

Speak, but consider well,—*thy sacred Use*,
And as they GOD must judge thee, *speak the Truth*."

Would not *our Patriot* have been safer *(in Respect to ungenteel Usage)* with the ancient Heathens,—with Turks,—Saracens—Moors,—or popish Spaniards;—or more safe and *kindly treated* with some of the wildest Indians in any Parts of the known World, than with *some of this inhuman* TORY FACTION *of* NEW-YORK *in* N. AMERICA?

AN ANONYMOUS WRITER: "A CARD TO THE SONS OF LIBERTY"

The Sons of Liberty did not keep a constant presence in the colonies. Instead, they appeared and disappeared from the Stamp Act on whenever their services were needed. As conflicts between America and England grew in the 1770s, the Sons of Liberty took on a more permanent visible presence. In this short card or letter of thanks, an unnamed New Yorker thanks the group for its role in fighting the tea tax.

Rivington's New-York Gazetteer; or Connecticut, New-Jersey, Hudson's River, and Quebec Weekly Advertiser, 11 November 1774

A CARD,
PRESENTING compliments to all the SONS of LIBERTY *in* AMERICA, particularly to those of New-York, to congratulate and acquaint them, that I sincerely rejoice to find such a numerous body of *high-spirited* people here, exerting themselves with the most essential *perseverance* in the good old cause of *General Liberty*;—am glad to find that Americans are still universal in the grand cause;—like strokes of lightning, in a moment, your sentiments are penetrating to the bottom of every iniquitous, dark, and futile, scheme [of Great Britain].

OPPOSED TO THE SONS OF LIBERTY

AN ANONYMOUS WRITER: "THE NOISIEST YELPERS IN THE WHOLE PACK"

Because the governors of the colonies were appointed in England, they were targets of attack. When Massachusetts Governor Thomas Hutchinson came under attack from an anonymous Boston writer, those loyal to the crown came to his defense. Here, an unknown writer defends the governor by attacking the Sons of Liberty, calling them the "noisiest yelpers in the whole pack."

The Censor (Boston), 23 November 1771

THERE are certain persons among us, who in the common concerns of life, do not exhibit any extravagant malignity of disposition, but no sooner do they enter the lists of *political* warfare, they strip themselves of all the social virtues, and become the noisiest *yelpers* in the whole *pack*. There are some I would candidly suppose are not led from a love of disorder of self-exaltation to become adventurers in this desperate game; but absurdly imagine themselves to be instruments of such little consequence, as not likely to do much mischief: such persons should remember, that *frogs, lice; vermine* the most *insignificant* and *despicable* have heretofore proved the most severe plagues to an unhappy kingdom. . . .

THERE are others . . . who for the vain purpose of creating a *temporary importance* to themselves . . . take pleasure in producing disorder in the machine of government, and wickedly seek occasion to endanger the shipwreck of the commonwealth. Every system of social regulation is pregnant with the seeds of its dissolution: in free governments a presumption of impunity cherishes the *brawler* FACTION, till it becomes that *destroying fiend* rank, rank REBELLION. No government perhaps has suffered such astonishing vicissitudes as our own, from the unbridled ambition, and daring phenzy [frenzy] of aspiring demagogues. . . . Remember my beloved countrymen! for the sake of yourselves and posterity remember, you have something to lose, but nothing to gain, by uniting in the cry of the *seditious*. . . . How despicable is the swagger of a presumptuous *demagogue!* Of what estimation all his pretence of *philanthrophy* and *patriotism!* when the measures he pursues, and so strenuously urges, appear evidently calculated to produce intestine commotions and publick calamity.

PATRICK MCADAM O'FLAGHARTY, ESQ. "I WANT TO BE AN ASSEMBLYMAN"

The pro-English Censor *specialized in essays and letters attacking efforts to separate America from Britain. In an anonymous letter, the writer pretends to be an Irish immigrant who wants to become a Massachusetts assemblyman by performing assorted "jobs" for the Sons of Liberty.*

The Censor (Boston), 29 February 1772

To the sweet ELECTORS of the TOWN of BOSTON.
   Friends and Brethren in one common cause.
   THOUGH I was not born in the country, yet I have a great many natural connections in it, my *Honies!* and having a great affection to *libertas* . . . and am come to live and die with you, so I am: I am told you have some

meetings here called *caucasses* do you see, or some such *outlandish* word, where they make all the Representative and Town-Officers. . . . I have a great itch to move in a *higher* sphere do you see, and long mightily to be a *Parliament Man*. . . . I will but just hint at my qualifications, with as much prolixity as may be: I can *tar* and *feather* any body with the best of you, ay and *cart* them to the D——l and all; In *dear Ireland* I was a *White-Boy*, so I was; what do you call them here? *High Sons*. . . . And many a brave merry prank we play'd too, like nothing at all: I was one of the foremost of our gang, and would rob my own Father to serve the *common cause*. . . . My dear Cousin *O'Connolly* is a sweet *Son of Liberty*, and man of fashion . . . so he is: And lives in *Boston*, poor soul! but he's dead; he informed me in a big letter he brought me, that this was the country for an honest industrious-like Gentleman to get his bread in, and rise in the world, so I am come to see you, *my Lovelies!* and love you mightily, so I do: So they tell me you have a vacancy for a Representative in this brave City, my *Lovelies!* . . . I have got a sweet *shillaly* for all sorts of Tories, faith! here's at them.

The Honourable
PATRICK MCADAM O'FLAGHARTY, Esq.

AN ANONYMOUS WRITER: "THE DOUGLIAD, NO. 1"

Few Americans chastised the Sons of Liberty for fighting the Stamp Act in 1765, and the writer of the Dougliad series was no different. He distinguished between that activity by the group and what it was now doing in New York. The writer of the Dougliad did not consider the Sons of Liberty currently in operation as true Sons of Liberty. True Sons of Liberty, he said, would fight for the freedom of all and of all to speak their own minds.

New-York Gazette; and the Weekly Mercury, 9 April 1770

To the READER.
THE *liberty of a man* in society, *as designed by the celebrated Mr. Lock, is to be "subject to no power, but that established* by consent, *in the common wealth; nor under the dominion of any will, or restraint of any law, but what the legislative shall enact*, according to the trust put in it." . . . THE SONS OF LIBERTY, *distinguished themselves by an early, and undisguised opposition to these, pernicious innovations. Far from censuring, I respect and applaud them; and am at all times devoted to their defence. They acted with firm and manly spirit, becoming the friends of their injured country*. . . . *Remember my gentle reader, to distinguish between them and the mock patriots who assume the flaming epithet of* TRUE *sons of liberty; in the same manner that you ought to distinguish between* social *and* natural *liberty. The first is subject to the*

controul of law, or those regulations wisely contrived for the peace and happiness of society: But the latter, to use the words of Mr. Lock, "is to be free from any power on earth, and not under the will or legislative authority of man."

No. 1. The DOUGLIAD.

TRUE liberty, or the principle of a TRUE son of liberty, consists in speaking and acting without restraint or controul; to be denied this privilege, is nothing better than Egyptian bondage; for how are we free, when our tongues are fettered by authority, or our actions limited by laws! The sentiments and inclinations of mankind, varying not less than their features; it must be clear, that this earling of a choice and elevated spirit, is by no means *common* to the sons of Adam. To it's [*sic*] proper exercise, a blind submission to our dictates is essential; for if our opinions are thwarted, or our views disappointed, we are no more *free, we cannot do what we please.* . . . True freedom is far more excellent than order or government; for tho' by the latter we are protected in our lives and properties; what are these benefits compared to the exquisite delight of *saying and doing as we please?* Nor can we be at a loss, to whom to assign this *natural* privilege. Not surely to the *legislature*; for they may not always have the complaisance to consult our humours, or obey our mandates (I speak of a TRUE son of liberty.) Instead of serving, they may, in our opinion, betray our cause; and put contempt on our best performances. . . .

The truth is, that to a TRUE sons of liberty only it belongs, *to speak and act without Controul*; to those, I mean, who contend for freedom in it's [*sic*] utmost latitude, as their own proper and peculiar inheritance, superior to all law and authority, and independent and unconfined as the light of Heaven, while at the same time, they have spirit enough to refuse the least indulgence to others; who by differing from them manifest that they are too weak and timid, to be significant.

AN ANONYMOUS WRITER: "TWO TYPES OF SONS OF LIBERTY"

Describing the nature of the opposing parties was fashionable in colonial times. One type of the Sons of Liberty, according to this writer, were willing to destroy their country for their wrongheaded cause. The other kind consisted of ministers who preached disobedience to the laws of England.

Rivington's New-York Gazetteer; or the Connecticut, New-Jersey, Hudson's River, and Quebec Weekly Advertiser, 9 March 1775

It is a remark that the high sons of Liberty consist of but two sorts of men. The first are those who by their debaucheries and ill conduct in life, are reduced almost to poverty, and are happy in finding a subsistence, though it is even on the destruction of their country; for on the turbulence of the times, and the heated imaginations of the populace, depends their existence. The latter are the ministers of the gospel, who, instead of preaching to their flocks meekness, sobriety, attention to their different employments, and a steady obedience to the laws of Britain, belch from the pulpit liberty, independence, and a steady perseverance in endeavoring to shake off their allegiance to the mother country.

QUESTIONS

1. What made the Sons of Liberty so attractive as heroes to so many Americans? Explain.
2. In the *Boston Gazette* article of February 24, 1766, the Sons of Liberty are referred to as "true born." Why might Patriots refer to themselves as "true born Sons of Liberty"? Use the Dougliad essay attacking the Sons of Liberty to explain your reasoning.
3. According to the writers in the *Censor* and *Rivington's New-York Gazetteer*, what were the real motivations of the Sons of Liberty?
4. According to the writer of the Dougliad, what is the essence of true freedom?

CHAPTER 19

Tories versus Patriots, 1768–1775

The ten to fifteen years leading up to the Revolution were filled with problems for Americans. The colonies entered an economic depression when the French and Indian War ended in 1763. Depression was accompanied by inflation, especially in food prices, and the lack of currency, which had been scarce in America for most of its existence, continued to compound the problem. In addition, moral and economic issues slowed the profitable slave trade that had provided a livelihood for many during the eighteenth century. The use of slaves and others in bound servitude was beginning to decline, particularly in non-Southern colonies.

Religious differences among Americans, which had been elevated by denominational divisions during the Great Awakening (see Chapter 8), grew. Many feared that the Anglicans wanted to establish an American bishopric. Such a move, those who opposed it felt, was the first step in establishing Anglicanism as the state church of America just as it was in England. The concept was abhorrent to many Americans whose ancestors, just a few generations earlier, had come to America to escape government-mandated religion.

Americans also found themselves at odds economically. Artisans and laborers, merchants and shippers, and, closer to the Revolution, importers and nonimporters were at odds concerning salaries, taxes, the sale of goods, and the sources of the items for sale. In this environment of hardship and controversy, Americans began to take sides. Those who believed that America needed to gain more autonomy over its own existence and escape the taxes and laws of England were called Patriots or Whigs. Those who favored British policy, the right to tax America, and did not want to see the colonies separate from the British Empire were referred to as Loyalists or Tories.

Just how many Americans were Tories before the Revolution may never be known, but about 100,000 left America for England and the Caribbean and never returned following the Battles of Lexington and Concord in 1775.[1] Newspaper advertisements announced the departure of many Tories from America. They left behind their property, and most never were compensated.

Most American newspapers were staunchly Patriot. Printers with Tory sympathies found themselves constantly attacked not only in print but in public, and most Tory printers went out of business as soon as the Revolution began. One, James Rivington, was able to reestablish himself in New Jersey in 1777 after he was run out of New York and forced to return to England in 1775. Rivington's newspaper, *Rivington's New-York Gazetteer*, was more objective in its approach to news than most other newspapers in pre–Revolutionary America. Following the Battles of Lexington and Concord, for example, Rivington printed both American and British versions of the confrontations. That, however, was enough to send an angry Patriot mob into his shop where its members destroyed the printer's press and type.

Another Tory printer, John Mein of Boston, entered into a battle in print with the *Boston Gazette* concerning nonimportation, or the practice of boycotting British goods (see Chapter 20). After one attack, Mein, who published the *Boston Chronicle*, demanded that *Gazette* printers Benjamin Edes and John Gill reveal the author of the disparaging remarks made about him. When they refused, Mein promised to cane the first one of them he met on the street. When Mein saw Gill the next day, he knocked Gill down and beat him on the head. Shortly after that, Mein was attacked on the street by angry citizens. While defending himself, Mein shot a bystander and subsequently fled to England rather than face prosecution.[2]

The chapter readings supporting Patriots and attacking Tories begin with an anonymous Connecticut letter that was written when America's first attempt at nonimportation began to deteriorate. It suggests that Tories should be tarred and feathered. It is followed by an anonymous letter describing the character of Tories. Interestingly, the traits ascribed to the Tories are similar to these ascribed to the Patriots by the Tories.

The next selection is a variation on one of the most popular tunes in American history, "Yankee Doodle." Originally, the song was sung in seventeenth-century England, but it quickly became popular in America during the Revolutionary period. The tune printed here pokes fun at Tories, the way they dress, and their strong loyalties to England. A macaroni was a slang term for Englishmen who put on airs, and as such it became a derogatory term for Loyalists. The next selection, a poem, is a reply to an attack on the "JOIN, or DIE" woodcut that was now being used by Patriots to represent America in the dispute with England. Compare this poem to the initial poem attacking the Patriots' use of the image that is included in the Tory section below.

The readings supporting Tories and attacking Patriots begin with a belittling view on the nature of Patriots. The men referred to at the end of the article are Thomas Young, Sam Adams, James Otis, and William Molineux, although one extra blank for his name appears in the article. The next selection, written by an unknown author, refers to the re-institution of the "JOIN, or DIE" snake woodcut created by Benjamin Franklin to represent colonial unity during the French and Indian War and resurrected during the Stamp Act crisis. It directly attacks the Patriot leaders of New England.

The final Tory selections appeared in *Rivington's New-York Gazetteer* following attacks made on the Tory printer. The first talks about tarring and feathering Tories. The second belittles Whigs, and the third, which includes a woodcut of Rivington hanged in effigy, attacks Patriots who suppress the freedom of the press.

FOR PATRIOTS AND AGAINST TORIES

A TRADER: "OUR CONTINENT'S LAST STRUGGLES FOR LIBERTY"

In 1768 and 1769, merchants in many of America's major ports agreed that they should ban together and refuse to import British products as a way to protest the Townshend Acts, taxes placed on tea, paint, lead, paper, and glass in 1767. The agreement, however, was not universal among merchants, and by 1770, nonimportation was falling apart. In this letter from the anonymous A Trader, Tories are called traitors who would sell out their own country for monetary gain.

Massachusetts Spy (Boston), 25 September 1770

WHEN this Continent are [*sic*] in the last Agonies and struggles for Liberty, and when they are so universally agreed in one plan to get rid of some unconstitutional arbitrary acts of parliament, it is astonishing and to the last degree intollerable, to see some few weak, selfish, traiterous Jacobites and Tories—(who for a single groat would sell their country) plead for breaking the non importation agreement . . . is not the universal voice of the people the best humane law that can be made?—But some are very virulent, and with their poisonous doctrines, would assist to overthrow a wholesome constitution; by influencing weak minds where they can have any influence, that it is a trick of the merchants to get off their old goods. But, blessed be God, there is virtue enough left in this government, to see and withstand them. . . . Let them know by woful experience what an evil thing and bitter it is to set up against the universal judgment of the people, better one man die (a political death) than the whole people perish. I would have them hooted by the rising generations, in whose cause the continent are struggling, and if that will not do, I would use what has proved effectual, viz. tar and feather in every town where such are to be found, and persist in it, I am, the public's most humble servant, A TRADER *that will not Import*.

P.S. I hope if any remain after the foregoing hints, to persist in such principles to encourage an importation . . . that the several towns to which they belong will adopt the plan of Boston, and send their names to be printed as base perfidious wretches in all the news papers in this colony.

CORNELIUS NEPOS: "THE GENERAL DENOMINATION OF TORIES"

In the newspaper battle between the Patriots and the Tories, name-calling and descriptions of the opposition commonly appeared. In this description of Tories, the anonymous writer describes two types of Tories. One was to be pitied; and the other was the doom of American trade.

Boston Gazette, and Country Journal, 10 January 1774

To the PRINTER,

THERE are two very different species of men that pass under the general denomination of *tories*. The one sort usually devoid of the very ideas of honor or virtue, are the most despicable beings, that ever appear'd in human shape; the other are men of honest hearts, but deluded not by "sounds and decsimations, but by the most palpable falshoods and fanciful existences, and possess so small a share of penetration and discernment, that they cannot (assisted by the united wisdom of the provinces) discover the imposition—these are rather objects of pity, than contempt. By the former, I mean those who are ever ready to prostitute their abilities on the altar of preferment, and to sacrifice their consciences, their Country, and their God to gratify the basest of all passions—an insatiable lust for gain—and consequently are exerting their influence to the utmost, to support measures of administration, which . . . will be fatal to the commerce, the liberties, and ultimately to the religion of this country. . . .

CORNELIUS NEPOS.

N.B. If any tory or more dirty creature, if dirtier there can be should have the effrontery to deny the above-mentioned facts, they shall be evinced to the satisfaction of the most prejudiced—and all the works of darkness of the whole group shall be exposed to light by C. N.

AN ANONYMOUS WRITER: "THE MACARONI"

The tune "Yankee Doodle," which dates to the seventeenth century, experienced a resurgence in eighteenth-century America. British troops first used it to deride Americans, but later, Americans turned the song into an attack on Tories. In this version, the macaroni—or English dandy who copied foreign dress and manners—is the Tory who struts about America disdaining anything colonial while praising all that is British.

Massachusetts Spy Or, Thomas's Boston Journal, 19 May 1774

The MACARONI.

TO please the bucks of this gay town,
    And give them something pretty,
Long time I've rambled up and down,
    Thro' country, and thro' city;
In ev'ry place I view'd each face,
    Some I saw fat, some boney,
But he who now doth shew his taste
    Is call'd a *Macaroni*. . . .
Upon his head a high toupee
    Stood foolishly erected;
A stranger sight I ne'er did see,
    Nor e'er to see expected; . . .
With breeches large and wond'rous wide;
    Like to a *Dutchman's* trowsers,
With simp'ring grin and haughty stride;
    And lies that saith were rousers . . .
Say what you can, 'tis not a man,
    'Tis but a *Macaroni*.
And yet the thing it did pretend
    To be a human creature,
But Heaven ever me defend
    From being of it's [*sic*] nature. . . .
A man we love, we must approve,
    If rich, or void of money;
But cur'd be she who'er can be
    Fond of a *Macaroni*.

AN ANONYMOUS WRITER: "A DEFENSE OF 'JOIN, OR DIE' "

Benjamin Franklin's "JOIN, or DIE" woodcut (see Chapter 14), created to unite the colonies at the outset of the French and Indian War, made its third appearance in 1774 in an effort to unite the colonies against British taxes, troop occupation, and port closings. The "snakes in the grass" in the poem is a reference to Tories. The poem is a response to one that appeared in Rivington's New-York Gazetteer, *which is also included in the chapter, and refers to Patriots as "sons of sedition." That writer says that the head of the snake—New England—deserves to be bruised, a reference to England's occupation and embargo against Boston.*

Pennsylvania Journal; and the Weekly Advertiser (Philadelphia),
31 August 1774

THAT New England's abus'd, and by the sons of sedition,
Is granted without either prayer or petition.
And that "tis a scandalous, saucy reflection,
That merits the soundest, severest correction,"
Is as readily granted, "How comes it to pass?"
Because she is pester'd with snakes in the grass,
Who by lying and cringing, and such like pretensions.
And you, Mr. Pensioner, instead of repentance,
(If I don't mistake you) have wrote your own sentence;
For by such Snakes as this, New-England's abused,
And the head of these serpents, "you know, should be bruised."

FOR TORIES AND AGAINST PATRIOTS

AN ANONYMOUS WRITER: "RECIPE FOR A MODERN PATRIOT"

In the continuing Tory and Patriot newspaper battle, members of both groups sought ever more clever ways to attack the other. Here, an unknown Tory provides the recipe for creating a Patriot. It includes enough unfounded abuse, endless writing, lack of conscience, plenty of atheism, and as many lies as necessary. According to the writer, the formula will produce the likes of Boston's Thomas Young, Samuel Adams, James Otis, and William Molineux, Patriot leaders of that city.

The Censor (Boston), 8 February 1772

The Publisher of the CENSOR is desired to insert the following *Recipe* to make a *modern* PATRIOT for the *colonies*, especially for the *Massachusetts*, to wit.

TAKE of impudence, virulence, and groundless abuse, *quantum suffi-cit*; of flowing periods, *half a drachm*; conscience a *quarter* of *a scruple*; atheism, deism, and libertinism, *ad libitum*; false reports well adapted, and plausible lies, with abuse of Magistracy, a pusillanimous and diabol-ical contempt of divine revelation and all its abettors *an equal quantity*; honour and integrity not quite an *atom*; fraud, imposition, and hypocrisy, and any *proportion* that may seem expedient; infuse these in the credulity of the people, *one thousand gallons* as a *menstrum*, stir in the *phrenzy* of the *times*, and at the end of a year or two, this judicious composition will probably bring forth a Y——, and A——, an O——, and a M——.

AN ANONYMOUS WRITER: "WHAT THE SNAKE DESERVES"

The snake, through Benjamin Franklin's efforts, developed into a meta-phor for the American colonies. When printer Isaiah Thomas resurrected the snake in 1774 in an effort to unite the colonies against English taxes, occupation, and embargoes, Tories attacked the concept. In this poem, the author agrees that the Patriots are surely like a snake in the grass. He also believes that England has been justified in bruising the head of the serpent, which was New England, for its rebellious acts.

Rivington's New-York Gazetteer; or the Connecticut, New-Jersey, Hudson's River, and Quebec Weekly Advertiser, 25 August 1774

YE Sons of Sedition, how comes it to pass,
That America's typ'd by a SNAKE—in the grass?
Don't you think 'tis a scandalous, saucy reflection,
That merits the soundest, severest Correction,
NEW-ENGLAND's the Head too;—NEW ENGLAND's abused;
For the *Head of the serpent* we know *should be* Bruised.

AN ANONYMOUS WRITER: "AN ATTACK ON PATRIOT SUPPRESSION OF THE PRESS"

Printer James Rivington was one of the most successful printers in co-lonial America; his New-York Gazetteer's *circulation reached around 3,600 issues weekly. Rivington, who was the son of a wealthy London printer, could have easily fit the description of a macaroni, as depicted in the song in the first section of this chapter. Rivington printed letters and essays from both Tories and Patriots. Patriots, however, wanted him to print only their point of view. Rivington balked and declared his press would remain open to all. This poem was written to support that position and to attack Patriots who, the writer said, feared an open and equal press in America.*

Rivington's New-York Gazetteer; or the Connecticut, New-Jersey, Hudson's River, and Quebec Weekly Advertiser, 8 December 1774

THEY tremble at an equal press,
For reasons, every dunce can guess. Without one single grain of
   merit,
Devoid of honour, sense and spirit
Treating all men as mortal foes,
Who dare their high behests oppose.
Stark raving mad, with party rage,
With coward arms, those foes engage,
And lurk in print, a nameless crew,
Intent to slander, rob, undo.
Consicious of guild, they hide their shame,
And stab conceal'd the printer's fame.
Dares the poor man impartial be.
He's doom'd to want and infamy.
Condemn'd by their imperial ire
To poison, daggers, pillage, fire;
Precarious lives in constant dread,
Tar, feathers, murder, haunt his bed;
Sees all he loves, a sacrifice,
If he dares publish, out—but lies.
What would you have the poor man do? . . .
Alas, vain men, how blind, how weak;
Is this the liberty we seek! . . .

AN ANONYMOUS WRITER: "THE WHIG SONG"

Whig was the political label given to Patriots. In this song, the traits of the Patriot are presented stanza by stanza. Patriots were the spawn of the Devil whose goal it was to damn all Americans.

Rivington's New-York Gazetteer; or the Connecticut, New-Jersey, Hudson's River, and Quebec Weekly Advertiser, 26 January 1775

The WHIG: A SONG. . . .

WOULD you know what a Whig is, and always was,
I'll shew you his face, as it were in a glass,
He's a *rebel* by nature, a *villain* in grain,
A *saint* by profession, who never had grace:
Cheating and *lying* are puny things,
Rapine and *plundering* venial sins,
His great occupation is *ruining nations*,
Subverting of Crowns, and *murdering Kings*.

2.

To she that he came from a wight of worth
'Twas *Lucifer's pride* that first gave him birth,
'Twas bloody *Barbarity* bore the elf,
Ambition the midwife that brought him forth:
Oh! *Judas* was tutor, until he grew *big*,
Hypocrisy taught him to *care not a fig*
For all that is *sacred*,—and thus was,
And brought in the world, what we call a Whig.

3.

Spew'd up among mortals by hellish jaws,
To strike he begins at *religion* and *Laws*,
With *pious Inventions*, and *bloody intentions*,
And *all* for to bring in the *good of cause*.
At *cheating* and *lying* he plays his game;
Always dissembling, and *never* the same;
Till he fills the whole nation with sins of d—n-t—n,
Then goes to the d-v-l, from *when* he *came*.

JAMES RIVINGTON: "MY PRESS WILL REMAIN OPEN TO ALL PARTIES"

James Rivington's New-York Gazetteer *boldly proclaimed "PRINTED at his OPEN and UNINFLUENCED PRESS" in its nameplate (front-page title). When Patriots threatened him for publishing Tory letters and essays, he refused to change his printing policies. Finally, irate New York Patriots hanged Rivington in effigy. Instead of backing down, the obstinate printer replied with an editorial on freedom of the press that attacked Patriots as the enemies of press freedom. The printer also added a wood-cut of himself hanging in effigy to emphasize his position.*

Rivington's New-York Gazetteer; or the Connecticut, New-Jersey, Hudson's River, and Quebec Weekly Advertiser, 20 April 1775

The Printer is bold to affirm, that his press has been open to publications from all parties; and he defies his enemies to produce an instance to the contrary. He has considered his press in the light of a public
office, to which every man has a right to have re-course. But the moment
he ventured to publish sentiments which were opposed to the dangerous
views and designs of certain demagogues, he found himself held up as
an enemy of his country, and the most unwearied pains were taken to
ruin him. In the country wherein he was born, he always heard the liberty
of the press represented as the great security of freedom, and in that
sentiment he has been educated; nor has he reason to think differently
now on account of his experience in this country. While his enemies

Hanging in Effigy. New York printer James Rivington angered many New Yorkers by printing pro-British letters and essays in his *Gazetteer*. In April 1775, a group of citizens threatened Rivington and then hanged a likeness of the printer. Rivington used the incident to promote his right to freedom of the press and emphasized the point by running a woodcut of his likeness hanging from a tree. He said his press had always been open to anyone, regardless of their political position. Now, he said, men wanted to establish "cruel tyranny" over the paper and dictate to him what he could print.

make liberty the prostituted pretense of their illiberal persecution of him, their aim is to establish a most cruel tyranny, and the Printer thinks that some very recent transactions will convince the good people of this city of the difference between being governed by a few factious individuals, and the good old law and constitution, under which we have so long been a happy people.

QUESTIONS

1. Why do you think Patriots were able to resort successfully to measures such as the tarring and feathering of Tories?

2. How are the ways that Tories and Patriots attacked each other in the news-papers similar? How are they different?

3. From the readings, can you determine the positions of Tories and Patriots politically?

4. From the readings, which of the two groups best used persuasion and emotional appeals to create animosity toward the other group?

NOTES

1. Francis G. Walett, *Patriots, Loyalists & Printers* (Worcester, Mass.: American Antiquarian Society, 1976), 74.

2. See *Boston Gazette, and Country Journal*, 28 August 1769; and 15 and 30 January 1770.

CHAPTER 20

Nonimportation Agreements, 1768–1775

Following the Stamp Act crisis of 1765, the relationship between America and England deteriorated. England levied taxes, and America responded with protests. Americans from South Carolina to New England quickly realized that the best way to get the attention of king and Parliament and to harm England was through economic pressure. Assorted nonimportation agreements in 1765 forced the 1766 repeal of the Stamp Act. What had worked once, many Americans reasoned, would work again: pressure the crown to repeal the latest set of taxes placed on the colonies, the 1767 Townshend Acts, which placed a levy on tea, lead, paper, paint, and glass.

In 1768 and 1769, various merchant associations throughout America produced a set of nonimportation agreements, which stated that the tradesmen of the town would no longer import items from England or other countries if the point of origin for the supplies was England. In addition to the prohibitions upon British goods, nonimportation agreements promoted the production and use of American-made items. If Americans could refrain from using British goods, especially tea, paint, lead, glass, and paper, which were the Townshend Act taxed items, America could force England to repeal the act and increase its own stature in the empire, or so the Patriot leaders thought.

Whether the boycott increased America's stature in England is debatable, but Benjamin Franklin declared that nonimportation was a win-win proposition for Americans. "It gives me great Pleasure to hear that our People are steady in their Resolutions of Non Importation," Franklin wrote from London. "They will soon be sensible of the Benefit of such Conduct."[1]

Early in 1770, Parliament did repeal most of the taxes levied by the Townshend Acts, ironically when many merchants—especially those in New York—tired of the burden nonimportation placed on them. With the repeal, nonimportation fell apart. The nonimportation agreements of 1769, which had been organized locally, had worked well, and colonial leaders realized that the economic and political implications of trade boycotts with England would make them powerful weapons if needed again.

The next time the colonies wanted to use nonimportation, however, the effort would have to be a unified one among all colonists. This happened in 1774 when the Continental Congress reinstituted the concept with a nonimportation, nonexportation, and nonconsumption agreement called the "Association." The Congress unanimously passed the declaration not to trade in any way with Great Britain or any of its colonies in the West Indies. Each county, city, or town was to set up a committee of correspondence to ensure that all complied with nonimportation. If any merchants did not, the Association stated, their names were to be "published in the Gazette, to the end that all such foes to the rights of British America may be publicly known, and universally contemned as the enemies of American liberty."[2] The colonies were organized, and the economic and political battle lines between America and Britain had been drawn.

The readings supporting nonimportation begin with the resolves of the New York merchants to abide by the nonimportation organized following the Townshend Acts. It is followed by an attack on those same merchants in 1770 for discontinuing the trade boycott. The letter originally appeared in the *Pennsylvania Gazette*. By 1770 many New York merchants had abandoned the agreement and were trading with England. This letter compares those merchants who ignored nonimportation to Judas Iscariot, the apostle of Jesus of Nazareth who betrayed Jesus for thirty pieces of silver.

The next entries deal with the 1774 nonimportation agreement. The first calls for a universal adoption of nonimportation. The second shows to what lengths committees of correspondence would go in order to enforce nonimportation once it was passed by the Continental Congress.

The chapter readings opposing nonimportation begin with one of Boston printer John Mein's attacks on a group he called "the Well Disposed." Mein, who strongly opposed nonimportation in 1769, said "the Well Disposed" forced nonimportation on many Boston merchants yet continued themselves to import British goods. For months, Mein printed on the front page of his paper, "A QUESTION FOR THE WELL DISPOSED." It named "John Hancock, Thomas Cushing, J. Rowe, Edward Payne, Wm.

Phillips, and Jno. Barrett" as the group of crooked merchants. The parody in this reading discusses duffil, a coarse Dutch wool material.

The next selection deals with the importation of tea and the Boston Tea Party and explains why nonimportation was bad for America. It is followed by a letter in a continuing series written to the inhabitants of North America by the Reverend Charles Inglis of New York. Here, Inglis calls for the nonimportation established by the Continental Congress to be rejected. Instead, Inglis suggests, America should seek political answers to the problems of taxes on imported goods.

FOR NONIMPORTATION

NEW YORK MERCHANTS: "RESOLVES"

Protests against the Stamp Act led to its repeal. The Townshend Acts increased the number of items on which Americans would have to pay a duty. Some of the merchants in New York decided that the best way to stop such taxes would be to fight back against the British pocketbook. They proposed a boycott against British goods. Because the boycott was voluntary, not all merchants in the city participated. Similar plans were put into operation in other colonies.

New-York Gazette; and the Weekly Mercury, 12 September 1768

A Copy of the RESOLVES subscribed by the Merchants in New-York, dated the 27th of August, 1768.

I. THAT we will not send for from Great-Britain, either upon our own Account or on Commission this Fall, any other Goods than what we have already ordered.

II. THAT we will not import any kind of Merchandize from Great-Britain, either on our own Account or on Commission, or any otherwise, nor purchase from any Factor or others, any kind of Goods imported from Great-Britain directly, or by Way of any of the other Colonies, or by Way of the West-Indies . . . until the *forementioned* Acts of Parliament imposing Duties on Paper, Glass, &c. be repealed. . . .

III. WE further agree, not to import any kind of Merchandize from Hamburgh and Holland, directly thence, nor by any other Way whatever, more than what we have already ordered. . . .

IV. WE also promise to countermand all Orders given from Great-Britain, on or since the 16th Inst. . . . ordering those Goods not to be sent unless the forementioned Duties are taken off.

V. AND we further agree, that if any Person or Persons, Subscribers hereto, shall take any Advantage by importing any kind of Goods that are herein restricted, directly or indirectly contrary to the true Intent and Meaning of this Agreement; such Person or Persons shall by us be deemed Enemies to their Country.

VI. LASTLY, we agree, that if any Goods shall be consigned or sent over to us, contrary to our Agreement in this Subscription; such Goods so imported, shall be lodged in some public Ware-House, there to be under Confinement until the forementioned Acts are repealed.

Subscribed by nearly all the Merchants and Traders in Town.

A JERSEY MAN: "AN ATTACK ON NEW YORK MERCHANTS"

By 1770 the boycott against British merchants was disintegrating. As more and more merchants discontinued their protest against Britain, the ability to fight taxes decreased, according to the writer of this letter, who called himself A Jersey Man. He declared that New Yorkers were letting down the rest of America by discontinuing the boycott.

Massachusetts Spy (Boston), 14 August 1770

TO THE PRINTER.

IT cannot be denied, but that the Non-importation Agreement, which was entered into by the merchants in the several colonies on this continent, has been much applauded by the most judicious and fast friends of America, on both sides of the water, as the only expedient to obtain a repeal of the odious Act of Parliament, imposing a duty on goods imported, for the purpose of raising a revenue in America. . . .

However the self-denial, or great the hardships may be in this matter, on the part of the merchants in particular, it is certain the cause, for which it is suffered, is infinitely greater; for no less than our civil rights and privileges, both for ourselves and posterity, are apparently at stake in this contest, and undoubtedly will be infringed upon, and finally taken away, if a bad ministry may have their ends.—Hence how must it grieve the hearts of all true undissembled friends of America, to behold the merchants of New York, even the committee or depositaires of that salutary measure, have violated and broke their plighted faith in this matter, and thereby have given cause to our inveterate enemies to exult and rejoice.—Shocking! to see New-York, before so high in esteem and reputation, who had the eyes of her sister-colonies fixed on her, as a strong pillar in this important struggle, just when brought to a crisis, fall through, and desert her cause. How can you (New-Yorkers) who were formerly renowned for asserting and supporting the cause of Freedom, answer for this conduct to God, your Country, and posterity? Alas! the love of Mammon has been too prevalent with you—to this idol you have prostituted you honour, and stained your character.—I will not compare your guilt to that of J——s; but the wound you have given to the common cause of America, is indeed dangerous. . . . The best you can now do, is, to do as St. Peter did, when he had denied his master, return instantly from whence you have so shamefully revolted, that your crime may be remitted.   A JERSEY MAN.

A CONNECTICUT FARMER: "FARMERS MUST SUPPORT NONIMPORTATION"

Before the First Continental Congress met in September 1774, talk circulated in the colonies about the possibility of a mandatory nonimportation agreement for all of America. The delegates to the congress approved just such a pact, which probibited imports and exports. In this letter, a Connecticut farmer outlines the hardships that such an agreement would create for farmers, but he insists that they must be willing to shoulder the burden for the good of America.

Massachusetts Spy Or, Thomas's Boston Journal, 25 August 1774

To the FARMERS *of the Colony of* CONNECTICUT.

GENTLEMEN.

AS one of your order I take the liberty to address you upon a subject of the last importance to you, and your posterity; the question is no less than this, whether you will quietly submit to the yoke of merciless tyranny and usurpation—let a wretched minister of the state lay a tax of a dollar a head on each of your polls, and tax your cattle and lands at such an exorbitant rate that you cannot pay, then take your land for the rates, and make you and your children slaves to him and his,—or whether you will nobly and resolutely refuse a compliance, and honestly and chearfully make a willing sacrifice of some little part of your property now, in defence of your and your children's liberty.—Life and death, in a political sense, are now set before you, and you certainly have your choice. . . .

I am determined to support, to the utmost of my property, the honest merchant who will punctually and religious observe such nonimportation and non-exportation agreement as may be come into by a congress from the colonies to meet at Philadelphia the first of September next: And on the other hand, I am determined to withdraw my trade, and all profits and advantages arising from it, from the merchant or merchants who either directly or indirectly goes counter to such agreement. . . .

I think the farmers can do more towards regaining and supporting the liberties of this country than any other set of men whatever, as they are the present Lords and proprietors of the lands and produce thereof, we must therefore insist upon and resolutely urge a non-importation and a non-exportation agreement to England, and the West-Indies: But methinks I hear some mercenary merchants say, that won't do for either of us, we must have our navigation go on; we must export lumber, horses, &c. else what will you do with your provision? and we must import salt, sugar, Molasses, &c. And some farmers of the like stamp, re-echo, true, we must put off our old horses, and we must have salt,—but let me tell you, without a total stop is put to the West-India trade, nothing can be done; for I am well informed, and I believe may venture to affirm it is true, that there is no less than seventy-four members of parliament that are West-India planters or proprietors; and I also am credibly informed that they were the means of fomenting these difficulties, by first getting a duty laid on all sugars, molasses, coffee, &c. not imported from the English West-India Islands; it will therefore be necessary to shew them of how much importance we are, by distressing them for want of our trade. . . .

I am sufficiently chagrined, and my indignation boils to hear some who call themselves prudent or moderate men talk,—'tis best, say they, to be moderate, to be well advised, to act cautiously, and to do nothing rashly: 'Tis true, the caution is good, but it is needless; for the temper of these men is to do nothing at all but calmly submit to every requisition of parliament.—They say why the voice of parliament makes all Europe to tremble; but I answer, it never made America to wink. . . . We have prayed and petitioned till we have been insulted and abused, and treated viler than any slave had a right to expect. . . . I hope my brother farmers will kindly receive the hints given them, and act accordingly.

I am a sincere friend to husbandry, navigation and trade.
    A CONNECTICUT FARMER.

THE COMMITTEE OF NORFOLK: "JOHN BROWN'S VIOLATION OF NONIMPORTATION"

As part of the Continental Congress' nonimportation agreement, which was called the Association by the delegates, all counties in America were authorized to elect committees to oversee nonimportation, seek out violators, and have their names published in newspapers. This newspaper report appeared after the committee in Norfolk, Virginia, discovered a ship owned by John Brown filled with slaves for sale.

Virginia Gazette (Williamsburg, Dixon and Hunter), 25 March
1775

To the FREEMEN *OF* VIRGINIA. . . .

TRUSTING in your sure resentment against the enemies of your country, we, the COMMITTEE elected by *ballot* for the *borough* of NORFOLK, hold up for your just indignation Mr. *John Brown*, merchant of this place. . . .

On Thursday the 2d of March this committee were informed of the arrival of the brig *Fanny*, Capt. *Watson*, with a number of SLAVES, for Mr. *Brown*; and, upon inquiry, it appeared that they were shipped from Jamaica, as his property, and on his account; that he had taken great pains to *conceal* their arrival from the knowledge of the committee, and that the shipper of the *slaves*, Mr. *Brown*'s correspondents, and the Captain of the vessel, were all fully apprized of the continental prohibition against that article. These circumstances induced a suspicion that Mr. *Brown* had given orders for the *slaves* himself, which he positively *denied*, asserting that he had expressly *forbidden* his correspondents to send any, as being contrary to the association. . . .

From the whole of this transaction, therefore, we, the *committee* for *Norfolk borough* do give it as our *unanimous* opinion that the said *John Brown* has *wilfully and perversely violated the Continental Association*, to which he had, wit his own hand, subscribed obedience; and that, agreeable to the 11th article, we are bound "forthwith to publish the truth of the case, to the end that all such foes to the rights of British America may be publicly known, and universally contemned as the enemies of American liberty, and that every person may henceforth break off dealings with him."

AGAINST NONIMPORTATION

JOHN MEIN: "THE WELL DISPOSED MERCHANT"

Printer John Mein opposed the voluntary nonimportation that began at the end of the 1760s. He felt that many of the advocates of the plan were really violating nonimportation while coercing less wealthy merchants to support it. In this dialogue, Mr. Well Disposed pretends that he does not sell imported British cloth, and the tailor pretends that the English broadcloth that he sees is really coarse Dutch wool duffil.

Boston Chronicle, 12 February 1770

SCENE. A Store.

Taylor. Pray Sir! have you any broad cloths to sell?

Mr. "Well Disposed." No: but I have very good Duffils which I dare say will suit you.

Taylor. I want a broad cloth, can you inform me where I can get some?

Mr. "Well Disposed." As my Duffils are of an extraordinary kind, you had better look at them.

[The supposed Duffils being by this time in sight, the Taylor had nigh cried out, Why! Sir! That's a broad cloth; but recollecting the *times*, and with *whom* he was about to deal, he suppressed the honest effusions of his heart, and, as he wanted the cloth, he then continued to act his part of the farce.]

Taylor. Really Sir! I never saw so fine a Duffil as this is, I believe it will do if the price is not too high.

The bargain is immediately made, by which Mr. *"Well disposed"* pockets thirty per cent. increase of profit, and the Taylor goes about his business *muttering.*—What a scoundrel is this Fellow! With what a sanctified face has this Pharisee been selling me a superfine broad Cloth for a Duffil? This is cheating the Devil with a witness! It does not signify, as Mr. Frebble must have his Cloaths whatever it may cost him, I may as well submit to the imposture as another.—I hope in GOD these *times* will not last long; if they do, LORD have mercy on my poor soul! . . .
A BOSTONIAN.

AN ANONYMOUS WRITER: "THE BURDEN OF NONIMPORTATION"

In the weeks following the Boston Tea Party (see Chapter 24), many Americans discussed the possibility of instituting a nonimportation agreement against British goods. This unknown writer to the Virginia Gazette *saw such a proposal as a threat to the liberty of all Americans and explained why.*

Virginia Gazette (Williamsburg, Purdie and Dixon), 20 January 1774

To Mr. PURDIE.
SIR,
    I PERCEIVE that one of your Correspondents . . . has been pleased to send you some Strictures upon . . . Importation or Non-importation. . . . I should think every Man in America highly interested that every Man's House (Storehouse or Warehouse) should be his Castle; that every Man's Property, not only in his Goods, but in his Life, more especially, should be sacred. . . . Is there no Danger to Liberty when every Merchant is liable to have his House, Property, and even Life, invaded or threatened by a Mob, who may be assembled at any Times, at the Call of unknown Leaders, by Ringing of the Bells (of all the Meeting Houses) and hanging out a Flag? Are their Leaders sure they can always train them only to fly at such as they may be directed to, in the Name of Liberty (I am sure not of Law or Order) or in the Name of the Lord!

A NEW-YORK FREEHOLDER: "WHY WE SHOULD OPPOSE NONIMPORTATION"

The New-York Freeholder was really the Reverend Charles Inglis, an Anglican minister. In an earlier writing, he warned that America was on the verge of civil war, being pushed toward it by the Patriotic leadership of the colonies. In this letter to all Americans, Inglis pleads for America to avoid nonimportation and other extreme measures. Instead, he says, Americans should use the political process to ease the tax burden. He reminds readers that most of the taxes placed on the colonies had been rescinded by Parliament.

New-York Gazette; and the Weekly Mercury, 10 October 1774

To the INHABITANTS of NORTH-AMERICA. . . .

I have always had great Doubts about the Expediency of a Non Importation Scheme, for which many are so zealous. To give it any Weight, it should be *general*, and religiously observed by all. Now supposing this practicable and that it took Place, there is the highest probability that our Exports would be prohibited, and our Ports shut up by Men of War. What would be the Consequence?—A total Stagnation to all Business—the Ruin of our Farmers, whole Wheat would scarcely sell for *Eighteen Pence* a Bushel, I mean what did not rot on their Hands; and this also would be the Case with other Grain. No Debts would be paid; and such as have Money lent out, would be in the utmost Danger of losing it intirely. In short, this Scheme seems to be big with numberless Evils to ourselves; and I apprehend would be considered in England as the Prelude of an Appeal to the Sword; and in Truth it should be so. I know it is commonly supposed that this Measure would compel Great Britain to submit to our Terms; and were this the Case, it would indeed be an Object of great Moment. But I have Reason to think, from the most authentic Information, that this is a groundless Notion—one of the vulgar Errors which prevail among us, owing to Ignorance of the true State of the British Commerce and Manufactures, and has contributed to lull us into Security and Confidence. . . .

But whatever Doubts I may have as to a *general* Non-Importation, I have none at all about one that is *partial*. It would be totally inadequate to the Purpose we have in View; and only serve to enrich a few Individuals at the Expence of the Public. Such a feeble Effort would manifest our own Weakness, irritate Government without serving ourselves, and make us a laughing Stock to the World. . . . Why should we have Recourse to any violent measures, till such as are mild and decent have been tried, and proved ineffectual? We know the Stamp-Act has been repealed—the Duty on Glass, Paint, &c. has been repealed—the Duty on Tea has been lowered. Why then not endeavour to have the Duty wholly taken off; or a free and regular CONSTITUTION fixed, which would put an End to these Troubles? What Reason is there to suppose that Government will not listen to us and to its own Interest, in this as well as in the former Instances? Were calm dispassionate Reason to preside in our Deliberations, there would not be Room to hesitate one Moment which Part we should Act in so plain a Case. . . .

A NEW-YORK FREEHOLDER.

QUESTIONS

1. Why might merchants such as those in New York agree to nonimportation agreements, and why might those same merchants renege on such agreements?

2. In what ways does the letter in the *Massachusetts Spy* that attacks New York merchants who have foregone nonimportation play upon emotional appeals and use logic in its appeal for nonimportation to be continued?

3. In what ways, according to the letter to the farmers of Connecticut, will nonimportation benefit farmers and other Americans?

4. In what ways do you think public announcements, such as the one in the *Virginia Gazette* against importers, deterred their actions?

5. In what ways does John Mein criticize Boston's nonimportation leaders in his questions for "the Well Disposed"?

6. What reasons did the writers to the *Virginia Gazette* and the *New-York Gazette* give for opposing the 1774 nonimportation? Do you believe their reasoning has credibility? Explain by comparing them to the reasons given in the chapter for supporting nonimportation.

NOTES

1. Benjamin Franklin to Timothy Folger, London, September 29, 1769, in *Benjamin Franklin, Writings*, ed. J. A. Leo Lemay (New York: Library of America, 1987), 847.

2. *Boston Gazette; and Country Journal*, 7 November 1774, 1.

CHAPTER 21

The Boston Massacre, 1770

The crisis created by the Stamp Act in America (see Chapter 16) never really subsided, at least not in Boston. The riots that accompanied that act were remembered annually. The British government added to the resentment in 1767 with the passage of the Townshend Acts, which placed duties on lead, tea, paint, paper, and glass; Americans would have to pay tax on any of these items imported from the mother country. During the month-long August 1768 anniversary of the Stamp Act riots, some Boston merchants proposed an agreement among all Boston merchants not to import any goods from England (see Chapter 20). Anti-British sentiment in Boston was so high that Governor Francis Bernard secretly requested that British troops be stationed in the city.

British troops had been living in New York since 1766 as part of the Quartering Act, which authorized the housing of troops in a town instead of in barracks, but in the year and a half before the Boston Massacre, on March 5, 1770, the troops stationed in Boston became the butt of the jokes and jeers of Americans. Adolescents and adults often taunted the soldiers, and the soldiers, likewise, resented their assignments and the "inferior" Americans. Newspaper articles reacted to the quartering of troops in Boston, and intimated that mob violence was the probable end of such an action. "Among a certain Set of People," a writer to the *Boston Gazette* warned, "I have observed that Mobs are represented as most hideous Things. I confess they ought not to be encouraged; but they have been sometimes useful. In a free Country I am afraid a standing Army rather occasions than prevent them."[1]

Despite the troops' presence in the city, Boston merchants continued their nonimportation of British goods, and relations between soldiers and citizens grew steadily worse in 1769. Nonimportation was hard on everyone, however, and early in 1770 nonimportation was in danger of failing. Some merchants began selling their imported goods. In response, threats were made against the importers and against known Tory informants. One of those Tories was named Ebenezer Richardson. On February 22, a mob surrounded his house, and Richardson, fearing for his life, fired his musket into the crowd, mortally wounding an eleven-year-old boy named Christopher Seider. His death exacerbated the hard feelings between Bostonians and soldiers.

With Seider's death still fresh in people's memory, rumors circulated through Boston that the soldiers planned to massacre large numbers of Boston citizens. Fights broke out between British troops and Boston citizens. One particularly violent one took place on March 2, and neither the troops nor the Bostonians sick of the troops' presence in the city had gotten over the incident, which took place in a Boston business, three days later. On March 5, a group of youths began to taunt a sentry on King Street. The sentry responded by beating one of the youths with his musket. Fire alarms sounded, and soon more than 400 people surrounded the sentry post at the customhouse, throwing snowballs and other items at the soldier.

Captain Thomas Preston soon arrived with seven soldiers. The taunts and assault grew. The crowd dared the soldiers to fire on them, and one did after he and Preston were hit with clubs. Other soldiers then fired. Four men died on the spot and a fifth died a few days later. Several people were wounded, and a horrified Lieutenant Governor Thomas Hutchinson ordered the British troops out of Boston to an island in the harbor.

The Boston Massacre, as the Patriots called the riot, was used to fuel the flames of sedition in America for the next five years. Four years later, on the anniversary of the massacre, John Hancock said in a fiery speech, "Let this sad tale of death never be told without a tear; let not the heaving bosom cease to burn with a manly indignation at the barbarous story through the long tracts of future time; let every parent tell the shameful story to his listening children until tears of pity glisten in their eyes, and boiling passions shake their tender frames . . . let all America join in one common prayer to heaven that the inhuman, unprovoked murders of the fifth of March, 1770 . . . may ever stand in history without parallel."[2] Similarly, Paul Revere produced an engraving of the massacre, which he had colorized, and he sold it to heighten the tensions between the British and Americans because it depicted the massacre as British soldiers firing on an innocent crowd.

The soldiers involved in the shooting were arrested. Their trial began on October 24. All were acquitted of murder charges. Two were convicted of manslaughter and branded as punishment.

The section of Patriotic responses to the Boston Massacre begins with the *Boston Gazette*'s version of the March 5 confrontation. It appeared on March 12 on pages two and three of the paper. The columns of text were outlined in black border, a traditional way to mark the death of important people. Page three also included a woodcut depicting four coffins and marked with the initials of the four men killed on the scene. When reading this section, pay special attention to the interpretation of the massacre in this account as compared to the *New-York Gazette; and the Weekly Mercury*'s presentation of the shootings, which appears in the second section of the chapter. From the newspaper accounts, it is hard to know exactly what happened in Boston, except that soldiers killed four Bostonians. Note, too, the *Gazette*'s account is vivid in its description of the mortal wounds, no doubt part of the writer's plan to stir up anti-British sentiment.

The next two entries come from the *Massachusetts Spy*, a newspaper that began publication in the summer following the March shootings. Its printer, Isaiah Thomas, was pro-Patriot. The first selection reports the results of the trial of the British soldiers who were arrested for the shootings. The second is the first of Thomas' commemoratives of the massacre. The *Spy* ran one and sometimes several every year until the Revolution. These stories attacked the British and reminded Americans of the innocent loss of lives. Here, Thomas placed this memorial in a black box with a skull and crossbones at the top.

The section of readings with a Loyalist or pro-British spin begins with John Mein's retelling of the event. Mein, a printer who opposed many Patriot activities especially the nonimportation agreements, called the shootings "a most unfortunate affair." His use of this terminology and the fact that his *Boston Chronicle* did not blame the British led to immediate repercussions for the printer. His paper, which had been successful and filled with advertisements and correspondence and was twice the size of most Boston papers at eight pages per week, quickly saw a downturn in advertising. Its correspondents also stopped writing. Almost immediately, the *Chronicle* stopped mentioning any of the controversial activities taking place in the colonies and replaced it with news from Europe. On June 25, the paper folded, and Mein moved to England.

The next entry, a letter written by British captain Thomas Preston, the officer in charge during the massacre, appeared in the *Boston Gazette* at the conclusion of its coverage of the event. The letter thanks those who supported Preston following his arrest. The section closes with the *New-York Gazette; and the Weekly Mercury*'s accounts of the shootings and the trial. Both were sent to an unnamed New York resident from Boston Tories.

PATRIOT RESPONSE TO THE BOSTON MASSACRE

AN ANONYMOUS REPORT: "THE BOSTON MASSACRE"

When the Boston Gazette *presented its version of the Boston Massacre, its printers portrayed the confrontation between the British soldiers and townspeople as a violent act perpetrated by oppressive soldiers against an innocent populace. Printers Benjamin Edes and John Gill outlined the borders of the story in black—a sign of mourning—and provided a woodcut of coffins with the initials of those killed on them. The report explains all that occurred prior to the March 5 incident and places the blame squarely on the British soldiers.*

Boston Gazette, and Country Journal, 12 March 1770

BOSTON, March 12.

THE Town of Boston affords a recent and melancholy Demonstration of the destructive Consequences of quartering Troops among Citizens in a Time of Peace, under a pretence of supporting the Laws and aiding Civil Authority; every considerate and unprejudic'd Person among us was deeply imprest with the Apprehension of their Consequences when it was known that a Number of Regiments were ordered to this Town under such a Pretext, but in Reality to inforce oppressive Measures; to awe & controul the legislative as well as executive Power of the Province, and to quell a Spirit of Liberty, which however it may have been basely oppos'd and even ridicule'd by some, would do Honor to any Age and Country. A few Persons amongst us had determin'd to use all their Influence to procure so destructive a Measure with a View to their securly enjoying the Profits of an American Revenue, and unhappily both for Britain and this Country they found a means to effect it. . . .

We have known a Party of Soldiers in the face of Day fire off a loaden Musket upon the Inhabitants, others have been prick'd with Bayonets, and even our Magistrates assaulted and put in Danger of their Lives, when Offenders brought before them have been rescued. . . . It is natural to suppose that when the Inhabitants of this Town saw those Laws which had been enacted for their Security, and which they were ambitious of holding up to the Soldiery, eluded, they should more commonly resent for themselves—. . . . What passed at Mr. Gray's Rope-walk, has already been given, the Public, & may be said to have led the Way to the late Catastrophe—That the Rope-walk Lads when attacked by superior Numbers should defend themselves with so much Spirit and Success in the Club-way, was too mortifying, and perhaps it may hereafter appear, that even some of their Officers were *unhappily* affected with this Circum-

stance. . . . The Evidences already collected shew, that many Threatnings
had been thrown out by the Soldiery, but we do not pretend to say that
there was any preconcerted Plan, when the Evidences are published, the
World will judge—We may however venture to declare, that it appears
too probably from their Conduct, that some of the Soldiery aimed to draw
and provoke the Townsmen into Squabbles, and that they then intended
to make Use of other Weapons than Canes, Clubs, and Bludgeons.

Our Readers will doubtless expect a circumstantial Account of the Tragical Affair on Monday Night last; but we hope they will excuse our being
so particular as we should have been, had we not seen that the Town
was intending an Enquiry & full Representation thereof.

On the Evening of Monday, being the 5th Current, several Soldiers of
the 29th Regiment were seen parading the Streets with their drawn Cutlasses and Bayonets, abusing and wounding Numbers of the Inhabitants.

A few minutes after nine o'clock, four youths, named Edward Archbald,
William Merchant, Francis Archbald, and John Leech, jun. came down
Cornhill together, and seperating at Doctor Loring's corner, the two former were passing the narrow alley leading to Murray's barrack, in which
was a soldier brandishing a broad sword of an uncommon size against
the walls, out of which he struck fire plentifully. A person of a mean
countenance armed with a large cudgel bore him company. Edward Archbald admonished Mr. Merchant to take care of the sword, on which the
soldier turned round and struck Archbald on the arm, then pushed at
Merchant and pierced thro' his cloaths inside the arm close to the arm-
pit and grazed the skin. Merchant then struck the soldier with a short
stick he had, & the other Person ran to the barrack & bro't with him two
soldiers, one armed with a pair of tongs the other with a shovel: he with
the tongs pursued Archbald back thro' the alley, collar'd and laid him
over the head with the tongs. The noise bro't people together, and John
Hicks, a young lad, coming up, knock'd the soldier down, but let him
get up again; and more lads gathering drove them back to the barrack,
where the boys stood some time as it were to keep them in. In less than
a minute 10 or 12 of them came out with drawn cutlasses, clubs and
bayonets, and set upon the unarmed boys and young folks, who stood
them a little while, but finding the inequality of their equipment dispersed.—On hearing the noise, one Samuel Atwood, came up to see what
was the matter, and entering the alley from dock-square, heard the latter
part of the combat, and when the boys had dispersed he met the 10 or
12 soldiers aforesaid rushing down the alley towards, the square, and
asked them if they intended to murder people? They answered Yes, by
G—d, root and branch! With that one of them struck Mr. Atwood with a
club, which was repeated by another, and being unarmed he turned to
go off, and received a wound on the left shoulder which reached the
bone and gave him much pain. Retreating a few steps, Mr. Atwood met

two officers and said, Gentlemen, what is the matter? They answered, you'll see by and by. Immediately after those heroes appeared in the square, asking where were the boogers? where the cowards? . . . Thirty or forty persons, mostly lads . . . gathered in Kingstreet, Capt. Preston, with a party of men with charged bayonets, came from the main guard to the Commissioners house, the soldiers pushing their bayonets, crying, Make way! They took place by the custom-house, and continuing to push to drive the people off, pricked some in several places; on which they were clamorous, and, it is said threw snow-balls. On this, the Captain commanded them to fire, and more snow-balls coming, he again said, Damn you, Fire, be the consequence what it will! One soldier then fired, and a townsman with a cudgel struck him over the hands with such force that he dropt his firelock; and rushing forward aimed a blow at the Captain's head, which graz'd his hat and fell pretty heavy upon his arm: However, the soldiers continued the fire, successively, till 7 or 8, or as some say 11 guns were discharged.

By this fatal maneuvre, three men were laid dead on the spot, and two more struggling for life; but what shewed a degree of cruelty unknown to British troops, at least since the house of Hanover has directed their operations, was an attempt to fire upon or push with their bayonets the persons who undertook to remove the slain and wounded!

Mr. Benjamin Leigh, now undertaker in the Delph Manufactory, came up, and after some conversation with Capt. Preston, relative to his conduct in this affair, advised him to draw off his men, with which he complied.

The dead are Mr. Samuel Gray, killed on the spot, the ball entering his head and beating off a large portion of his skull.

A mulatto man, named Crispus Attucks, who was born in Framingham, but lately belonged to New-Providence and was herein order to go for North-Carolina, also killed instantly; two balls entering his breast, one of them in special goring the right lobe of the lungs, and a great part of the liver most horribly.

Mr. James Caldwell, mate of Capt. Morton's vessel, in like manner killed by two balls entering his back.

Mr. Samuel Maverick, a promising youth of 17 years of age, son of the widow Maverick, and an apprentice to Mr. Greenwood, Ivory-Turner, mortally wounded, a ball went through his belly, & was cut out at his back: He died the next morning. . . .

The People were immediately alarmed with the Report of this horrid Massacre, the Bells were set a Ringing, and great Numbers soon assembled at the Place where the tragical Scene had been acted; their Feelings may be better conceived than express'd; and while some were taking Care of the Dead and Wounded, the Rest were in Consultation what to do in those dreadful Circumstances. . . .

Tuesday Morning presented a most shocking Scene, the Blood of our

Fellow Citizens running like Water thro' King-Street, and the Merchants Exchange the principal Spot of the Military Parade for about 18 Monts past. Our Blood might also be track'd up to the Head of Long-Lane, and through divers other Streets and Passages.

At eleven o'clock the inhabitants met at Faneuil-Hall, and after some animated speeches becoming the occasion, they chose a Committee of 15 respectable Gentlemen to wait upon the Lieut. Governor in Council, to request of him to issue his Orders for the immediate removal of the troops.

The Message was in these Words:

THAT it is the unanimous opinion of this meeting that the inhabitants and soldiery can no longer live together in safety; that nothing can rationally be expected to restore the peace of the town & prevent further blood & carnage, but the immediate removal of the Troops; and that we therefore most fervently pray his Honor that his power and influence may be exerted for their instant removal. . . .

Last Thursday, agreeable to a general Request of the Inhabitants, and by the Consent of Parents and Friends, were carried to their *Grave* in Succession, the Bodies of *Samuel Gray, Samuel Maverick, James Caldwell*, and *Crispus Attucks*, the unhappy Victims who fell in the bloody Massacre of the Monday Evening preceeding!

On this Occasion most of the Shops in Town were shut, all the Bells were ordered to toll a solemn Peal, as were also those in the neighboring Towns. . . . The several Hearses forming a Junction in King-Street, the Theatre of that inhuman Tragedy! proceeded from thence thro' the Main-Street, lengthened by an immense Concourse of People, so numerous as to be obliged to follow the Ranks of six, and brought up by a long Train of Carriages belonging to the principal Gentry of the Town. The Bodies were deposited in one Vault in the middle Burying-ground: The aggravated Circumstances of their Death, the Distress and Sorrow visible in every Countenance, together with the peculiar Solemnity with which the whole Funeral was conducted, surpass Description.

ISAIAH THOMAS: "THE VERDICT IN THE MASSACRE TRIAL"

The soldiers involved in the shootings were arraigned, and their trial began at the end of October. Thomas reported the verdict to his readers, but his displeasure with it is easily detected. He used all capitals to emphasize that most of the soldiers were found not guilty. He did the same with the fact that two of the soldiers were convicted only of manslaughter.

The Massachusetts Spy (Boston), 7 December 1770

FRIDAY, December 7. BOSTON.

On Wednesday last ended the trial of the Soldiers, for the *Murder* of

Samuel Gray, Patrick Carr, James Caldwell, Samuel Maverick, and Crispus Attucks, on the evening of the fifth of March last, after being continued for *nine* days, successively, Sunday excepted. The jury went out about two o'clock in the afternoon, and in about two hours after brought in their verdict; Seven were found "NOT GUILTY," the other two (Montgomery and Kilroy) were convicted of MANSLAUGHTER *only*, and *are to be* branded in the hand. Thus ended this long expected and important trial!

ISAIAH THOMAS: "BE IT FOREVER REMEMBERED"

While many events may have created a rift between Americans and British from the Stamp Act to the Revolution, none seemed to galvanize opinion against England more than the Boston Massacre, according to newspapers. Every year on the anniversary of the tragedy, newspapers ran memorials to those slain; towns such as Boston held public memorials with speeches. Below is Isaiah Thomas' first commemorative that attributes what happened to British tyranny.

The Massachusetts Spy (Boston), 7 March 1771

As a solemn and perpetual Memorial of the Tyranny of the British Administration of Government in 1768, 1769 and 1770:

Of the fatal and destructive Consequence of quartering Armies, in Time of Peace in populous Cities: . . .

Be it forever Remembered

That this day, the Fifth of March, is the Anniversary of Preston's Massacre, in King-Street Boston, New-England, 1770; in which Five of his Majesty's Subjects were slain, and Six wounded by the Discharge of a Number of Muskets from a Party of Soldiers under the Command of Capt. Thomas Preston.

GOD Save the PEOPLE!

LOYALIST RESPONSES TO THE BOSTON MASSACRE

JOHN MEIN: "A MOST UNFORTUNATE AFFAIR"

Printer John Mein, unlike his counterparts at the Boston Gazette, *refused to point a finger of blame about the Boston Massacre when his paper came out three days after the incident. Mein had already made his stand in Boston by opposing Patriot merchants who called for the non-importation of British goods. Instead, Mein called the shootings "a most unfortunate affair." He promised to provide more information later and called the British who had been arrested "unfortunate prisoners." This account of the massacre, however, was the only one that Mein printed. He and his paper became the target of incensed Patriots. After advertisers stopped using the paper, all controversial issues were avoided. The paper ceased publication at the end of June 1770.*

Boston Chronicle, 8 March 1770

BOSTON.

For some days bye-past, there have been several affrays between the inhabitants, and the soldiers quartered in this town.

Last Monday, about 9 o'clock at night a most unfortunate affair happened in King-street: The centinel posted at the Custom-house, being surrounded by a number of people, called to the main-guard, upon which Capt. Preston, who was Captain of the day, with a party went to his assistance: soon after which some of the party fired, by which the following persons were killed and wounded.

Mr. Samuel Gray, ropemaker, killed.—A Molatto man named Johnson, killed.—Mr. James Caldwell, mate of Capt. Morton's vessel, killed.—Mr. Samuel Maverick, wounded, and since dead.—A Lad named Christopher Monk, wounded.—A lad named John Clark, wounded.—Mr. Edward Payne, Merchant, standing at his entry-door, wounded in the arm.—Mr. John Greene, taylor, wounded.—Mr. Patrick Cole, wounded.—David Parker, wounded.

A meeting of the Inhabitants was called at Fanueil-hall that forenoon; and the Lieutenant-Governor and Council, met at the Council-chamber, where the Colonels Dalrymple and Carr were desired to attend, when it was concluded upon, that both regiments should go down to the barracks at Castle-William, as soon as they were ready to receive them.

We decline at present, giving a more particular account of this unhappy affair, as we hear the trial of the unfortunate prisoners is to come on next week.

THOMAS PRESTON: "THANK YOU FOR YOUR SUPPORT"

Captain Thomas Preston was the officer in charge of the British troops that fired on the angry crowd on King Street on March 5. Arrested with some of his men, Preston used one of the more staunchly Patriot papers, the Boston Gazette, *to issue this word of thanks to the people of Boston for treating him with civility after his arrest.*

Boston Gazette, and Country Journal, 12 March 1770

Boston Goal [*sic*], Monday 12th March 1770.
Messieurs Edes and Gill,

PERMIT me thro' the channel of your paper, to return my thanks in
the most publick manner to the inhabitants in general of hits town—who
throwing aside *all* party and prejudice, have with the utmost humanity
and freedom stept forth advocates for truth, in defence of my injured
innocence, in the late unhappy affair that happened on Monday night
last: And to assure them, that I shall ever have the highest sense of the
justice they have done me, which will be gratefully remembered by their
    much obliged, and obedient humble servant,
THOMAS PRESTON.

AN ANONYMOUS WRITER: "AN ACCOUNT OF THE LATE UNHAPPY AFFAIR IN BOSTON"

While the Boston Gazette's *version of the Boston Massacre reflected a
Patriot slant, this interpretation, supplied to the* New-York Gazette *by a
Boston Tory, puts the blame for the shooting squarely on the mob. Compare this account with the* Gazette's *to see the similarities and differences in the two.*

New-York Gazette; and the Weekly Mercury, 2 April 1770

Extract of a Letter from Boston, dated March 19, 1770.
    Dear Sir,
I Received your Favour of the 12th, wherein you desire a particular Account of the late unhappy Affair here.—Before we enter into a minute
Detail of that unhappy Transaction, it may be necessary to take up Matters
a little higher, to shew that the People of this Town, have not upon all
Occasions, been so innocent, and so free from Aggression, as they represent themselves.

The Measures of Government you knew was odious to them, Magistracy either join'd with them, or fell into Contempt, every Nerve of Civil
Authority was unstrung; to support insulted Government, his Majesty was
pleased to order Troops to Boston. Designing Men of sour Minds and
Principles, will make Use of every Art, to agitate and inflame the unwary
Multitude to their Purposes, whilst they keep snug behind the Curtains,
pee[r]ing thro' their Fingers at the mischievous Event.

The Troops arrive, and sure no Troops ever arrived in any Country
with less hostile Intentions than they did; they landed, march'd and in-
camp'd, without a single Act of Violence.

What was the Consequence? The lower sort of People, whose Minds
were poisoned to that End, instead of looking on the Soldiers as fellow
Subjects, and Countrymen, they viewed them with the malignant Eye of
Detestation, and Insult, as a mercenary Banditti, in the Hands of most

benevolent Majesty, ready to perpetrate every Act of Devastation and Cruelty.

Is this the Portrait of British Troops, the natural Enemies of their Country? Say no. For they have experienced as many Instances of their Humanity as their Valour. . . .

So much by Way of Preface, now we come to the Particulars relating to poor Preston.—

The Temper above hinted at, occasion'd many Bickerings between Parties of the Town People and stragling Soldiers. On the 2d ult. two of the 29th going thro' a Rope Walk, belonging to one Gray, the Rope-makers insultingly asked them, if they would empty a Little House; this unfortunately had the desired Effect. Soldiers are as irritable as Browncoats, Words and Blows ensued, both Sides suffered in the Affair; the Officers did every Thing in their Power on the first Notice of it, to prevent any ill Consequences; however they had several private Quarrels.

The 5th and 6th Instant was agreed upon for a general Attack upon the Troops, and great Numbers came in with Arms from the Country, to join their Friends in Town. On the 5th in the Evening, two Soldiers were attack'd and beat, and the Town's People, agreeable to their Plans, broke open two Meeting Houses, and rang the Alarm Bells, which was supposed to be for Fire. Soon after some of the Guard came to Capt. Preston, who was Captain of the Day, and informed him the Inhabitants were assembling to attack the Troops, that the Bells were ringing for that Purpose, and not for Fire.

Preston as the regulating Officer of the Day, on such a Report being made to him, was bound in Duty, instantly to repair to the Main Guard; in his Way thither, he saw the People in great Commotion, uttering terrible Threats against the Troops; soon after he reached the Guard, a Number of People passed it, and went towards the Custom-House, they instantly surrounded the Centry there, and threatened to execute their Vengeance upon him. This Centry being posted at a small Distance from the Guard, Preston to prevent any ill Accidents, sent a Serjeant and twelve Men to bring him off. He sent them without loading in their Pieces, and for fear the Insults of the Mob should provoke them to any rash Act, he followed them himself.

The Mob was assembled in great Numbers, extremely outrageous, striking their Clubs one against the other, crying out, Come on you Rascals, you Bloody Backs, you Lobster Scoundrels, Fire if ye dare, G—d Dam'n you, Fire and be damned; we know you dare not. Captain Preston all this time, was between the Soldiers and the Mob, parlying with them, and making Use of every conciliating Method, to persuade them to retire. In the mean Time, the Men loaded without Orders from Preston, He could not prevail on the People to go off peaceably, they advanced to the Points of the Bayonets; and endeavour'd to close with the Soldiers. At this time, some among them asked Preston, if he intended to order the Men to Fire, he reply'd, by no Means, and observed to them he stood between the Troops and them.

While Preston was thus speaking, one of the Solders received a severe Blow with a Stick, who instantly stept on one Side and fired.

Preston turn'd round to see who fired without his Order, and in doing it received a blow with a Club aimed at his Head, upon his Arm, which for some Time, deprived him of the use of it. The Mob persisted pelting and striking at the Soldiers, the Rear of them crying out, Damn you, why don't you fire? The Soldiers were pressed, their Lives in Danger, three or four of them fired one after another, and again three more in the same Hurry and Confusion.

The Mob ran off, except three unhappy Men that fell, among whom was Mr. Gray, at whose Rope-Walk the prior Quarrel happened. In their returning again to bring of the Dead Bodies, the Soldiers thinking they were coming to renew the Attack, prepared to fire, which Preston prevented by striking up their Firelocks. . . . The Justice issued a Warrant to apprehend Preston and eight Soldiers, he heard of it, and surrendered himself; conscious of Innocence he did so; for if he could have reproached himself with the least Degree of Guilt, he had Time enough to Escape. . . .

Malice and Revenge, (for the Honour of human Nature) are transient Passions, while we are agitated by them only, we are blind to Reason, Truth and Justice. But what sort of a Monster must he be, who comes in cool Blood, in a judicial Way too, to pronounce on the Life and Honour of his Countryman, with a Particle of Vengeance in his Heart.

No, Sir, tho' I lament the Catastrophe of the poor People that fell, and feel with you for the anxious Situation in which poor Preston is; who conscious of his Innocence has confided himself to their Justice; I have Reason to think, Truth and Innocence, will prevail; that blind Vengeance will not intrude itself in his Tryal.

AN ANONYMOUS WRITER: "THE VERDICT BASED ON THE EVIDENCE"

In this Tory version of the Boston Massacre trial, the unknown writer emphasizes that the evidence was weighed carefully by the jury. According to this story, the massacre was the result of a careful plan to attack the few soldiers on duty.

New-York Gazette; and the Weekly Mercury, 17 December 1770

Extract of a Letter from Boston, dated December 6, 1770.

"Yesterday the Jury gave in their Verdict, and found two of the Soldiers guilty of Manslaughter only, and the other six not guilty. There was not one Inhabitant of the Town upon the Jury. The Country People are not under such strong Prejudices. . . . A Gentleman lately from the West-Indies, who was in Court at the Trial of the Soldiers, told me, he overheard one of the — of the Town several Times speak so loud that the Jury might hear him, making his Remarks as the Witnesses were giving Evidence, and when something was said, which seemed to bear hard upon one of the Prisoners, he declared that Fellow ought to be hanged. I have been told that the Jury laid great Stress upon the Evidence, of a Plan having been laid by the Inhabitants to attack the Soldiers, a great Number having met together in the Market Place, breaking the Stalls to furnish them with Clubs, such as were not before provided, and amongst the rest, there was one with a white Wig, and a Boston red Cloak, encouraging them to make the Attack."

QUESTIONS

1. How do you explain the differences in the two accounts of what happened on King Street on March 5?

2. Which account of the Boston Massacre do you believe is the more accurate? Why?

3. How does the use of capitalization and italics in the *Massachusetts Spy* account of the Boston Massacre trial establish prejudice on the part of its printer, Isaiah Thomas? Compare this version of the trial to that found in the *New-York Gazette*.

4. Find a copy of the Bill of Rights. What effects might the Boston Massacre have had on them?

5. Do you think the *Boston Chronicle*'s account of the massacre is biased, or is it objective reporting?

6. How does the *Boston Chronicle*'s version of the massacre differ from those found in the *Boston Gazette* and *New-York Gazette*?

7. Truth is considered of vital importance in most situations. Do you think the truth mattered in the retelling of the massacre, or were the actual events of less importance than the repercussions created by the event? Explain.

NOTES

1. *Boston Gazette; and Country Journal*, 12 September 1768.

2. John Hancock, "Boston Massacre Oration," in *American Voices: Significant Speeches in American History*, ed. David Zarefsky (New York: Longman, 1989), 41–48.

CHAPTER 22

Religious Liberty: Baptists Call for Toleration, 1770–1776

In 1771 four Baptist preachers in Virginia were given five-month jail sentences for holding unlawful religious meetings—that is, services that were not approved by the general assembly and did not use the liturgy of the Church of England. The ministers' plight was not unusual. Baptists had been the target of attacks in Virginia since they migrated in large numbers into the colony following the Great Awakening (Chapter 8). Some Baptists faced more dire consequences for their worship and preaching than imprisonment. Some were beaten or stoned. One minister, David Thomas, was grabbed while preaching, dragged outdoors, and beaten. When his attacker pulled a gun to execute the stunned Baptist, a bystander wrenched it from the would-be assailant's hand.[1]

In Virginia, as in most of the other Southern and New England colonies, colonial law established one denomination as the official religion. Citizens paid taxes to support worship in the state church, Anglicanism in the South and Congregationalism in New England. Virginia's ties with the Church of England were established in the colony's 1606 charter, which required mandatory Anglican worship. As John Smith explained, "When I first went to Virginia, I well remember . . . wee had daily Common Prayer morning and evening, every Sunday two sermons, and every three moneths the holy Communion."[2]

The fact that the settlers in any part of America established a preferred form of religion within a colony seems ironic. After all, many of America's first settlers were themselves religious dissenters in England and braved Atlantic passage to obtain freedom of worship. But worshipers who had been persecuted and were in the minority in Europe, like the Puritans, became the majority in places such as Massachusetts Bay and quickly grew intolerant of worship that varied from their own. Furthermore, no two colonies possessed exactly the same religious composition. The concept of religious liberty, therefore, was not part of the typical colonial mind-set. Most who emigrated from England believed as Presbyterian Richard Baxter, believed: "I abhor unlimited liberty and toleration for all,"[3] he said. In a few instances, American colonial governments attempted to counter the concepts of Baxter and others and grant religious freedom to settlers. Maryland, for example, passed "An Act Concerning Religion" in 1649 that provided for religious liberty, but by 1654, the colony's freeholders voted to ban free worship, a move aimed specifically at the Roman Catholics who originally had settled the colony.

How did Americans go from state-supported religions to the First Amendment of the Constitution, which says, "Congress shall make no law respecting an establishment of religion or prohibiting the free exercise thereof?" The answer may be discovered in part by observing the activities of certain religious groups, especially the Baptists.

Baptists grew out of the English Separatist tradition of the late sixteenth and early seventeenth centuries. From the beginning, Baptists in England advocated freedom to worship as one pleased, and in 1612 they issued a confession of faith that stated, "That the magistrate is not by virtue of his office to meddle with religion, to force or compel men to this or that form of religion or doctrine: but to leave Christian religion free, to every man's conscience."[4] When Baptists emigrated to America, they brought this concept with them, and it was given its American form in 1644 by Roger Williams, who said there must be a "wall of separation" between the church and government in order to keep the magistrate's hand out of the affairs of religion.[5]

Despite their belief in separation of church and state, Baptists were forced to pay taxes to support state churches in both New England and the South. When the Great Awakening caused Americans to refocus on their religious life and denominations to split off, the Baptist church began to flourish. Baptists began to migrate south, especially from Pennsylvania where they had been allowed to worship freely, and Virginia became a battleground for Baptists over religious liberty. Encouraged by the success of George Whitefield and other itinerant preachers (see Chapter 8), the Baptists ignored Virginia's licensing law, which required all ministers and worship to be approved by the government. Instead, Baptists simply moved into all areas of the colony, addressing their message not to the elite in the capital of Williamsburg but to the commoners of the colony.

The battle for religious liberty in Virginia continued throughout the Revolutionary War and into the beginnings of the young republic. The principal Baptist spokesman, John Leland wrote to the political leaders of Virginia, including James Madison, about the necessity of freedom of conscience in worship, and Leland spearheaded the Baptist Petition Movement in 1784, which sent numerous petitions for toleration to the Virginia legislature. Within a year, Madison penned "A Memorial and Remonstrance on the Religious Rights of Man," which stated that religious liberty was an individual right, and Virginia passed Thomas Jefferson's "Bill for Establishing Religious Freedom," which legally separated religion and government in the commonwealth.

The readings supporting religious toleration begin with an essay from 1735, said to have been written by Cato, the pseudonym of the British champions of liberty John Trenchard and Thomas Gordon. It is followed by a New York essay written by William Livingston, a young lawyer and aspiring writer. It defends the rights of Moravians to worship as they please. The next entry is a Presbyterian petition to Virginia Governor Botetourt, who promised them full protection of the 1689 Act of Toleration. The act, which marked the passing of the English throne from the Catholic James II to the Protestant William and Mary, allowed dissenters the right to worship so long as they paid tithes to the Church of England and registered their meeting places with Anglican bishops, something Presbyterians and Baptists in Virginia refused to do.

The Presbyterian petition is followed by a sympathetic letter from Philadelphia in support of New England Baptists' quest for free worship. The next two entries are calls by Baptists to send all examples of their being denied free worship to local Baptist associations, or groups of churches. The second is an advertisement written by Isaac Backus, the Baptists' chief organizer for religious liberty in New England. In his advertisement, Backus threatened to take Baptist pleas to a higher authority, that is, to the king and Parliament, which in all likelihood would have resulted in the revulsion of Massachusetts' colonial charter. The next letter comes from a Connecticut dissenter calling himself "A PROTESTANT." The letter attacks the colony's law that allowed the confiscation of property if one refused to support the government-prescribed form of religion.

The final selections in the section on religious toleration come from the period of the Revolution. In the first, the Continental Congress approves exemptions from military service based on religious reasons. In the second, a company of Virginia militiamen demand religious freedom in Virginia, asserting that the Declaration of Independence guarantees it.

The letters opposing toleration come from the decades' long battle to stop Baptist preaching and proselytizing in Virginia. The first, signed by the unknown Thomas Telltrutha, uses analogy to explain why Baptists should not be tolerated. In one comparison, the Baptist migration to the colony is equated with cancer spreading through the body. The second is a letter written by an unknown lawyer to the Baptist preachers arrested in 1771. The letter attempts to explain why toleration is dangerous and how the ministers violated the Act of Toleration. The final letter, appearing late in 1776, ties toleration to the fight for independence from England. It defends an establishment of religion as a necessity for a government and the backing of the established religion as another means of supporting the government of Virginia and the newly formed confederation in its fight against England.

FOR RELIGIOUS TOLERATION

AN ANONYMOUS WRITER: "EVERY MAN'S RELIGION IS HIS OWN"

Even in colonial times, New York City's harbor made it a natural port of entry for immigrants. As a result, people with many different religious traditions lived there. The first signs of the religious revival that culminated in the Great Awakening also occurred in nearby New Jersey among the Dutch-speaking residents. These facts, taken with the tendency for colonies to establish a preferred or state-supported church, led to statements such as the one below made by an anonymous writer who chose the pseudonym Cato for this letter. Cato was the name used by writers when discussing issues of freedom and toleration. It was based on the use of the name by Englishmen John Trenchard and Thomas Gordon, who penned a series of essays on freedom of the press and other similar subjects.

New-York Weekly Journal, 25 August 1735

From CATO's Letters. . . .

Every Man's Religion is his own; nor can the Religion of any Man, of what Nature or Figure soever, be the Religion of another Man, unless he also chuses it; which Action utterly excludes all Force, Power, or Government. Religion can never come without Conviction, nor can Conviction come from civil Authority. . . . It is a Relation between God and our own Souls only, and consists in a Disposition of Mind to obey the Will of our great Creator. . . . It is independent upon all human Directions, and superior to them; and consequently uncontrouable by external Force. . . . Religion therefore, which can never be subject to the Jurisdiction of another, can never be alienated to another, or put in his Power. . . . This Power therefore which no Man has, no Man can transfer to another.

WILLIAM LIVINGSTON: "A DEFENSE OF MORAVIANS"

Moravians were pietists, which means they believed that individuals need to experience God personally, depend upon the Bible for guidance, and work to reform church and society. Most Moravians emigrated to America from Germany and settled in Pennsylvania, the Carolinas, and Georgia. They also moved into New York to start missions among the Indians and were successful. Moravian success, however, meant a decrease in trade among Native Americans, especially in liquor. Traders complained. On top of that, Moravians opposed slavery and military service, and they would not swear allegiance to any human oath including one to King George. As a result, they were regarded as troublemakers. As opposition to the Moravians living in New York grew, Livingston, a lawyer and the force behind the Independent Reflector, *wrote about religious liberty in an effort to defend Moravians from other Protestants who wanted toleration for themselves but not for Moravians.*

Independent Reflector (New York), 4 January 1753

TO engage in controversial Points of Divinity, and commence a flaming Zealot in religious Debates, is beneath the Character of a Writer, animated with a Love of Mankind . . . entertaining a nobler Idea of Religion, than to confine it, to the speculative Opinion of a particular Set of Christians. . . . In such Disputations, I am not ambitious of carrying the Prize. But to defend every Sect, of whatever Denomination, in the undisturbed Enjoyment of their civil and religious Liberties, and to repress every persecuting Spirit that offers them Violence. . . .

It is indeed astonishing, that Dissenters, who *so much*, and *so justly*, magnify the Reasonableness of *Toleration*, when themselves are concerned, should at the same Time treat as Hereticks, a People whom the Parliament hath acknowledged as *good Christians*; which, perhaps, is more than can be said for any Church in this Province. . . .

Nothing can be more unmannerly, as well as unchristian, than for any Protestant Minister, within his Majesty's Dominions, to stigmatize and vilify, a numerous Body of People, protected by the same Laws, and incorporated under the same Constitution with himself. . . .

If in any Case I could recommend it to the Civil Magistrate, to interfere in Matters of Religion, it would be in this; for he should not only avoid persecuting his Subjects, for differing from him in their Opinions; he should also prevent their persecuting each other. . . . Z. & B.

VIRGINIA PRESBYTERIANS/LORD BOTETOURT: "PLEA FOR TOLERATION IN VIRGINIA"

The Great Awakening in the 1730s and 1740s signaled a growth and movement in some denominations. Presbyterians and Baptists moved south into Virginia and the Carolinas where they successfully gained followers. Anglicanism was the religion of Virginia, and dissenters, including Presbyterians and Baptists, were by Virginia law required to register their meeting places, something both refused to do. In this letter to Governor Botetourt and his reply, Presbyterians are assured they will receive religious protection based on the Act of Toleration.

Virginia Gazette (Williamsburg, Rind), 4 May 1769

WILLIAMSBURG, *May* 4.

To his Excellency the Right Honourable NORBORNE Baron De BOTETOURT. . . . The humble ADDRESS of the Presbyterian Clergy in *Virginia*.

May it please you Excellency, . . .

As we will ever study to make your Excellency's residence in this colony agreeable, and your government easy, we doubt not but your Excellency will secure to us the free use of our religion in doctrine and discipline, as practised in the church of Scotland, to which we believe we have a right by the act of toleration. . . .

To which his Excellency was pleased to return the following ANSWER.

Gentlemen, . . .

It is the King's express command, that liberty of conscience be allowed to all his subjects, so they be contended with a quiet and peaceable enjoyment of the same: And I can venture to promise that the advantages marked out in the act of toleration will all be continued to you in their fullest extent.

AN ANONYMOUS WRITER: "GIVE BAPTISTS FREE WORSHIP"

Just as dissenters ran into problems with worship in the Southern colonies, they found the same resistance in New England. This letter from an unknown Philadelphian calls on all New England colonies to provide free worship for Baptists. Readers should be aware that calls for religious toleration in the 1770s and the general push toward independence from England was not a mere coincidence. Many dissenters, such as Baptists Isaac Backus and John Leland, were friends with the patriotic leaders of the country. Backus was a delegate to the First Continental Congress in 1774 (see Chapter 25). These men regarded America's efforts in the 1770s to be free of British control as the right time for dissenting worshipers to do the same with state-sponsored religion and restrictions on any Protestant religious group.

Pennsylvania Chronicle, and Universal Advertiser (Philadelphia), 19 March 1770

YOUR Letterwriter-general informs us, that the Baptists are now making preparations once more to apply to Old England for Liberty of Conscience, which they have never been able to obtain in New-England.——
—I am sorry that ever any denomination of christians, when vested with civil power, has acted so far beneath their characters as to deprive any man, or society of men, of the privilege of worshipping GOD according to the best of their judgment, and the light of their consciences; or that any peaceable subjects, that were loyal to their King, and willing and able to serve the public, should have ever been deprived of this privilege, or excluded from all places of honour and trust, on the account of their religious opinions. . . . All the protestant churches at the reformation, emerging out of the thick darkness of popery, did not well understand the civil or religious rights of mankind. . . . If the Baptists are deprived of their rights, in any of the New-England governments, they have taken the proper method to obtain a redress of grievances, by applying to the Governor and Assembly, who, according to their own confessions, seemed ready almost at all times to hear them kindly, until they fell into the hands of the present Lieutenant-Governor and his associates.

THE WARREN ASSOCIATION: "A CALL TO PROTEST"

Isaac Backus led the Warren Baptist Association of New England. For years, Baptists and other dissenters paid taxes in Massachusetts that were used to build Congregational meeting houses and to pay Congregational preachers. Now, Baptists were asked to come together in protest of these taxes, a redress of grievances against the colony. Whether Backus and other Baptist leaders really believed they would be reimbursed by the colony is not known, but he probably felt that his growing group could force the repeal of taxes to support the state church.

Providence Gazette; and Country Journal, 11 August 1770

Boston: TO the BAPTISTS in the Province of Massachusetts-Bay, who are and have been oppressed in any Way on a religious Account:

IT would be needless to tell you, that you have long felt the effects of the laws, by which the religion of the government in which you live, is established; your purses have felt the burthens of ministerial rates, and when these would not satisfy your enemies, your property hath been taken from you, and sold for half its value: These are things you cannot forget——you will therefore readily hear and attend, when you are all desired to collect your cases of suffering, and have them well attested; such as, the taxes you have paid to build meeting-houses, to settle ministers, and support them; with all the time, money and labour you have lost, in waiting on courts, seeing lawyers, &c.——And bring or send such cases to the Baptist Association, to be held at Bellingham, the Tuesday next after the first Wednesday in next September: When measures will be resolutely adopted for obtaining redress from another quarter, than that to which repeated application hath been made, unsuccessfully: Nay, complaints however just, and grievous, have been treated with indifference, and scarcely, if at all, credited. We deem this our conduct perfectly justifiable, and hope you will pay a particular regard to this desire, and be exact in your account of your sufferings, and punctual in your attendance at the time and place above mentioned.

ISAAC BACKUS: "TO BAPTISTS, OPPRESSED BECAUSE OF RELIGION"

Issac Backus believed that the time was right in the summer of 1770 for Baptists to win religious toleration from Massachusetts. Five Bostonians had died in the Boston Massacre of March (see Chapter 21), which generated calls for an end to tyranny. From the Stamp Act on, Americans had rallied behind the phrase "no taxation without representation" (see Chapter 17). Backus and the Baptists built on these ideas by applying them to religious toleration. The next years were difficult because, following the meeting called for below, Baptists stopped paying religious taxes to the colony. In response, Massachusetts disrupted Baptist meetings, confiscated Baptists' property, and hindered Baptists in their efforts to license churches. In many ways, Massachusetts Baptists were fighting for independence just as Patriots were fighting for independence from Britain.

Boston Evening-Post, 20 August 1770

To the Baptists of the Province of Massachusetts Bay, who are, or have been oppressed in any way on a religious account. It would be needless to tell you that you have long felt the effects of the laws by which the religion of the government in which you live is established. Your purses have felt the burden of ministerial rates; and when these would not satisfy your enemies, your property hath been taken from you and sold for less than half its value. These things you cannot forget. You will therefore readily hear and attend, and when you are desired . . . and bring or send such cases to the Baptist Association to be held at Bellingham; when measures will be resolutely adopted for obtaining redress from another quarter than that to which repeated application hath been made unsuccessfully.

A PROTESTANT: "THE RIGHT TO BE FREE IN THE CHOICE OF
RELIGION"

*Just like Massachusetts, Connecticut taxed its citizens to support the
state church. In this letter, the unknown A Protestant complains about
the practice. Note that he sent his letter to a paper in Rhode Island, not
one in Connecticut.*

Providence Gazette; and Country Journal, 13 October 1770

That mankind have a right to be free in the choice of religion, is a truth
that can't be denied, and is a privilege dearer to every sober Christian
than any civil privilege whatsoever; and no authority on earth have a right
to deprive their subjects of the same; nor can without being guilty of
assuming that power or dominion over others that God never gave them:
For, to allow mankind, as individuals, the free choice of their own religion, and yet to take by force their estates from them, to support a
religion or worship that they do not choose, is a piece of oppression that
would make even a moral heathen blush. Yet many instances of the same
have we had, and still have!
A PROTESTANT

CONTINENTAL CONGRESS: "EXEMPTION FROM MILITARY
SERVICE FOR RELIGIOUS REASONS"

*Americans realized in the summer of 1775 that they would need a large,
strong army if they were to fight Great Britain. In an act of recognizing
religious right, the congress agreed that those who rejected to bearing
arms as a matter of religious beliefs would be excused from this type of
service.*

Essex Journal: or, the New-Hampshire Packet (Newbury,
Massachusetts), 18 August 1775

As there are some people, who from religious principles cannot bear
arms in any case, this Congress intend no violence to their consciences,
but earnestly recommend it to them to contribute liberally in this time
of universal calamity to the relief of their distressed brethren in the several colonies, and to do all other services to their oppressed country,
which they can consistent with their religious principles.

ANONYMOUS WRITERS: "EQUAL LIBERTY FOR ALL WHO FIGHT"

*A number of men serving in the Virginia militia found it ironic that they
were fighting for the freedom of Virginia and America yet were still*

prohibited from free worship. They wrote this letter as a petition to the Virginia assembly.

Virginia Gazette (Williamsburg, Purdie), 18 October 1776

The sentiments of several companies of militia . . . to their representatives in the General Assembly of the commonwealth.

GENTLEMEN,

WE have chose you at a very critical juncture to represent us in the General Assembly of our commonwealth, and need not tell you that we place great confidence in you. . . .

Our independence on Great Britain, and every other nation, we are determined upon, without a nice calculation of costs; for if possible to effect and preserve liberty for ourselves and unborn generations, we think it will be a noble equivalent for much blood and treasure, and we trust a full balance of all our losses.

Attempts, unnatural, cruel, and unjust, to rob us of our most valuable rights and privileges, have roused almost all America to defend them forgetting the illiberal treatment which a difference in religious sentiments; in some misguided places, has produced. All denominations have unanimously rushed to arms, to defend the common cause. Their unanimity has made them formidable to their enemies; their unanimity will be ever preserved by giving *equal liberty* to them all; nor do the[y] crave this as their patrimony, they cannot be withheld from them without the most flagitious [shamefully wicked] fraud, pride, and injustice, which, if practised, may shake this continent, and demolish provinces.

This we think our representatives in Convention, last June, had fully in view. Besides other things, they declared, "that all men are equally entitled to the free exercise of their religion, or the duty they owe to their creator, and the manner of discharging it according to the dictates of their consciences." We take this to be the true and full meaning of their words, without any unjust view of favouring some to the hurt of others, and view their declaration in this light as a most happy proof of their wisdom and virtue.

Hereby men, how different soever in their religious opinions, are united in defence of our invaluable inheritance, which they can equally call their own. . . .

We do, gentlemen, as our representatives, most solemnly require you, and positively command you, that, in the General Assembly of this commonwealth, you declare it the ardent desire and unanimous opinion of your constituents, should such a declaration become necessary, that all religious denominations within this dominion be forthwith put in the full possession of equal liberty, without preference or pre-eminence, which, while it may favour one, can hurt another, and that no religious sect whatever be established in this commonwealth.

AGAINST RELIGIOUS TOLERATION

TOM TELLTRUTHA: "THE CANCER OF UNIVERSAL TOLERATION"

Baptists used Philadelphia and the Great Awakening as points of departure in their efforts to spread the denomination in America. The anonymous Tom Telltrutha compared Baptists to a cancer spreading throughout Virginia. One would not readily accept a cancer, Tom reckons. To accept universal toleration would be to allow a religious cancer to spread in the colony.

Virginia Gazette (Williamsburg), 3 April 1752

The SPEECH of Tom Telltrutha. . . .

THE Love of Truth obliges me to oppose the Motion, which you have heard made . . . . I am against this Scheme of universal Toleration; for which I shall offer a few plain Reasons. . . .

A State, composed of many little Parties, each with different Ends and Aims, and such as interests with one another, is rather a disjointed Assemblage of various States, than one compact and regular Whole. . . . Some things are better learn'd from the Experience of others than our men among which Things I reckon those, which concern Government, and the Affair under Consideration in particular, of whose pernicious Nature we may see plentiful Proof in the History of the Mother Country. A Cancer may be stopped, it is said, if taken in Hand at it's [*sic*] first Appearance, but if you let it alone a while to spread, it will quickly get above the Skill of the ablest Surgeon. . . . But in Relation to this Point, I will, if you please, tell you an old Story. Once upon a Time, a poor big-bellied Bitch ready to lie in, and destitute of any Habitation, or Lodging, humbly intreated an old Dog, that he would in all Love lend her his Kennel, only 'til she had *littered*, and her Month should be out: Her Request was immediately granted by by the *compassionate* old Dog. He appeared again, at the Time appointed, to demand the Restoration of his Kennel, but she put him off from Time to Time, with Pretences, that her dear tender Brood were not yet strong enough to go abroad, and endure the Inclemency of the Weather, till at least, when they were grown pretty sturdy she plucked up her Spirits and plainly told him, that it was not the Custom of *her Family to resign to the Weaker*, and that if he thought herself capable of bringing into the World any such *Puppies* as would do that, she would not be at the Trouble to rear them: Upon which, what could the terrified old Dog do, but troop off to seek a *new dwelling Place*, with his Tail between his legs, muttering, all the Way he went, Curses and wise Maxims, between his Teeth such as *Pox take all Ingrat-*

itude, and *beware whom you trust*, or to that Effect, as you surely see at large in old *æsop*. . . .

If we must have the *Dissenters*, I should be rather for importing them from *Scotland*, than *Pennsylvania*, Because I am apt to fancy, that this latter will only send such, as *she can very well spare*, and almost as *useless Lumber*. . . .

With Regard to Toleration, I propose, that Care be taken, that we have not a Bit more of it than is *unavoidably* pinned down upon us by *Act of Parliament*, which may happen to be full enough, if not too much; for it is possible, that in this Point, the Interest of the Mother may run counter to that of the Daughter.

AN ANONYMOUS WRITER: "THE DANGERS OF TOLERATION"

The four Baptist ministers arrested for holding services drew attention to the issue of toleration in Virginia. Not all people, however, sympathized with them or their cause. In this letter addressed to them, a lawyer explains how dissenters are given the right to worship, how they have violated the British Act of Toleration, and how Virginia's laws do not violate that act.

Virginia Gazette (Williamsburg, Purdie and Dixon), 20 February 1772

An ADDRESS *to the* ANABAPTISTS *imprisoned in* Caroline *County*, August 8, 1771. . . .

You have, I hear, desired to see the Law by which you are condemned. This is what you have a Right to, and in which I propose to give you Satisfaction. . . .

When a Legislature is fixed, they have the Power of judging what Laws will best promote the true Ends of Society, and Submission becomes the Duty of all other Members; which may surely be more cheerfully allowed in our happy Constitution, where a Part of them are chosen by ourselves, are subject to be changed as often as they betray their Trust. . . . This Legislature would meet in a new Society to very little Purpose if they did not for a *religious* as well as a *civil* Establishment, not only because their Union has ever been found necessary to support Government, but that a State could not expect to thrive which should seem to rely on her own Strength, by providing State Regulations only, without endeavouring to conciliate the Divine Favour, by establishing Modes of Piety and Devotion. To these religious Establishments it becomes the Duty of every good Member of Society to submit; and an Opposition to them must be considered as Heresy and Schism, and Breach of the Laws.

I do not mean to exclude Toleration to scrupulous Consciences: I am for that upon the broadest Bottom a due Regard to the publick Peace will admit of; but of that the Legislature are to judge, and to fix its Limits, to which Dissenters must conform.

I would also desire not to be misunderstood in these my Notions of Heresy: The private Opinions of Men are not the Objects of Law or Government; while they keep those to themselves, they may enjoy them without Interruption from the civil Magistrate. But if they go about publickly preaching inculcating their Errours, raising Factions tending to disturb the publick Peace, or utter Doctrines which in their Nature are subversive of all Religion or Morality, they become obnoxious to civil Punishment.

That you may not rely on my Word for this, I will read you some Authorities in Support of it. . . . "Although Offences against Religion are, strictly speaking, of ecclesiastical Conusance [sic], yet where a Person, in Maintenance of his Errours, sets up Conventicles, or raises Factions which may tend to disturb the publick Peace, or where the Errours are of such a Nature as subvert all Religion and Morality, which are the Foundation of Government, they are punishable by the temporal Judges with Fine and Imprisonment, and also such other corporal infamous Punishment as to the Court in Discretion shall seem meet, according to the Heinousness of the Crime, lest the Publick should suffer a Detriment." . . .

"Seditious Words in Derogation of the established Religion are indictable, as tending to a Breach of the Peace; such as these, your Religion is a new Religion, and preaching is but prattling, and Prayer once a Day is more edifying." . . .

Here you must see plainly that you are liable to be indicted, fined, and imprisoned, nay, if we had that persecuting Spirit we are charged with, we might have gone farther, and added infamous corporal Punishment, instead of which we only endeavour to prevent these Mischiefs in future, by requiring Security for your good Behaviour, fairly letting you know that preaching at Houses or Places not licensed will be considered as a Breach of your Bond; and your Imprisonment is your own seeking, as it is only in Consequence of your obstinately refusing to give this Security.

But you say for yourselves, that you have a Call from GOD to preach, and deny that your Doctines or Practiceds are hurtful to Society. As to your Call, produce your Credentials; and, I will engage for the Court, they shall not be opposed. . . .

Have we Reason to expect, and therefore from Probability to believe, any such Calls? We are told that false Prophets will come, but no Hint given that we are to look for any True Ones.

And for what should you be called? Have you a new Redeemer to preach, or a new Revelation of GOD'S WILL to make the World? You do not pretend it, but only that you are to preach that Saviour, and explain those Scriptures, with which the World have been acquainted for upwards of seventeen Hundred Years. Can you pretend to be better acquainted with them than others. . . . Can you be so well able to expound them as those Teachers provided by the State, who have Educations suited to such a Work, and have no Interest in deceiving us, and therefore we cannot suspect them of such an Inclination? . . .

Your Doctrines and Practices tend to disturb, if not to sap, the very Foundations of Society, and will fully justify the Proceeding against you. Indeed your publick Preaching at all as Dissenters subjects you to worse Punishment by the common Law than we have attempted, unless it be true that you are exempted and justified by the Act of Toleration, which you claim the Benefit of; and I am one among the few Lawyers in the Country who think you are entitled to all the Benefit of that Act, provided you comply with the Terms of it. I will endeavour to state that Matter faithfully to you. . . .

By that Statute, "the Book of Common Prayer and Church Liturgy was to be used in all Places of Worship; and every Person was to resort to his Parish Church every Sunday and Holiday, under the Penalty of twelve-pence, and Church Censures." . . .

Thus stood the Law when the Statute was made commonly called "The Act of Toleration," and from that Title is supposed to be an universal Indulgence to Men to be of what Religion, or to practice what Mode of Religion, their Whims may suggest, and to make Converts to their Visions, running to and fro and uttering them, and disturbing Society as much as they please. But this will appear to be a Mistake . . . "that all Dissenters shall be exempted from the Penalties of the several Statutes before mention, and others about Religion . . . provided they take the Oaths to Government, and make a Declaration against Transubstantiation . . . and come to some Congregation for religious Worship, in a Place registered in the Bishop's Court . . . the Doors whereof shall not be locked, barred, or bolted."

"Teachers are to be qualified by taking the Oaths to Government, making the same Declaration, and subscribing Part of the thirty nine Articles. . . .

The General Court have exercised this Power; and while none but qualified Teachers assume that Office, and they meet only unlicensed Houses, you will meet with Protection, not Interruption, from Magistracy here; but as often as you break those Limits, and *every One* undertakes to preach *every Where*, you may expect to be proceeded against as the Law directs, and can derive no Advantage from the Act of Toleration.

AN ANONYMOUS WRITER: "GOVERNMENT NEEDS RELIGION AND TAXES"

While America fought the Revolution, the battle over religious toleration continued. In this unsigned letter, the writer points out that govern-

ments must tax to run properly. They must also have ties to religion for the same purpose. Whenever someone pays a tax to support an established religion, they are, in reality, supporting government.

Virginia Gazette (Williamsburg, Purdie), 13 December 1776

To the PUBLICK, . . .

Every system of religion, that has been hitherto instituted, is equally false and foolish; from the Roman Catholick with his host, down to the African with his fettish. Individually, therefore, the sectaries are right; that each should be foolish in his own way, without contributing to the folly of others. Collectively, they are wrong; for recent experience has taught, that some particular sects hold principles not only incompatible with the prosperity, but even the very existence of established governments. Does the state summon all its members to arms, for mutual defence? Their faith forbids their bearing arms, on any occasion whatsoever. Does its safety demand a rigid authority over a proportion of its inhabitants? Their religion teaches, that the souls of all men are equal in the sight of God; and, for religious purposes, they level so indiscriminately, with those they should command, that all subordination must be destroyed by it.

Religious evils have no remedy, but counteracting each other; and hence the expedience of an established church, which, while it receives protection from government, always pays a due obedience to its authority, and does remotely, though feebly, lay some restraint on systems more noxious than its own. The sectaries, then, are mistaken when they suppose they are taxed for the support of a foreign church; they only contribute to the support of government, for no government can be well regulated which turns every religious order, uncontrouled, loose on society.

QUESTIONS

1. What were the principal reasons proposed for an established religion in colonies?

2. Why would religious toleration as guaranteed by the Act of Toleration, promised by Virginia Governor Botetourt, not be acceptable to Baptists, Presbyterians, and other dissenting religious groups?

3. Read the First Amendment to the Constitution. How much do you think religious dissenters had to do with its inclusion in the Bill of Rights? Explain.

4. Why did the group of Virginia militiamen believe the Declaration of Independence gave them religious liberty?

5. What was Tom Telltrutha's real concern about allowing dissenters free worship in Virginia?

6. How did Baptists violate the Act of Toleration, according to the Virginia lawyer who wrote to them in prison?

7. What was the relationship between religion and government in the colonial era? Use the *Independent Reflector* essay of 1753 and the *Virginia Gazette* letter of December 1776 as your key to answering this question.

NOTES

1. David Benedict, *A General History of the Baptist Denomination in America and Other Parts of the World*, 2 vols. (Boston: Manning and Loring, 1813), 2: 30–31.

2. Captaine John Smith, *Advertisements for the unexperienced Planters of New England, or any where. Or The Path-way to experience to erect a Plantation* (London, 1631), 32.

3. Richard Baxter, *Plain Scripture Proof* (London, 1651), 251.

4. *Propositions and Conclusions concerning True Christian Religion, containing a Confession of Faith of certain English people, living at Amsterdam* (1612), reprinted in William L. Lumpkin, ed., *Baptist Confessions of Faith* (Valley Forge, Pa.: Judson Press, 1959), 140.

5. Roger Williams, "Mr. Cottons Letter Lately Printed, Examined and Answered" (1644), in *The Complete Writings of Roger Williams*, 7 vols. (New York: Russell & Russell, 1963), 1:108.

CHAPTER 23

The Somerset Case and the Anti-Slavery Controversy, 1772

In 1772 the case of James Somerset went before England's highest common law court, the King's Bench. When the chief justice rendered his decision following five days of testimony, Somerset was free—literally—from the laws that had enslaved him for years.

James Somerset, an American slave, was sold to a customs official named Charles Stewart. Stewart bought Somerset in Virginia and took him to Massachusetts, where Stewart worked for the British government. In 1769 Stewart sailed to England on business and took his slave with him. Somerset used the trip as an opportunity to escape, but he was recaptured. Stewart decided the best thing to do with a rebellious slave was to sell him back into slavery, and he made plans to ship Somerset to Jamaica.

At this point, British abolitionists learned of Somerset's plight, and an outspoken advocate of manumission, or freedom for slaves, Granville Sharp, contacted Somerset. With the abolitionist's help, the slave petitioned the court for his freedom. The chief justice, in ruling that Somerset must be set free, said, "[N]o Master ever was allowed here to take a Slave by Force to be sold . . . therefore the Man must be discharged."[1] The decision to free Somerset was handed down not because slavery was illegal, but because England had no laws that pertained to his particular situation.[2]

Even though the decision did not end slavery in Britain and its colonies, many in England and America believed that the Somerset verdict was the beginning of the end for slavery in the English-speaking world. As a writer in the *London Chronicle* noted on June 20, 1772,

Some generous humane persons subscribed to the expence of obtaining liberty by law for Somerset the Negro.—It is to be wished that the same humanity may extend itself among numbers; if not to the procuring liberty for those that remain in our Colonies, at least to obtain a law for abolishing the African commerce in slaves, and declaring the children of present Slaves free after they become of age.

The trial of James Somerset coincided with a movement in America toward ending slavery. As Benjamin Franklin, who was in London during the hearing, wrote in a letter following the decision, "I am glad to hear that the Disposition against keeping Negroes grows more general in North America. . . . I hope therefore you and your Friends will be encouraged to proceed."[3] Most Americans who favored manumission lived in New England or in Pennsylvania, the colony founded by the religious group known as the Society of Friends. Friends, or Quakers as they were known to many, were the first in America to call for the end of slavery. For nearly 100 years before the Somerset decision, Quakers publically opposed slavery, and they began publishing anti-slavery tracts in 1700 with Samuel Sewell's *Selling of Joseph.*

The Quaker call for the abolition of slavery in the first two-thirds of the eighteenth century went unheeded for a number of reasons. Principally, slaves were seen as necessary for the survival of the British colonies, and they had been viewed in such a way almost from the beginning of colonization. As a letter to Massachusetts Bay Governor John Wintrop pointed out in 1645, "The colony will never thrive untill we gett . . . a stock of slaves sufficient to doe all our business."[4] The Southern colonies depended upon slaves to work the fields of large plantations. In the Middle and New England colonies, slaves filled any number of positions, but for New England merchants and shippers, the slave trade was a prime source of revenue. In fact, two-thirds of Rhode Island's ships and sailors directly took part in the slave trade,[5] and profits from the slave trade grew by more than 321 percent from the beginning of the century to 1740.[6] Slaves entered America at all ports; more than 35 percent of the immigrants coming to America through New York from the 1730s to the 1760s were Africans destined for slavery.[7] More than a quarter of a million Africans were sold into American slavery during the eighteenth century.[8]

The American dialogue on slavery had its roots in religion and the concepts of freedom and liberty. Americans of the 1770s were seeking both from England, and some saw a natural corollary in their own plight and that of the slaves. But curtailing such a popular and profitable practice as slavery would not be easy. In 1775 Rhode Island became the first colony to prohibit the importation of slaves, and by 1800 all New England states had outlawed slavery. Still, it took the Civil War to end slavery in all parts of America.

The anti-slavery section of this chapter begins with a pair of letters related to the Somerset trial. The first says that African slaves now had achieved equality in Great Britain. The second recommends sending all Africans back to Africa. These letters are followed by Rhode Island's "An ACT for prohibiting the Importation of Negroes into this Colony, and asserting the Right of Freedom of all those hereafter born or manumitted within the same," America's first governmental outlawing of slavery. The next selection is the first anti-slavery essay to appear in newspapers, George Whitefield's letter to the Inhabitants of the Southern colonies, written in 1740. After it comes an essay that points out the hypocrisy of white Americans demanding liberty while enslaving Africans. The last anti-slavery entry is a rare letter from a Southern newspaper opposing bondage and servitude for Africans. The letter writer, who used a pseudonym, is unknown.

The first pro-slavery entry, a reaction to the Somerset decision, declares that the repercussions from it will be greater than the reaction to the Stamp Act in America. Two pro-slavery letters, which are unsigned, follow. They outline the religious foundations used in colonial America to support slavery. Even though these letters sound like pro-slavery arguments, they were in reality printed to demonstrate what their authors—and probably the printers—saw as the foolishness of the pro-slavery argument. Identical arguments, however, appeared in pamphlets printed during the period but were not presented as parody. The arguments on both sides of the issue were the same as those used by abolitionists in the nineteenth century. The third letter, which is signed with a pseudonym, comes from the *Virginia Gazette*. It specifically uses the book of Genesis to legitimize slavery.

ANTI-SLAVERY DIALOGUE

AN ANONYMOUS WRITER: "THE GREAT NEGRO CAUSE"

American newspapers did not discuss in great depth the Somerset trial. Instead, papers concentrated more on the overall debate on the validity of slavery. In this letter from an unknown Londoner, the writer thinks that freedom for African slaves was greatly enhanced by the Somerset decision.

New-York Journal; or, the General Advertiser, 3 September 1772

Extract of a letter from London, dated July 2.

The great Negro cause was determined a few days ago, and the consequence was, the negro obtained his freedom. The poor fellow was present in the court at the decision, as were likewise a great many other blacks, all of whom, as soon as Lord Mansfield had delivered the opinion of the court, came forward, and bowed first to the Judges, and then to the bar, with symptoms of the most extravagant joy. Who can help admiring the genius of that government, which thus dispenses freedom to all around it? No station or character is above the law, nor is any beneath protection. The Monarch and the Beggar are alike subject to it . . . are equally guarded by it.

AN ANONYMOUS WRITER: "SEND ALL NEGROES BACK TO THEIR OWN COUNTRY"

Any time slaves or issues surrounding slaves appeared in newspapers, reports of slave problems increased. This letter from an anonymous New Jersey writer, written while news of the Somerset trial was still occasionally being printed, suggests that the best thing for white America would be to send all slaves back to the point of their origin. The letter is not an anti-slavery one as are many of the readings in this section of the chapter; instead, it proposes freedom for slaves as a means to protect white Americans.

New-York Journal; or, the General Advertiser, 5 November 1772

AN anonimous correspondent who dates his letter in East New-Jersey, has sent money to pay for an advertisement, signifying his apprehensions, of a conspiracy among the Negroes, which he supposes has been long in agitation, to set themselves free: He grounds this conjecture on speeches that he has heard, were made by two Negroes . . . "That it was not necessary that they should endeavour to please their masters, for, that they should not have any masters long." He therefore hopes all the Colonies will take proper measures for their security, and particularly, that they will put in execution the laws which prohibit Negroes, who are become vastly numerous, from meeting together in companies. And tho' he has 7 of his own, he prays that the King and parliament would make a law, to send all Negroes back to their own country, at the expense of their owners; and he desires, that this caution may not seem to any, as coming *from one that mocketh!*

GENERAL ASSEMBLY OF RHODE ISLAND: "AN ACT PROHIBITING THE IMPORTATION OF NEGROES"

The Revolution had begun, and Rhode Island's legislature took a bold step to end slavery there with this act. Now, it was against the law to

*import slaves to Rhode Island. The act also talked in terms of freedom
and liberty for slaves.*

Providence Gazette; and Country Journal, 9 September 1775

An ACT for prohibiting the Importation of Negroes into this Colony,
and asserting the Right of Freedom of all those hereafter born or manumitted within the same.

WHEREAS the inhabitants of America are generally engaged in the preservation of their own rights and liberties, among which that of personal
freedom must be considered as the greatest; and as those who are desirous of enjoying all the advantages of liberty themselves, should be willing
to extend personal liberty to others:

Therefore be it enacted by this General Assembly, and by the authority
thereof it is enacted, that for the future no Negro or Mulatto slave shall
be brought into this colony; and in case any slave shall hereafter be
brought in, he or she shall be, and are hereby, rendered immediately
free, so far as respects personal freedom, and the enjoyment of private
property, in the same manner as the native Indians.

Provided nevertheless, that this law shall not extend to servants of persons travelling through this colony, or that come to settle within the
same, provided the masters of such servants do not presume to sell or
alienate them as slaves. And to prevent any slave or slaves from being
clandestinely brought into this colony, in order that they may be free,
and liable to become chargeable, be it further enacted by the authority
aforesaid, that all persons so offending shall be liable to and pay a fine
of One Hundred Pounds lawful money, for each and every one so
brought in, to and for the use of the colony, to be recovered in the same
manner that other fines and forfeitures usually are by the laws of this
government; and also all persons who shall be convicted of receiving,
harbouring or concealing any such Negro or Mulatto slave within this
colony, he or they so offending shall be liable to the like penalty, to be
recovered and applied in the same manner; and such Negro or Mulatto
shall be sent out of the colony as other poor persons are by law. . . . And
whereas by the charter of this colony, and by the declarations of our
rights at sundry times since asserted, all persons born within this colony
are as free, to all intents and purposes, as though born within the realm
of England, where the laws expressly exclude personal slavery; be it further enacted by this General Assembly, and by the authority thereof it is
hereby enacted, that for the future all Negroes, as well as other persons,
hereafter born within this colony, be, and they are hereby, declared free,
and intitled to the same personal privileges as the native inhabitants at
the usual age of twenty-one years, and usage or custom to the contrary
in any wise notwithstanding. . . . And to prevent he public becoming
chargeable, by reason of the master or mistress of any slave or slaves (not

manumitted as aforesaid) being unable to support them, be it enacted by the authority aforesaid, that in such case the preceding possessor; of such slave or slaves shall be liable to and pay the whole expence of such Negro or Mulatto, if of ability, and there be any such to be found, and so back, or the preceding master or mistress shall be liable, until there be a former possessor found (if any) who may have estate sufficient to indemnify and free the town (where such indigent Negro or Mulatto may fall) from said expence.

GEORGE WHITEFIELD: "A LETTER TO THE INHABITANTS OF MARYLAND, VIRGINIA, NORTH AND SOUTH-CAROLINA"

George Whitefield (see Chapter 8) rarely backed down when he believed in an issue, and the itinerant minister from England thought slavery was wrong. He spent a considerable amount of time during his first preaching tour in the Southern colonies and wrote this open letter to the inhabitants of them on the sins of slavery.

Pennsylvania Gazette (Philadelphia), 17 April 1740

"A Letter form the Rev. Mr. GEORGE WHITEFIELD, to the Inhabitants of Maryland, Virginia, North and South-Carolina."

As I lately passed through your Provinces, in my Way hither, I was sensibly touched with a Fellow-feeling of the Miseries of the poor Negroes. . . . Whatever be the Event, I must inform you, in the Meekness and Gentleness of christ, that I think God has a Quarrel with you for your Abuse of and Cruelty to the poor Negroes. Whether it be lawful for Christians to buy Slaves, and thereby encourage the Nations from whence they are brought, to be at perpetual War with each other, I shall not take upon me to determine; sure I am, it is sinful, when bought, to use them as bad nay worse than as though they were Brutes; and whatever particular Exceptions there may be. . . . I fear the Generality of you that own Negroes, are liable to such a Charge; for your Slaves, I believe, work as hard if not harder than the Horses whereon you ride. . . . Your Dogs are caress'd and fondled at your Tables–But your Slaves, who are frequently stiled Dogs or Beasts, have not an equal Privilege. They are scarce permitted to pick up the Crumbs which fall from their Masters Tables. . . . I have wondered, that we have not more Instances of Self-Murder among the Negroes, or that they have not more frequently rose up in Arms against their Owners. . . . For God is the same to Day as he was Yesterday, and will continue the same forever. He does not reject the Prayer of the poor and destitute, nor disregard the Cry of the meanest Negroes! The Blood of them spilt for these many Years in your respective Provinces, will ascend up to Heaven against you.

AN ANONYMOUS WRITER: "THE SHAMEFUL, SHOCKING SLAVE-TRADE"

Americans during the tumultuous period from the Stamp Act crisis of 1765 to the beginning of the Revolution in 1775 looked at a number of issues through the lens of their own situation. Patriots used the rhetoric of their rights to freedom and liberty juxtaposed against their own oppression and slavery to England. As a result, some Americans realized that within America some groups were just as depressed because of their religion (see Chapter 22) or because of their station—they were slaves. In this anonymous letter, the writer uses liberty and religion to criticize the slave trade.

New-London Gazette, 10 August 1770

A prognostic of the loss of Liberty, is, the shameful, shocking Slave-Trade, so long carried on by a nation that makes her boast of Liberty, that calls herself Protestant and Christian!—It is said England supplies her American colonies yearly with more than 100,000 slaves. In order to procure such, they encourage the African princes to go to war with one another, and to spread wretchedness among their own humane, innocent well-disposed subjects. What adds to the horrid barbarity, no less than 10,000 of these unhapppy humans creatures die in the voyage, and one fourth of an hundred thousand, in, what is called, the seasoning. It is affirmed of Liverpool, that her vessels alone import to America more than 30,000 slaves yearly.

ASSOCIATOR HUMANUS: "SLAVERY IS LIKE MINISTERIAL TYRANNY"

Anti-slavery literature in Southern newspapers was rare, but in this anonymous letter published in the Virginia Gazette, *the writer suggests that Americans despise tyranny by the ministry of England. But America's condoning of slavery, he says, is tyranny, too, and it should be stopped.*

Virginia Gazette (Williamsburg, Purdie and Dixon), 18 July 1771

GENTLEMEN,

I HAVE often thought that we should have been more strenuous in our Opposition to ministerial Tyranny, spoken out with more Boldness against it, and manifested a more genuine Abhorrence of Slavery, had we not been too familiar with it, or had we not been conscious that we ourselves were absolute Tyrants, and held Numbers of the poor Souls in the most abject and endless State of Slavery. . . . Let us endeavour to discourage a Practice which must for ever prevent our Country from flourishing as the northern Colonies have done, a Practice which is a neverfailing Source of Ignorance and Vice, of Indolence and Cruelty, amongst us; in short, a Practice which Prudence should guard against and Humanity forbids, and which, above all, is directly contrary to the fundamental Principles of our holy Religion. Let us endeavour to make the Lives of those we are unfortunate enough to have already among us as comfortable as we can. Let us treat them as unfortunate Men; but let us never heighten their Misfortune by Cruelty, nor aggravate it by Insult. Let us not even mention the Name of Slavery before them. And let us never shock them with the dreadful Sight of free born Men dragged from their native Country, and forced to work among them. Let us beware how we remind them that this was once their Case. If we will resolve to import no more, and determine to treat those we have humanely, so that they cannot perceive the Yoke of Slavery, nor accuse us of Tyranny, then, and then only, may we, with Confidence, step forth and boldly assert our own Liberty and Independence.

I am, your humble Servant,
ASSOCIATOR HUMANUS.

PRO-SLAVERY DIALOGUE

AN ANONYMOUS REPORT: "THE SOMERSET DECISION WILL CAUSE PROBLEMS"

When Lord Mansfield ruled that Somerset was free, some feared the repercussions for England's American and Caribbean colonies would be worse than the reaction to the Stamp Act. Although that was not the case, this London writer passed on that report.

New-York Journal; or, the General Advertiser, 27 August 1772

The late decision with regard to Somerset the Negro, a correspondent assures us, will occasion a greater ferment in America (particularly in the islands) than the Stamp Act itself; for the slaves constituting the great value of (West-Indies) property (especially) and appeals lying from America in all cases of a civil process to the mother-country, every pettifogger will have his neighbour entirely at his mercy, and by applying to the King's Bench at Westminster, leave the subject at Jamaica or Barbados wholly without a hand to cultivate his plantations.

AN ANONYMOUS WRITER: "SCRIPTURE FORETOLD SLAVERY OF AFRICANS"

Scripture was used by colonial writers to support or refute a number of issues. It was central to the dialogue on slavery. In this anonymous letter, the writer states all the usual scriptural rationales for accepting slavery. The letter, as included here, sounds very much like the pro-slavery pamphlets that circulated during the era. In reality, the letter ended with refutation to the argument. It is included here because it contains the standard pro-slavery argument, which generally appeared in publications other than newspapers.

Connecticut Journal, and New-Haven Post-Boy, 6 July 1770

IT is strange that any persons should be so infatuated, as to deny the right of enslaving the black inhabitants of Africa. I cannot look on silently and see this inestimable privilege, which has been handed down inviolable from our ancestors, wrenched out of our hands, by a few men of squeamish consciences, that will not allow them, or others peaceably to enjoy it. I therefore engage in the dispute and make no doubt of proving to every unprejudiced mind, that we have a natural, moral, and divine right of enslaving the Africans. . . . It is positively foretold in the scriptures, that the children of Ham, should be servants of servants to their brethern. Now if our adversaries will but allow these two points, that a prophecy concerning any thing that shall be done, may be construed into a permission for the doing of it, and that the Africans are the children of Ham, which is plain from their being servants of servants to their brethren; the controversy is brought to a point, and there needs nothing further to be said upon the subject.

Besides, was not the slave trade carried on exactly in the same manner, by Abraham and several other good patriarchs, whom we read of in antient history? Those Gentlemen will doubtless be allowed to have been perfect patterns and examples. . . . The whole world is the property of the righteous; consequently the Africans, being infidels and heretics, may rightly be considered as lawful plunder.

I come now to the most weighty part of the argument. . . . Is not the enslaving of these people the most charitable act in the world? With no other end in view than to bring those poor creatures to christian ground, and within hearing of the gospel, we spare no expence of time or money, we send many thousand miles across the dangerous seas, and think all our toil and pains well rewarded.

AN ANONYMOUS WRITER: "AFRICANS ARE BROUGHT HERE TO CHRISTIANIZE"

Slaves were brought to America for their own welfare, according to some pro-slavery advocates. In this letter, the writer outlines the basic reasons why Africans are slaves. Three main ones are used: Slaves are bought with rum money; slaves are descended from the biblical Ham and are, therefore, to be slaves, and slaves are enslaved and brought to America to be Christianized.

Connecticut Gazette; and the Universal Intelligencer (New London), 6 January 1775

Mr. GREEN,

Almost every person who has ingenuity enough to form into a combination half a dozen ideas, has communicated them to the public on the favorite theme of slavery—Among the rest, I think I have a right to say something on the matter, and if the world will be at the trouble of reading these remarks, I promise never to trouble them with any thing more on the topic.

Scarcely one, amidst all the performances on this popular subject, has been written with a proper degree of candor. It is a sure mark of an imperious mind, when it has the advantage in any contest, to behave with insolence, or cast unpolite reflections on its adversary. . . . I have ever been an avowed enemy to enslaving the Africans, till a few days since meeting with a remarkable champion for the cause of slavery, the very weighty suggestions and reasons which he introduced in support of it, broke through every objection, and struck so clear a conviction of truth in my mind, as over-powered the prejudices and prepossessions which along and (as I supposed) a warrantable opinion would naturally create; and now instead of opposing him, I am become the most enthusiastic abetter of his sentiments.

In vindication of slavery he argued copiously and pertinently. The three most striking and ingenious intimations were—That the Africans were purchased with Rum—That they were descendants of Ham, and therefore by divine decree ought to be reduced to a state of servitude—That bringing them into a land of civilization and religion contributed to moralize and christianize them. These were his principal, these his most penetrating and invicible arguments. . . . Slaves are frequently purchased with RUM—with Rum—with New-England Rum—with New-England rum suitably attempered and molified, that I may not prove detrimental to their constitutions. . . . Can perpetual and horrid wars, can final and the most abject kind of servitude, can quitting their native country and all the comforts which result from friends, from relations and from acquaintance, be too great reprisals on the part of Negroland, for so excellent a commodity as rum?—Even Liberty itself is to be disdained in competition with it—Place them both upon the same parallel and Rum would share the amplest company of votaries. Don't then complain of African slavery, nor charge its encouragers with barbarity or injustice.

The next, and a still more powerful argument, is deducible from the denunciation of Noah upon Canaan. We may take for granted that the

Negroes are the descendants of Ham. It is also an incontestible fact that curses were denounced against them—And by a kind of inspiration we are induced to believe we are authorized to put them in execution, as the Jews were to accomplish the prophecies concerning the crucifixion of our Saviour. It is no less our duty to enslave the Africans, than it was the Jews to crucify Christ.—We may expect a reward for it. . . . If a negro were manumitted by his master, any person by virtue of Noah's prediction may as rightly enslave him as the first man might, and so on *ad infinitum*; for no human institution ought to violate the decrees of God. It is too plain to need any more said on this head.

Here comes the capital, the irresistable argument.—The Africans are brought here to be christianized.—Let us here pause and admire!—We are to judge of Christians by their fruits. Negroes are Arminians, to be saved by their works.—In what set of men are many of the moral and some of the christian virtues so illustriously exhibited?

A CUSTOMER: "THE BEASTS OF ETHIOPIA SHALL BOW DOWN TO THEE"

As the attack on slavery increased, the arguments in support of it endeavored to find biblical support. In this anonymous letter, the writer postulates that the book of Genesis validates the enslavement of Africans in this strained interpretation of Genesis 1:28–30. The writer's quote of the verses, however, does not agree with the King James version of scripture.

Virginia Gazette (Williamsburg, Purdie and Dixon), 2 December 1773

SIR,

IN looking over the latter Part of the first Chapter of Genesis, I find an Account of God's having granted to Adam, and his Posterity, not only a Dominion over "the Fish of the Sea, the Fowl of the Air, Cattle and every Thing that *creepeth* upon the Earth," but likewise, in a particular Manner, over the Negroes of Africa.* I beg therefore you would mention this, in your Paper, to silence those Writers who insist upon the Africans belonging to the same Species of Men with the white People, and who will not allow that God formed them in common with Horses, Oxen, Dogs, &c. for the Benefit of the white People alone, to be used by them either for Pleasure, or to labour with their *other* Beasts in the Pasture of Tobacco, Indigo, Rice, and Sugar.   A CUSTOMER.

"And the Beasts of Ethiopia shall bow down to thee, even those [with] Figure and Speech are like unto thine own."

QUESTIONS

1. Why do you think the 1775 Rhode Island anti-slavery act did not completely ban slavery?

2. What were George Whitefield's reasons for thinking slaves should be set free?

3. How did America's desire to be free from England figure into the abolition dialogue?

4. What were the foundations of the pro-slavery argument as presented in the newspapers?

5. How might you refute the pro-slavery argument as outlined in the question above?

NOTES

1. *Virginia Gazette* (Williamsburg, Dixon and Purdie), 22 August 1772, 3.

2. David Brion Davis, *The Problem of Slavery in the Age of Revolution, 1770–1823* (Ithaca, N.Y.: Cornell University Press, 1975), 498.

3. "To Anthony Benezet," in *Benjamin Franklin, Writings*, ed. J. A. Leo Lemay (New York: Library of America, 1987), 876.

4. Quoted in Lorenzo J. Greene, *The Negro in Colonial America, 1620–1776* (New York, 1942), 60.

5. Steven Deyle, " 'By farr the most profitable trade': Slave Trading in British Colonial North America," *Slavery & Abolition* 10 (1989): 112.

6. James F. Shepherd and Gary M. Walton, *Shipping, Maritime Trade, and the Economic Development of Colonial North America* (Cambridge: Cambridge University Press, 1972), 42, note 2.

7. David Brion Davis, "The Comparative Approach to American History: Slavery," in *Slavery in the New World: A Reader in Comparative History*, ed. Laura Foner and Eugene D. Genovese (Englewood Cliffs, N.J.: Prentice-Hall, 1978), 62.

8. David Hackett Fischer, *Albion's Seed: Four British Folkways in America* (New York: Oxford University Press, 1989), 810.

CHAPTER 24

The Tea Act and the Boston Tea Party, 1773–1774

On December 16, 1773, about fifty members of the Sons of Liberty (see Chapter 18) dressed as Native Americans and boarded the *Dartmouth*, a ship docked in Boston harbor. Methodically, the men dumped 342 chests of tea into the harbor destroying £9,659[1] worth of private property. While the act of destroying the tea may have been a simple one, its causes and repercussions were anything but simple.

Tea was the principal drink of Americans and the British, and in 1698, Parliament gave exclusive rights to import tea into Great Britain to the East India Company. In 1721 Parliament prohibited the colonies from importing tea from any source other than the East India Company. Even though Americans often ignored the law and smuggled tea, especially from Holland, the East India Company thrived.

The Stamp Act crisis of 1765 (see Chapter 16) and the passage of the Townshend Acts (see Chapter 20), which levied taxes on lead, tea, paint, paper, and glass, triggered a change in American thinking, and in 1767, angry Bostonians proposed that Americans stop using British commodities. Many merchants and others in the colonies rallied behind this plan of nonimportation (see Chapter 20). As a result, the amount of tea shipped by the East India Company to America decreased from 1768 to 1772 from approximately 562,281 pounds per year to 213,417.[2]

Even though not all Americans joined in nonimportation, enough did that Parliament lifted the Townshend Acts in 1770 with one exception—the duty on tea. In 1773 Parliament decided that, in order to bolster the East India Company, which now was on the verge of collapse, it would allow the company to export tea to America duty free. This did not mean that Americans would no longer pay a tax on tea; it meant that the East India Company would be reimbursed for the initial taxes it paid to bring the tea to England and store it. The East India Company's tea would now be much cheaper than that currently being sold by American merchants, much of which had been obtained from the Dutch during nonimportation. The East India Company appointed men throughout America to act as tea distributors and successfully excluded any merchants who had acted previously as middlemen between distributor and consumer.

Many Americans argued that the Tea Act of 1773 placed America in a precarious position. If Parliament could effectively create a tea monopoly for the East India Company, what other commodity and company would be next to be given sole rights to American trade? And, these same people argued, Americans were still being required to pay a tax that was levied on them without their consent (see Chapter 17). "If the East India company can establish warehouses in America for the sale of TEA, *on which a duty is imposed for the purpose of raising a revenue in America*, they may vend, in like manner any other articles of their trade," a writer to the *Boston Gazette* explained. "Thus the imposition may be increased at pleasure; and America be subjugated without the possibility of redemption."[3]

Some in Boston wrote about the dangers of the Tea Act; others decided to act. What better way to get Britain's attention than empty her purse, they no doubt figured. So while some citizens were meeting with Governor Thomas Hutchinson, who told them the tea tax would not be lifted, others were proceeding to Griffin's Wharf, dressed as Indians, to dump British tea into the harbor.

Parliament responded to the Boston Tea Party with a series of acts aimed exclusively at the port of Boston. First, the port was closed to all trade on June 1, 1774. Next, the Massachusetts Government Act changed the colony's charter and took away the colonial legislature's right of appointing the governor's council, giving it, instead, to the king. Parliament also revised the Quartering Act, which had been partly responsible for the Boston Massacre (see Chapter 21). Following the Tea Party, troops could be quartered in the city rather than in barracks outside town. The number of soldiers stationed in Boston was increased, and General Thomas Gage was temporarily made governor of the colony. A new act, the Administration of Justice Act, allowed any government or customs official accused of a crime to be tried in England and not by a Boston jury.

Collectively, Bostonians referred to the new measures placed on them by Parliament as the Intolerable or Coercive Acts. The Intolerable Acts not only failed to bring Boston into line, they created sympathy for Boston throughout America. Colonials in other ports staged protests against East India Tea and found ways to assist the struggling citizens of Boston.

The section containing the Patriot views of the Tea Act and Boston Tea Party begins with two articles from *Rivington's New-York Gazetteer*. Usually considered the strongest of the Tory newspapers in America, printer James Rivington often published pro-Patriot articles as a way to balance the content of his paper. The first is a set of queries and answers aimed at the Tory writer Poplicola. One of Poplicola's letters supporting the Tea Act is included in the second set of readings in the chapter. The queries are followed by a public notice that importers of East India tea could expect acts of violence directed at them, a prediction that came true in Boston a little more than two weeks after this notice appeared in the New York paper.

The next selections come from Boston's two Patriot newspapers, the *Massachusetts Spy* and the *Boston Gazette*. The *Gazette* presents an account of the Boston Tea Party written supposedly by an impartial Rhode Island observer. The articles from the *Spy* included here appeared both before and after the tea was thrown into Boston harbor. The first intimated that the ship and the tea were infested with smallpox. In its post–Tea Party newspapers, the *Spy* first laid the blame for the tea's destruction on Governor Thomas Hutchinson in a letter written under the pseudonym E. Ludlow. This letter is followed by an announcement that Bostonians had no alternative but to dump the tea. The final entry in this section is a call for the return of the Indians who dumped the tea into the harbor because more tea would soon be arriving from England.

Writers to Tory newspapers tended to ignore the actual Tea Party. Instead, the writers focused on what they deemed to be the positive aspects of the Tea Act and the quality of English tea versus Dutch tea. The first letter, by the unknown Poplicola, demonstrates the complexities of the politics of the age. The letter points out that buying East India tea is a patriotic activity. The letter also counsels Americans on the relationship between the colonies and Great Britain. The letter stresses the good of the whole—the British Empire—versus the welfare of its separate parts.

The next two selections, from the *Massachusetts Gazette*, discuss the actions of those in Boston who dumped the tea without ever mentioning the Boston Tea Party. The first attacks the actions of the tea dumpers who said they were acting for all citizens of the colony, something the letter writers denounce. The second, a letter from England, discusses the destruction of private property. The final selection suggests that Boston repay the East India Company for its losses as a way to avoid the closing of Boston harbor on June 1, the date the Boston Port Act was to go into effect.

PATRIOT VIEWS

AN OLD PROPHET/THE MOHAWKS: "WE WILL NOT BE ENSLAVED"

When a writer using the name Poplicola wrote to the New-York Gazetteer *in support of the Tea Act, others responded. In these two letters, the writers declare that Americans will not be enslaved to intolerable British taxes. In an ironic preview to the Boston Tea Party, the writers of the second letter signed themselves The Mohawks, perhaps a veiled reference that they were Sons of Liberty, but those who took part in the Boston tea dumping were dressed like Mohawk Indians.*

Rivington's New-York Gazetteer; or Connecticut, New-Jersey, Hudson's River, and Quebec Weekly Advertiser, 2 December 1773

QUERIES.
Respecting the TEA ACT, *submitted to the* most serious consideration of every person in AMERICA.

QUERY. As there is an act of the British Parliament in being, that would subjugate America to *three pence sterling duty* upon every pound weight of tea imported from Britain . . . what ought to be done unto every one of those *traiterous persons* who shall aid or abet the importation of, *or landing*, the said tea in any port of America, till that act is totally repealed, *jointly by King, Lords, and Commons?*

ANS: Such base *traitors* to this country, without exception, should be immediately and *resolutely* be dragged from concealment; they should be transported, or forced from every place in America, loaded with the most striking badges of disgrace; particularly, we ought not to forget . . . LYING, *infamous* POPLICOLA; for in this case, all such may absolutely and justly be deemed as *public robbers* of our LIBERTY, PROPERTY, *and* PEACE. . . .

QUERY. What will be the consequence of a *ministerial illegal suspension* of the TEA ACT, of receiving or storing the said *tea* in any way or manner whatever, until the British Parliament shall be pleased to recognize the matter?

ANS: It will be *dreadful*—it will be productive of innumerable and excessive bad consequences;—a *suspending power is the most dangerous of all powers*;—we must universally bear our testimony, and hold up our hands *firmly* against it;—reject the tea firmly—for when it is landed, there will be inevitably be an incessant uproar . . . for, if the *accursed tea* should once gain such a footing as this, in America, our situation would be deplorable, *as we should then be at the precarious mercy of others*, and incontestibly forfeit, *by rapid degrees*, our invaluable blessings, our *Birthrights*, Liberty, Property, *and* Peace.   AN OLD PROPHET.

WHEREAS our nation have lately been informed, that the fetters which have been forged for us, (by the parliament of Great-Britain) are hourly expected to arrive, in a certain ship, belonging to, or chartered by, the East India Company. We do therefore declare, that we are determined not to be enslaved, by any power on earth; and that whosoever shall aid, or abet, so infamous a design, or shall presume to let their store, or stores, for the reception of the infernal chains, may depend upon it, that we are prepared, and shall not fail to pay them an unwelcome visit, in which they shall be treated as they deserve; by The MOHAWKS.

AN ANONYMOUS REPORT: "TEA AND SMALLPOX ARRIVE IN BOSTON"

In a brief notice, printer Isaiah Thomas informed citizens that a ship with tea and smallpox was now in the Boston port. Bostonians were warned to avoid the tea because it might have absorbed the disease.

Massachusetts Spy Or, Thomas's Boston Journal, 16 December 1773

BOSTON.
   Since our last arrive here Capt. Coffin, not only with the Plague (TEA) on board, but also with the small pox—As tea is of a drawing quality, it is suspected it has sucked in the distemper; and therefore if permitted to be landed, it is presumed there would be no purchaser.

AN IMPARTIAL OBSERVER: "THE TEA PARTY"

Following the Boston Tea Party, a number of accounts of what happened on December 16 appeared. In this one, the writer calls himself An Impartial Observer, meaning he is neither from Boston nor on the side of any party involved the controversy. It is doubtful that the writer of this report, however, was not from Boston or impartial. The letter is sympathetic with the Patriot cause.

Boston Gazette, and Country Journal, 20 December 1773

Messieurs Edes & Gill,
   HAVING accidentally arrived at Boston upon a visit to a Friend, the Evening before the meeting of the body of the People on the 29th of November . . . I must confess I was very disagreeably affected with the conduct of Mr. Hutchinson, their pensioned Governor, on the succeeding day, who very unseasonably, and as I am informed, very arbitrarily . . .

framed and executed a Mandate to disperse the people, which in my opinion, with a people less prudent and temperate, would have cost him his head: The force of that body was directed to effect the return of the Teas to Great-Britain; much argument was expended, much entreaty was made use of to effect this desirable purpose. . . . The Consignees have behaved like Scoundrels in refusing to take the consignment; or indemnify the owner of the ship which conveyed this detestable commodity. . . . The Body once more assembled, I was again present; such a collection of the people was to me a novelty; near seven thousand persons from several towns, Gentlemen, Merchants, Yeomen and others. . . . Previous to the dissolution, a number of persons supposed to be the Aboriginal Natives from their complection, approaching near the door of the assembly, gave the War Whoop, which was answered by a few in the galleries of the house where the assembly was convened; silence was commanded, and a prudent and peaceable deportment again enjoined: The Savages repaired to the ships which entertained the pestilential Teas, and had begun their ravage previous to the dissolution of the meeting— They applied themselves to the destruction of this commodity in earnest, and in the space of about two hours broke up 342 chests, and discharged their contents into the sea—A watch as I am informed was stationed to prevent embezzlement, and not a single ounce of Tea was suffered to be purloined or carried off.—It is worthy of remark, that although a considerable quantity of goods of different kinds were still remaining on board the vessels, no injury was sustained; such attention to private property was observed, that a small padlock belonging to the Capt. of one of the ships being broke, and there was procured and sent to him.—I cannot but express my admiration at the conduct of this people! I presume I shall not be suspected of misrepresentation. . . . That American virtue may defeat every attempt to enslave them, is the warmest wish of my heart. I shall return home doubly fortified in my resolution to prevent that deprecated calamity, the landing the teas in Rhode-Island, and console myself with the happiest assurances that my brethren have not less virtue, less resolution than their neighbours.   An Impartial Observer.

E. LUDLOW: "MR. HUTCHINSON COULD HAVE STOPPED THE TEA PARTY"

E. Ludlow blamed Governor Thomas Hutchinson for the Boston Tea Party. After all, the governor said the tea would not be returned, leaving Boston citizens with little choice but to destroy it. This letter, like the one above, provides a glimpse into the acts of December 16 from the Patriot point of view.

Massachusetts Spy Or, Thomas's Boston Journal, 23 December
1773

For the MASSACHUSETTS SPY.
To Mr. HUTCHINSON.

AT Length, Sir, your politics have arrived at maturity, and a noble crop you have reaped. Twelve to fifteen thousand pounds sterling of the East-India company's property, is a pompous sacrifice to the avarice and obstinacy of their worthy directors on this side of the water. . . .

Reflect a little, Mr. Hutchinson, what could they do but destroy it? What step did that wise and determined body leave unessayed to preserve it, consistent with the public safety? They refused to have it stored, you answer. They certainly did, and that from the beginning well knowing that if it were landed their blood-suckers were entitled to the tribute. . . . But you know, Mr. Hutchinson, the body met at the Old South meeting-house endeavoured to the last moment to return the teas. They encountered every block your craft and power could throw in their way, and finally were in full meeting, when a party of heroes, exasperated beyond measure with your unparalleled abuse, took the matter out of their hands. . . .

Yet notwithstanding all this forbearance and the inevitable necessity under which the people lay to rid themselves of this bane of their civil constitution, can you still retain the tyrannic port, the infernal impudence to avow your disposition to have them hanged, drawn and quartered for effecting it? If such an effort as this be not sufficient to put your character out of all dispute, the Resitator must be incapable of conviction by any evidence whatsoever. But few, I am persuaded will now pretend to deny, that in the persons of Thomas Hutchinson, Andrew Oliver, Charles Paxton, Benjamin Hallowell, Richard Clark, and the remaining small fry of Tea-Sellers, are contained the most obstinate, obdurate and determined enemies to the Rights and Liberties of this country, that ever existed above ground: And how such persons ought in future to dispose of themselves, should, in my humble opinion, be with them a very serious question. Were I in the predicament of either of them, it would be so with   E. LUDLOW.

P.S. Men who can sell Teas, subject to unconstitutional tribute, in peace, hatchets, scalping knives, &c. in time of war, and solicit troops to cut the throats of their fellow citizens, are dangerous inmates!

AN ANONYMOUS WRITER: "FOR THE FRIENDS OF AMERICAN LIBERTY"

The Boston Tea Party, at least from the point of view of those in beleaguered Boston, was an act committed for all Americans. In this short statement, the Massachusetts Spy *affirms that fact.*

Massachusetts Spy Or, Thomas's Boston Journal, 30 December
1773

The News of the destruction of the Tea, as it was the ONLY way left to prevent the chains prepared for us, from being riveted, we are well informed, gave satisfaction to all the Friends of American Liberty, who heard of it.

AN ANONYMOUS WRITER: "WE MAY NEED THE INDIANS AGAIN"

The repercussions of the Boston Tea Party lingered long after the dumping of the tea. Britain imposed more sanctions on the city, and more tea arrived from England. In this letter, the writer warns that the sachems, or Indian leaders, may have to round up their warriors again because taxed tea has returned to the harbor.

Boston Gazette, and Country Journal, 7 March 1774

Messi'rs Edes & Gill, PUBLISH THIS!

IT is said that Capt. Gorham who is just arrived from London, has brought Forty Chests of that *baneful, detested, dutied Article* TEA, shipped by the East-India Company, their Brokers of Employers, and consigned to HENRY LLOYD, Esq; of this Town, Merchant. Justice to ourselves and to AMERICA—Justice even to the *other* Consignees—A Regard to our own Reputation and Honor—Every Obligation binds us most SOLEMNLY, at once to DETERMINE ABSOLUTELY to oppose its Landing—Experience has fully convinced us that the Governor and the Custom-House Officers concern'd *will* lay INSUPERABLE Bars in the Way of sending it back to London. The Consent of the Consignee to have it return'd would be to no Purpose, if he be waited upon to request it. The SACHEMS must have a *Talk* upon this Matter—Upon THEM we depend to extricate us out of this *fresh* Difficulty; and to their Decisions all the GOOD People will say, AMEN!

TORY VIEWS

POPLICOLA: "THE TEA DUTY IS OUR DUTY"

The anonymous Poplicola supported the belief that America could be taxed by England because the colonies were part of the empire, owned and protected by British law and military. Poplicola also believed that America had a responsibility to help the struggling East India Company, which held the rights to tea sales in the colonies.

Rivington's New-York Gazetteer; or Connecticut, New-Jersey,
Hudson's River, and Quebec Weekly Advertiser, 18 November
1773

To Mr. James Rivington.

SIR,

Since you have inserted several pieces relative to the intentions of the
East-India Company . . . I presume you will not refuse to print in your
next Gazetteer. I have enclosed a bill of Three Pounds to pay for insert-
ing it; if that should not be sufficient let me know by the bearer how
much more is required,

   I am, Sir,

     Your humble Servant,

      POPLICOLA.

TO THE worthy Inhabitants of the City of NEW-YORK. 'Tis to the exertion of the common wisdom and power in the pursuit of a common
good, that he owes the security of his life, liberty and property; and he
will of course feel himself under an obligation of contributing his share
to the promotion of public happiness. . . . For when men unite in civil
society, a common interest of the whole is formed, and each member
obliges himself to act jointly with the rest for this common interest. The
doctrine holds with equal pertinency, when applied to the larger or more
complex members of the body politic, as when applied to individuals.
The good of the whole society must then also be the leading object, and
an attention to this greater good, is the criterion by which the patriot is
distinguished. With what countenance, then, fellow citizens, can they assume the character of patriots, who endeavour to separate (what in nature can never be disjoined) the good of particular branches of the
community from the good of the community itself? . . . You love your
country, and this affection is your duty, your honour; but remember that
not this, or any other province, is your country, but the *whole British*
empire. Its strength and superiority over its rival neighbours, are the
strength and glory of every part of its dominions, and its injuries, the
injuries of us all. On this ground let us test the pretensions of some men
to patriotism. . . .

No human institution whatsoever is totally free from imperfection and
abuse; but none but weak or fraudulent minds would conclude from
accidental perversions, that the general and natural tendency of any constitution was prejudiced. One useful consequence, however, you can
draw from the virulent attack on the East-India company, that those violent partizans are enraged, not through any jealously, as they pretend,
for your liberties, but through an enmity to the company itself, which in
their addresses they have held up in the most odious colours, and loaded
with the most illiberal and cruel invectives.

But notwithstanding the insidious arts which have been used to bias your minds, I am convinced, that no honest man, who is fully acquainted with the infinite importance of the Company to the commercial interests of his country, and who is also sensible of his duty, as a member of society, to study its welfare, can be at a loss what course he ought to pursue.

The British Company is at this time in extreme distress, tottering on the verge of ruin. Its fall would be fatal to our trading interest. In this season of danger, the Legislature, among other methods of assistance, has granted the liberty of exporting some of that immense quantity of teas which they have on hand, free from all duties, to their fellow subjects in America. At the same time, a few of your merchants have their stores crouded [*sic*] with teas from the Dutch Company, the sale of which would be injur'd by the sale of the English, which is better in quality, and can be afforded at a much cheaper rate. In this dilemma, can it be a matter of doubt to a *lover of his country*, to an *honest man*, whether he should encourage the *illicit trader*, who crams his coffers with wealth, at the expence of the consciences of numbers of deluded dependents, and to the support and exaltation of a foreign Company, which is a rival to that of his own country: or by purchasing from the *fair trader*, to assist in this extremity an institution on which the commercial interest of the state so greatly depends? Is it the office of a patriot to encourage an unlawful traffic, to the prejudice of the common wealth, from which a few individuals (for to the honour of our country and virtue, only a few have thus sacrificed their consciences to this pockets) will accumulate wealth, by extorting what price they please from the public for their illicit commodities; or to support the commercial interest in general of the State of which he is a member, by encouraging a trading company, whose welfare is so necessary to keep herein a balance with their neighbours? . . .

But every measure of the cabal, fellow citizens! is an undoubted proof, that not your liberties, but their private interest is the object. To create an odium against the British company is the main point at which they have laboured. . . . To liberty they can pretend no friendship. Every step they have hitherto taken has been introductive of the most fatal tyranny; a tyranny of so high a nature as not to permit a fellow citizen even to think differently from them without danger.

It is the part of every man who values the blessings of social life, to be jealous of his civil liberties; and, in order to their preservation to be watchful that no members of the community usurp a tyrannical power of trangressing the laws. No man can be in a more abject state of bondage, than he whose Reputation, Property and Life, are not under the security of law; but exposed to the discretionary violence of any part of the community. . . .

Ought not therefore every good citizen, who values his liberty, to oppose the arbitrary incroachments of some men among us, who have assumed the legislative power of the colony, arrogated, the privilege of decreeing what is right or wrong, and assumed the *judicial* and *executive* power of determining on the actions of any of the community, and punishing these whom they may deem offenders? . . . Are we to know our rights by the laws, are *they* to be the rule of our actions; or must we regulate our conduct by, and have our civil liberties dependent on, the fluctuating and capricious decisions of a giddy cabal? Even in the purest and simplest *democracy* nothing is obligatory except by consent of the majority constitutionally given. But among US the crude decrees of a small cabal, who are actuated by self interest, are to be binding on the whole community; and whoever ventures to contradict them, or even express a doubt of their validity and propriety, must be exposed to violence, and, unheard, without a tryal, must be condemned to infamy and disgrace.

Every friend to *liberty* must be alarmed at such procedures; and even the promoters of such measures should tremble, lest they kindle a civil conflagration, which, becoming ungovernable, may end in the destruction of their own property. Your own house is in danger when your neighbour's is in flames. On points that concern us all, every man in the province has a right of judging, and whatever body of men, without being chosen representatives of the rest, presume, to determine and act for them, effectually *deprive* us of our liberties. While we are watchful against *external* attacks on our freedom, let us be on our guard, lest we become *enslaved* by *dangerous* tyrants within.   POPLICOLA.

EVERY good citizen will be inclined from duty as well as interest, to love his country, and to be zealous in advancing its welfare.

AN ANONYMOUS WRITER: "A PROTEST AGAINST THE ACTS IN BOSTON"

Patriots initiated meetings to oppose the tea tax and the tea arriving from England early in December 1773. In this letter, the writer protests the assumption that those who decided to dump tea in the harbor acted on behalf of all Bostonians. The writer never mentions the actual tea party but does talk about those who operate under the "masque of patriotism."

Massachusetts Gazette, and Boston Weekly News-Letter, 23 December 1773

THAT IT is not only our right but our duty frankly and freely to express our sentiments on every matter which essentially concerns the safety and welfare of our country, is a trust which we apprehend cannot be denied.

Therefore, We who are inhabitants of the town of Plymouth neither captivated by sounds and declamations, nor deceived by the cunning stratagems of men who under the specious masque of patriotism have attempted to delude an innocent and loyal people; But firmly and steadily fix'd and determined to defend our rights and privileges, and to endeavour to hand to our posterity the blessings of peace and good government which were procured by our fathers and transmitted to Us,—Having taken into serious consideration the dangerous and fatal consequences which may arise from the late resolves pass'd at a meeting of this town on the seventh day of this instant December; Fearing that they may bring upon us the vengeance of affronted Majesty and his insulted authority, We cannot answer it to our God and our consciences unless we protest against the proceedings of said meetings, and publish to the world that we were not instrumental in procuring those mischiefs which may naturally be expected from such conduct.—And we do by these presents solemnly protest against the whole of said resolves as being repugnant to our ideas of Liberty, law and reason. With the first of said resolves we will not concern ourselves further than to observe that we cannot see the necessity of this town's adopting similar measures with the citizens of Philadelphia. . . .

We say that we think it an affront to the common sense of mankind and to the dignity of the laws, to assert that such a meeting as was held in the town of *Boston* on the first of this instant December, was either lawful or regular: And further that the said meeting and the conduct and determination therein do not appear to us to be either necessary or laudable, or in any degree meriting the Gratitude of those who wish Well to America: But in our opinion those who by constitutional and lawful means have endeavoured to hinder their proceedings and to prevent the bad effects thereof, have in this instance shewn themselves to be firm friends to the freedom and *true* interests of this Country. . . .

[W]e must observe,

That we do not think ourselves bound either in duty or gratitude to acknowledge any obligations to the body who composed that meeting, nor to aid and support them in carrying their votes and resolves into execution, nor do we intend to hazard our lives and fortunes in their defence: But on the contrary We suppose it our indispensable duty (as the faithful and loyal subjects of his most gracious Majesty King GEORGE the third) to manifest our abhorrence and detestation of every measure which has a tendency to introduce anarchy, confusion, and disorder into the state, whether the same be proposed by Bodies of Men or by an individual.

AN ANONYMOUS WRITER: "DESTROYING PROPERTY"

Printed in the Massachusetts Gazette *eleven months after the Boston Tea Party, this letter from a writer in London looks at the dumping of the tea as a property violation. The issue is not whether laws are invalid or harsh but that personal rights were violated with the destruction of the tea.*

Massachusetts Gazette, and Boston News-Letter, 17 November 1774

Whenever a factious set of People rise to such a Pitch of Insolence, as to prevent the Execution of the Laws, or destroy the Property of Individuals, just as their Caprice or Humour leads them; there is an end of all Order and Government, Riot, and Confusion must be the natural Consequence of such Measures. It is impossible for Trade to flourish where Property is insecure.

AN ANONYMOUS WRITER: "PAY FOR THE DAMAGES"

England responded to the Boston Tea Party with a series of harsh laws called the Intolerable Acts by Patriots. In this letter, the anonymous writer suggests that perhaps Boston could avoid having its port closed if the city paid for the destroyed tea.

New-York Gazette; and the Weekly Mercury, 16 May 1774

A British American, who is a Lover of Peace, as well as a Hater of every Species of Tyranny, whether Monarchial or Parliamentary, proposes to the Consideration of the Publick of Boston, whether it would not be their wisest Course in the present critical Situation of Affairs, to raise immediately, by Subscription, a Sum equal to the estimated Value of the drowned Teas, and deposit it in some publick Office, ready to be tendered to his Excellency General Gage, immediately on his first Requisition for Restitution of the India Company's Loss, with a solemn Declaration . . . that they make the Reimbursement with sincere Pleasure, as they thereby have at once an Opportunity of testifying their Readiness to repair every private Loss that Individuals may sustain in the present unhappy Struggle for the Maintenance of their just Rights. . . .

The Querist presumes that by adopting some such Mode of Management as this, "Good may be brought out of Evil," and that hasty Act of Violence which moderate Men now look on with high Disapprobation, be thereby rendered a Circumstance honourable to the Bostonians in particular, and advantageous to the Colonies in general, who doubtless would chearfully bear their Proportions in the Sum to be raised.

QUESTIONS

1. According to the readings, what bothered colonists more, the tea monopoly of the East India Company or the tax on tea? Explain.

2. Why might the *Massachusetts Spy* mention smallpox as a way of justifying refusal to bring the tea on land?

3. How were those who destroyed the tea portrayed as noble and honest individuals in the *Boston Gazette* and *Massachusetts Spy*?

4. What were Poplicola's reasons for supporting the Tea Act? Are they logical and valid? Explain.

5. What can you tell about the unanimity of Massachusetts colonists from these articles?

6. Why does the writer in the *New-York Gazette* believe Boston should make restitution to the East India Company? Do you think the destruction of private property could be justified? Explain.

NOTES

1. Figure based on East India Company records. Cited in Bernard Knollenberg, *Growth of the American Revolution, 1766–1775* (New York: Free Press, 1975), 100.

2. Benjamin W. Labaree, *The Boston Tea Party* (New York: Oxford University Press, 1964), 33.

3. *Boston Gazette, and Country Journal*, 25 October 1773, 2.

CHAPTER 25

The Continental Congress, 1774–1775

In the early months of 1774, the tensions between England and the colonies increased. Following the dumping of tea into the harbor in December 1773, Boston, especially, suffered through a series of British decrees that Americans referred to as the Intolerable or Coercive Acts (see Chapter 24). Throughout the colonies, individuals began to suggest that all the colonies should select representatives to attend an intercolonial congress to discuss ways to voice grievances for British actions toward America. Some of those who suggested a congress also intimated that perhaps Americans should find a way to hurt the British pocketbook through trade embargoes so that British merchants could feel the same economic sting just as those in Boston.

Finally, on May 17, 1774, the town of Providence, Rhode Island, issued a decree that the town and colony should push for a general meeting of all the colonies. The town leaders, the resolution stated, were "*to use their Influence, at the approaching session of the General Assembly of this Colony, for promoting a CONGRESS, as soon as may be, of the Representatives of the General Assemblies of the several Colonies and Provinces of North-America.*"[1] Within a week, Pennsylvania and Virginia passed similar measures, and within a month nearly every colony had done so. While John Adams was moderating a meeting in Boston on June 17, the town voted to use the Committees of Correspondence in America to set up a Continental Congress.[2]

All the American colonies except Georgia voted to send delegates to the Congress. Philadelphia was selected as the site for the meeting, which was set to begin early in September. Eventually, fifty-six delegates attended the First Continental Congress, which lasted from September 5 to October 26 and met in Carpenter's Hall in the Pennsylvania capital. The Congress worked diligently to establish a framework in which it could operate. The representatives elected Peyton Randolph of Virginia as president, set up committees, and decided on voting methods.

The Congress, like America, was divided among those who favored reconciliation with Britain and those who favored separation. James Galloway of Pennsylvania led the conservatives who sought to mend any tears in the American-British relationship. Galloway, especially, opposed a nonimportation agreement, which proposed the cessation of trade with England and the West Indies (see Chapter 20). His plan, however, was defeated, and the delegates voted to begin the trade boycott on December 1.[3] This nonimportation was to be enforced by another creation of the Congress, the Association, which was established to ensure that each municipality took part in the boycott.

Before adjourning, the Congress agreed that a second meeting should take place in May 1775 unless England repealed the Intolerable Acts. Before the delegates could return for the meeting, however, shots were fired at Lexington and Concord. British troops had marched out of Boston toward Concord where colonials stored military supplies. Patriots met the regulars at the bridge in Lexington. Exactly who fired first is unknown, but before April 19 ended, America was in rebellion against the mother country (see Chapter 29). When the representatives returned to Philadelphia, talk centered around fighting, war preparations, and the appointment of a commander in chief, George Washington of Virginia. The delegates, led by John Dickinson, the writer of the Letters from a Pennsylvania Farmer (see Chapter 28), made one more attempt at reconciliation with England. For most present, though, there was little doubt that the colonies would never remain under the dominion of Great Britain. On June 7, Richard Henry Lee of Virginia proposed that the colonies ought to be free. After a three-week recess, the delegates agreed. Delegates selected Thomas Jefferson and several others to produce a document. This document, the Declaration of Independence, was presented and unanimously approved on July 4, and the fighting between colonials and British regulars became a war for independence (see Chapter 31).

The first two selections supporting a continental congress appeared in the *Boston Gazette* in 1773. Boston was essentially in a state of occupation and siege by England. The port was closed, and British troops were stationed in the city for control. The first entry was written by Samuel Adams as part of "Observations," views of what was happening in the colonies which were shared with other Americans through newspapers. In his observations, Adams called for a Bill of Rights for America. In the second letter, signed by the anonymous Union, the writer calls for a congress of colonies because the freedom of America is at stake. The writer argues that Americans must act to obtain their God-given rights, which he explains were once the property of Americans but are no longer.

The next selection is simply an insertion by printer John Holt into the *New-York Journal* of the fact that colonies throughout America are calling for a congress of all the colonies. A version of this news account also appeared in Boston. It is followed by an anonymous letter to *New-Hampshire Gazette* printer Daniel Fowle supporting the decision of the colonies to hold a general congress. Another anonymous letter, with the Sydney pseudonym, follows. It insinuates that a continental congress is what America must convene to protect the rights of Americans. The next two selections, one from New York but written by B. N. of New Jersey and the other from Boston but reprinted from the *Pennsylvania Gazette*, explain why a general congress is necessary. The first explains what the congress can do for the colonies; the second describes what England has done to America to justify the meeting. All of these news items demonstrate how the calls for a continental congress increased during the summer of 1774.

The readings opposing the formation of the Continental Congress begin with an anonymous letter to all Americans written during the summer of 1774. The letter declares that a convention of delegates would be the worst possible action the colonies could take to end their disputes with England. The letter obviously worried printer James Rivington who appended a note to the letter stating his intention to insert any reply to this letter in his newspaper. In the next letter, an anonymous writer using the name Phileleutherus Caesariensis argues that an assembly comprising representatives from all the colonies is impracticable. His comments were included in a letter attacking America's claims that it needed representatives in Parliament. The letter also discusses the fact that the New York representatives to the Congress could not approve that revenue from the colony for use by the Congress. In fact, New York's representatives had little power in the Continental Congress. When the Declaration of Independence was passed, for example, the New York delegation did not have the power to approve it. Instead, they took it back to the New York Assembly, which ratified the Declaration on July 9.

The next entry is a letter written by an anonymous author to the people of New Jersey. It describes the actions of the recently concluded First Continental Congress. It states that all the Congress has done is exacerbate the situation between the colonies and England. The letter from New Jersey is followed by a letter to the citizens of New York, which warns against appointing delegates to another congress. The first congress having adjourned, its delegates recommended that a second be held in Philadelphia beginning on May 10, 1775. Each colony was to elect new representatives. In this letter from the anonymous A Citizen of New

York, the writer suggests that the representatives to the first congress moved the colonies to verge of anarchy and war with England. He also suggests the congress and newly created provincial congresses violate the powers given to colonial assemblies and are destroying America's legal system.

IN SUPPORT OF A CONTINENTAL CONGRESS

SAMUEL ADAMS: "OBSERVATIONS"

Samuel Adams was as close as America came to having a professional agitator in the colonial era. The former brewer and Harvard graduate worked closely with the printers of the Boston Gazette, *Benjamin Edes and John Gill. Adams seemed to have a hand in every act of resistance and rebellion against England from the Stamp Act forward. In this essay, part of a feature called "Observations" written by him, Adams issues a call for a colonial congress well before the idea became popular in America.*

Boston Gazette, and Country Journal, 27 September 1773

This very important dispute between Britain and America has, for a long time, employed the pens of statesmen in both countries, but no plan of union is yet agreed on between them; the dispute still continues and everything floats in uncertainty. As I have long contemplated the subject with fixed attention, I beg leave to offer a proposal to my countrymen, namely, that a CONGRESS OF AMERICAN STATES shall be assembled as soon as possible, draw up a Bill of Rights, and publish it to the world; choose an ambassador to reside at the British Court to act for the United colonists; appoint where the congress shall annually meet, and how it may be summoned upon any extraordinary occasion, what further steps are necessary to be taken, &c.

UNION: "HOW SHALL FREEDOM BE PRESERVED?"

The anonymous Union remembers everything that America had once had—free trade, tax-free commodities, and so on. Now, he sees colonies where all these have been lost to British tyranny. The only way to regain these things, he said, was to establish a congress of the colonies.

Boston Gazette, and Country Journal, 27 December 1773

Messieurs EDES & GILL, . . .

THE mind of an intelligent and inquisitive creature naturally runs from causes to their effects, and from action to its consequences. . . . Freedom

was given by God as an important requisite to the happiness of man, and
the preservation of it is the indispensable duty of every rational being. As
this proposition has never been controverted or denied with success, I
shall take it for granted, and the supreme question in America is, How
shall it be preserved? . . . Must we not act prudently? . . . This province
has lost much, they have therefore much to regain; we had a first charter,
we have not; we had free trade, we have not; we had all our commodities
from England without duty; we have not; we had streets free from slaves
and pensioners, we have not; we had judges free from an undue influence, have we now? We had an independent governor, we have not; we
had affection for the mother country, we have not; we had a castle, we
have not; enough! For if ever human patience was tortured to resentment, the patience of this country is. We have already suffered with too
much pusillanimity, we can redress ourselves if we will; and what the
people wills shall be effected.

> *Let senseless slaves embrace the tyrant's rod,*
> *A state of* FREEDOM *is the reign of* GOD.

There is no time to be lost, a Congress or meeting of the American
states is indispensable. Let the Gordian knot be tied, and whatsoever the
people do shall prosper. . . . If we have not a free fair equitable government, we will have; and what the people wills shall be effected. . . .

The politician and general act from the simple principles, though in
different departments; and neither has much to fear from action, when
there is a probability of defeating the designs of their enemy. And when
the consequence resulting from a failure, cannot be worse than what
would have happened in the course of the enemy's operations without
the attempt.
UNION.

JOHN HOLT: "ALL WANT A CONGRESS"

*Printers shared their newspapers with each other. In the summer of
1774, New York printer John Holt told his readers what he had discovered from looking at papers from throughout America: All Americans
wanted a general congress of the colonies. A Patriot printer, Holt said
that Americans wanted to cease trade and relations with England,
something that the Continental Congress moved toward with its nonimportation agreement.*

New-York Journal; Or, the General Advertiser, 30 June 1774

The News Papers from all Quarters, in every British American Colony,
so far as we have yet received Intelligence, are chiefly filled with Accounts
of Meetings and Resolutions of Towns and Counties, all to the same

Purpose—complaining of Oppression, proposing a general Congress, and Cessation of Intercourse with Great-Britain, and a Contribution for Relief of the Poor of Boston, so that it now evidently appears, that all the Colonies are unanimous in Sentiment and will be so in Conduct.

These Accounts of Facts are so lengthy, that we have not had Room to insert the Reflections upon them—which must be the Subject of future Papers.

AN ANONYMOUS WRITER: "A CONGRESS WILL REVIVE DROOPING SPIRITS"

When news reached Americans that a congress of the colonies was planned for September 1774, most rejoiced. In this anonymous letter from New Hampshire, the writer suggests that such an action by America would revive spirits in the colonies, which had been dampened by England's taxes and other oppressive laws.

New-Hampshire Gazette, and Historical Chronicle (Portsmouth), 22 July 1774

Mr. Fowle,

IT must revive the drooping Spirits of every desponding AMERICAN, to see all the Provinces *uniting* to withstand Oppression: And as a GENERAL CONGRESS of DELEGATES is proposed, and will shortly meet, whatever is by them concluded upon, for the Benefit of the whole, let every Man, who values Life, Liberty and Property, sacredly abide by their Determination. And whoever shall dare to act counter, let them be stigmatized by the Sons of true Americans, and their Names handed down with Infamy to the latest Posterity; and may every Female detest a Connection with them.

SYDNEY: "ENGLAND HAS SCHEMED TO TAKE AWAY OUR LIBERTIES"

By 1774 George III was a tyrant, and Britain was a bully ready to snatch away all American freedoms. When the anonymous Sydney wrote, he called on the Reverend George Whitefield, who had died in 1770 (see Chapter 8). Whitefield was still revered in America, and when the writer quoted the minister concerning a British plot to take away the rights of Americans, he was using as powerful an ally as could be imagined in America.

Massachusetts Spy Or, Thomas's Boston Journal, 4 August 1774

To the AMERICANS.

TRUTH and liberty are not afraid of tyrants, therefore I shall speak freely. No one has now any reason to doubt the truth of what the excelled Mr. *Whitefield* told a gentleman in this country ten years since, "that a scheme was laid in Britain as deep as hell, to deprive the people of New-England of all their rights, civil and sacred"—this infernal plot now appears in full view; and the wisdoms of America is in exercise to defeat it. The CONGRESS is the grand leading step, they will be the front rank of America's sons, therefore they must be supported and the measures which they may adopt, carried into execution with the utmost vigor. . . .

It is understood by the good people of this country, that no man of *any virtue*, will contenance the execution of acts of parliament to destroy the free constitution of any colony.—Should any be guilty of *treason against their country*, by assisting to destroy your constitutional freedom, no doubt they will be *noticed*, and in some future time *rewarded* according to their deeds, for *such crimes cannot*, they *ought not* to be pardoned.—"Steady, Americans, steady," be firm, persevering: "*To be, or not to be*," now "is the question."—Do not *too soon* resent an insult, but *never* pardon an *enemy* to American Liberty.   SYDNEY.

AN ANONYMOUS WRITER: "WHAT A GENERAL CONGRESS CAN DO FOR AMERICA"

Many Americans wanted independence from England; few wanted to obtain it through war. They believed that a general congress with delegates from all the colonies was the best way to obtain the first and avoid the second, as this writer suggests.

New-York Journal; Or, the General Advertiser, 4 August 1774

Mr. PRINTER. . . .

IT seems now to be a matter past doubt, that there will be a general congress of delegates from the several British colonies in America. A very important assembly it will be. The weal of America, yea and of Britain too, will very much depend upon their proceedings. Never in this country, has more depended upon an assembly of men, than depends upon this. Liberty or oppression, if not abject slavery, depends upon the turn that things shall now take. . . .

The delegates should go to the congress with hearts deeply affected with the weight and vast importance of their business: With a proper concern, if not anxiety of mind, considering how much is depending, and how difficult it may be to determine matters in the best manner. . . .

The delegates from the province ought to be the most hearty friends to America, men that will give up their own private interest for the public good, when these two come in competition. He that will not do this is no real friend to the public. This important assembly will be in danger from false or pretended friends. There are a few in almost every province, who, from one reason or other, would be glad to bring America to submit to the ministerial unconstitutional measures which we are now threatened with. . . .

Considering the vast importance of this congress, the long train of most interesting consequence that may follow from their advice or determinations; considering the need they have of wisdom, as well as integrity, it might be proper for the several provinces to observe a day of fasting and prayer about the time that the delegates meet; and if the provinces as such do not, yet it may be proper for as many persons, or societies, as can, to do it.

AN ANONYMOUS WRITER: "WE NEED HARMONY WITH ENGLAND"

Just as the writer above believed that a congress was the way to achieve harmony with England, so, too, did this anonymous writer to the Massachusetts Spy. *This writer believed the constitutional foundation upon which England and her colonies were based was the salve to heal the wounds between colony and mother country.*

Massachusetts Spy Or, Thomas's Boston Journal, 11 August 1774

THE dissentions between Great-Britain and her colonies on this continent, commencing about ten years ago, since continually increasing, and at length grown to such an excess, as to involve the latter in deep distress and danger, have excited the good people of this province to take into their serious consideration the present situation of public affairs. . . .

To us therefore it appears, at this alarming period, our duty to God, to our country, to ourselves, and to our posterity, to exert our utmost ability in promoting and establishing harmony between *Great-Britain* and these colonies, on A CONSTITUTIONAL FOUNDATION.

For attaining this great and desirable end, we request you to appoint a proper number of persons to attend a Congress of deputies from the several colonies, appointed, or to be appointed, by the Representatives of the people of the colonies respectively in Assembly, or convention, or by delegates chosen by the counties generally in the respective colonies, and met in the provincial committee, at such time and place as shall be generally agreed on: And that the deputies from this province may be induced and encouraged to concur in such measures, as may be devised for the common welfare, we think it proper particularly to inform you, how far, we apprehend, they will be supported in their conduct by their constituents.

The assumed parliamentary power of internal legislation, and the power of regulating trade, as of late exercised and designed to be exercised, we are thoroughly convinced, will prove unfailing and plentiful sources of dissentions to our mother country and these colonies, unless some expedients can be adopted to render her secure of receiving from us every emolument that can in justice and reason be expected, and us secure in our lives, liberties, properties, and an equitable share of commerce. . . .

We therefore desire of you . . . that the deputies, you appoint, may be instructed by you strenuously to exert themselves, at the ensuing Congress, to obtain a renunciation, on the part of Great-Britain, of all powers . . . imposing taxes or duties internal or external—and of regulating trade, except with respect to any new articles of commerce . . . a repeal of all statutes for quartering troops in the colonies, or subjecting them to any expence on account of such troops—of all statutes imposing duties to be paid in the colonies, that were passed at the accession of his present Majesty, or before this time. . . .

If all the terms above-mentioned cannot be obtained, it is our opinion, that the measures adopted by the congress for our relief should never be relinquished or intermitted, until those relating to the troops,—internal legislation,—imposition of taxes or duties hereafter . . . be obtained. . . .

In order to obtain redress of our common grievances, we observe a general inclination among the colonies of entering into agreements of non-importation and non-exportation. . . .

Upon the whole, we shall repose the highest confidence in the wisdom and integrity of the ensuing Congress. . . . We should be glad the deputies chose by you could, by their influence, procure our opinions hereby communicated to you to be as nearly adhered to, as may be possible: But to avoid difficulties, we desire that they may be instructed by you, to agree to any measures that shall be approved by the Congress; the inhabitants of this province having resolved to adopt and carry them into execution.

IN OPPOSITION TO A CONTINENTAL CONGRESS

AN ANONYMOUS WRITER: "A GENERAL CONVENTION IS NOT THE ANSWER"

Most Tories could not conceive of an America not aligned with England, and they assumed that a "permanent union," as this writer referred to it, was the colonies' natural relationship with the mother country. Such a union could never take place if a congress met to discuss other things, such as economic boycotts. In this letter, the writer pleads for colonial assemblies not to send representatives to a general congress, but instead to have each legislature petition the king for representatives to Parliament.

Rivington's New-York Gazetteer; or the Connecticut, New-Jersey, Hudson's River and Quebec Weekly Advertiser, *7 July 1774.*

To the INHABITANTS *of the* BRITISH COLONIES *in* AMERICA.

NEVER did AMERICA behold so alarming a time as the *present.* The *parent state* is big with resentment against us for our late proceedings; and seems determined, at all events, either to make us obedient to the laws of the *British Parliament,* or to cast us off. . . . How shall the dispute between us be adjusted? How shall a FIRM FOUNDATION be laid for a *future* PERMANENT UNION? Surely not by opposing a *military force,* which, in the event, must infallibly overpower us;—and *then* we shall have no *claim of right,*—as being a *conquered country.* Surely not by making resolves in *town,* and *country,* and *parish* meetings;—for they can do nothing. . . . Surely not by a GENERAL CONVENTION; for *that* is a measure which *never* should be adopted, unless we have *resolved* on the *last extremes.* Whatever may be the proceedings of such a body, it is too much to be apprehended that they will have no salutary influence on the British policy; because the *convention itself* will be deemed unconstitutional; and having no existence in *law,* it may also be judged to be *illegal.* . . .

Let every COLONY *instruct its* REPRESENTATIVES *in* GENERAL ASSEMBLY, *to present an* humble address *to the* KING, *requesting the liberty of sending a certain number of their body to England, at a fixed time, for the* express purpose *of settling, with the national Council, a* CONSTITUTION FOR AMERICA; *which hitherto we have not enjoyed, but in idea; and let that settlement be* FINAL.

PHILELEUTHERUS CAESARIENSIS: "COLONIAL PLANS ARE IMPRACTICAL"

The anonymous Phileleutherus Caesariensis wrote on occasion to the New-York Gazette *about the state of America. In this letter, he says that Patriot leaders do not want direct parliamentary representation because that would mean that Parliament would have the right to tax America. As long as virtual representation was in effect (see Chapter 17), taxes could be fought, protested, and resisted.*

New-York Gazette, and the Weekly Mercury, *3 October 1774*

PHILELEUTHERUS CAESARIENSIS.

The colony advocates tell us, that by refusing to accept our offer of representatives, they only mean to avoid giving parliament a pretence for *taxing* them. . . .

I have thus far followed the colonies in their own paths; and, instead of exposing the absurdity of their idea of a *polypus* government, where a head sprouts out of every joint, I have endeavoured to make the best of it, and even in that view shewn it to be monstrous and impracticable. Little less so indeed than it would be in England, where are but fifty-two *counties*, should the crown make requisitions to each of their *grand juries*, who have authority to assess money for *local purposes*, upon the respective inhabitants, as well as the colony assemblies, instead of applying to parliament, to provide for the exigencies of the state? And what sort of public revenue or credit we should then have, is easy to be imagined.

Indeed to do justice to the candour of the New-York Assembly, they give strong intimation of its being their opinion, that the raising of a revenue for *general* purposes, by grants from the several colony assemblies, is impracticable; and that either it must be done by parliament, or cannot be done at all.

AN ANONYMOUS WRITER: "THE DAMAGE DONE BY THE CONTINENTAL CONGRESS"

The actions of the Continental Congress were decidedly pro-Patriot. In this letter, the writer points out that the Congress did not represent all Americans and actually exacerbated the situation between England and America.

Rivington's New-York Gazetteer; or the Connecticut, New-Jersey, Hudson's River and Quebec Weekly Advertiser, 1 December 1774

TO THE PEOPLE OF NEW-JERSEY.

My Friends and Countrymen,

I Had once some hope that the resolutions of the Congress, would have been such as to produce some good to the colonies, but I find my fears verified by their proceedings: chosen, on one side, they seem to have had no other view, than to please their electors, and to forward confusion among us. They have formed no system by which the present differences might be solved, and future contention avoided, but deliberately have made bad worse, left us in retreat, nor the mother country any opening to advance to reconciliation.

With sovereign contempt, they have overlooked the legislature of Great Britain, and appealed to the people; will not this people take offence at the indignity so manifestly shewn to their legislature, and receive the appeal with disgust? especially when they see that we have forbid all intercourse with them, and that with as much seeming authority as if we were an independant state, and determining on rupture with them? Nay, will not this conduct be construed as open enmity to the British name?

. . . Thus by raising new contentions, and drawing us into new controversies, what end can this serve but to create confusion? From confusion, my Countrymen, is to be reared the new republic. . . . I suspect that felling their influence, and elated with power, new and unconstitutional, they apprehended the application would be successful, and their authority at an end; they therefore have made their appeal to the people, hoping to strike up rebellion and strife again; they have tickled you by encreasing the number of your committees, that you may appear to have a great share in this new government, and at the same time that they hold out to you an abhorrence of the laws of trade, and take upon themselves to give power to Heaven knows who.

A CITIZEN OF NEW-YORK: "WE DO NOT NEED ANOTHER CONTINENTAL CONGRESS"

As the First Continental Congress closed, its delegates voted that a second should be held in late spring 1775. The writer of this letter, however, strongly opposed yet another meeting. He points out that only the New York Assembly and Parliament had the power to make laws for the colony. Now, the Continental Congress was making laws that affected all America, something he felt was illegal.

New-York Gazette, and the Weekly Mercury, 6 March 1775

To the RESPECTABLE INHABITANTS of the City of New-York.
   Friends and fellow Citizens,
   BY the general tenor of your conduct since the commencement of our unhappy disputes with Great-Britain, you have uniformly and fully evinced yourselves to be possessed of an inviolable attachment to the cause of constitutional liberty; as well as of unshaken loyalty to our gracious sovereign, and a just abhorrence of such irregular proceedings as indicated a spirit of disaffection or independency in any of the colonists. These virtues, always valuable in a high degree, are peculiarly so in times like the present—when a dangerous infatuation has seized so many—when discord and tyranny, in the guise of liberty, stalk forth among us; and under specious pretences, would entail misery, ruin, and the most abject slavery upon us. These virtues, which you have nobly exerted on several occasions, will soon be called to another trial.
   A summons has been issued . . . for the purpose of *chusing Delegates* to go to the next Continental Congress. Considering our late transactions here relative to this matter, I am sure you must be greatly surprised at such a step as this. Especially, when you are not called to deliberate on the *expediency or propriety* of appointing delegates for the above purpose; but *actually* to *chuse* them! and this in consequence of an edict from the late congress, whose views and proceedings you most cordially

disapprove! *willing*, or *unwilling*, you are required to comply with this mandate!

Our *only* legal, constitutional representatives, the members of our assembly, to whom we have voluntarily committed the guardianship of our liberties, and the direction of our public affairs, and who are vested with full authority for these important ends, have absolutely refused to appoint any delegates for the ensuing congress. Would not such an attempt in you therefore, be an open violation of their just authority, and a glaring insult on them?

Whatever reasons might have existed for sending delegates to the former congress, there are none such now; but many cogent reasons to the contrary. Our assembly have taken the subject of our grievances into consideration, and are vigourously pursuing the most effectual methods for obtaining their redress. The proceedings of the late congress were violent and treasonable. Instead of healing the unnatural breach between us and the parent state, which was the ardent wish of every honest, good man, they shut up every avenue to an accommodation. An adherence to their proceedings must have infallibly involved us in all the horrors of a civil war, and ended in our ruin. Fully sensible of this, and of the unjust tyrannical power usurped by that congress over North-America, our assembly, to their immortal honour be it spoken, had virtue and fortitude enough to reject those proceedings. . . .

Now reflect, my fellow citizens, will not your sending delegates to the next congress, directly tend to frustrate these laudable endeavours, of whose success we have a moral certainty? will it not place this province in the most absurd, inconsistent point of light, as bursting the bands of all government, both with respect to Great-Britain, and our own legislature? may I not aver with truth, that you hold the violent proceedings of the late congress in abhorrence? what can you expect from the next congress, but such measures as were adopted by the last, when you know the same delegates are generally appointed by the other colonies? few alterations have been made; and where any have taken place, they were for the worst—persons more violent, if possible, being chosen. . . .

But this proposed meeting on Monday is replete with further mischief; for you are to *assemble* not only for *chusing delegates*; but also *to signify your sense whether you will appoint a certain number of persons to meet such deputies as the counties may elect, for that purpose, and join with them in appointing out of their body, delegates for the next congress*. Here you may perceive the first outlines of a Provincial Congress— the first artful advance towards bringing on us one of the heaviest curses. If the abettors of republicanism can gain this advantage over the friends of our constitution, the consequences must be terrible. Our constitutional assembly will become a mere cypher, and all order subverted.

I beseech you, fellow citizens, to think for yourselves. Turn your eyes to those colonies where *provincial congresses* are chosen; see the effects produced by them, and judge from those facts. In South Carolina, the *provincial congress* has shut up all the courts of justice. No man dare attempt to recover a just debt, unless graciously permitted by the committee of the county. . . .

These are notorious, indubitable facts. They cannot be denied. Say then, fellow citizens, do you chuse to bring yourselves into a similar situation?

I am very sensible that no gentleman, or man of character among us, would, as matters are now circumstanced, accept of the appointment of delegate to the *Continental*, or of deputy to a *Provincial Congress*. But you very well know that there are several here who are under no restraints of delicacy, or regard to decorums and order on this head. . . .

That wisdom, loyalty, firm attachment to your excellent constitution, and zealous assiduity may guide you at this most important crisis, is the unfeigned wish of

A CITIZEN OF NEW-YORK.

QUESTIONS

1. Why did letter writers advocate a congress of colonies?

2. What role did God play in the cause of American freedom, according to the newspapers?

3. What does the fact that newspapers were filled with calls for a general congress say about the mood of Americans? Or, do the newspaper accounts represent propaganda? Explain.

4. According to the writers to the *New-York Journal* and the *Massachusetts Spy* in August, what would the congress do for the colonies?

5. Why did the writer who addressed "the Inhabitants of the British Colonies in America" oppose any act by the Continental Congress that might be seen as anything less than a move of reconciliation?

6. Why do you think the writer to the people of New Jersey worried about a new form of government?

7. Why did the writer to the *New-York Gazette* so oppose the Second Continental Congress?

NOTES

1. *Boston Gazette, and Country Journal*, 30 May 1774, 2.

2. Ibid., 20 June 1774, 2.

3. *Journals of the Continental Congress*, ed. Worthington C. Ford and G. Hunt (Washington, D.C., 1904–1937), I:43.

CHAPTER 26

The Edenton Tea Party and Perceptions of Women, 1774

By 1774 protest and confrontations against British rule in America had become commonplace. The Tea Act of May 1773 produced a series of reactions, especially among merchants who saw the act as a way of removing them from America's vital and profitable tea market. In December 1773, Boston citizens had dressed as Indians and dumped all the tea on the ship in Boston harbor into the water (see Chapter 24).

Support of the actions in Boston spread throughout the colonies. In the North Carolina port of Edenton, however, backing came from what might be considered an unlikely source. On October 25, fifty-one women—members of the Edenton Ladies' Patriotic Guild—gathered at the home of Penelope Barker and made this promise: "We, the Ladys of Edenton, do hereby solemnly engage not to conform to the Pernicious Custom of Drinking Tea. . . . We Ladys will not promote ye wear of any manufacturer from England until such time that all acts which tend to enslave our Native country shall be repealed."[1] Their actions produced responses, including a belittling editorial woodcut that appeared in British papers and this sarcastic comment from an Englishman to his brother in the town: "I see by the Newspaper that the Edenton Ladies have signalized themselves by their Protest against Tea-drinking," Arthur Iredell wrote to his brother James. "Is there a Female Congress in Edenton too? I hope not, for we Englishmen are afraid of Male Congress, but . . . the Ladies . . . have ever, since the Amazonian Era, been esteemed the most formidable Enemies; . . . the only Security on our Side to prevent the im-

No More Tea. When they met in October 1774, women of the North Carolina port town of Edenton vowed not to drink British tea. The Edenton Tea Party was one of the first organized political acts by American women and caught the attention of a British cartoonist who produced this woodcut for a London newspaper. In the cartoon, the woman with the gavel bears a likeness to King George. The cartoonist shows his disdain for the women's action by having a dog urinate on one of the women.

pending Ruin, that I can perceive, is the probability that there are few Places in America which possess so much Female Artillery as Edenton."[2]

The Edenton Tea Party was one of the first organized political acts undertaken by women in America, but as Arthur Iredell's letter suggested, women were increasingly becoming involved in the politics of the 1770s; at least 300 in the Boston area had promised to give up imported tea in 1770.[3] Some groups of women had been making their collective opinions

known for decades. The *American Weekly Mercury* of Philadelphia reported weekly meetings of women in the 1720s,[4] and when women from
nearby Chester County in 1735 found that one abused wife could get no
relief in court, they took measures into their own hands and tried and
punished the man themselves. "The Women form'd themselves into a
Court," the *Pennsylvania Gazette* reported, "and order'd him to be apprehended by their Officers and brought to Tryal: Being found guilty he
was condemn'd to be duck'd 3 times in a neighbouring Pond, and to
have one half cut off, of his Hair and Beard."[5]

While American men may have tacitly and sometimes publicly approved
of women's protests in the tumultuous politics of the pre-Revolutionary
era, they did not always condone women's involvement in the affairs of
politics and society in colonial America. Many men felt that women
should remain at the hearth, taking care of family and home, and leave
other affairs to men. In fact, women were routinely criticized in newspapers for frittering away time on idleness, something a gathering of
women such as the Edenton Tea Party would have been considered thirty
years earlier. Many men felt that as women turned away from their duties
at home, they endangered society; furthermore, women, could in no way
be equal to men politically, socially, or religiously. Each sex had its role
in society, and women, according to historian Mary Beth Norton, were
viewed as inferior to men by both males and females.[6] Their role was
one of service.

The basis for colonial understanding of the role of women was rooted
in the Protestant Christian thought of the era. Women caused humankind's fall in the Garden of Eden making women evil. At the same time,
a woman gave birth to Jesus. Or, as Boston minister Cotton Mather explained, "As a woman had the Disgrace to go first in that horrid and woful
Transgresson of our first Parents. . . . A Woman had the Saviour of Mankind in the Circumstances of an Infant Miraculously Conceiv'd within
her."[7]

Colonial society, therefore, often viewed women in a Jekyll-and-Hyde
way. Women were virtuous because of their selfless commitment to service. They could also be seen as vicious if they veered from the path of
service or did anything that made them less than subservient to men.[8]
The fifty-one Edenton women were certainly performing a service-
oriented act with their tea party, but no doubt more than one American
man wondered how these women from the wealthiest and the not-so-
wealthy parts of the town could find time to hold such a meeting.

The readings in this chapter examine the perceptions of women as they
were presented in newspapers. They look at how women were considered virtuous for service to family and society. They also look at how
women were considered vicious for ignoring their nurturing role, fritter-

ing away time in idle activities, subverting society through crime, and breaking the mold of traditional patterns of behavior for women.

The first, unsigned letter criticizes women and speaks directly to women's activities in politics, stating that women have neither the mental capabilities nor the free time to engage in politics if they are caring properly for their families. The second selection, which originally appeared in London's *Spectator*, is an assault on women that simply belittles them. It demonstrates how women could be considered vicious simply by not serving. In the third entry, an unknown New York man explains how women are destroying society.

The fourth entry describes the arrest of a woman for the murder of her infant, born out of wedlock. Having a child out of wedlock in America was a crime, a violation of bastardy laws. These laws could be traced to sixteenth-century England where religious and social implications helped create the statutes. The church viewed such births as sin. The state regarded the births as a way for the poor to defraud charities, especially when the parent would maim or disfigure the child to enhance money that might be made from begging on the streets. Because of bastardy laws, unwed, pregnant women hid their pregnancies. The fact that women would have children out of wedlock and then kill those children after they were born to escape punishment was another example of what some saw as the viciousness of women.

The final selection in the section critical of women is related to the above story because it deals with the deaths of children. This graphic account describes the execution of a midwife convicted of murdering the children she was hired to deliver. The commentary in this news story from Paris refers to the woman as a "monster of iniquity," justifies her torture, and enforces the concept that women could sometimes be inhuman in their actions against humankind.

Works on virtuous women often appeared in newspapers as poetry because it was felt that lines of verse were the best way to reach females. The assumption was that women would not be—nor should be—as interested in the political stories in newspapers. Since printers wanted as many readers as possible, however, they provided selections of poetry, which sometimes appeared in a feature called the Poet's Corner and was aimed principally at a female audience.[9]

The first selection that points women toward virtue, from the *American Weekly Mercury* of Philadelphia, describes the ideal wife. It displays much of what was expected of women in the eighteenth century by men. The second poem, published forty years after the *Weekly Mercury*'s, again lists the attributes of the good wife. The third piece comes from a Poet's Corner that appeared in a New York paper in 1770. It advised women to make no pretenses at achieving goals within society. Women should, the poet suggested, seek "Domestick worth." All the poems were printed without the names of those who submitted or wrote them.

NEGATIVE PERCEPTIONS OF WOMEN

AN ANONYMOUS WRITER: "POLITICS DOES NOT BECOME WOMEN"

New York in 1734 was filled with political turmoil and discussion surrounding the government of Governor William Cosby (see Chapter 5). New York's female population was evidently speaking out on the issue, too, and the anonymous writer of this letter did not find such talk proper. He advised that women should leave governing to men because it was too difficult for them—obviously forgetting his history and the queens of his ruling country, Elizabeth I and Anne, to name two.

New-York Weekly Journal, 19 August 1734

Mr. Zenger;

As Many of your Readers are of the female Sex, I hope they won't take it ill, if they should be the told, that Policks [politics] is what does not become them; the Governing of Kingdoms and Ruling Provinces are Things too difficult and knotty for their fair Sex, it will render them grave and serious, and take off those agreeable Smiles that should always accompany them.

It is with the utmost concern that I daily see Numbers of fair Ladies contending about some abstruce Point in Politicks, and running into the greatest Heats about they know not what. I must say that unluckily the other Day I fell into Company with some Ladies, and one of them said, that for her Part, she thought such a one was a very sad Creature. Another of the Company said, she was of a different Opinion, being well acquainted with the Lady, and thought her to be a very discreet Woman. *Pray how can that be* (says the first) *when her Husband has signed the Address to the Governour?* Finding them to grow warm, I endeavoured to mitigate Matters, and said, the Woman might be a very discreet Woman, tho' her Husband had been so indiscreet as to do such a Thing. But all I could say was in vain, and I luckily got clear without being scalded with the hot Tea.

And what I think still worse, is, they can't help shewing their Resentments in the publick Streets. The other Day I saw one of the Courtiers walking along the Streets, and being obliged to pass by the Door of one of the contrary Party, she speaks to her Children who were with her, that at their Perils they should not bow when thy pass'd by such a Door, and when she got home could not help exulting at that great Mark of Disrespect that she had shewn, and how pretty the Children had behaved.

Men indeed ought to exert themselves in Defence of their Liberties, and shew a just Disregard for all those Tools of Power that endeavour to contribute to their Slavery; and had I the Happiness of being a fair Lady, I should always treat with Contempt any Man that appear'd a Tool in any Shape; yet I think a Woman never appears more agreeable then when she is discharging the Duties incumbent upon a Mistriss of a Family, when through her Management her Friends partake of a Genteel Frugality. I would not have you imagine I design by this to perswade the Ladies from reading your Journals; by no means, let them read them, and teach their Children the Principles of Liberty and good Manners, which will redound much more to their Honour than by Discommoding their pretty Faces with Passion and Resentment.

AN ANONYMOUS WRITER: "WOMEN"

Essays that provided a community with discussion were a staple of colonial newspapers. This one directly attacks the character of women. While it may have appeared in Benjamin Franklin's newspaper as humor, the examples of types of women certainly placed blame on women for domestic problems and belittled any female activity that did not serve society.

Pennsylvania Gazette (Philadelphia), 26 November 1730

The Subject of this Satyr is Woman. . . .

In the Beginning God made the Souls of Womankind out of different Materials, and in a separate State from their Bodies.

The Souls of one Kind of Women were formed out of those Ingredients which compose a Swine. A Woman of this make is a Slut in her House, and a Glutton at her Table. She is uncleanly in her Person, a Slattern in her Dress, and her Family is no better than a Dunghil.

A second Sort of Female Soul was formed out of the same Materials that enter into the Composition of a Fox. Such an one is what we call a notable discerning Woman, who has an Insight into every Thing, whether it be good or bad. In this Species of Females there are some virtuous and some vicious. . . .

The Sixth Species were made up of the Ingredients which compose an Ass, or a Beast of Burden. These are naturally exceeding slothful, but upon the Husband's exerting his Authority, will live upon hard Fare, and do every Thing to please him. They are however far from being averse to Venereal Pleasure, and seldom refuse a Male Companion. . . .

The Mare with a flowing Mane, which was never broke to any servile Toil and Labour, composed an eighth Species of Women. These are they who have little Regard for their Husbands, who pass away their Time in Dressing, Bathing and Perfuming; who throw their Hair into the nicest Curls, and trick it up with the fairest Flowers and Garlands. A Woman of this Species is a very pretty Thing for a Stranger to look upon, but very detrimental to the Owner, unless it be a King or Prince who takes a Fancy to such a Toy.

AN ANONYMOUS LETTER: "LETTER TO A LADY"

The writer of this letter did not like what he saw happening around him. Gender roles seemed to be changing, and he did not like women invading the traditional sphere of men. Women were perverting society, he said. The key to his comments may be found in his opening sentence: women were leaving the duties *of their sex for the* privileges *granted to males.*

Parker's New-York Gazette; or the Weekly Post-Boy, 4 December 1760

LETTER TO A LADY;

Women famed for their valour, their skill in politicks, or their learning, it is to be fear'd have left the duties of their own sex in order to invade the privileges of our's [*sic*].

The modest virgin, the prudent wife, or the careful mother, are much more serviceable than petticoated philosophers, blustering heroines, or virago Queens. She who makes her husband and her children happy, who reclaims the one from vice, or trains up the others to virtue, is a much greater character than the finest lady that ever existed in poetry, or romance, whose whole occupation it has been to murder mankind with the shafts from her quiver, or her eyes.

Women, it has been observed, are not naturally formed for great cares themselves, but to soften our's. Their tenderness is the proper reward for the dangers we undergo for their preservation; and the ease and cheerfulness of their conversation, our desirable retreat from the fatiques of study, war, or business. They are confined within the narrow limits of domestick assiduity; and when they stray beyond them, they move excentrically, and consequently without grace.

Fame has been very unjustly dispensed, therefore, among the female sex; those who least deserved to be remembered, meet our admiration and applause, while many who have been an honour to humanity, are passed over in silence. Perhaps no period has produced a stronger instance of the blindness of same in this respect than the present.

AN ANONYMOUS REPORT: "UNWED WOMAN MURDERS CHILD"

Colonial society depended to a great extent upon laws that had developed in England. The bastardy laws of sixteenth-century England were still enforced in eighteenth-century America, and an unwed, pregnant woman faced condemnation from civil and religious authorities. As a result, women hid such pregnancies and sometimes killed the child after its birth. This story is but one example of many that appeared in colonial newspapers. The women involved were damned with any decision they made. If their pregnancy was discovered, they violated bastardy laws. If they hid the pregnancy and then killed the child, they were guilty of murder. In either case, the woman's action reinforced ideas like those expressed in the second essay above—that women were the part of society that caused evil to happen.

American Weekly Mercury (Philadelphia), 28 August 1735

We hear from Providence in this County, that a young Woman about 19 Years of Age, is now under Confinement, for concealing the birth of her Bastard Child; and burying it in the Orchard. It seems her Master & Mistress had suspected her being with Child, but she constantly deny'd it; and they being from Home on the 4th Instant, she was Delivered by herself, and bury'd the Child about 9 Inches under Ground: After this, his Mistress observing her to appear smaller put it close to her that she had be deliver'd of a Child, but she would own nothing, 'til ten Days after, when Milk being found in her Breasts, and a Constable threatned to be sent for, she confess'd the whole.

AN ANONYMOUS REPORT: "THE MURDEROUS MIDWIFE"

Humans are drawn to the odd, the different, and the sensational. That is why they often slow down and look at wrecks and why print and broadcast tabloids are so popular. This story is an example of eighteenth-century sensational reporting. The fact that a woman entrusted with such an important job as delivering children could intentionally kill them was unthinkable. The brutality of her execution probably, was due to the expectation that women should be nurturers and servers of society.

Boston Evening-Post, 11 March 1765

The murderous Midwife. . . . It happened that a gentleman who lived next door to the midwife had observed, that although many pregnant women went to be delivered at her house, yet very few children were brought out, and his suspicion of foul play towards the infants increasing daily, he at length consulted with some of his neighbours, who joined him in requesting a warrant from a magistrate to search. . . . When they came to her place of abode, she affected the utmost concern, desiring the gentlemen not to hurry themselves, but to proceed in their search, with all possible circumspection,—they did so—and on their coming to the necessary-house, they put down a hook, which they had brought with

them on purpose, which bro't up the body of a child newly destroyed.—
They continued their search, till they found no less than sixty-two children—some of whom were in great measure decayed, but many of them
appeared to have been deposited in that place within a very few weeks
at the most. . . . She was sentenced to be executed in the following manner. . . . A gibbet was erected under which a fire was made, and the prisoner being brought to the place of execution, was hung up in a large
iron cage, in which were placed sixteen wild cats, that had been catch'd
in the woods for the purpose. When the heat of the fire became too great
to be endured with patience, the cats flew upon the woman, as the cause
of the intense pain they felt.—In about fifteen minutes they had pulled
out her intrails, though she continued yet alive, and sensible, imploring,
as the greatest favour, an immediate death from the hands of the charitable spectators. No one however dared to afford her the least assistance;
and she continued in this wretched situation for the space of thirty-five
minutes, and then expired in unspeakable torture.

However cruel this execution may appear with regard to the poor an-
imals, it certainly cannot be thought too severe a punishment for such a
monster of iniquity, as could proceed in acquiring a fortune by the deliberate murder of such numbers of un-offending innocents. And if a
method of executing murderers, in a manner somewhat similar to this
was adopted in England, perhaps the horrid crime of murder might not
so frequently disgrace the annals of the present times.

The above story is strictly true in every part of it.

POSITIVE PERCEPTIONS OF WOMEN

AN ANONYMOUS WRITER: "THE BATCHELOR'S CHOICE"

*The first letter in this chapter's readings states that women constituted
a large portion of newspaper readership in colonial America. One newspaper feature aimed directly at women was the inclusion of poetry. In
this poem, the writer outlines all the traits he thinks unmarried men
desire in women. Each characteristic is one of virtuous service to her
husband and future family.*

American Weekly Mercury (Philadelphia), 3 January 1739–1740

The Batchelor's Choice.

If Marriage gives a Happiness to life,
Such be the Woman who shall be my Wife:
Beauteous as the height of fancy can express,
Meek in her Nature cleanly in her dress;

Wife without pride, and Pleasing without Art,
With chearful Aspect and with honest Heart.
To sooth my Cares, most high, most sweet her Song,
To blame my Faults most low, most kind her Tongue:
In looser Hours, in Hours more dull, still dear,
A gay Companion, and a Friend sincere:
Fond without folly, spirit'ous without rage,
and as in youth shall seem the same in Age.
Ye pow'rs above, if such a Woman be,
(Such cou'd y make) that such a Woman give to me:
She as a Wife must please, and she alone.
O! give me such a Wife or give me none.

AN ANONYMOUS WRITER: "THE GOOD WIFE"

Thirty years after "The Batchelor's Choice" appeared in a newspaper, another writer submitted "The Good Wife." The concepts are for the most part identical. Women are to serve husband and family. It was a woman's job to make sure that all in the home had everything they needed. This poem appeared in a feature called the Poet's Corner, which became a regular feature in newspapers in the second half of the eighteenth century with subject matter aimed at female readers.

Massachusetts Gazette, and Boston Post-Boy and Advertiser, 20
August 1770

The GOOD WIFE
HAPPY the man whoe'er shall find
Among the race of women kind,
A Wife with every virtue grac'd,
Industrious, prudent, generous, chaste:
In her his ravish'd soul shall prove
The purest joys of nuptial love,
      His welfare, happiness, and ease
She meditates in all her ways,
And daily adds a chearful share
Of prudent industry and care.
      Like the wing'd bark from eastern shores,
That brings her load of coastly stores,
She with her diligence at home
Enriches all within her dome.

AN ANONYMOUS WRITER: "ADVICE TO A LADY"

In 1770 America was embroiled in turmoil with England over taxes, representation, and trade. In this poem, however, women are advised not to think about the problems of the day but about seeking "Domestick worth," a phrase that meant women were to serve society. They were not to think too much about the issues of the day because, as the poet says, their brains were not made for such serious thought.

New-York Journal; or the General Advertiser, 9 August 1770

ADVICE to a LADY.

DO you, my fair, endeavour to possess
An elegance of mind, as well as dress:
Be that your ornament, and know to please,
By graceful nature's unofficiated case.
Bless'd is the maid, and worthy to be bless'd,
Whose soul entire, by him she loves, possess'd,
Feels every vanity in fondness lost,
And asks no power but that of pleasing most.
Nor make to dangerous wit a vain pretence,
But wisely rest content with modest sense;
For wit, like wine, intoxicates the brain,
Too strong for feeble woman to sustain:
Of those who claim it more than half have none;
And half of those who have it are undone.
Be still superior to your sex's arts,
Nor think dishonesty a proof of parts;
For you the plainest is the wisest rule,
A cunning woman is a knavish fool,
Be good yourself, nor think another's shame
Can raise your merit, or adorn your fame;
Virtue is amiable, 'tis mild, serene,
Without, all beauty, and all peace within.
Seek to be good, but aim not to be great,
A woman's noblest station is retreat;
Her fairest virtues fly from public sight,
Domestick worth, that shuns too strong a light.
To this great point direct your constant aim,
This makes your happiness, and this your fame.

QUESTIONS

1. What can you tell about gender roles in the eighteenth century from these essays, letters, and poems?

2. Why was the writer of the letter "Politics Does Not Become Women" really so concerned that women not become involved in politics?

3. What do you think the writers meant by the term virtuous?

4. According to the letter published in *Parker's New-York Gazette*, what was woman's purpose and chief crime?

5. What assumptions might one make about the changing role of women in society from these newspaper articles?

6. The explanation of women in the *Pennsylvania Gazette* article describes the vicious type. What made these women, according to this description, evil?

7. Although the bastardy laws of colonial America have long been banished, do their implications have any effects today? Explain.

NOTES

1. Quoted in "Edenton, North Carolina," http://www.edenton.com.

2. Don Higginbotham, ed., *The Papers of James Iredell* (Raleigh, N.C., 1976), I: 282–86n.

3. *Boston Evening-Post*, 12 February 1770.

4. *American Weekly Mercury* (Philadelphia), 30 September 1725, 2.

5. *Pennsylvania Gazette* (Philadelphia), 17 April 1735, 4.

6. Mary Beth Norton, *Liberty's Daughters: The Revolutionary Experience of American Women, 1750–1800* (Boston: Little, Brown 1980), xiv.

7. Cotton Mather, *Ornaments for the Daughters of Zion, Or, The Character and Happiness of a Virtuous Woman* (Boston, 1692), 1–2.

8. David A. Copeland, "Virtuous and Vicious: The Dual Portrayal of Women in Colonial Newspapers," *American Periodicals* 5 (1995): 60.

9. David A. Copeland, *Colonial American Newspapers: Character and Content* (Newark: University of Delaware Press, 1997), 170–71.

CHAPTER 27

Arguments over Going to War with England, 1774–1776

In March 1775, the Virginia Convention met in Richmond. The delegates, who met to discuss the crisis with Britain, moved approximately fifty miles inland from Williamsburg to keep their business from being interrupted by the governor and the British troops stationed in the capital. The meeting might be considered a gathering of who's who in the formation of the United States with men such as Thomas Jefferson, George Washington, Richard Henry Lee, and Peyton Randolph in attendance.

While all of these men played crucial roles in what Virginia did during the eight-day convention, none were more vocal or more bellicose than Patrick Henry. Already in 1774, Henry, who became an outspoken proponent of American rights during the Stamp Act crisis, had admitted that the colonies must fight England if taxation and virtual control over the colonies by Parliament could not be removed from America.[1] Now with Virginia's delegates meeting in convention, Henry demanded and the convention approved the raising of militias in every county of Virginia and providing them with the tools of war.[2] Henry felt the time had come for the colonies to go to war with England.

Not all of the Virginia delegates agreed with Henry's demands that the colony prepare for war, but few could speak as eloquently as the 38-year-old lawyer. On the fourth day of the convention, he told all the delegates exactly how he felt:

This is no time for ceremony. The question before the House is one of awful moment to this country. For my own part, I consider it as nothing less than a question of freedom or slavery. . . . Should I keep back my opinions at such a time, through fear of giving offence, I should consider myself as guilty of treason towards my country, and of an act of disloyalty toward the majesty of heaven, which I revere above all earthly kings. . . .

Has Great Britain any enemy, in this quarter of the world, to call for all this accumulation of navies and armies? No, sir, she has none. They are meant for us; they can be meant for no other. . . . Sir, we have done everything that could be done, to avert the storm which is now coming on. We have petitioned; we have remonstrated; we have supplicated; we have prostrated ourselves before the throne, and we have implored its interposition to arrest the tyrannical hands of the ministry and Parliament. . . . There is no longer any room for hope. I wish to be free . . . we must fight! I repeat it, sir, we must fight! An appeal to arms and to the God of Hosts is all that is left us! . . . There is no retreat but in submission and slavery! Our chains are forged! Their clanking may be heard on the plains of Boston! The war is inevitable—and let it come! I repeat it, sir, let it come.

It is vain, sir, to extenuate the matter. Gentlemen may cry, Peace, Peace—but there is no peace. The war is actually begun! The next gale that sweeps from the north will bring to our ears the clash of resounding arms! Our brethren are already in the field! Why stand we here idle? What is it that gentlemen wish? What would they have? Is life so dear, or peace so sweet, as to be purchased at the price of chains and slavery? Forbid it, Almighty God! I know not what course others may take; but as for me, give me liberty or give me death![3]

The readings begin with those opposed to war with England. The first entry is a letter written by the Reverend Charles Inglis, the assistant rector of Trinity Church, who signed it A New-York Freeholder. The staunch Anglican was a strong supporter of Britain and opposed the independence movement in America. The letter attempts to paint a picture of the horrors of going to war with Britain and what Americans would lose in such a confrontation.

The second selection is one part of seventeen essays written by Daniel Leonard under the pen name Massachusettenis for the *Massachusetts Gazette*. Leonard was solicitor general of the customs board in Boston. His essays brought responses from John Adams in the *Boston Gazette*, who wrote under the name Novanglus. The third letter was written by William Smith to the people of Pennsylvania. As in the rest of his letters in this series, the Provost of the College of Philadelphia attacks Thomas Paine's *Common Sense*. Here, Smith also discusses how wrong and bad it would be for America to fight Great Britain. The final reading opposing war with England is a poem that declares that many Americans are ready to fight for the king. It was printed with a woodcut of the British flag with a declaration of loyalty to the king by his faithful subjects.

The readings advocating war with England begin with a biting declaration from an unknown Boston writer. It declares that Americans are millions strong and that Britain should be prepared, "*for the* Herculean

Arm *of this* New World *is lifted up—and Woe be to them on whom it falls!"* The next selection talks about the vastness of America's resources and what could be offered to allies in war. Compare this letter to Inglis' letter, in the chapter's first section, which approaches the possibilities of war from the opposite point of view.

The next reading is one of the more popular songs of the early part of the war that appeared in several newspapers. It is followed by a letter written by an anonymous soldier. The letter equates the actions of those fighting for America with doing God's will. It asserts that fighting England is a noble act that will win favor for all those who fought into future generations. The letter discusses how America can produce all it needs, and asserts that its soldiers have the advantage over those of Britain.

AGAINST WAR WITH BRITAIN

A NEW-YORK FREEHOLDER: "WARS BRING A HIDEOUS TRAIN OF MISERIES"

A New-York Freeholder was really the Reverend Charles Inglis, an Anglican minister. Using this pseudonym, he wrote several letters to New York newspapers in support of England during the 1770s. In this letter, Inglis paints a picture of the horrors of war. Like many Americans, Inglis knew war was inevitable if the Patriot leaders, principally from Boston, continued to control colonial actions. This letter, with its descriptions, is an attempt to sway people not to follow policies that would place America on a collision course with England's military.

New-York Gazette; and the Weekly Mercury, 19 September 1774

To the Inhabitants *of* NORTH-AMERICA.

Brethren, Friends and Fellow Subjects,

CIVIL war is one of the most tremendous judgments that can befall a nation. Foreign wars bring a hideous train of miseries with them; but the former is infinitely more bloody, cruel and destructive. When permitted to range long and uncontrolled, perhaps Heaven has not in store a severer Scourge for guilty mortals. . . .

O my country! how gladly would I wrench from the hand of this fiend, the poisonous dagger which she is now aiming at thy bosom! how gladly would I teach thy children to beware of her approaches, and not suffer her to infest thy happy borders! . . .

In case these people [those stirring up insurrection in Massachusetts] should persist in the same steps and spirit, and the other colonies should be so infatuated as to join them which must necessarily terminate in an open rupture with Great-Britain, let us calmly consider how we are prepared for such a contest. I shall not knowingly exaggerate a single circumstance, but represent things as they really are.

The naval power of Great-Britain is undoubtedly at this day the greatest in the world. . . . Have we a fleet to look this formidable power in the face, and defend our coasts? no—not one ship. The inevitable consequence then must be, that all our sea-port towns will be taken, and all our trade and commerce destroyed, at the very first shock. As many troops as government pleases may be poured in: and all hopes of foreign succour, even if we had any, intirely cut off. Have we disciplined troops to encounter those veterans that are now in America, or that may be sent hereafter?—Not a single regiment. We must leave our farms, our shops and trades, and *begin* to learn the art of war at the very same we are called to practise it, and our ALL is at stake. We indeed have great numbers of people in America—some compute upwards of two millions; but these are the peaceful sons of industry, employed in agriculture and commerce. As yet they are unpractised in the rugged scenes of war; tho' I doubt not but under proper discipline they would make as good soldiers as any in the British dominions. Supposing then we had a disciplined army of these, have we funds to support that army? or military stores to carry on warlike measure? no—neither of these. We are indebted to the mother country for all military stores; which we cannot look for in case of a civil war. Commerce and agriculture are our great sources of wealth—the former would be utterly ruined, the latter greatly languish. An American army then could only subsist on the plunder of the wretched inhabitants, who must be equally harassed and pillaged by friends and foes. It might require several years to decide the contest; and so long this pillage must continue.

Thus matters would be circumstanced along our sea coast. If we turn our eyes west to that vast tract of country which skirts our back settlements, and where some promise themselves a sanctuary, the case will not be much mended. The Quebec bill cuts off that refuge. By that bill, which I highly disapprove in all respects . . . the province of Canada extends south as far as Carolina, and surrounds all our colonies from thence to Nova Scotia. In a petition presented by the French inhabitants of Canada to his Majesty . . . they assert their number to be more than ONE HUNDRED THOUSAND. Every man in Canada is a soldier, and may be commanded on any service, or at any time when government pleases. To that may be added the Indians, whose warriours in Canada and the Six Nations amount at least to FIVE THOUSAND, and who are equally at the beck of government. In case of a civil war, all these Canadians and Indians would infallibly be let loose on our back-settlements, to scalp, ravage and lay every thing waste with fire and sword; so that we should be hemmed in on all sides.

What has been said hitherto is on the supposition that *all* the British Americans would unite in a war against Great-Britain, but can any man be so weak and credulous as to believe this would really happen? are not several provinces as much in the hands of government as Canada? . . . Were a civil war to break out, the Americans themselves would be divided. There could be no such thing as standing neuter. One side or other must be chosen. Men of property would naturally incline to that where there was most safety, and they must be blind indeed who cannot see which that is. Besides, separate from these considerations, I am confident there are many thousands in America who would suffer any thing— even death—rather than take arms against our gracious sovereign, whom I may pronounce the best prince in christendom. . . .

I would leave the reader's imagination to paint the rest. It can afford me no pleasure to enter on a minute description of my country's miseries—the thousands that must perish by sword, by famine and other deaths. . . .

Shall we, then, notwithstanding the clearest light and conviction, madly pursue violent measures that would plunge our country into all the horrors of a civil war? Shall we desperately risque our lives, liberties and property in so unequal a contest, and wantonly drench this happy country with the blood of its inhabitants, when our liberties and property may be effectually secured by prudent, pacific measures?—Forbid it humanity! Forbid it loyalty, reason and common sense!

A NEW-YORK FREEHOLDER.

MASSACHUSETTENIS: "THE SEED OF SEDITION IS PLANTED BY THE VILEST REPTILES"

Massachusettenis was the pseudonym of Daniel Leonard, the solicitor general of the Boston customs board. His series of essays published in the Massachusetts Gazette *produced reactions from many Patriots. In this letter, he explains how men such as Samuel Adams planted the mustard seed of sedition among the people, watered it, and watched it grow. He now worries about the fruits of that planting: violence.*

Massachusetts Gazette and Boston Post-Boy, 1 January 1775

To the Inhabitants of the province of Massachusetts-Bay. . . .

I saw the small seed of sedition, when it was implanted; it was, as a grain of mustard. I have watched the plant until it has become a great tree; the vilest reptiles that crawl upon the earth, are at the root; the foulest birds of the air rest upon its branches. I would now induce you to go to work immediately with axes and hatchets, and cut it down, for a two-fold reason: because it is a pest to society, and lest it be felled by a stronger arm and crush its thousands in the fall. . . .

I appeal to your good sense, I know you have it, and hope to penetrate to it, before I have finished my publications. . . . I do not address myself to whigs or tories, but to the whole people. I know you well; you are loyal at heart, friends to good order, and do violence to yourselves, in harbouring one moment, disrespectful sentiments towards Great-Britain, the land of our forefathers nativity, the sacred repository of their bones: but they have been most insidiously induced to believe, that Great Britain is rapacious, cruel and vindictive, and envies us the inheritance purchased by the sweat and blood of our ancestors. Could that thick mist that hovers over the land . . . be but dispelled, that you might see our sovereign, the provident father of all his people, and Great-Britain, a nursing mother to these colonies as they really are; long live our gracious King, and happiness to Britain, would resound from one end of the province to the other.

MASSACHUSETTENIS.

CATO: "LETTER III-COMMON SENSE WILL KEEP US FROM GOING TO WAR WITH ENGLAND"

Cato, the pseudonym of freedom among English-speaking people, was used by William Smith of Philadelphia to argue against going to war with England, against separating from England (see Chapter 28), and against Thomas Paine's Common Sense *(see Chapter 30). Smith was the provost of the College of Philadelphia. Here, he states that peace is always the purpose of war. Since America and England are now at peace, why go to war to gain what already exists?*

New-York Gazette; and the Weekly Mercury, 1 April 1776

To the PEOPLE of Pennsylvania.
LETTER III.
. . . It will be *asserted*—indeed it has been already *asserted*—that the animosities between Great-Britain and the Colonies are now advanced to such a height, that RECONCILIATION is impossible. But *assertions* are nothing, when opposed to the nature of things. . . . There never was a war so implacable, even among states naturally rivals and enemies, or among savages themselves, as not to have *peace* for its object as well as end! And, among people naturally friends, and connected by every dearest tie, who knows not that their quarrels (as those of *lovers*) are often but a stronger renewal of *love*? . . .

It has been further asserted—that we are able, with our land forces, to defend ourselves against the whole world; that if commerce be an advantage, we may command what foreign alliances we please; that the moment we declare ourselves an *independent people*, there are nations ready to face the British thunder, and become the carriers of our commodities for the sake of enriching themselves; that, if this were not the case, we can soon build navies to force and protect a trade; that a confederacy of the Colonies into one great *republic* is preferable to *Kingly government*, which is the appointment of the *Devil*, or at least reprobated by God; that those denominated *wise men*, in our own and foreign countries, who have been so lavish of their encomiums upon the English constitution, were but egregious *fools*; that it is nothing better than a bungling piece of machinery, standing in need of constant *checks* to regulate and continue its motions; that the nation itself is but one mass of corruption, having at its head a *Royal Brute*, a hardened *Pharaoh*, delighting in blood; that we never can enjoy liberty in connection with such a country, and therefore all the hardships mentioned above, and a thousand times more, if necessary, are to be endured for the preservation of our rights.

If these things had been as fully proved, as they are boldly asserted by the authors of what is called COMMON SENSE, I should here drop my pen; and through the short remainder of life, take my chance of whatever miseries Providence may have in reserve for this land, as I know of none else to which I can retire. But as these doctrines contradict every thing which we have hitherto been taught to believe respecting government, I hope you, my dear countrymen, have yet kept *one ear open*, to hear what answer may be given in my future letters.   CATO

AN ANONYMOUS WRITER: "LOYALTY TO THE KING"

One way Tories used to sway public opinion away from war was to suggest the strength of Great Britain. In this poem, the unknown writer also points out that many Americans support the king and will fight for England, not America, if war erupts. The writer no doubt hopes that the poem will keep some who have not yet decided that war is the proper course for the colonies from siding with Patriots pushing for war.

Rivington's New-York Gazetteer; or Connecticut, New-Jersey, Hudson's-River, and Quebec Weekly Advertiser, 2 March 1775

IN TESTIMONY

Of our unshaken loyalty, and incorruptible fidelity, to the best of Kings;

Or our inviolable affection, and attachment, to our parent state, and the British constitution;

Or our abhorrence of, and aversion to, a republican government;

Or our detestation of all treasonable associations, unlawful combinations, seditious meetings, tumultuous assemblies, and execrable mobs; and of all measures that have a tendency to

alienate the affections of the people from their rightful sovereign, or lessen their regard for our most excellent constitution;

And to make known to all Men,

That, we are ready, when properly called upon, at the hazard of our lives, and of every thing dear to us, to defend the KING, support the magistrates in the execution of the laws, and maintain the just rights and constitutional liberties of freeborn Englishmen.

IN FAVOR OF WAR WITH BRITAIN

AN ANONYMOUS WRITER: "THE HERCULEAN ARM OF THIS NEW WORLD IS LIFTED UP"

Few American newspapers printed statements as strong as this one this early, but the Boston Gazette *was the newspaper of choice of Samuel Adams, the most outspoken of all American Patriots. Whether Adams penned this threat to Great Britain is not known, but with the first paper of 1774, the* Gazette *issued a warning that the strength of America should never be underestimated and that it was ready to let its Herculean arm fall upon any who challenged it.*

Boston Gazette, and Country Journal, 3 January 1774

To all Nations under HEAVEN,

Know Ye,

THAT the PEOPLE *of the* AMERICAN WORLD, *are Millions strong,—countless Legions compose their united* ARMY *of* FREEMEN—*whose intrepid Souls sparkle with Liberty, and their Hearts are steeled with Courage to effect what their Wisdom dictates to be done—*AMERICA *now stands with the Scale of* JUSTICE *in one Hand, and the Sword of* VENGEANCE *in the other, and whatever Nation or People who dares to lift a hostile Hand against her, to invade her serene Region, or sully her Liberty, shall— — —Let the Britons fear to do any more so wickedly as they have done, for the* HERCULEAN ARM *of this* NEW WORLD *is lifted up—and Woe be to them on whom it falls!—At the Beat of a Drum, she can call five Hundred Thousand of her* SONS *to* ARMS—*before whose blazing Shields none can stand—Therefore, ye that are Wise make Peace with Her, take Shelter under Her Wings, that ye may shine by the Reflection of Her Glory.*

May the NEW YEAR *shine propitious on the* NEW WORLD—*and* VIRTUE, *and* LIBERTY, *reign here without a Foe, until rolling Years shall measure* TIME *no more.* MARLBOROUGH.

SOLON: "TO THE PEOPLE OF ENGLAND"

Writers knew that the letters they wrote to American newspapers often ended up in London prints. The unknown Solon wrote this letter to the people of England. He wanted them to know that America's resources were vast and that Americans were ready to defend their rights, even if it meant death.

Massachusetts Spy Or, Thomas's Boston Journal, 20 October 1774

To the PEOPLE *of* ENGLAND.

IF you suffer your tyrannical *Ministers* to proceed much farther, in their execrable plan for enslaving America, they will plunge the nation into the gulph of political perdition, and that very soon—there is now but a *step between them and death.*—The Americans are unalterably determined to defend their rights—they will soon be well prepared for the *last appeal.* . . . Weigh well the consequences of a civil war—be not hasty to take this *last step*, after which you can go neither *forward* nor *backward* without *destruction.*—The moment you commence war with America, you *stab your own vitals*, and will inevitably bleed to death at *these three wounds*; First, The *increase of national expence*: Second, *The Sources of your wealth will be cut off*: Third, *In this exhausted state, while your fleets and armies are* in America, *you will be an easy prey to* France and Spain, *and lie open to the attacks of your enemies in every part of the world.*— THEREFORE you have nothing to expect in this situation but TOTAL RUIN.

The Americans have such a vast country, with so many advantages for defending it, and extensive *trade* to give to their *allies*, LAND to give to all foreign soldiers, and others who will join in the cause of liberty, and half a million of hardy determined men, great part of which are now prepared for action—that no wise man can suppose they will ever be conquered. But were it possible for Britain to conquer them it must be the work of many years, which would be such an expence of blood and treasure as totally to ruin her.   SOLON.

AN ANONYMOUS WRITER: "A SONG OF FREEDOM"

To discuss the current political situation, writers often borrowed the tunes of popular songs and added their own words. This is was done in this selection. The anonymous writer adds words that call for brave Americans to fight for liberty.

New-Hampshire Gazette (Portsmouth), 26 May 1775

A Song. . . .
Hark! 'tis Freedom that Calls, come patriots awake!

To arms, my brave boys, and away:
'Tis Honour, 'tis Virtue, 'tis Liberty calls,
And upbraids the too tedius delay.
What pleasure we find in pursuing our foes;
Thro' blood and thro' carnage we'll fly;
Then follow, we'll soon overtake them, huzza!
The tyrants are seized on, they die.

A SOLDIER: "TO THE AMERICAN SOLDIERY"

In December 1775, America was locked in war, and it appeared that Great Britain held the upper hand. The writer of this letter to all American soldiers wants his fellow warriors to know how important their task is. He looks ahead to the year 2000, predicting America's population and condition. He reminds those who read the letter that, unless they are successful, America is doomed to slavery.

Virginia Gazette (Williamsburg, Pinkney), 20 December 1775

To the AMERICAN SOLDIERY. . . .

WHEN I take a view of . . . these once dreary wastes blossoming as the rose, and teeming with an ample supply of all the conveniencies of life; in fine, when I attend to the almost incredible rapidity of population in the American colonies, I am struck with astonishment at the bountiful rewards of the industry of our worthy forefathers, and cannot forbear anticipating the future grandeur of this western world.

The number of inhabitants, according to the most accurate estimates that have been made, doubles in every period of twenty five years. The continental congress have estimated the number of inhabitants in eleven colonies at three million, equal to about three fifths of those in the whole island of Great Britain. . . . Let us stretch our ideas to the year 2000, and our computation furnishes us with the number of one thousand five hundred and thirty six millions, a computation which almost exceeds human conception. . . . To this pleasing portrait, if we add the proportionable improvements in agriculture, the military, and polite arts and sciences, together with the encrease of wealth and importance which will result from an unconfined trade, they may perhaps render this once DESPICABLE COUNTRY the most POWERFUL and AUGUST EMPIRE which the annals of history can boast. Let us look around us then, my fellow soldiers; let us contemplate this pleasing figure; let us make a solemn pause, and then ask ourselves whether we are willing to relinquish not only our present enjoyments, but all hopes of securing happiness and freedom for our children, and thereby spurn those privileges which the God of nature has conferred upon us in such beneficient profusion; let us ask ourselves whether we will see our wives, with every thing that is dear to us, subjected to the merciless rage of controuled despotism; or are any of us at a loss concerning our duty in this day of general distress? . . . let us drop a grateful tear in tribute to the memory of men, the very relation of whose disinterested exertions, and unparalleled sufferings, should be sufficient to inspire us with an heroic ardour in the glorious enterprize of transmitting to our children those sacred rights to which we ourselves were born; let us fly to the only means left for our defence, and swear to those venerable shades that their sons will never disgrace their unsullied names with the execrable epithet of *slavery*.

But if these considerations are not sufficient to inspire us with fortitude and resolution, there are still higher motives, which cannot fail to unite us in this noble struggle. We are engaged, my fellow soldiers, in the cause of virtue, of liberty, of God: For God's sake, then let us play the man for God's sake, let us neglect no requisite precautions to frustrate the cruel attempts of our remorseless foes. . . .

Our cruel enemies have forced us to pass the rubicon; we have begun the noble work, and there is no retreating; the king of Britain has proclaimed us rebels. The sword is drawn, the scabbard must be thrown away; there is no medium between a glorious defence and the most abject slavery. If we fail in our endeavours to repel the assaults of tyranny, we are to expect no mercy. . . . Our enemies have ridiculed our courage and military skill; but, by dear-bought experience, they have been convinced of their error; they are obliged to submit to the mortification of being confined within a few acres of lend [*sic*], miserably fed upon a beggarly pittance of half starved animal food. We are driving them from our fortresses in the west; our privateers are daily seizing valuable cargoes of provisions, and other articles upon the seas, where we least expected success. In fine, we are supplying ourselves with every thing necessary to support the war. New schemes of œonomy [economy] are inventing, and I doubt not but we shall find our calamities, in a short time, considerably alleviated, if not by foreign trade, yet by industry and frugality, which are making such rapid progress throughout the continent. Approving Heaven has hitherto smiled upon almost every enterprize. . . . A few more noble exertions, my brave fellow soldiers, a few more spirited struggles, and we secure our liberties; a few more successful battles, and we are a free and happy people. We will then retire to our families, and, whilst we are regaling ourselves with social festivity, entertain our listening children with the fatigues and dangers to which they owe their freedom, and shew the scars of the honourable wounds we received in the field of battle. Happy the man who can boast that he was one of those heroes that put the finishing stroke to this arduous work; in serenity may he pass his future days, and, when satisfied with life, and expiring under the smiles of an approving conscience, bequeath the inestimable patrimony to this grateful children.   A SOLDIER.

QUESTIONS

1. How did Charles Inglis, writing as A New-York Freeholder, underestimate America's ability to fight?

2. Why does Massachusettenis believe Americans do not really want to fight England?

3. According to Cato, what are the reasons being put forth for America's going to war with England?

4. What is the rationale in the *Boston Gazette* letter of January 3, 1774, for England to fear war with America?

5. Do you think the writer Solon is correct in expecting other European countries to come to America's assistance if war breaks out with England? How does the writer support this claim?

6. Why will America defeat England according to the letter by A Soldier?

7. Compare the reasons that America should not go to war with those of why America can expect to win a war with England. Which side presents the more persuasive argument? Why?

NOTES

1. Pauline Maier, *From Resistance to Revolution: Colonial Radicals and the Development of American Opposition to Britain, 1765–1776* (New York: Alfred A. Knopf, 1973), 254.

2. Peter Force, *American Archives: A Documentary History of the English Colonies in North America* (Washington, D.C., 1844), II: 167–70.

3. Henry's speech was reconstructed in William Wirt, *Sketches of the Life and Character of Patrick Henry* (Philadelphia, 1836).

CHAPTER 28

Separation from England, 1768–1776

With the Stamp Act crisis of 1765 (see Chapter 16), most Americans began thinking about the relationship between the American colonies and Great Britain. Americans protested that they were not directly represented in Parliament, and some concluded that the colonies should seriously consider a separation from Britain.

Charles Townshend, Britain's Chancellor of the Exchequer (or finance), decided shortly after the Stamp Act's repeal in March 1766 that America's share of the British budget had to increase, as did America's ability to pay its own way as part of the British Empire. Townshend believed England had the right to tax the colonies directly or indirectly and discounted the arguments that had arisen during the Stamp Act concerning actual and virtual representation in America (see Chapter 17). Most members of Parliament concurred with Townshend and passed the Townshend Acts in June 1767, which levied a tax on imported tea, lead, paint, glass, and paper.

Most Americans reacted negatively to the Townshend Acts, but they soon discovered that there was little room for a redress of grievances politically for the new taxes because of the Declaratory Act, passed in 1765 on the heels of the Stamp Act and to a great extent ignored in America because of the Stamp Act furor. The Declaratory Act gave Parliament sole authority to make laws for the colonies, and it gave Parliament the right to dissolve colonial legislatures.

When the New York legislature reacted negatively to another of Britain's new policies, the Quartering Act, according to which troops could be housed in taverns, barns, and uninhabited homes at colonial expense, Americans saw how powerful the Declaratory Act really was. They also realized that repeal of the Townshend Acts would not come about as quickly as that of the Stamp Act.

In the midst of the controversy concerning the Townshend Acts and Parliament's new flexing of its power over America, a Philadelphia lawyer, John Dickinson, issued a series of twelve letters that ultimately questioned who held the political power over America and, to a certain extent, within the entire British Empire. Dickinson wrote his letters under the heading "Letters from a Farmer in Pennsylvania." Even though he professed that all Americans should retain loyalty and subjugation to the king, his letters suggested that perhaps separation from England was America's prerogative and right. "Let these *truths* be indelibly impressed on our minds—*that* we *cannot be* HAPPY, *without being* FREE—that we cannot be secure in our property, *if, without our consent, others may, as by right, take it away*," Dickinson said in his final letter and added, " 'SLAVERY IS EVER PRECEDED BY SLEEP.' *Individuals* may be *dependent* on ministers, if they please. STATES SHOULD SCORN IT."[1]

Others joined Dickinson's debate, which continued even while the first shots were being fired at Lexington and Concord in 1775 (see Chapter 29). Questions surrounding separation from England heightened with the publication of Thomas Paine's *Common Sense* in 1776, which declared that it made common sense for England and America to separate (see Chapter 30). Those questions continued even after the signing of the Declaration of Independence (see Chapter 31).

The readings begin with those opposing separation from Britain. The first letter, probably written by someone in England, offers a proposal for the continuance of the union between Great Britain and America. The second letter, written by the anonymous Rusticus, discusses the advantages America has gained and will continue to gain by being a part of the British Empire. The final entry is a statement made by freeholders from White Plains, New York, who opposed any move of separation from England. It is typical of many such announcements that appeared in newspapers following the colonial conventions proposing separation.

The entries that advocate separation begin with John Dickinson's final Pennsylvania Farmer letter. Nearly every newspaper in America ran the series, even those with Tory leanings. Dickinson's letter is followed by one probably written by William Livingston, a New York lawyer who opposed any increases in governmental control over the colonies.

The next selections play on familiar forms of expression in America—songs, poetry, and drama. The first is John Dickinson's "Liberty Song," which, just as the "Letters from a Farmer in Pennsylvania," appeared in papers throughout America. The next entry, a poem from the *Virginia Gazette*, suggests separation from England should occur even if it means bloodshed. The third is printer Isaiah Thomas' paraphrase of Hamlet's soliloquy, which begins "To Be, or Not To Be." The speech focuses upon taxation but equates England's actions with slavery.

The next selection builds upon the slavery theme. It also compares the times in America to those of the latter Stuarts' reign—Charles II and James II—in seventeenth-century England. The comparison would not have been missed by Americans who would see this discussion intimating that America should expect total political and religious control by Britain unless the colonies separated from England.

The next selection comes from a book written by Josiah Quincy, Jr., following the Tea and Port acts. The excerpt alleges that freedom or separation from England is America's only recourse. Quincy was a lawyer who successfully defended the soldiers during the Boston Massacre trial. Despite this, he ardently worked for America's cause and died in April 1775 while returning from England where he had been pleading America's case.

The last two entries are songs for independence. The first appeared just months before shots were fired at Lexington and Concord. The second appeared several months after hostilities had begun.

AGAINST SEPARATION FROM BRITAIN

AN ANONYMOUS WRITER: "A PLAN TO PERPETUATE THE UNION
BETWEEN GREAT BRITAIN AND AMERICA"

Americans and Britons alike realized in the years just before the Revolution that the colonies and the mother country were on a course that would probably lead to separation unless drastic steps were taken. In this letter, probably written in London, the writer offers a plan to continue the union between the two. He believed the common interests of the two were enough to keep the colonies as a part of Great Britain.

Virginia Gazette (Williamsburg, Purdie and Dixon), 29 April 1773

A PLAN *to perpetuate the* UNION *between* GREAT BRITAIN *and* AMERICA, *to the latest Period of Time.*

IT is a just Observation, that the most simple Propositions are hard to be rendered more intelligible by any Explanation. This Remark is applicable to the present Dispute between Great Britain and America; although the Truth is obvious to common Sense, yet there have been Volumes written on the Subject. . . . The great Question now is, how shall the Union between Great Britain and America be preserved? The Answer is easy: Common Interest is the Bond of Union; the People of each Country must treat the other in such a Manner as to make it their Interest to preserve Connexion. The People of both Countries are united in the King, who is the Head of the Empire; and Interest, the only Comment of political Bodies, must preserve Union between the Members of the Empire, and between their Head. . . .

Union and Harmony between the two Countries, founded on Freedom and common Interest, the British Empire may continue firmly united, and flourish to the latest Age.

RUSTICUS: "THE INESTIMABLE PRIVILEGES OF BRITISH SUBJECTS"

The anonymous Rusticus believed that if Americans truly thought about all they gained from being British citizens, they would never separate from Great Britain. In this letter, Rusticus outlines the advantages of being British.

Pennsylvania Packet, or the General Advertiser, 2 January 1775

To the PRINTER. . . . RUSTICUS.

My Friends and Countrymen, . . .

Enjoying the inestimable privileges of British subjects, this once desart [*sic*] and howling wilderness has been converted into a flourishing and populous country, and by the happiness of its climate, and the industry and virtue of its inhabitants, has attained to a degree of improvement not to be paralleled in the annals of history in the same space of time. But, has not this been owing to the manner in which the Colonies have been treated from the beginning? Is it not from the readiness which Great-Britain has ever shewn to encourage our industry and protect us from foreign injuries, that we have attained this growth? If so, surely some returns of gratitude, such as become a free and liberal people, are justly due for favours received. . . .

I cannot nor will imagine that any of my countrymen entertain even a secret wish, that America shall be freed from all political connections with Great-Britain. The peace and security we have already enjoyed under her protection, before the mistaken system of taxation took place, must make us look back with regret to those happy days whose loss we mourn, and which every rational man must consider as the golden age of America. Even that future independancy which, in the course of human affairs, these colonies must arrive at, cannot for our true interest be too long delayed. History informs us that the constitutions of few or no governments have been established without a vast effusion of blood: and I need not remind you how much has been shed to obtain that happy constitution we now possess. Let us not, therefore, wantonly sport with our inestimable privileges, but virtuously endeavour to deliver the fair inheritance entire and unsullied to our posterity; and whilst with unremitting ardor we pursue this grand and important object, let us cautiously pursue it by constitutional measures. . . .

Let us then, my friends and countrymen, patiently attend this expected important period, in the mean time avoiding all inflammatory publications, and such as are disrespectful to our most gracious Sovereign, still looking forward with an anxious hope to an happy termination of our present disputes, and a cordial reconciliation with our mother country, on constitutional principles, as a consummation most devoutly to be wished for by every true and sincere lover of his country.

THE FREEHOLDERS OF WHITE PLAINS: "WE ARE NOT PART OF A DISPUTE WITH ENGLAND"

In 1774 and 1775, the freeholders—or male voters—of many American towns met together to discuss the political crisis between the colonies and England. In a number of colonies, groups such as the Sons of Liberty or other patriotic organs passed resolves listing their differences with England and declaring separation from the Britain would be the only recourse if relief to their list of complaints was not met. In this announcement, the freeholders of White Plains, New York, declare that they have not entered into such an agreement. In fact, the declaration states, they want to remain British subjects forever.

Rivington's New-York Gazetteer; or Connecticut, New-Jersey, Hudson's-River, and Quebec Weekly Advertiser, 12 January 1775

To the PRINTER.

Sir,

WE the subscribers, freeholders and inhabitants in the White Plains, in the county of Westchester, think it our duty to our King and country, to declare, that we have never given our consent to any Resolves touching the disputes with the mother country, nor are we any ways concerned in any measures entered into relative to them. . . . We also declare that we desire to live and die peaceable subjects to our gracious Sovereign King *GEORGE* the Third, and his laws. This is to inform the public, that the above declaration was signed by forty-five freeholders and inhabitants, in the small precinct of the White Plains, against the proceedings of the New-York Committee.

FOR SEPARATION FROM BRITAIN

A FARMER FROM PENNSYLVANIA: "LETTER XII"

Pennsylvania lawyer John Dickinson stirred American thought in 1767 and 1768 with a series of letters he wrote and signed A Farmer from

Pennsylvania. His letters were a reaction to the Townshend Acts. In this letter, Dickinson suggests that Americans deserve to be freemen, not slaves to Great Britain.

Pennsylvania Chronicle, and Universal Advertiser (Philadelphia), 15 February 1768

My dear Countrymen,

Some states have lost their liberty by *particular accidents*: But this calamity is generally owing to the *decay of virtue*. A *people* is travelling fast to destruction, when *individuals* consider *their* interests as distinct from *those of the public*. Such notions are fatal to their country, and to themselves. . . .

Our *vigilance* and our *union* are *success* and *safety*. Our *negligence* and our *division* are *distress* and *death*. They are *worse*—They are *shame* and *slavery*. . . . Let us consider ourselves as MEN—FREEMEN—CHRISTIAN FREEMEN—*separated from the rest of the world, and firmly bound together* by the *same rights, interests* and *dangers*. Let *these* keep our attention inflexibly fixed on the GREAT OBJECTS, which we must CONTINUALLY REGARD, in order to *preserve those rights, to promote those interests*, and to *avert those dangers*. Let these *truths* be indelibly impressed on our minds—*that* we *cannot be* HAPPY, *without being* FREE—that we cannot be secure in our property, *if, without our consent, others may, as by right, take it away*—that *taxes imposed on us by parliament*, do thus take it away. . . .

What have these colonies to *ask*, while they continue free? Or what have they to *dread*, but insidious attempts to subvert their freedom? . . .

Let us take care of our *rights*, and *we therein* take care of *our prosperity*. "SLAVERY IS EVER PRECEDED BY SLEEP." *Individuals* may be *dependent* on ministers, if they please. STATES SHOULD SCORN IT. . . .

ALMIGHTY GOD himself will look down upon your righteous contest with gracious approbation. You will be a *"band of brothers,"* cemented by the dearest ties,—and strengthened with inconceivable supplies of force and constancy, by that sympathetic ardor, which animates good men, confederated in a good cause. Your *honor* and *welfare* will be, as they now are, most intimately concerned; and besides—*you are assigned by divine providence*, in the appointed order of things, the *protectors of unborn ages*, whose *fate* depends upon your *virtue*. Whether *they* shall arise the *generous* and *indisputable heirs* of the noblest patrimonies, or the *dastardly and hereditary drudges* of imperious task-masters, YOU MUST DETERMINE.

To discharge this double duty to *yourselves*, and to your *posterity*, you have nothing to do, but to call forth into use the *good sense* and *spirit* of which you are possessed. . . . You will convince the world of the *justice of your demands*, and the *purity of your intentions*.—While all mankind must, with unceasing applauses, confess, that YOU indeed DESERVE lib-

erty, who so *well understand* it, so *passionately love* it, and so *wisely, bravely,* and *virtuously assert, maintain,* and *defend* it. . . .
A Farmer

WILLIAM LIVINGSTON: "THE DAY DAWNS ON THE FOUNDATION OF A MIGHTY EMPIRE"

William Livingston's writings served as stimulation for discussion in New York from the early 1750s through the beginning of the Revolution in 1775. The lawyer, one-time newspaper printer, and agitator believed that America needed its own constitution and that it was God's providence that America be its own empire, and he stated that in this unsigned essay.

New-York Gazette: or the Weekly Post-Boy, 11 April 1768

Courage, then Americans! liberty, religion, and sciences are on the wing to these shores: The finger of God points out a mighty empire to your sons. . . . The day dawns in which the foundation of this mighty empire is to be laid, by the establishment of a *regular American Constitution*. All that has hitherto been done, seems to be little beside the collection of materials, for the construction of this glorious fabrick. 'Tis time to put them together . . . before seven years roll over our heads, the first stone must be laid.—Peace or war; famine or plenty; poverty or affluence; in a word no circumstance, whether prosperous or adverse, can happen to our parent . . . no conduct of hers . . . no possible temper on her part . . . will put a stop to this building. There is no contending with Omnipotence, and the *predispositions* are so numerous, and so well adapted to [the] rise of America, that our success is indubitable.

JOHN DICKINSON: "THE LIBERTY SONG"

As others did in times of controversy, lawyer John Dickinson discovered that one of the best ways to permeate society with his message was to put that message into a song. The "Liberty Song" turned out to be a popular song. Sometimes, its verses were altered to create a pro-English song. The version here, which appeared in the Boston Chronicle, *was the pro-Patriot and separation rendering.*

Boston Chronicle, 5 September 1768

The LIBERTY SONG. In FREEDOM we're born &c.

COME join hand in hand brave AMERICANS all,
And rouse your bold hearts at fair LIBERTY'S call; No tyrannous
   acts shall suppress your just claim,

Or stain with dishonour AMERICA's name
  In FREEDOM we're born and in FREEDOM we'll live,
Our purses are ready,
    Steady, Friends, steady,
    Not as SLAVES, but as FREEMEN our Money we'll give.
  Our worthy Forefathers—Let's give them a cheer—
To Climates unknown did courageously steer;
Thro' Oceans, to Deserts, for FREEDOM they came.
And dying bequeath'd us their FREEDOM and Fame.
  In Freedom we're born, &c. . . .
  Then join Hand in Hand brave AMERICANS all,
By uniting we stand, by dividing we fall;
IN so RIGHTEOUS a Cause let us hope to succeed,
For Heaven approves of each generous Deed. . . .
  All Ages shall speak with Amaze and Applause,
Of the Courage we'll shew in support of our LAWS;
To die we can bear—but to serve we disdain,
For Shame is to FREEDOM more dreadful than pain. . . .

AN ANONYMOUS WRITER: "AMERICA SHALL BLAST HER FIERCEST FOES"

When writers talked of separation from England, they did not necessarily assume that separation and bloodshed went hand in hand. The writer of this poem, however, did not rule out a bloody war but accepted that the loss of life would be worth what America would gain from independence from England.

Virginia Gazette (Williamsburg, Purdie), 19 May 1774

Thus we shall see, and triumph in the Sight,
While Malice frets and fumes, and gnaws her Chains;
AMERICA shall blast her fiercest Foes,
Shall brave the dismal Shocks of Bloody War,
And in unrivall'd Pomp resplendent rise,
And shine *sole* Empress of the WESTERN WORLD.

ISAIAH THOMAS: "A PARODY ON SHAKESPEARE"

Using the well-known to present new ideas was popular in colonial America. Here, printer Isaiah Thomas placed his ideas on separation in Hamlet's soliloquy, "To Be, or Not To Be." Thomas used the same speech to convey other patriotic ideas, too.

Massachusetts Spy (Boston), 14 August 1770

A PARODY on SHAKESPEAR.

BE taxt, or not be taxt, that is the question:
Whether 'tis nobler in our minds to suffer
The sleights and cunning of deceitful statesmen,
Or to petition 'gainst illegal taxes,
And by opposing them end them?—
To live, to act, no more, and fast asleep,
To say we and Assemblies, and the thousand
Liberties that Englishmen are heirs to,
'Tis a determination directly to be crush'd:
To live, to act, perchance to be all SLAVES,
Aye, there's the rub.

CANDIDUS: "THE SLAVERY ADMINISTERED ON US BY ENGLAND"

In the 1770s, ideas about freedom spread throughout America. Often, those who wrote of America's relationship with England discussed it in terms of slavery, which is what the anonymous Candidus did. He suggested that if the yoke of slavery could not be lifted from America, its citizens had the right to separate themselves from Britain.

Boston Gazette; and Country Journal, 7 October 1771

Is it impossible to form an idea of *slavery* more complete, more miserable, more *disgraceful*, than that of a people where justice is administer'd, government exercis'd, and a standing army maintain'd at the expense of the people, and yet without the least dependence upon them? If we can find no relief from this infamous situation,—I repeat it, *"if we can find* no relief from this infamous situation,—let the ministry, who have stripped us of our property and liberty deprive us of our understanding too; that, unconscious of what we have been or are, and ungoaded by tormenting reflections, we may tamely bow down our necks with all the stupid serenity of servitude to any drudgery which our lords and masters may please to command."—I appeal to the common sense of mankind to what a state of infamy and misery must a people be reduced! . . . Whenever the relentless enemies of America shall have completed their system, which they are still, though more silently pursuing, by subtle arts, deep dissimulation, and manners calculated to deceive, our condition will then be more humiliating and miserable, and perhaps more *inextricable too*, than that of the people of England in the infamous reigns of the Stuarts, which blackens the pages of history. . . .

Your's [*sic*],
CANDIDUS

JOSIAH QUINCY, JR.: "OBSERVATIONS ON THE TIMES IN BOSTON"

Josiah Quincy, Jr., was a lawyer, and he could hardly be considered a radical. After all, he defended Colonel Thomas Preston and the other British soldiers arrested following the Boston Massacre (see Chapter 21). In 1774 Quincy wrote a pamphlet, Observations on the Act of Parliament for Blocking up the Harbour of Boston. *In it, he stated that America should rid itself of the yoke of bondage—be free from a tyrannical government. This selection comes from an advertisement in the* Boston Gazette, *inserted by printers Benjamin Edes and John Gill to promote one of their own publications and their ideas of separation and liberty for America.*

Boston Gazette, and Country Journal, 16 May 1774

OBSERVATIONS ON THE ACT OF PARLIAMENT For Blocking up the Harbour of *Boston*; with THOUGHTS on civil society and STANDING ARMIES. By *JOSIAH QUINCY*, Jun. . . .

"*YET be not amused, my Countrymen!—the extirpation of bondage, and the re-establishment of freedom are not of easy acquisition. The worst passions of the human heart and the most subtle projects of the human mind are leagued against you; and principalities and powers have acceded to the combination. Trials and conflicts you must, therefore, endure;—hazards and jeopardies—of life and fortune—will attend the struggle. Such is the fate of all noble exertions for public liberty and social happiness.——Enter not the lists without thought and consideration, lest you arm with timidity and combat with irresolution. Having engaged in the conflict, let nothing discourage your vigour, or repel your perseverance:—Remember that submission to the yoke of bondage is the worst that can befall a people, after the most fierce and unsuccessful resistance. What can the misfortune of vanquishment take away, which despotism and rapine would spare? It had been easy . . . to repress the advances of tyranny, and prevent its establishment, but now it is established and grown to some height, it would be* MORE GLORIOUS *to demolish it.*

AN ANONYMOUS WRITER: "A NEW LIBERTY SONG"

John Dickinson penned a liberty song in 1768 (see above). Now, an anonymous writer added another liberty song to the repertoire of America's Patriots. In this song, the inevitability of war is assumed, but the

writer concludes that America has right on its side. The colonies' rights
will be protected when sensible people in England realize America is
serious about separation.

Massachusetts Spy Or, Thomas's Boston Journal, 3 November
1774

LIBERTY SONG.

Tune, Smile Britania.
YE Sons of Freedom smile!
    America unites!
And Friends in Britain's Isle
    Will vindicate our Rights;
In spite of Ga—e's hostile Train,
We will our Liberties maintain.
Boston be not dismay'd,
    Tho' Tyrants now oppress;
Tho' Fleets and Troops invade:
    You soon will have redress:
The resolutions of the brave
Will injur'd Massachusetts save. . . .
Our Charter-Rights we claim,
    Granted in ancient Times,
Since our Forefathers came
    First to these Western Climes:
Nor will their Sons degenerate,
They Freedom love—Oppression hate.
If Ga—e shou'd strike the Blow,
    We must for Freedom fight,
Undaunted Courage show,
    While we defend our Right:
In Spite of the oppressive Band,
Maintain the Freedom of the Land.

AN ANONYMOUS WRITER: "ALL THE WORLD SHALL KNOW,
AMERICANS ARE FREE"

After the Battles of Lexington and Concord and the other confrontations
in the early months of the Revolution, Americans based their patriotic
songs on the moral rights that they believed were theirs. This song evokes
that concept when it states that all the world will know that Americans
are free.

New-Hampshire Gazette and Historical Chronicle (Portsmouth),
12 September 1775

What! Can those British Tyrants think
    Our Fathers cross'd the main;
And savage Foes and Dangers met,
    To be enslav'd by them?
If so, they are mistaken,
    For we will rather die;
And since they have become our Foes,
    Their Forces we defy.
        And all the world shall know,
        Americans are free;
        Nor slaves nor cowards we will prove—
        Great Britain soon shall see.

QUESTIONS

1. What were the basic reasons for America to remain a part of the British Empire, according to the writers of the first three letters in this chapter?

2. Why did citizens such as those in White Plains, New York, feel it necessary to declare their loyalty to King George?

3. Why do you think the concept of slavery was so prominent in discussions of America's separation from England. How did writers use the slavery theme?

4. Why might those seeking separation and independence from England choose songs, poetry, and drama as the means of spreading their message? Think about the power of these forms of expression today as you answer this question.

5. What are the prevalent themes in the poetry of these readings?

NOTE

1. *Pennsylvania Chronicle, and Universal Advertiser* (Philadelphia), 15 February 1768.

CHAPTER 29

The Battles of Lexington and Concord, 1775

The colony of Massachusetts was not the only site of insurrection and hard feelings toward the British government in America, but for ten years Boston had served as the center for protest against nearly every action taken by England. Following the Boston Tea Party in 1773, England had saddled the colony with a series of punishments by passing acts that placed burdens upon all Massachusetts citizens.

The Boston Port Act, which closed the harbor to all shipping, was joined by parliamentary actions that forced Bostonians to house troops, changed the basic charter of the colony, and usurped much of the colony's control over its judicial system. Parliament even passed the Quebec Act, which essentially gave Canada control of lands from the Ohio River to the Mississippi River. Not only did the Quebec Act remove control of western territories from the colonies, it granted the thousands of French living in America's western territories the right to practice Roman Catholicism. Even though many Americans in the 1770s supported freedom of religion, few if any believed that such freedoms applied to Catholics (see Chapter 22). Catholicism was equated with intolerance, oppression, and warfare.

Taken together, Britain's actions against Massachusetts in particular and America in general in 1774 were viewed as intolerable, and Americans labeled all of these British laws as the Intolerable Acts. From Britain's point of view, the purpose of the acts was to punish Boston for such hostile actions as the Boston Tea Party and to coerce Americans into being obedient Britons.

King George III and others believed that Americans might revolt, but they believed the revolt would be small and probably confined to Massachusetts. Others, notably the British commander in America, Thomas Gage, thought otherwise. Having been stationed in Boston since a few months after the Boston Tea Party and serving as the colony's interim governor, Gage knew that support for Boston's actions was not confined to Massachusetts or even New England. He knew that Patriots were stockpiling weapons and gunpowder in magazines throughout the colonies, and he knew that the main storehouse for volatile Massachusetts was in Concord, a town about twenty miles from Boston.

Since he had arrived in Boston, Gage had been strategically maneuvering troops and ships in case of trouble. Now the general decided it was time to destroy the Concord supplies. On April 18, 1775, he ordered Colonel Francis Smith to take about 700 troops to go "with the utmost expedition and Secrecy to Concord." There, the troops were to seize and destroy "a Quantity of Ammunition, Provision, Artillery, Tents and small Arms, having been collected . . . for the Avowed Purpose of raising and supporting a Rebellion against His Majesty."[1]

Even though the British troops left Boston by ferry instead of marching out, their movement was observed, and messengers rode toward Lexington and Concord to warn of the approaching troops. The first shots of April 19 were fired before sunrise, and their importance quickly recognized. Just who fired first, the Americans or the British, was never determined, and it became fodder for speculation in newspapers. Printers produced newspapers on a weekly basis, and none were printed in Boston during the latter part of the week, except the *Boston News-Letter*. The paper gave no facts about the confrontations in Lexington and Concord, but it did accurately predict the questions that would surround the skirmishes and their repercussions. "The Reports concerning this unhappy Affair, and the Causes that concurred to bring on an Engagement," the *News-Letter* stated, "are so various, that we are not able to collect any Thing consistent or regular, and cannot therefore with certainty give our Readers any further Account of this shocking Introduction to all the Miseries of a Civil War."[2]

Even though the *Boston News-Letter* could not offer any facts surrounding what had happened in Lexington and Concord, reports were soon made available through handbills first, and then through the newspapers. The colonies were in rebellion, and in the weeks following the incidents at Lexington and Concord, that news spread down the Atlantic seaboard as printers announced the fact to their readers.

The writings supporting American actions at Lexington and Concord begin with the *Essex Gazette*'s extended explanation of the events of April 19 that appeared in the Salem, Massachusetts, newspaper six days later. Compare it with General Thomas Gage's letter recounting what happened at Lexington and Concord in the chapter's second section. The next American account of the fighting describes the day's events in less detail but offers an editorial interpretation of the British troops' "DESIGN of MURDER and ROBBERY!"

The next selection comes from a Tory newspaper, *Rivington's New-York Gazetteer*, which includes affidavits by American eyewitnesses. These reports were followed by a speech made by Tory Governor William Franklin of New Jersey and a letter written by General Thomas Gage, commander of the British troops in America.

The British interpretation of Lexington and Concord begins with Governor Franklin's speech. Its purpose was to reconcile Americans to British rule. The chapter closes with Gage's explanation of the events that occurred at Lexington and Concord. The principal issue was who initiated the fighting by firing the first shot. As one might suspect, the general placed the blame on the Americans. The American reports and affidavits placed the blame squarely upon the British. Also, Gage's letter describing the fighting, which was sent to Connecticut Governor Jonathan Trumbull, was written after many Patriot accounts of the battles had already appeared in colonial newspapers.

IN SUPPORT OF THE AMERICANS AT LEXINGTON AND CONCORD

AN ANONYMOUS REPORT: "BRITISH TROOPS COMMENCE HOSTILITIES"

News of Lexington and Concord may have spread faster by word of mouth than by newspapers because most newspapers in New England had already published for the week when the confrontations occurred. Most New England newspapers, therefore, had enough time to gather a sizable amount of information about Lexington and Concord before publishing an account of the event. The strongly pro-American Essex Gazette's *version blames British troops for starting the hostilities.*

Essex Gazette (Salem, Massachusetts), 25 April 1775

Last Wednesday, the 19th of April, the Troops of His Britannick Majesty commenced Hostilities upon the People of this Province, attended with Circumstances of Cruelty, not less brutal than what our venerable Ancestors received from the vilest Savages of the Wilderness. The Particulars relative to this interesting Event, by which we are involved in all the

Horrors of a civil War, we have endeavoured to collect as well as the present confused State of Affairs will admit.

On Tuesday Evening a Detachment from the Army, consisting, it is said, of 8 or 900 men, commanded by Lieut. Col. Smith, embarked at the Bottom of the Common in Boston, on board a Number of Boats, and landed at Phipps's Farm, a little way up Charles River, from whence they proceeded with Silence and Expedition on their way to Concord, about 18 Miles from Boston. The People were soon alarmed, and began to assemble in several Towns, before Day-Light, in order to watch the Motion of the Troops.

At Lexington, 6 Miles below Concord, a Company of Militia, of about 100 Men, mustered near the Meeting-House; the Troops came in Sight of them just before Sun-rise; and running within a few Rods of them, the Commanding Officer accosted the Militia in Words to this effect:—'Disperse, you Rebels—Damn you, throw down your Arms and disperse': Upon which the Troops huzza'd, and immediately one or two Officers discharged their Pistols, which were instantaneously followed by the Firing of 4 or 5 of the Soldiers, and then there seemed to be a general Discharge from the whole Body: Eight of our Men were killed, and nine wounded.

In a few Minutes after this Action the Enemy renewed their March for Concord; and which Place they destroyed several Carriages, Carriage Wheels, and about 20 Barrels of Flour, all belonging to the Province. Here about 150 Men going towards a Bridge, of which the Enemy were in Possession, the latter fired, and killed 2 of our Men, who then returned the Fire, and obliged the Enemy to retreat back to Lexington, where they met Lord Percy, with a large Reinforcement, with two Pieces of Cannon.

The Enemy now having a Body of about 1800 Men, made a Halt, picked up many of their Dead, and took Care of their wounded. . . .

In Lexington the Enemy set Fire to Deacon Joseph Loring's House and Barn, Mrs. Mulliken's House and Shop, and Mr. Joshua Bond's House and Shop, which were all consumed. They also set Fire to several other Houses, but our People extinguished the Flames. They pillaged almost every House they passed by, breaking and destroying Doors, Windows, Glasses, &c. and carrying off Cloathing and other valuable Effects. It appeared to be their Design to burn and destroy all before them; and nothing but our vigorous Pursuit prevented their infernal Purposes from being put in Execution. But the savage Barbarity exercised upon the Bodies of our unfortunate Brethren who fell, is almost incredible: Not contented with shooting down the unarmed, aged and infirm, they disregarded the Cries of the wounded, killing them without Mercy, and mangling their Bodies in the most shocking Manner.

We have the Pleasure to say, that notwithstanding the highest Provocations given by the Enemy, not one instance of Cruelty, that we have heard of, was committed by our victorious Militia; but, listening to the merciful Dictates of the Christian Religion, they 'breathed higher sentiments of humanity.' . . .

The public most sincerely sympathize with the friends and relations of our deceased brethren, who gloriously sacrificed their lives in fighting for the liberties of their Country. By their noble and intrepid conduct, in helping to defeat the forces of an ungrateful tyrant, they have endeared their memories to the present generation, who will transmit their names to posterity with the highest honour.

ISAIAH THOMAS: "FOREVER BEAR IN MIND THE BATTLE OF LEXINGTON"

Printer Isaiah Thomas and other Patriot printers were forced to flee Boston following the events at Lexington and Concord. Other printers in the city shut down operation and never again printed. Thomas moved his newspaper to Worcester, Massachusetts, and delivered this editorial in his first issue from there. Notice the inflammatory language and exaggeration he uses to introduce and interpret the events of April 19.

The Massachusetts Spy; or, American Oracle of Liberty
(Worcester, Massachusetts), 3 May 1775

AMERICANS! forever bear in mind the BATTLE of LEXINGTON!—where British Troops, unmolested and unprovoked, wantonly, and in a most inhuman manner fired upon and killed a number of our countrymen, then robbed them of their provisions, ransacked, plundered and burnt their houses! nor could the tears of defenceless women, some of whom were in the pains of childbirth, the cries of helpless babes, nor the prayers of old age, confined to beds of sickness, appease their thirst for blood!— or divert them from their DESIGN of MURDER and ROBBERY! . . .

A few days before the battle, the Grenadier and Light-Infantry companies were all drafted from the several regiments in Boston, and put under the command of an officer, and it was observed that most of the transports and other boats were put together, and fitted for immediate service. This manœuvre gave rise to a suspicion that some formidable expedition was intended by the soldiery, but what or where the inhabitants could not determine—however, the town watches in Boston, Charlestown, Cambridge, &c. were ordered to look well to the landing-places. About ten o'clock on the night of the 18th of April, the troops in Boston were discovered to be on the move in a very secret manner, and it was found they were embarking in boats (which they privately brought to the place in the evening) at the bottom of the Common; expresses set off immediately to alarm the country, that they might be on their guard. When the expresses got about a mile beyond Lexington, they were stopped by about fourteen officers on horseback, who came out of Boston in the afternoon of that day, and were seen lurking in the bye-places in the country till after dark. One of the expresses immediately fled, and was pursued two miles by an officer, who, when he had got up with him presented a pistol, and told him he was a dead man if he did not stop, but he rode on till he came up to a house, when stopping of a sudden his horse threw him off, having the presence of mind to halloo to the people in the house, *Turn out! Turn out! I have got one of them!* The officer immediately retreated and fled as fast as he had pursued. The other express, after passing through a strict examination, by some means got clear. The body of the troops in the meantime, under the command of Lieut. Colonel Smith had crossed the river and landed at Phipp's Farm." They immediately to the number of 1000 proceeded to Lexington, 6 miles below Concord, with great silence: A company of militia, of about 80 men, mustered near the meeting-house; the troops came in sight of them just before sun-rise; the militia upon seeing the troops began to disperse; the troops then set out upon the run, hallooing and huzzaing, and coming within a few rods of them, the commanding officer accosted the militia in words to this effect, *"Disperse you dam'd rebels!—damn you disperse!"* Upon which the troops again huzzaed, and immediately one or two officers discharged their pistols, which were instantaneously followed by the firing of four or five of the soldiers, and then there seemed to be a general discharge from the whole body; it is be noticed they

fired upon our people as they were dispersing, agreable to their command, and that we did not even return the fire: Eight of our men were killed and nine wounded;—the troops then laughed, and damned the Yankees, and said they could not bear the smell of gun-powder. A little after this the troops renewed their march to Concord, where, when they arrived, they divided into parties, and went directly to several places where the province stores were deposited. . . .

A young man, unarmed, who was taken prisoner by the enemy, and made to assist in carrying off their wounded, says, that he saw a barber who lives in Boston, thought to be one Warden, with the troops, and that he heard them say, he was one of their pilots; he likewise saw the said barber fire twice upon our people, and heard Earl Piercy order the troops to fire the houses. . . .

Immediately upon the return of the troops to Boston, all communication to and from the town was stopped by Gen. Gage. . . . The troops in Boston are fortifying the place on all sides, and a frigate of war is stationed up Cambridge river, and a sixty-four gun ship between Boston and Charlestown. . . .

They pillaged almost every house they pass'd by, breaking and destroying doors, windows, glasses, &c. and carring off cloathing and other valuable effects. It appeared to be their design to burn and destroy all before them; and nothing but our vigorous pusuit prevented their infernal purposes from being put in execution. But the savage barbarity exercised upon the bodies of our unfortunate brethren who fell, is almost incredible: Not content with shooting down the unarmed, aged and infirm, the disregarded the cries of the wounded, killing them without mercy, and mangling their bodies in the most shocking manner.

We have the pleasure to say, that not withstanding the highest provocations given by the enemy, not one instance of cruelty, that we have heard of, was committed by our Militia; but, listening to the merciful dictates of the Christian religion, they, "breathed higher sentiments of humanity."

JOHN PARKER: "THE BRITISH FIRED FIRST"

John Parker was the militia commander at Lexington. He, as well as numerous others present, offered affidavits as to who fired first and what occurred in Lexington and Concord. Parker's testimony, which appeared in several papers including the version here from James Rivington's Tory New-York Gazetteer, *put the blame squarely upon the British. Rivington ran the affidavits and followed them with a Tory speech on the events, an effort on Rivington's behalf to present balanced news on this critical event.*

Rivington's New-York Gazetteer; or Connecticut, New-Jersey,
Hudson's River, and Quebec Weekly Advertiser, 25 May 1775

PHILADELPHIA, MAY 13.
AFFIDAVITS and depositions relative to the commencement of the late hostilities in the province of Massachusetts-Bay. . . .
Lexington, April 25, 1775.
I JOHN PARKER, of lawful age, and commander of the militia in Lexington, do testify and declare, that on the 19th instant, in the morning, about one of the clock, being informed that there was a number of regular officers riding up and down the road, stopping and insulting people as they passed the road; and also was informed that a number of regular troops were on their march from Boston, in order to take the province stores at Concord; ordered our militia to meet on the common in said Lexington, to consult what to do, and concluded not to be discovered, nor meddle or make with said regular troops (if they should approach) unless they should insult or molest us, and upon their sudden approach I immediately ordered our militia to disperse and not to fire; immediately said troops made their appearance and rushed furiously, fired upon and

killed eight of our party, without receiving any provocation therefore from us.

IN SUPPORT OF THE BRITISH AT LEXINGTON AND CONCORD

WILLIAM FRANKLIN: "A RESOLUTION TO RESTORE HARMONY WITH GREAT BRITAIN"

William Franklin, the brother of Benjamin Franklin, was the governor of New Jersey and a staunch Tory. He made this speech to the New Jersey assembly following the affidavits of soldiers present at Lexington (an example of which appears at the end of the previous set of readings). Including Franklin's speech was part of printer James Rivington's effort to balance news of the outbreak of war for his readership, which included many Tories. Franklin called on the assembly to restore friendly relations with England.

Rivington's New-York Gazetteer; or Connecticut, New-Jersey, Hudson's River, and Quebec Weekly Advertiser, 25 May 1775

NEW-JERSEY, MAY 16.—
SPEECH of his Excellency WILLIAM FRANKLIN . . . Governor and Commander in Chief, in and over the Province of NEW-JERSEY. . . .
Gentlemen of the General Assembly.

THE sole occasion of my calling you together at this time is to lay before you a resolution of the House of Commons wisely and humanely calculated to open a door to the restoration of that harmony between Great-Britain and her American colonies on which their mutual welfare and happiness so greatly depend. . . .

His Majesty, ardently wishing to see a reconciliation of the unhappy difference by every means through which it may be obtained without prejudice to the just authority of Parliament, which his Majesty will never suffer to be violated, has approved the resolution of his faithful Commons, and has commanded it to be transmitted to the governors of his colonies, not doubting that this happy disposition to comply with every just and reasonable wish of the King's subjects in America will meet with such a return of duty and affection on their part as will lead to a happy issue of the present dispute, and to re-establishment of the public tranquility on those grounds of equity, justice and moderation which this resolution holds forth.

THOMAS GAGE: "OFFICIAL REPORT—LEXINGTON AND
CONCORD"

*In 1774 General Thomas Gage was appointed governor and military
commander of Massachusetts. Decidedly unpopular in Boston because
of his strict enforcement of the closing of Boston's port and other laws
aimed at punishing patriotic Boston, he ordered troops to find the Patriots' storehouses of military supplies. This news report is his version
of the events that led up to the battles Lexington and Concord and the
events of April 19. Gage lays the blame for the first shots being fired on
the Americans.*

New England Chronicle: or, the Essex Gazette (Salem,
Massachussets), 18 May 1775

ON Tuesday the 18th of April, about half past ten at night, Lieut. Col.
Smith of the 10th regiment, embarked from the Common at Boston, with
the grenadiers and light infantry of the troops there, and landed on the
opposite side, from whence he began his march towards Concord. . . .

The Colonel called his officers together, and gave orders that the
troops should not fire, unless fired upon; and after marching a few miles,
detached six companies of light infantry, under the command of Major
Pitcairn, to take possession of two bridges on the other side of Concord:
Soon after they heard many signal guns, and the ringing of alarm bells
repeatedly, which convinced them that the country was rising to oppose
them, and that it was a preconcerted scheme to oppose the King's troops,
whenever there should be a favourable opportunity for it. . . .

About three o'clock the next morning, the troops being advanced
within two miles of Lexington, intelligence was received, that about five
hundred men in arms, were assembled, and determined to oppose the
King's troops; and on Major Pitcairn's galloping up to the head of the
advanced companies, two officers informed him, that a man . . . had presented his musket, and attempted to shoot them, but the piece flashed
in the pan: On this, the Major gave directions to the troops to move
forward, but on no account to fire, nor even to attempt it without orders.
When they arrived at the end of the village, they observed about two
hundred armed men, drawn up on a green, and when the troops came
within a hundred yards of them, they began to file off towards some stone
walls, on their right flank: The light infantry observing this, ran after
them; the Major instantly called to the soldiers not to fire, but to surround and disarm them; some of them who had jumped over a wall, then
fired four or five shot at the troops, wounded a man of the 10th regiment,
and the Major's horse in two places, and at the same time several shots
were fired from a meeting house on the left: Upon this, without any order
or regularity, the light infantry began a scattered fire, and killed several

of the country people; but were silenced as soon as the authority of their officers could make them. . . .

After this, Col. Smith marched up with the remainder of the detachment, and the whole body proceeded to Concord . . . but vast numbers of armed people were seen assembling on all the heights . . . and fired upon the King's troops, killed three men, wounded four officers, one serjeant, and four private men. . . . [W]hen Captain Parsons returned with the three companies over the bridge, they observed three soldiers on the ground, one of them scalped, his head much mangled, and his ears cut off, though not quite dead; a sight which struck the soldiers with horror; Captain Parsons marched on and joined the main body, who were only waiting for his coming up, to march back to Boston; Colonel Smith had executed his orders, without opposition, by destroying all the military stores he could find; both the Colonel and major Pitcairn, having taken all possible pains to convince the inhabitants that no injury was intended them, and that if opened their doors when required, to search for said stores, not the slightest mischief should be done; neither had any of the people the least occasion to complain, but they were sulky, and one of them even struck Major Pitcairn. . . . As soon as the troops had got out of the town of Concord, they received a heavy fire from all sides, from walls, fences, houses, trees, barns, &c. which continued without intermission. . . . Notwithstanding their numbers, they did not attack openly during the whole day, but kept under cover on all occasions The troops were very much fatigued, the greater part of them having been under arms all night. . . .

The troops had above fifty killed, and many more wounded: Reports are various about the loss sustained by the country people, some make it very considerable, others not so much.

Thus this unfortunate affair has happened through the rashness and imprudence of a few people, who began firing on the troops at Lexington.

QUESTIONS

1. The news accounts of Lexington discussed who fired first. How much difference do you think it mattered who initiated the hostilities? Explain.

2. Why do you think both news accounts included graphic descriptions of death and mutilation?

3. Why might accuracy in the *Massachusetts Spy* version of the battles be less important than in the other accounts? Explain.

4. Why might a printer such as James Rivington, who was considered to be pro-British, feel compelled to run affidavits that placed the blame for Lexington and Concord squarely upon the British?

5. Why do you think William Franklin worked so hard to bridge the differences between the colonies and the crown?

NOTES

1. Allen French, *General Gage's Informers: New Material upon Lexington and Concord* (Ann Arbor: Michigan University Press, 1932), 31–32.

2. *Boston News-Letter*, 20 April 1775.

CHAPTER 30

Thomas Paine Publishes
Common Sense, 1776

"*Common Sense* was the work of an 'original genius,'" an unknown writer calling himself "An Independent Whig" declared in the *New-York Journal; or the General Advertiser* on February 22, 1776. Whether Thomas Paine's pamphlet, published anonymously on January 10, 1776, was the work of a genius is not as important as the influence the tract had on Americans. Even though America and Britain had been in open confrontation since April 1775, many Americans were still unsure about whether a war with Britain and independence were the right courses to pursue. One month after its publication, *Common Sense* had sold a half million copies and was in its third printing.[1] In it, Paine advocated as "common sense" a complete separation from England via a declaration of independence. These ideas grew in popularity.

Common Sense motivated Americans. "I find Common Sense is working a powerful change in the minds of men," George Washington said.[2] The commander in chief was correct. Paine had taken ideas current in America and succinctly structured them into a logical argument against continuing as colonies to Great Britain subservient to the monarchy. Within six months of the publication of *Common Sense*, the American colonies had declared their independence from England and were ready to face the world as a sovereign nation.

For Thomas Paine, the transformation from Englishman to rebellious colonist happened quickly. After talking to Benjamin Franklin in London, Paine emigrated to America with a letter of recommendation from the renowned Pennsylvania doctor. In America, Paine got a job working for the *Pennsylvania Magazine*, which began publication in January 1775. Paine quickly felt empathy for the American cause, and in October he suggested, in a writing condemning the growing British slave trade in the colonies, that independence was God's will for America. "I hesitate not for a moment," Paine wrote in a letter he signed Humanus and published in the *Pennsylvania Journal* on October 18, 1775, "to believe that the Almighty will finally separate America from Britain. Call it independence or what you will, if it is the cause of God and humanity it will go on."

Paine believed strongly enough in the American cause to volunteer for service in the colonial army. While serving with Washington's troops in December 1776, he penned the first in a series called "The American Crisis." The crisis papers were designed to bolster the sagging morale of American soldiers. The first sentence of the first crisis paper, "These are the times that try men's souls," became one of the most repeated statements in America.

Even though *Common Sense* may have been the single largest factor in pushing America toward independence, Paine's ideas were not universally accepted. A number of writers attacked the reasoning in *Common Sense*. Paine's chief antagonist was the Provost of the College of Philadelphia, William Smith. Writing under the pseudonym Cato, Smith launched a series of letters, "To the People of Pennsylvania," which refuted Paine's rationale for American independence. Paine replied directly to Smith through a series of four letters written with the name The Forester. Others joined in the debate, which continued into May and June of 1776 setting the stage for Richard Henry Lee's call for American independence from England on June 7 on the floor of the Continental Congress (see Chapter 25).

The readings by Paine begin with excerpts from *Common Sense* that were published in the *Virginia Gazette*. The second selection is from the first Forester letter. In it, Paine answers Cato's first four letters. The final Paine writing is the first American Crisis circular.

The reading opposing Paine and *Common Sense* comes from Smith's fourth letter "To the People of Pennsylvania." In this letter, Smith refers to Paine's pamphlet as "common nonsense." It was after this letter that Paine began to write as The Forester.

IN SUPPORT OF THOMAS PAINE'S *COMMON SENSE*

THOMAS PAINE: "COMMON SENSE"

Common Sense *was a pamphlet, but some printers took excerpts from it to create newspaper articles. Williamsburg printer John Pinkney pulled what he considered the essence of Paine's work to print in his* Virginia Gazette.

Virginia Gazette (Williamsburg, Pinkney), 3 February 1776

EXTRACTS from a most excellent pamphlet, lately published, and addressed to the Americans, *entitled, COMMON SENSE.*

HOWEVER strange it may appear to some, or however unwilling they may be to think so, matters not, but many strong and striking reasons may be given to shew that nothing can settle our affairs so expeditiously as an open and determined declaration for independence. Some of which are:

First. It is the custom of nations, when any two are at war, for some other powers, not engaged in the quarrel, to step in as mediators, and bring about the preliminaries of a peace. . . .

Secondly. It is unreasonable to suppose that France or Spain will give us any kind of assistance if we mean only to make use of that assistance for the purpose of repairing the breach, and strengthening the connection, between Britain and America. . . .

Thirdly. While we profess ourselves the subjects of Britain, we must, in the eye of foreign nations, be considered as rebels. . . .

Fourthly. Were a manifesto to be published, and dispatched to foreign courts, setting forth the miseries we have endured, and the peaceable methods we have ineffectually used for redress, declaring, at the same time, that not being able any longer to live happily or safely, under cruel disposition of the British court, we had been driven to the necessity of breaking off all connections with her; at the same time assuring all such courts of our peaceable disposition towards them, and of our desire of entering into trade with them. Such a memorial would produce more good effects to this continent than if a ship were freighted with petitions to Britain.

Under our present denomination of British subjects we can neither be received nor heard abroad; the custom of all courts is against us, and will be so, until, by an independence, we take rank with other nations. . . .

I challenge the warmest advocate for reconciliation to shew a single advantage that this continent can reap by being connected with Great Britain. I repeat this challenge; not a single advantage is derived. Our corn will fetch its price in any market in Europe, and our imported goods must be paid for, buy them where we will.

But the injuries and disadvantages we sustain by that connection are without number, and our duty to mankind at large, as well as to ourselves, instruct us to renounce the alliance, because any submission to, or dependence on Great Britain, tends directly to involve this continent in European wars and quarrels. As Europe is our market for trade, we ought to form no political connection with any part of it. It is the true interest of America to steer clear of European contentions, which she can never do while, by her dependence on Britain, she is made the make-weight in the scale of British politics.

Every thing that is right or reasonable pleads for separation. The blood of the slain, the weeping voice of nature, cries *'tis time to part*.

O ye that love mankind! ye that dare oppose not only the tyranny, but the tyrant stand forth. Every spot of the old world is over-run with op-pression. Freedom hath been hunted round the globe. Asia and Africa have long expelled her. Europe regards her like a strange, and England hath given her warning to depart. O! receive the fugitive, and prepare in time an asylum for mankind.

THE FORESTER: "REPLY TO CATO"

Thomas Paine defended attacks on Common Sense *by writing a series of letters using the Forester pseudonym. Cato was the name used by William Smith, provost of the College of Philadelphia. Paine believed that the Cato series was wrong because it advocated reconciliation with England, and Paine felt the events of the past months made that im-possible.*

Pennsylvania Journal; and the Weekly Advertiser (Philadelphia),
3 April 1775

To Cato

TO BE *nobly wrong* is more manly than to be *meanly right*. Only let the error be disinterested—let it wear *not the mask*, but the *mark* of prin-ciple, and 'tis pardonable. It is on this large and liberal ground, that we distinguish between men and their tenets, and generously preserve our friendship for the one, while we combat with every prejudice of the other. But let not Cato take this compliment to himself; he stands excluded from the benefit of the distinction; he deserves it not. . . .

Four letters have already appeared under the specious name of Cato. What pretensions the writer of them can have to the signature, the public will be determine. . . . The moment he explains his terms of reconcilia-tion the typographical Cato dies. If they be calculated to please the Cab-inet they will not go down with the colonies: and if they be suited to the colonies they will be rejected by the Cabinet: The line of the no-variation is yet unfound; and, like the philosopher's stone, doth not exist. "I am bold," says Cato, "to declare and yet hope to make it evident to every honest man, that the true interest of America lies in *reconciliation* with Great Britain on *constitutional principles*."

This is a curious way of lumping the business indeed! And Cato may as well attempt to catch lions in a mousetrap as to hope to allure the public with such general and unexplained expressions. It is now a mere

bugbear to talk of *reconciliation* on *constitutional principles* unless the terms of the first be produced and the sense of the other be defined; and unless he this he does nothing. . . .

Cato, by way of stealing into credit, says, "that the contest we are engaged in is founded on the most noble and virtuous principles which can animate the mind of man. We are contending (says he) against an arbitrary ministry for the rights of Englishmen." No, Cato, we are *now* contending against an arbitrary king to get clear of his tyranny. While the dispute rested in words only, it might be called "contending with the ministry," but since it is broken out into open war, it is high time to have done with such silly and water-gruel definitions. . . . Alas poor Cato! . . .

For the present, Sir, farewell. I have seen thy soliloquy and despise it. Remember thou has thrown me the glove, Cato, and either thee or I must tire. I fear not the field of fair debate, but thou hast stepped aside and made it personal. Thou hast tauntingly called on me by name; and if I cease to hunt thee *from* every lane and lurking hole of mischief, and bring thee not a trembling culprit before the public bar, then brand me with reproach, by naming me the list of your confederates.   THE FORESTER.

COMMON SENSE: "THE CRISIS"

In December 1776, Britain held the upper hand in the fighting for America. British troops and ships had successfully burned ports and captured vital cities. Paine enlisted in the army and joined George Washington's troops, who were fleeing across New Jersey. While seated at a campfire, Paine wrote the first in "The Crisis" series on the head of a drum and signed it Common Sense. Washington ordered it read to his troops. Soon, all Americans had the opportunity to read Paine's essay when the printers reproduced it. Paine added three more installments of "The Crisis" in 1777.

Dunlap's Pennsylvania Packet (Philadelphia), 27 December 1776

THESE are the times that try men's souls. The summer soldier and the sunshine patriot will, in this crisis, shrink from the service of their country; but he that stands it *now*, deserves the love and thanks of man and woman. Tyranny, like hell, is not easily conquered; yet we have this consolation with us, that the harder the conflict, the more glorious the triumph. What we obtain too cheap, we esteem too lightly: it is dearness only that gives every thing its value. Heaven knows how to put a proper price upon its goods; and it would be strange indeed if so celestial an article as FREEDOM should not be highly rated. Britain, with an army to enforce her tyranny, has declared that she has a right (*not only to tax*) but "to BIND *us in* ALL CASES WHATSOEVER," as if being *bound in that man-*

ner, is not slavery, then is there not such a thing as slavery upon earth. Even the expression is impious; for so unlimited a power can belong only to God. . . .

I call not upon a few, but upon all: not on *this* state or *that* state, but on every state: up and help us; lay your shoulders to the wheel; better have too much force than too little, when so great an object is at stake. Let it be told to the future world, that in the depth of winter, when nothing but hope and virtue could survive, that the city and the country, alarmed at one common danger, came forth to meet and to repulse it. . . . It matters not where you live, or what rank of life you hold, the evil or the blessing will reach you all. The far and the near, the home counties and the back, the rich and the poor, will suffer or rejoice alike. The heart that feels not now is dead; the blood of his children will curse his cowardice, who shrinks back at a time when a little might have saved the whole, and made them happy. I love the man that can smile in trouble, that can gather strength from distress, and grow brave by reflection. . . .

There are cases which cannot be overdone by language, and this is one. There are persons, too, who see not the full extent of the evil which threatens them; they solace themselves with hopes that the enemy, if he succeed, will be merciful. It is the madness of folly, to expect mercy from those who have refused to do justice; and even mercy, where conquest is the object, is only a trick of war; the cunning of the fox is as murderous as the violence of the wolf, and we ought to guard equally against both.

COMMON SENSE.

IN OPPOSITION TO THOMAS PAINE'S *COMMON SENSE*

CATO: "TO THE PEOPLE OF PENNSYLVANIA"

Cato, the pseudonym of the College of Pennsylvania Provost William Smith, was long used to represent the name of freedom among English-speaking people. Dating to the early years of the eighteenth century, the British advocates of free press, John Trenchard and Thomas Gordon, signed their essays Cato. Americans quickly copied the practice whenever discussing issues of freedom. Smith believed Common Sense *steered America along the wrong course. He believed that Paine was an agitator who wanted war. Smith believed the best course for America lay in reconciliation and peace with England. Paine's ideas were not common sense to Smith, but common nonsense.*

New-York Gazette; and the Weekly Mercury, 8 April 1776

TO THE PEOPLE OF PENNSYLVANIA.
LETTER IV.

The authors—or (if I must say) author of what is called *Common Sense*, has certainly had fair play. Full time has been allowed him by the sale of his pamphlet to reap the fruits of his labours, and gratify that avidity with which many are apt to devour doctrines that are out of the common way—bold, marvellous, and flattering. What was intended as a compliment to the publick—to give them time to gaze with their own eyes, and reason with their own faculties, upon this extraordinary appearance—the author's vanity has construed wholly in his own favour. . . . If what is called *Common Sense* be really *common sense*, it is invulnerable, and every attack upon it will but add to the author's triumph. If it should be proved, in any instances to be *nonsense*, millions will be interested in the discovery; and to them I appeal. . . .

One side of a great question has been held up to us. We are told that it can never be our interest to have any future connection with *Great Britain*, and are pressed immediately to declare our total separation; for now is the time and the time has found us. Could it be expected that all *America* would instantly take a leap in the dark? or that any who had not a predilection for the doctrine, or were capable of reasoning upon it, would swallow it in the gross, without wishing to hear the arguments on the other side? I am sure this is the wish of multitudes of good men— particularly of those who may be principally concerned in deciding the question, and whose earnest desire it is not only to know the sense of individuals, but the clear sense of their country upon it; without which, they could not think themselves at liberty to give their decision. . . .

In my remarks in the pamphlet before me, I shall first consider those arguments on which the author appears to lay his chief stress; and these are collected under four heads, in his conclusion:

"It is the custom of nations, when any two are at war, for some other Powers, not engaged in the quarrel, to step in as mediators, and bring about the preliminaries of peace. But while *America* calls herself a subject of *Great Britain*, no Power, however well disposed she may be, can offer her mediation."

Is this *common sense* or common nonsense? Surely peace with *Great Britain* cannot be the object of this writer, after the horrible character he has given us of the people of that country, and telling us that reconciliation with them would be ruin. The latter part of the paragraph seems to cast some light upon the former, although it contradicts it; for these mediators are not to interfere for making up the quarrel, but to widen it, by supporting us in a declaration that we are not subjects of *Great Britain*. A new sort of business, truly, for mediators!

But this leads us directly to the main inquiry, What foreign Powers are able to give us this support? Whether they can be persuaded to engage with us? What will be their terms? Is an alliance with them safe; or is it to be preferred to an honourable and firm renewal of that ancient connection under which we have so long flourished? . . .

Not a word shall be drawn from me to discredit our own strength or resources: although the accounts given of them by the author of *Common Sense* appear incredible to some, I will even go beyond him in expressing my good opinion of our situation. He thinks foreign assistance necessary to us. I think we should be injured by it. We are able to defend our own rights, and to frustrate the attempt of any nation upon earth to govern us by force. For my part, I would risk my all in resisting every attempt of this kind at every hazard.

But let us see what assistance he offers us: and we find *France* and *Spain* held out for that purpose, although not as mediators to "strengthen the connection between *Great Britain* and *America*," but wholly to dissolve it.

As to *Spain*, it is well known that the Government of her own unwieldy Colonies is already a weight which she can hardly bear. . . . But our author mentions *France*, as well as *Spain*, and thus proposes that both branches of the *Bourbon* family, so long the terrour of Protestants and freemen, should now join as their protectors. By what means, or at what price, is this marvellous revolution in the system of politicks, religion, and liberty, to be accomplished? How are these two Powers to divide these Colonies between them? Is their guardianship to be joint or separate? Under whose wing is *Pennsylvania* to fall—that of the most Catholick, or most Christian King? . . .

And of all nations in the world, *France* is the last from which we should seek assistance, even if it were necessary. What kind of assistance do we expect from her? Gold and silver she can but ill afford to give us; her men we have no occasion for; and, in a word, until she has a fleet able to contend with that of *England*, she can do us no essential service. . . . Can any Protestant—can you, my countrymen, ever wish to see her possessed of such a fleet, assist her in attaining it, or willingly give her footing in *America*? Would she then be contented to be the humble ally of these Colonies; or would she not, in her own right, resume *Canada*, which, according to the limits she formerly claimed, is larger than all our Provinces together? . . .

This consideration is truly alarming; and *France* has never shown herself so worth of confidence among the nations of *Europe*. . . . It could scarce have been imagined that the author of *Common Sense*, after telling us that "the blood of the slain, the weeping voice of nature, cries, 'tis time to part"—eternally to part—from the limited monarchy of *Great Britain*, (whatever future terms might be offered us,) would so soon have recommended to us a new alliance with the arbitrary monarchs of *France* and *Spain*. Bloody massacres, the revocation of sacred edicts, and the most unrelenting persecutions, have certainly taught *American* Protestants . . . what sort of faith we are to expect from Popish Princes, and from nations who are strangers to liberty themselves, and envy the enjoyment of it to others.

In short, I am not able, with all the pains I have taken, to understand what is meant by a Declaration of Independence; unless it is to be drawn up in the form of a solemn abjuration of *Great Britain*, as a nation with which we can never more be connected. And this seems the doctrine of the author of *Common Sense*. But I believe he has made but few converts to this part of his scheme; for who knows to what vicissitudes of fortune we may yet be subjected? . . .

We have long flourished under our Charter Government. What may be the consequences of another form we cannot pronounce with certainty; but this we know, that it is a road we have not travelled, and may be worse than it is described.   CATO.

QUESTIONS

1. According to *Common Sense*, why should America declare its independence from England?

2. Why did Paine believe that reconciliation with England was impossible?

3. Communication can use logic and/or emotion to persuade. Which do you think is best used in "The American Crisis"? Why?

4. According to Cato, what are the problems with the reasoning of *Common Sense*?

NOTES

1. Mary Margaret Roberts, "Introduction: Paine's *Common Sense*," in *Pamphlets and the American Revolution: Rhetoric, Politics, Literature, and the Popular Press*, ed. G. Jack Gravlee and James R. Irvine (Delmar, N.Y.: Scholars' Facsimiles & Reprints, 1976), i.

2. Quoted in Wm. David Sloan and Julie Hedgepeth Williams, *The Early American Press, 1690–1783* (Westport, Conn.: Greenwood Press, 1994), 172.

CHAPTER 31

The Declaration of Independence, 1776

When the bells announcing the new year rang on January 1, 1776, America and Britain had been at war for nearly nine months, and reconciliation between the colonies and the mother country seemed unlikely. Many Americans had for years believed that America should separate itself from England (see Chapter 28), but most who believed, for example, that America should have its own constitution and pass its own laws still envisioned America as part of the British commonwealth.

January 1776, however, brought more than just more hostilities between the colonies and England. On January 10, Thomas Paine published the pamphlet *Common Sense* (see Chapter 30), in which he not only advocated total separation from Great Britain but also urged the colonies to declare their independence from England. In May, the Virginia Convention took the first step on the road to all colonies declaring their independence when it adopted the Virginia Declaration of Rights. Written by George Mason, the document stated,

That all men are by nature equally free and independent and have certain inherent rights . . . namely, the enjoyment of life and liberty, with the means of acquiring and possessing property, and pursuing and obtaining happiness and safety. . . . And that, when any government shall be found inadequate or contrary to these purposes, a majority of the community has an indubitable, inalienable, and indefeasible right to reform, alter, or abolish it, in such a manner as shall be judged most conducive to the public weal.[1]

At least seven other colonies before month's end declared that should the American colonies agree to declare their independence from England, they would support the decision.

In Philadelphia, the Continental Congress began to take steps toward declaring independence. The congress was comprised of delegates from all the colonies except Georgia. They met in the Fall of 1775 in Philadelphia to seek a solution to the continuing difficulties with the British government. The delegation passed resolutions allowing colonists to outfit privateers to seize ships belonging to enemies of the colonies and opening American ports to other nations. In May, the congress passed a resolution allowing colonies to establish their own governments. Finally, in June, Virginia delegate Richard Henry Lee spoke these words, "Resolved: That these United Colonies are, and of right ought to be free and independent States, that they are absolved from all allegiances to the British Crown, and that all political connection between them and the State of Great Britain is, and ought to be, totally dissolved."[2] The motion was seconded, but consideration of the bill was postponed until July 1.

The Congress appointed a group to look into preparing such a declaration: the Committee of Five, composed of Thomas Jefferson, John Adams, Benjamin Franklin, Robert R. Livingston, and Roger Sherman. The committee members assigned the duties of writing the document to Thomas Jefferson. Using concepts he drew from the Virginia Declaration of Rights, Jefferson prepared the Declaration of Independence and gave it to Adams and Franklin to edit. When the Continental Congress was back in session, the delegates of twelve colonies unanimously approved the Declaration on July 4, 1776. The New York delegation, which could not officially vote on the document because it had not been given the power to do so by the colony, officially approved the Declaration of Independence on July 9.

Echoing the words of his fellow Virginian George Mason, Jefferson proclaimed and the colonies assented to the dissolution of ties between the American colonies and England:

We hold these truths to be self-evident, that all men are created equal, that they are endowed by their Creator with certain unalienable Rights, that among these are Life, Liberty, and the pursuit of Happiness. . . . That whenever any Form of Government becomes destructive of these ends, it is the Right of the People to alter or to abolish it, and to institute new Government, having its foundation on such principles and organizing its powers in such form, as to them shall seem most likely to effect their Safety and Happiness. . . . We, therefore . . . solemnly publish and declare, That these United Colonies are, and of Right ought to be Free and Independent States; that they are Absolved from all Allegiance to the British Crown, and that all political connection between them and the State of Great Britain, is and ought to be totally dissolved.

The articles, letters, and essays supporting independence begin with an unsigned letter, written in 1773, probably by Samuel Adams. Adams, perhaps the most fiery of all Patriots, started pushing for independence shortly after the passage of the Townshend Acts in 1767. Even though Adams proposed the formation of an independent commonwealth, he was still willing—at least in 1773—to consider that America remain a part of England.

The second selection outlines the benefits of independence from Britain. It is followed by a letter written by Thomas Paine using the pseudonym The Forester. Paine wrote this series of letters to answer the attacks made on *Common Sense* by William Smith, provost of the College of Philadelphia, who used the name Cato. The next entry is a news story from Williamsburg calling for the drafting of a declaration of rights and independence from England. The final selection in this part of the chapter offers colonial response to the adoption of the Declaration of Independence.

The readings in the chapter opposing independence all appeared before the adoption of the Declaration of Independence. By July 1776, few media outlets that supported the Tory cause existed. Even those with Tory leanings, such as the *New-York Gazette*, hailed the Declaration of Independence. The first selection opposing independence, from Fairfield, Connecticut, is a statement made by 141 freeholders unwilling to support any move toward making America an independent country. The next selection, from New Jersey, requests that the colony's representatives to the Continental Congress not vote for independence.

The third letter was written by William Smith, the provost of the College of Philadelphia under the pseudonym Cato. Smith opposed any separation from England before the Declaration of Independence but supported the split after it occurred. The Cato pseudonym had long been used in England and America to signify the right to speak one's opinion on controversial subjects. This letter is part of Smith's attack on Thomas Paine's *Common Sense*. Written in the spring of 1776, it states that those pushing so hard for independence from England were doing so for personal reasons. Part of Paine's reply to Smith is included in the first set of chapter readings under the pseudonym The Forester.

IN SUPPORT OF INDEPENDENCE

AN ANONYMOUS WRITER: "AN AMERICAN COMMONWEALTH"

Boston was the center of dissent to English rule in America, and the Boston Gazette, *the prime voice of Patriots in the city, facilitated the protest. Samuel Adams was probably the best of the agitators, and he probably wrote this unsigned essay. Nearly three years before the Declaration of Independence, it called for independent American states and an American commonwealth.*

Boston Gazette, and Country Journal, 11 October 1773

How shall the Colonies force their oppressors to proper terms? This question has often been answered, already by our politicians: 'Form an independent state,' 'AN AMERICAN COMMONWEALTH.' This plan has been proposed, and I can't find that any other is likely to answer the great purpose of preserving our liberties. I hope, therefore, it will be well digested and forwarded, to be in due time put into execution, unless our political fathers can secure American liberties in some other way. As the population, wealth, and power of this continent are swiftly increasing, we certainly have no cause to doubt our success in maintaining liberty by forming a commonwealth, or whatever measure wisdom may point out for the preservation of the rights of America.

AN ANONYMOUS WRITER: "THE BENEFITS OF INDEPENDENCE"

In the months following the Battles of Lexington and Concord (see Chapter 29), many Americans realized that reconciliation and peace with England were impossible. They also understood that the wealth of America, if allowed to be developed by Americans, could make America a powerful player on the world stage. In this unsigned letter, the writer points out the benefits America would receive from being independent from England.

Pennsylvania Evening Post (Philadelphia), 17 February 1776

What will be the probable benefits of independence? A free and unlimited trade; a great accession of wealth, and a proportionable rise in the value of land; the establishment, gradual improvement and perfection of manufactures and science; a vast influx of foreigners, encouraged by the mildness of a free, equal, and tolerating government to leave their native countries, and settle in these Colonies; an astonishing encrease of our people from the present stock. Where encouragement is given to industry, where liberty and property are well secured, where the poor may easily find subsistence, and the middling rank comfortably support their families by labour, there the inhabitants must enrease rapidly; to some of these causes we owe the doubling of our numbers in somewhat more than twenty-five years. If such hath been the progress of population under the former restraints on our trade and manufactures, a population still more rapid may be reasonably expected when these restraints come to be taken off. . . . WE CANNOT PAY TOO GREAT A PRICE FOR LIBERTY,

AND POSTERITY WILL THINK INDEPENDENCE A CHEAP PURCHASE AT
EIGHTEEN MILLIONS.

THE FORESTER: "THE TIME OF RECONCILIATION IS PAST"

*The Forester was Thomas Paine's pseudonym for a series of letters he
wrote defending his pamphlet* Common Sense. *In this letter, he states
that America and Britain can no longer exist in the relationship they
once had. Instead, he pushes for the organization of an independent
American government.*

Pennsylvania Journal; and the Weekly Advertiser (Philadelphia),
24 April 1776

. . . TO THE PEOPLE.

IT is not a time to triffle. Men, who know they deserve nothing from
their country, and whose hope is on the arm that hath sought to enslave
ye, may hold out to you, as Cato hath done, the false light of reconciliation—There is no such thing. 'Tis gone! 'Tis past!—The grave hath
parted us—and death, in the persons of the slain, hath cut the thread of
life between Britain and America.

Conquest, and not reconciliation is the plan of Britain. . . . *we will
make peace with you as with enemies, but we will never re-unite with
you as friends. . . .*

Can this continent be happy under the government of Great-Britain or
not? . . . [C]an she be happy under a government of our own? To live
beneath the authority of those whom we cannot love, is misery, slavery,
or what name you please. In that case, there will never be peace. Security
will be a thing unknown, because, a treacherous friend in power, is the
most dangerous of enemies. The answer to the . . . question, can America
be happy under a government of her own, is short and simple, viz. as
happy as she please; she hath a blank sheet to write upon. Put it not off
too long. . . .

The FORESTER.

VIRGINIA CONVENTION: "CALL FOR A CONFEDERATION OF
COLONIES"

*Virginia's Patriot leaders pushed as hard as any group in America for
independence in 1776. In May, they issued a set of resolves calling for
America to declare itself free and independent states. The delegates, under the guidance of George Mason, produced the Virginia Declaration
of Rights, which Thomas Jefferson used as a guide in writing the Declaration of Independence.*

Virginia Gazette (Williamsburg, Purdie), 17 May 1776

FORASMUCH as all the endeavours of the UNITED COLONIES, by the most decent representations and petitions to the king and parliament of Great Britain, to restore peace and security to America under the British government, and a re-union with that people upon just and liberal terms, instead of a redress of grievances, have produced, from an imperious and vindictive administration, increased insult, oppression, and a vigorous attempt to effect our total destruction. By a late act, all these colonies are to be in rebellion, and out of the protection of the British crown, our properties subjected to confiscation, our people, when captivated, compelled to join in the murder and plunder of their relations and countrymen, and all former rapine and oppression of Americans declared legal and just. Fleets and armies are raised, and the aid of foreign troops engaged to assist these destructive purposes. . . . In this state of extreme danger, we have no alternative left but an abject submission to the will of those overbearing tyrants, or a total separation from the crown and government of Great Britain, uniting and exerting the strength of all America for defence, and forming alliances with foreign powers for commerce and aid in war: Wherefore appealing to the SEARCHER OF HEARTS for the sincerity of former declarations, expressing our desire to preserve the connexion with that nation, and that we are driven from that inclination by their wicked councils, and the external laws of self-preservation,

RESOLVED, unanimously, that the delegates appointed to represent this colony in General Congress be instructed to propose that respectable body TO DECLARE THE UNITED COLONIES FREE AND INDEPENDENT STATES, absolved from all allegiance to, or dependence upon, the crown or parliament of Great Britain; and that they give the assent of this colony to such declaration, and to whatever measures may be thought proper and necessary by the Congress for forming foreign alliances, and A CONFEDERATION OF THE COLONIES, at such time, and in the manner, as to them shall seem best. Provided, that the power of forming government for, and the regulations of the internal concerns of each colony, be left to the respective colonial legislatures.

RESOLVED unanimously, that a committee be appointed to prepare A DECLARATION OF RIGHTS, and such a plan of government as will be most likely to maintain peace and order in this colony, and secure substantial and equal liberty to the people. . . .

The resolution being read aloud to the army, the following toasts were given, each of them accompanied by a discharge of the artillery and small-arms, and the acclamations of all present:

1. *The American independent states.*

2. *The Grand Congress of the United States, and their respective legislatures.*

3. *General Washington, and victory to the American arms.*

AN ANONYMOUS REPORT: "THE DECLARATION OF
INDEPENDENCE"

News of the passage of the Declaration of Independence spread throughout America at the usual speed of news, reaching Williamsburg, Virginia, more than two weeks after its ratification in Philadelphia. Here, printer Alexander Purdie provides his readers with a series of reactions to the Declaration by Americans.

Virginia Gazette (Williamsburg, Purdie), 26 July 1776

TRENTON, *July 8.*

THE DECLARATION of INDEPENDENCE was this day proclaimed here, together with the new constitution of the colony of late established, and the resolve of the Provincial Congress for continuing the administration of justice during the interim.

The members of the Provincial Congress, the gentlemen of the committee, the officers and privates of the militia under arms, and a large concourse of the inhabitants, attended on this great and solemn occasion. The declaration, and other proceedings, were received with loud acclamations.

The people are now convinced, of what we ought long since to have known, that our enemies have left us no middle way between *perfect freedom* and *abject slavery.*

In the field, we hope, as well as in council, the inhabitants of New Jersey will be found ever ready to support the *freedom* and *independence* of America.

NEW YORK, *July 8. . . .*

On Wednesday last the DECLARATION of INDEPENDENCE was read at the head of each brigade of the continental army posted at and near New York, and every where receive with loud huzzas and the utmost demonstrations of joy.

The same evening the equestrian statue of George III, which Tory pride and folly raised in the year 1770, was, by the sons of freedom, laid prostrate in the dirt, the just desert of an ungrateful tyrant! The lead wherewith the monument was made is to be run into bullets, to assimilate with the brain of our infatuated adversaries, who to gain a pepper corn have lost an empire. . . .

WILLIAMSBURG, *July 26.*

YESTERDAY afternoon, agreeable to an order of the Hon. Privy Council, the DECLARATION OF INDEPENDENCE was solemnly proclaimed at the

Capitol, the Courthouse, and the Palace, amidst the acclamations of the people, accompanied by firing of cannon and musketry, the several regiments of continental troops having been paraded on that solemnity.

OPPOSED TO INDEPENDENCE

FAIRFIELD, CONNECTICUT, FREEHOLDERS: "WE OPPOSE INDEPENDENCE"

Towns and counties throughout America often held open meetings among those who could vote—those who owned property. This resolution from Fairfield offers one example of a set of resolves that opposed independence from England, citing among its reasons the protection afforded them by the English constitution.

Rivington's New-York Gazetteer; or Connecticut, New-Jersey, Hudson's-River, and Quebec Weekly Advertiser, 23 February 1775

Mr. Rivington,

Sir,

IN the present critical situation of public affairs, we, the subscribers, freeholders and inhabitants of the town of Reading, and the adjoining parts, in the county of Fairfield, and colony of Connecticut, think it necessary . . . to assure the public, that we are open enemies to any change in the present happy constitution, and highly disapprove of all measures, in any degree calculated to promote confusion and disorder . . . adopted for the purpose of opposing British government, we have entered into the following resolves and agreements, viz. . . .

Resolved, that whilst we enjoy the privileges and immunities of the English constitution, we will render all due obedience to his most gracious Majesty King George the third; and, that a firm dependance on the mother country is essential in our political safety and happiness. . . .

Resolved, that the privileges and immunities of this constitution are yet . . . continued to all his Majesty's American subjects, except those, who . . . have justly forfeited their title therein. . . .

Resolved, that notwithstanding, we will, in all circumstances, conduct with prudence and moderation, we consider it as an indispensible duty we owe to our King, our constitution, our country, and posterity, to defend, maintain, and preserve, at the risk of our lives and properties, the prerogative of the crown, and the privileges of the subject from all attacks, by any rebellious body of men, and any committees of inspection, correspondence, &c.

Signed by 141 inhabitants.

ANONYMOUS WRITERS: "DO NOT SEEK INDEPENDENCE"

Several people in New Jersey prepared this message, which was sent to the colony's delegates at the Continental Congress. It sought to convince the representatives not to vote for independence, but to seek reconciliation with England.

New-York Gazette; and the Weekly Mercury, 24 January 1776

We trust that you will be too deeply impress'd with the Recollection of the peculiar Happiness and Prosperity heretofore enjoyed by the Inhabitants of this Continent, connected with and subject to the government of Great-Britain, not to dread the Consequences of a declar'd Separation from that Country . . . a change of government will prevent a safe, honourable, and lasting Reconciliation with Great-Britain on constitutional Principles.

CATO: "INDEPENDENCE IS A CAUSE AIMED AT SUBVERTING OUR COUNTRY"

Cato was William Smith, the provost of the College of Philadelphia. He wrote this letter in opposition to Thomas Paine's ideas in Common Sense, *which advocated independence from England. Smith thought that America's best interests lay in retaining its current relationship with England. He explains his reasoning in this letter.*

New-York Gazette; and the Weekly Mercury, 25 March 1776

To the PEOPLE of Pennsylvania.

LETTER II. . . .

The account which we have already received of *Commissioners* being appointed in England, and ready to embark for America, in order to negociate [*sic*] a settlement of the present unhappy differences, has engaged the attention, and exercised the speculations of many among us. . . .

We are contending, at the risk of our lives and fortunes, against an arbitrary ministry, for the rights of Englishmen. The eyes of all Europe are upon us, and every generous bosom, in which the pulse of liberty yet beats, sympathises with us and is interested in our success. Our cause, therefore, being the cause of virtue, it will be expected that all our steps should be guided by it, and that where the flock is so fair, the fruit will be proportionably perfect. Let us not disappoint these sanguine expectations by the smallest deviation from those liberal and enlarged sentiments, which should mark the conduct of freemen; and when the faithful HISTORIC page shall record the events of this GLORIOUS STRUGGLE, may not a single line in the bright annals be stained by the recital of a disgraceful action, nor future Americans have cause to blush for the failings of their ancestors. . . .

And shall Americans, glorying in the attachment to the rights of humanity, be the first to violate obligations which have been thus universally held sacred? No! Let us never give that advantage to those who have been striving to excite the indignation of mankind against us as faithless people, ferocious, barbarous, and uninfluenced by those humane sentiments and finer feelings which, in modern times, have, in some measure, softened the horrors of war. We know that such a charge is a malicious as it is groundless. . . .

As we have long professed an ardent desire of peace, let us meet those who bring the terms, with that virtuous confidence, which is inseparable from an upright conduct. . . . If what they offer be such as *freemen* ought to accept, my voice shall be for an immediate reconciliation; as I know of no object so worthy of patriot as the healing our wounds, and the restoring of peace, if it has for its basis an *effectual* security for the liberties of *America*. . . .

I am bold to declare, and hope yet to make it evident to every honest man, that the true interest of America lies in *reconciliation*, with Great-Britain, upon *constitutional principles*, and I can truly say, I wish it upon no other terms. . . .

Perhaps it was thought best, where an *appeal* was pretended to be made to the COMMON SENSE of this country, to leave the people for a while to the free exercise of that good understanding which they are know to possess. . . . If little notice has yet been taken of the publications concerning independence, it is neither owing to the popularity of the doctrine, the unanswerable nature of the arguments, nor the fear of opposing them, as the vanity of the author would suggest. I am confident that nine tenths of the people of Pennsylvania yet abhor the doctrine.

If we look back to the origin of the present controversy, it will appear that some among us at least, have been constantly enlarging their views, and stretching them beyond their first bounds, till at length they have wholly changed their ground. From the claim of Parliament to tax us sprung the first resistence on our part. Before that unjust claim was set on foot, not an individual, not one of all the profound legislators with which this country abounds, ever held out the idea of independence. We considered our connections with Great-Britain as our chief happiness— we flourished, grew rich, and populous, to a degree not to be paralleled in history. Let us then act the part of the skilful physicians, and wisely adopt the remedy to the evil.

Possibly some men may have harboured the idea of independence from the beginning of this controversy. Indeed it was strongly suspected there were individuals whose views tended that way; but as the scheme was not sufficiently ripened, it was reckoned slanderous, inimical to America, and what not, to intimate the least suspicion of this kind. . . .

I doubt not to make it appear that independence is not the cause in which America is now engaged, and is only the idol of those who wish to subvert all order among us, and rise on the ruins of their country!
CATO

QUESTIONS

1. What were the reasons for turning the colonies into an independent nation?
2. What were Thomas Paine's reasons for declaring independence when he wrote as The Forester?
3. Why did the delegates to the Virginia Convention believe the colonies had to declare themselves independent of Great Britain?
4. Was England justified in its war against America following the Declaration of Independence? Consider answering this question in the larger framework of American history.
5. What did the freeholders of Connecticut and New Jersey fear if the colonies declared independence?
6. Why did Cato long for a reconciliation with England?

NOTE

1. "The Virginia Declaration of Rights," *The Proceedings of the Convention of Delegates, Held at the Capitol, in the City of Williamsburg, in the Colony of Virginia on Monday the 6th of May, 1776* (Williamsburg, 1776), 100–103.

2. Quoted in Oscar Theodore Barck, Jr. and Hugh Talmage Lefler, *Colonial America* (New York: Macmillan, 1958), 594.

Chronology of Events

1607	First English settlement in North America at Jamestown, Virginia
1608	First French settlement in North America at Quebec, Canada
1619	African slaves brought to Jamestown
1620	Pilgrims settle in Plymouth, Massachusetts
	America's population reaches 2,000
1629	British capture Quebec; French retake Quebec in 1632
1636	America's first college, Harvard, opens
1638	Printing press brought to Cambridge, Massachusetts
1639	First publication in America, the *Freeman's Oath*
1650	America's population reaches 50,000
1661	First New Testament printed in America—in Algonquin as translated by Puritan John Eliot
1675	King Philip's War—Wampanoag Indians attack Massachusetts settlers for encroaching on Native American lands
1686	America's first almanac, *Kalendarium Pennsilvaniense*, published in Philadelphia
1689	King William's War begins (first English-French war involving fighting in America)
1690	*New England Primer* published, America's principal book for teaching reading for 100 years
	Publication and suppression of *Publick Occurrences*, America's first newspaper

1693	College of William and Mary begun in Williamsburg to train Anglican clergy
1697	King William's War ends
1700	America's population surpasses 250,000
1702	Queen Anne's War begins (second English-French war with fighting in America)
1704	*Boston News-Letter* published (first continuously published newspaper in America)
1711	Tuscarora War—nearly 5,000 Tuscarora declare war on the whites of North Carolina; more than 100 whites and 900 Tuscaroras are killed or captured
1713	Queen Anne's War ends
1719	Newspaper competition begins with introduction of the *Boston Gazette* and *American Weekly Mercury*
1721	Boston smallpox epidemic leads to inoculation controversy; more than 800 die
1732	Benjamin Franklin publishes *Poor Richard's Almanac*
1733	Six colonies have a total of eleven newspapers
1735	Trial of John Peter Zenger
1739	Stono Rebellion in South Carolina; more than 100 slaves and colonists are killed
	George Whitefield begins to preach in America
	Great Awakening
1740	King George's War begins (third English-French war with fighting in America)
1744	British and American troops capture the French stronghold, Louisbourg, on Cape Breton
1748	King George's War ends
1750	America's population surpasses 1 million
	Eleven English-language newspapers printed in America
1752	Benjamin Franklin proves lightning is electricity by flying a kite in a storm
	England and America switch from the old Julian or Roman calendar to the Gregorian calendar, losing eleven days in September and changing the first of the year from March 25 to January 1
1754	George Washington's *Journals* are published, giving Americans a first-hand account of French and Indian aggression in the Ohio Valley

1754	French and Indian War begins
	Albany Congress
	Washington's forces defeated at Fort Necessity
1755	French defeat General Edward Braddock's forces near Fort Duquesne (Pittsburgh)
1756	England declares war on France beginning the Seven Years' War, a war fought on nearly every continent and body of water in the world
1759	Cherokee War begins in the Southern colonies
	Quebec captured
1760	France surrenders Canada, effectively ending French settlement in North America
	Nineteen English-language newspapers printed in America
1761	Cherokee War ends
1763	Peace of Paris ends French and Indian, Seven Years' wars
1764	Sugar Act passed to raise revenue to pay for wars by taxing lumber, molasses, and rum
1765	Stamp Act places a tax on paper goods, especially newspapers, to help defray England's war debt
1766	Stamp Act repealed
1767	Townshend Acts place taxes on paint, tea, lead, paper, and glass
1770	America's population surpasses 2 million
	Boston Massacre
	Townshend Acts repealed
1773	Boston Tea Party
1774	Intolerable Acts close Boston's port and place occupation troops in the city
	First Continental Congress meets in Philadelphia
	Rhode Island prohibits importation of slaves
1775	Forty English-language newspapers printed in America
	Patrick Henry tells the Virginia legislators, "Give me liberty or give me death"
	Battles of Lexington and Concord
	Battle of Bunker Hill
	George Washington named commander in chief of America's army
1776	*Common Sense* published by Thomas Paine
	America receives military aid from France and Spain

1776   Virginia adopts the Declaration of Rights, calling for American independence with the right to life, liberty, and the pursuit of happiness

Declaration of Independence

Thomas Paine writes *The Crisis*, announcing, "These are the times that try men's souls"

Washington wins a stunning victory at Trenton, New Jersey

Selected Bibliography

Aldridge, A. Owen. *Thomas Paine's American Ideology*. Newark: University of Delaware, 1984.

"Archiving Early America." http://earlyamerica.com/.

"Avalon Project at the Yale Law School: 18th Century Documents." http://www.yale.edu/lawweb/avalon/18th.htm.

Axtell, James. *Beyond 1492: Encounters in Colonial North America*. New York: Oxford University Press, 1992.

Bailyn, Bernard. *The Ideological Origins of the American Revolution*. Cambridge: Harvard University Press, 1967.

Barck, Oscar Theodore, Jr., and Hugh Talmage Lefler. *Colonial America*. New York: Macmillan, 1958.

Bonomi, Patricia U. *Under the Cope of Heaven: Religion, Society, and Politics in the Colonial Era*. New York: Oxford University Press, 1986.

Boorstin, Daniel J. *The Americans: The Colonial Experience*. New York: Vintage Books, 1958.

Canfield, Cass. *Sam Adams' Revolution 1765–1776*. New York: Harper & Row, 1976.

Cassedy, James H. *Medicine in America: A Short History*. Baltimore: Johns Hopkins University Press, 1991.

"Colonial America and the Eighteenth Century." http://bigsun.wbs.net/homepages/n/y/m/nymas1/nymas3colamer. htm.

Copeland, David A. *Colonial American Newspapers: Character and Content*. Newark: University of Delaware Press, 1997.

Dowd, Gregory Evans. *A Spirited Resistance: The North American Indian Struggle for Unity, 1745–1815*. Baltimore: Johns Hopkins University Press, 1992.

Evans, Sara M. *Born for Liberty: A History of Women in America*. New York: Free Press, 1989.

Ferguson, Robert A. *The American Enlightenment, 1750–1820*. Cambridge: Harvard University Press, 1997.

Fradin, B. Brindell. *Samuel Adams: Father of the American Revolution*. New York: Houghton Mifflin, 1998.

Franklin, Benjamin. *Autobiography*. Edited by J. A. Leo Lemay and P. M. Zall. New York: W. W. Norton, 1986.

Gibson, Arrell Morgan. *The American Indian: Prehistory to the Present*. Lexington, Mass.: D. C. Heath, 1980.

Higginbotham, A. Leon. *In the Matter of Color: Race and the American Legal System*. New York: Oxford University Press, 1978.

Hoffer, Peter Charles. *Law and People in Colonial America*. Baltimore: Johns Hopkins University Press, 1992.

Hoffer, Peter Charles, ed. *Early American History: Colonial Women and Domesticity*. New York: Garland Publishing, 1988.

Humphrey, Carol Sue. *"This Popular Engine": New England Newspapers During the American Revolution*. Newark: University of Delaware Press, 1992.

Jennings, Francis. *Empire of Fortune: Crowns, Colonies & Tribes in the Seven Years War in America*. New York: W. W. Norton, 1988.

Kobre, Sidney. *The Development of the Colonial Newspaper*. 1944; reprint, Gloucester: Peter Smith, 1960.

Labaree, Benjamin Woods. *The Boston Tea Party*. 1964; reprint, Boston: Northeastern University Press, 1990.

Lemay, J. A. Leo. "Benjamin Franklin: A Documentary History." http://www.english.udel.edu/lemay/franklin/.

Maier, Pauline. *American Scripture: Making the Declaration of Independence*. New York: Random House, 1998.

Malone, Patrick M. *The Skulking Way of War: Technology and Tactics among the New England Indians*. Baltimore: Johns Hopkins University Press, 1993.

May, Henry F. *The Enlightenment in America*. New York: Oxford University Press, 1976.

Mayer, Henry. *A Son of Thunder: Patrick Henry and the American Republic*. Charlottesville: University Press of Virginia, 1991.

McCusker, John J., and Russell R. Menard. *The Economy of British America, 1607–1789*. Chapel Hill: University of North Carolina Press, 1985.

Morgan, Edmund S. *American Slavery, American Freedom: The Ordeal of Colonial Virginia*. New York: W. W. Norton, 1975.

Morgan, Edmund S., and Helen M. Morgan. *The Stamp Act Crisis: Prologue to Revolution*. Chapel Hill: University of North Carolina Press, 1953.

Nash, Gary B. *The Urban Crucible. Social Change, Political Consciousness, and the Origins of the American Revolution*. Cambridge: Harvard University Press, 1979.

Norton, Mary Beth. *Founding Mothers and Fathers: Gendered Power and the Forming of American Society*. New York: Alfred A. Knopf, 1996.

———. *Liberty's Daughters: The Revolutionary Experience of American Women, 1750–1800*. Boston: Little, Brown, 1980.

Peckman, Howard H. *The Colonial Wars, 1689–1762*. 1964; reprint, Chicago: University of Chicago Press, 1990.

Quinn, Arthur. *A New World: An Epic of Colonial America from the Founding of Jameston to the Fall of Quebec*. New York: Berkley Publishing Group, 1995.

Rae, Noel. *Witnessing America. The Library of Congress Book of Firsthand Accounts of Life in America, 1600–1900*. New York: Viking, 1996.

Roux, Larry. "1755: The French and Indian War." http://web.syr.edu/~laroux/.

Schlesinger, Arthur M. *Prelude to Independence: The Newspaper War on Britain 1764–1776*. New York: Random House, 1958.

Sloan, Wm. David, and Julie Hedgepeth Williams. *The Early American Press, 1690–1783*. Westport, Conn.: Greenwood Press, 1994.

Smith, Jeffery A. *Printers and Press Freedom: The Ideology of Early American Journalism*. New York: Oxford University Press, 1988.

Stout, Harry S. *The Divine Dramatist: George Whitefield and the Rise of Modern Evangelism*. Grand Rapids, Mich.: William B. Eerdmans, 1991.

Thomas, Isaiah. *The History of Printing in America*. 1810; reprint, New York: Weathervane Books, 1970.

Tindall, George Brown. *America*. New York: W. W. Norton, 1984.

Tourtellot, Arthur B. *Lexington and Concord*. New York: W. W. Norton, 1994.

Ulrich, Laurel Thatcher. *Good Wives: Image and Reality in the Lives of Women in Northern New England 1650–1750*. New York: Alfred A. Knopf, 1982.

Walmsley, Andrew Stephen. *Thomas Hutchinson and the Origins of the American Revolution*. New York: New York University Press, 1999.

Wood, Gordon S. *The Radicalism of the American Revolution*. New York: Vintage Books, 1993.

Wood, Peter H. *Black Majority*. New York: W. W. Norton, 1974.

Wright, Louis B. *The Cultural Life of the American Colonies 1607–1763*. New York: Harper & Row, 1962.

Wroth, Lawrence. *The Colonial Printer*. Portland, Me.: Southworth-Anthoensen Press, 1938.

Zobel, Hiller B. *The Boston Massacre*. New York: W. W. Norton, 1970.

Index

About the Author

DAVID A. COPELAND is Associate Professor of Mass Communication at Emory & Henry College. He is the author of book chapters in *Colonial American Newspapers: Character and Content* (1997) and journal and encyclopedia articles on the colonial press and religion and the media. He is Vice-President of the American Journalism Historians Association and was named the 1998–1999 Carnegie Foundation for the Advancement of Teaching Virginia Professor of the Year.